Coastal Cruising Under Power

Coastal Cruising Under Power

How to Choose, Equip, Operate, and Maintain Your Boat

Gene and Katie Hamilton

INTERNATIONAL MARINE / MCGRAW-HILL

Camden, Maine • New York • Chicago • San Francisco • Lisbon • London • Madrid • Mexico City • Milan • New Delhi • San Juan • Seoul • Singapore • Sydney • Toronto

The McGraw·Hill Companies

2 3 4 5 6 7 8 9 DOC DOC 1 5 4 3 2 1

© 2006 Gene and Katie Hamilton

Library of Congress Cataloging-in-Publication Data
Hamilton, Gene.
Coastal cruising under power : how to choose, equip,
operate, and maintain your boat / Gene Hamilton
and Katie Hamilton.
p. cm.
Includes bibliographical references and index.
ISBN 0-07-144514-5 (pbk. : alk. paper)
1. Motorboats. 2. Boats and boating. I. Hamilton, Katie.
II. Title.
GV835.H26 2006
797.1—dc22
2005037577

Questions regarding the content of this
book should be addressed to
INTERNATIONAL MARINE
P.O. Box 220
Camden, ME 04843
www.internationalmarine.com

Questions regarding the ordering of this
book should be addressed to
THE McGRAW-HILL COMPANIES
Customer Service Department
P.O. Box 547
Blacklick, OH 43004
Retail customers: 1-800-262-4729
Bookstores: 1-800-722-4726

Photos by authors unless otherwise noted. Title page credits,
top to bottom, left to right: authors, Silverton, Regal Boats,
authors, authors, authors, Grand Banks. Part opener credits,
clockwise from top left: Sea Ray, Silverton Marine Corporation,
Monticello Yachts, authors.

Contents

Part VI Cruise These Great Destinations

Foreword

In July 1977, I became the editor of *Inland Sea*, a Chicago, Illinois-based Midwestern regional edition of the nationally circulated *Sea Magazine*. I met Gene and Katie Hamilton by chance, walking across the street to McCormick Place to attend IMTEC, the largest recreational marine trade show of its day. When they told me that they had returned just the year before from a cruise that took them through the Great Lakes, along the Erie Canal, down the Hudson River, south along the eastern U.S. coastline, and through the Intracoastal Waterway (ICW) to winter in the Bahamas, I wanted to know more—much, much more.

On a cold, wind-whipped afternoon later that fall, Gene and Katie visited my office in downtown Chicago, and we walked across Michigan Avenue to find a bit of lunch. It was the beginning of a friendship that has spanned 28 years. Their stories rang with authenticity, and I soaked up their experiences like a student musician attending a Master class. They explained that they were both teachers, and that they had taken a year off to make their cruise over the winter of 1975. They hoped to make a living writing for recreational marine magazines, and they had a few book ideas to develop along the same lines.

"You *had* to go cruising to write authoritative cruising stories," Gene said. Their first coastal voyage was in a Rhodes 41, which they sold in Annapolis, Maryland in the summer of 1976, after enjoying the Bicentennial activities taking place in the nation's capital and in cities and towns along the Chesapeake shoreline.

Gene and Katie returned to Chicago in 1976, bought a house in need of tender loving care, and began writing about their home improvement experiences as well as their cruising adventures.

I moved to California in November 1979, to take the helm of *Pacific Skipper*. Gene and Katie continued to write for *Sea*, and also did stories for *Lakeland Boating*. Katie's monthly column, "First Mate's Forum," was a staple for Midwestern women who loved boating. Even though their fame was spreading for their home improvement articles, they never lost their love for the water, nor their desire to go cruising again.

In 1985, after being land-bound and boatless for several years, Gene and Katie bought a wooden Grand Banks 42 located on the east coast, named her *Old Grand Dad*, rented out their Chicago-area home, took a year off, and went down to Florida for the winter. On their return trip the following summer, they spent some more time in the Chesapeake, liked it, and stayed, living aboard for a time in Castle marina, Kent Island, on Maryland's Eastern Shore. But because they were working on a book project (as well as articles for *Popular Mechanics*, *Popular Science*, and *Family Handyman* magazines), and needed the reliable phone connection that wasn't easily available in their marina, they made the decision to move ashore and rented a house nearby. I had moved to Annapolis in 1982 and, when I found that they were living in the area, I urged them to stay. They settled on St. Michaels as their new home.

Gene and Katie sold the GB42 in 1989, bought a J/24, and raced it around the buoys near St. Michaels. Meanwhile they launched a home improvement website that proved to be a huge success. They purchased a C&C 35, a boat they had lusted after since their days in Chicago, and took it to Florida for a winter in 2000. On their return to the Chesapeake the following spring, they sold it and bought a Grand Banks 36, which they still own and cherish. As I write, they are moving it up the Waterway for the third year.

Transiting the ICW and cruising along the coast in the fall and spring they experienced changeable weather firsthand. "The difference was windshield wipers," they quipped, referring to the difference between a sailboat and powerboat. Having made that trip a few times myself, I can tell you that cold and wet seem adventurous for only so long. "You get

a different perspective sitting above the waterline," said Gene, "but the speeds from point to point are not that much different. It's very comfortable."

Now, hundreds of boating articles later, Gene and Katie have penned *Coastal Cruising Under Power* to pass along the knowledge and experience they've garnered from numerous coastal passages. It comes just in time, as more and more boatowners turn to displacement and semi-displacement powerboat designs as platforms from which to view and enjoy this country's coastlines—to view America from a perspective most landlubbers hardly know exists.

Coastal cruising is hardly all flat water and bluebird weather. Being knowledgeable and prepared, mentally and physically, is vital. The prudent mariner relies on all sources of printed and electronic information to ensure the safety of crew and vessel. The book you hold in your hand is just such a source.

John Wooldridge
Managing Editor
Yachting magazine

Acknowledgments

We're grateful to so many boating friends who encouraged, nudged, and cajoled us to write this book. We want to thank all of them, especially these kind folks who shared their wit and wisdom with us: Brenda and Mike Appel, Martha and Captain Jack Austin, Nancy and Bob Bartell, Ken and Ardy Bridges, Mary Bowar and Mike Lurie, Ted and Jo Clark, Suellen and John Gargalli, Judy and Jerry Gaston, Gail Greco and Tom Bagley, Debby and Tony Greenwood, Laura and Tim Hanlon, Barb and Vic Hansen, Sheri and Captain Frank Herbert, Jayne and Irv Hetherington, Pepper and Geoff Holmes, Dalton and Louise Marks, Kathy McMahon and Sterling Neale, Debbie and Captain Roger Roark, Millie and Jack Rose, Linda and Harry Seemans, Mimi and Barry Starke, Annie and Sam Thompson, Sandy and Chivey Wieland, Sally and Neville Williams, Peg and Captain John Wooldridge, and Kay and Jack Wurst.

We sincerely appreciate the fine pen and direction of our editor Bob Holtzman, who so kindly guided and supported our efforts along the way.

We're also grateful to Captain Bob Armstrong, whose technical expertise enhanced our work.

We appreciate the work of Ben McCanna, the project editor who guided our book through the publication process, and all the members of the design and production staff at International Marine who took our words and pictures and created this book.

And as always we are grateful to our agent, Danielle Egan-Miller, who has for many years been a good friend and advisor.

Introduction
An Invitation to Come Cruising

Picture this scene: you're at anchor in a quiet cove under a starlit sky with a nice breeze to cool the cabin and keep the bugs away. In the forward cabin you're lulled to sleep by the peaceful sound of water lapping against the hull. This is cruising.

You're underway, enjoying crisp weather under sunny skies just a short distance from your destination, a new town and marina never visited before. This is cruising.

The boat is tied to a dock, it's pouring rain, the wind is pitching the boat back and forth making you feel like you're inside a blender. This is cruising, too.

Cruising on a powerboat can be anything from weekend boat camping on a 24-footer to a month or more aboard a 50-foot yacht. The spectrum of cruising styles is as varied as the spectrum of boats and cruisers—of whom we've met plenty in all our years at the helm. Some, who take a leisurely pace, are happy to make 50 miles a day at 7 knots, others are fast-track cruisers interested in getting to new cruising grounds in a hurry. Slowpokes or go-fasts, we all find our niche.

We've been boating since 1969, when we bought our first boat while living in Chicago, and we've been "messing about in boats" ever since. In this book we want to share our enthusiasm and experience of cruising the coastal waters of the United States, and hope

it encourages you to do the same. The thousands of miles of shoreline in and around the United States offer an endless number of destinations—close-to-home harbors and protected anchorages—where you can cruise comfortably and safely, without crossing wide oceans.

The book begins with a section on choosing a cruising boat, with a look at all the aspects you need to consider. In Part I we show how the shape of the hull determines the way a boat moves through the water, and how its engine and drive system power it at slow or fast speeds. We also provide an overview of different interior layouts and of a boat's electrical and freshwater systems. Then we discuss the nuts and bolts of buying a boat and how to choose a marina.

A boat is an empty shell until you load it with gear and equipment that help you navigate and communicate, so in Part II we outline how to outfit a cruising boat. We take a serious look at what safety gear to have aboard. To round out this section we review the documents and paperwork necessary to operate and register a boat, and how to keep them organized on board.

In Part III we lay out the necessary skills of operating and using a boat, with a review of the Rules of the Road and the basics of boat handling, anchoring, piloting, and navigation. Since weather can have such a profound effect on your boating, we include a primer on understanding weather and how to read present and upcoming conditions.

A routine of maintenance and cleaning is necessary to keep all the systems and components of a boat working at their best. Part IV includes three key chapters with our take on keeping a boat working, and what tools and spare parts to carry on board.

Over the years we've met many boaters who enjoy different styles of cruising, so the cruising lifestyle is the focus of Part V. We look at the creative ways people use to pay for cruising, how they cruise with kids and pets, and the many things we've learned from all of them.

The last part of the book, Part VI, features our favorite coastal areas for cruising—charming harbor towns with marinas and safe anchorages for gunkholing—destinations we know and enjoy.

At the end of the book, in the appendices, we list resources and contact information you can use to find out more about many of the topics we discuss in the book.

We hope you'll find the book helpful and use it as a starting point to venture out on your boat, exploring coastal waters. As your experience of operating your boat grows, and your confidence builds, you may want to learn more about specifics like navigation and piloting or how your engine works. You'll find plenty of good books about every aspect of boating.

Anyone who cruises aboard a boat will agree it can provide hours of contentment interrupted by moments of sheer terror, but most of the time cruising is being free to go where you want to go, at the speed and comfort level you choose. And that's what we like about it.

A sense of humor, a sense of adventure, and a boat are the key ingredients to attainable cruising along the coastal waters of the United States. In this book we'll tell you what we've learned about cruising and how to enjoy it any way you can.

PART I

Choose Your Cruising Powerboat

CHAPTER 1
Choosing a Boat Design

Over the past 35 years we've owned seven boats, from a J/24 racing sailboat to a 42-foot wooden trawler—and just about every type in between. We didn't start small and work our way up the food chain with larger and larger boats. Each boat was perfect for us at the time, but every time our life situation changed and the boat we had no longer fit our needs, we went shopping.

No boat can be all things to all people and no matter how clever the naval architect, all designs are at best a compromise. Only a finite number of objectives—such as adequate accommodation, good boat speed, and adequate fuel and water capacity—can be achieved with any given design. A change in one area will affect other aspects of the boat, and some compromises prove better than others. Successful designs are the ones that meet or exceed their stated objectives.

In the following sections, we'll present our take on the types of powerboat that we think are suitable for coastal cruising—boats that meet or exceed their stated objectives.

But before we get into the particulars let's make one point clear: it's not the boat that makes a cruise successful, it's the attitudes of the people on board. Anyone can successfully cruise coastal and inland waters in almost any boat. We've met people on modest boats enjoying the cruising life to its fullest, and those on elegant yachts not having any fun at all. Life and boats, as they say, are what you make of them.

IS THERE A BEST BOAT?

The answer is no. Every boat has both its qualities and its limitations. When you evaluate your present boat, or shop for a new one, it's important to envision how you will use it.

A slow-moving displacement hull (we'll explain what that is in a moment), for example, is relatively inexpensive to operate, but the deep *draft* (depth of the boat below the waterline) can limit your choice of cruising areas, especially in the shallow waters of the Bahamas and Florida Keys.

High-speed cruising boats generally have a shallower draft and a wider choice of cruising areas, but they are expensive to operate. As technology evolves, however, boats are being built lighter without sacrificing strength, and engines are becoming more fuel efficient. These developments could result in lower operating costs.

Tank capacity is another major consideration when choosing the right design. If you plan to cruise where fuel, water, and food are readily available, then tremendous load-carrying capacity isn't necessary. However, if you plan to cruise in remote areas where facilities are limited, then fuel and water capacities are a serious consideration.

There are dozens of questions that you must ask yourself before you decide what type of boat is right for you, and there no simple answers, but the more you learn about boat design, the better you'll be able to select a boat that truly suits you.

WHAT'S IT MADE OF?

Most production boats these days are made of fiberglass. Few wooden boats are built anymore, though there is usually a selection of older ones on the market. Whether an older wooden boat is a wise choice depends on the maintenance it has received. Some are still solid and seaworthy, while others are really only suitable for firewood. Aluminum and steel cruising boats are also available, but usually only in larger custom or semi-custom models. Here's a quick rundown of the characteristics of the major boatbuilding materials.

WOOD

Wood has long been an excellent material for boatbuilding. It still is, and you can't beat the quiet ride of a wooden hull. But few builders currently have the knowledge and skilled labor to produce a quality wooden boat by traditional methods.

Modern epoxy coatings and adhesives allow a skilled builder to create a boat that is essentially wood but is more durable and requires much less maintenance than traditional wood construction. These contemporary hulls are usually described as *cold molded,* and we'll have more to say about them later.

A wooden boat can have a long life expectancy if it's maintained properly, but will quickly deteriorate if it's neglected. There are still good used wooden boats around and they can represent good value when compared to a fiberglass boat of the same size, though they will require more expense and effort when it comes to maintenance.

In the mid-1980s we bought a 21-year-old, well-maintained wooden Grand Banks 42, *Old Grand Dad.* She'd had only one previous owner, she had a good survey, and she cost us about a quarter of the price the fiberglass version was selling for at the time. For five years, she served us well. We lived aboard her during the first year and then cruised on long vacations for another four years. We sold her for what we had paid, but during those five years we did most of the maintenance. We had the yard do some major repairs (like new shafts and engine work), which came to about $20,000.

All boats require maintenance but you can skip buffing or waxing a fiberglass boat for years with little but cosmetic damage. If a wood boat is neglected for any length of time it will quickly deteriorate. All protective hull and cabin paint must be maintained on a regular schedule. Wood is constantly expanding or contracting so chasing down small leaks around ports, doors, hatches, or in the deck is a continuing process. Most of the maintenance you can do yourself and if you keep on top of it, it's not overwhelming.

FIBERGLASS

The introduction of fiberglass construction to the mass marine market in the 1950s and 1960s revolutionized boatbuilding. The evolution continues, as new combinations of materials are introduced to make boats lighter and stronger. Today, fiberglass boats dominate the cruising boat market. The boats are strong—but not indestructible—and require far less maintenance than most other materials, though they are far from being "maintenance free."

One of the big advantages of fiberglass construction is that this material can be molded into just about any shape. Fiberglass boats can also be quite roomy inside, since the structure doesn't require frames, as is usually the case in wood, steel, or aluminum construction.

A typical fiberglass laminate consists of layers of different types of glass fabric bonded together with *polyester, vinylester,* or *epoxy* resin. This construction method allows builders to lay up thicker, heavier laminated sections where the hull stresses are the greatest like under the engine mounts, and thinner, lighter sections where the stresses are lower in the side portions of the hull.

Fiberglass, however, technically known as *fiberglass reinforced plastic* or FRP, can have its problems. Variations in quality are introduced by the builder's selection of the types and amounts of reinforcing material he uses and the type (or types) of plastic resin he chooses to bind them.

Quality control doesn't stop with the selection of materials: critical care in their application is important too. Unless the builder precisely controls the mixing of the resins and their application to the fiberglass reinforcing structure, small air voids or areas of uncured resins are created, which reduce the strength of the entire laminate. If the voids are large enough, the structure can delaminate under stress.

Another problem with fiberglass is that laminates thick enough to withstand high stress can become quite heavy. Builders are conquering this drawback by introducing lighter cores, such as end-grain balsawood or closed-cell PVC foam, between thinner skins of reinforcing glass. Today, many boats are no longer "solid" FRP from the waterline up. The hull sides, decks, cabin sides, and interior *bulkheads* (walls) are all cored.

In a further effort to maintain strength without weight, builders are now using other materials besides fiberglass for reinforcing various areas of laminate. Carbon-fiber rods, with a tensile strength six times that of a piece of steel of the same weight, are used to add rigidity to keels, *chines* (where the bottom of the hull meets the sides), and *gunwales* (the top edges of the hull). Stronger materials such as Kevlar are also used in the reinforcing fabrics instead of (or in addition to) fiberglass. And even among fiberglass fabrics, there are now many nonwoven options, such as unidirectional knitted cloth, that provide extra strength without the added weight of more layers.

Fiberglass boats are constantly improving in many ways. But a unique problem in using FRP for boatbuilding remains: a condition known as *blistering.* Blistering occurs when, over the passage of time, water penetrates the outer *gelcoat* by a process known as *osmosis* and mixes with water-soluble materials in the fiberglass layers beneath it. The seawater mixes with the laminate particles and then becomes a more complex solution that cannot flow back out through the passage it entered. As a result, it builds up pressure as it tries to escape, and then explodes, causing blister domes to appear on the outside of the hull.

Not all resins are equally impervious to water. The polyester resins known as *orthophthalic* are the most permeable. *Isophthalic* polyesters are denser and more resistant to water intrusion. Vinylester resins are more resistant still, and epoxy resins are *almost* totally impervious. Of course, increasing the resistance of a hull to water intrusion comes at a cost, but builders will usually tell you the types of gelcoat and resins they use, and paying for the more water-resistant versions can be worth it in the long run.

Blistering is largely a cosmetic problem at first, but the liquid within a blister can eventually penetrate deeper into the fiberglass and ultimately result in at least partial delamination of the affected area. So blisters must be repaired. Fortunately, epoxy-based barrier coats can be applied over the basic laminate to reduce further water intrusion and, most often, eliminate further blistering. But this treatment, too, is not cheap.

Finally, let us add that fiberglass boats are not expensive to repair. The work is relatively easy and readily handled by most boatyards. In many cases you, the owner, can even do it yourself. No boatbuilding material is perfect but the thousands of old boats built of fiberglass that still exist are a testament to its longevity.

COLD-MOLDED WOOD

Although wood is the major component of cold-molded boats, this method of boatbuilding has many similarities to fiberglass construction. Cold-molded wooden structures are made of many very thin layers of wood, crisscrossed over the form of a male mold and bonded together with epoxy resin. The process is called *cold* molding because the modern epoxy adhesives do not require the application of heat to cure properly. Stainless steel staples may be used to hold the strips in place until the resin cures, but it is the epoxy, not metal fasteners, that eventually holds everything together. The final result is a totally unified plywood structure that is very light for its strength.

Cold-molded construction is even more labor intensive than "hand laid" fiberglass and is more often used for custom-built boats—It is not conducive to production building. For this reason, cold-molded boats are generally more expensive than fiberglass when new, though used models are often available at an attractive price simply because custom-built boats do not have the broader appeal of production designs offered in glass.

STEEL AND ALUMINUM

In the United States, steel and aluminum construction is limited mostly to commercial boats or custom yachts, though the Dutch and other Europeans have been building steel cruising boats for decades. A skilled builder can fabricate either material into a beautiful yacht. Steel is heavy, so you won't find many boats under about 35 feet LOA (length overall) built from this material. Aluminum is lighter but more expensive, and is usually used to build custom yachts, especially those of 80 feet LOA and up.

Steel construction is usually associated with workboats, but when a hull is built to yacht specifications it's difficult to distinguish steel from other hull materials. Steel is extremely strong for its weight and can be bent and stretched without losing this strength. This makes for a resilient hull that can take severe punishment. In a hard grounding or collision it will most often be dented rather than punctured or cracked.

If not properly maintained, rust and corrosion can attack steel and damage the structural integrity of the boat, especially if relatively thin plate has been used to reduce the boat's weight. But modern paints and other rust-preventive coatings can reduce the maintenance required to keep a steel boat in Bristol condition.

Aluminum is lighter than steel, and more expensive to purchase and fabricate, but it doesn't rust and requires less maintenance. Like steel, aluminum can be formed into a beautiful, fair hull. It's often used for cabinhouses and for the superstructure on steel yachts since it is lighter. Aluminum is also used in high-speed, lightweight boats. The weight savings enable such boats to carry more cargo for a given displacement.

Aluminum is not without its drawbacks, however. One of them is a tendency for galvanic corrosion in a saltwater environment.

The common copper-based antifouling bottom paints cannot be used on an aluminum boat (unless a non-conductive barrier coat is applied to the hull first), because aluminum is higher on the galvanic scale (less *noble*) than, say, copper or bronze. (There's more on this in Chapter 4, Electrical Systems and Generators). Also, commonly available bronze through-hulls for fittings, such as seawater intakes, must be electrically isolated from the hull. But these are small considerations given the general desirability of aluminum as a material for large custom yachts.

HULL TYPES

While boat hulls sitting side by side in the water may look alike from the dock, they may be very different below the waterline. Hull shapes come in three varieties: displacement, planing, or semi-displacement. Hull shape greatly affects a boat's performance, so it's important to know the pros and cons of each type.

DISPLACEMENT HULLS

Until the invention of modern high-powered engines, most boats were designed as displacement hulls. A displacement hull pushes through the water, not over it. Most cruising sailboats still have displacement hulls, as do most commercial fishing and cargo vessels. The hull of a displacement-style cruising powerboat typically has a rounded, wineglass shape and a keel that extends the full length of the boat. The rounded shape gives the hull an easy motion in a seaway. This shape does not pound into a head sea but is instead pushed through it for a more comfortable ride. It will roll in a *beam sea* (waves coming at the boat from the side)—as will any other powerboat—but the motion of a displacement

hull is smoother. Depending on the size of the waves, this type hull may roll 10 to 20 degrees but the motion is smooth as it moves back and forth. The hard chined planing hull will roll the same but the roll will be faster with a snap that may send objects flying about.

Displacement hulls are designed to operate at slow speeds and usually have efficient, large diameter propellers that require a draft of 4 feet of more. Since the hull is pushed through, rather than over the water, boat speed is limited by the energy that gets wasted making waves and by the friction between water and hull. More horsepower will push the boat faster, but there is a certain speed beyond which the extra power needed to increase it any further is so great that it becomes impractical.

This is the boat's *hull speed*. For most displacement powerboats it's around 1.2 to 1.6 times the square root of the load waterline (LWL)—the boat's length when loaded on the waterline at which it is designed to float under a normal load, measured in feet. The formula is $S = 1.2 \times \sqrt{LWL}$. For example, our 36-foot trawler has a LWL of 35 feet so it has a theoretical hull speed of $S = 1.2 \times \sqrt{35}$ or 7.09 knots.

This is very close to the situation we actually experience underway. If we keep the speed at about 7.5 knots, our fuel consumption is less than 2 gallons of diesel per hour (GPH). Push the boat at more than 8 knots and the fuel consumption soars to 5 GPH. A displacement boat is economical to run only at or below its hull speed.

Since the waterline length of the hull is the largest single factor determining hull speed, the longer the hull the faster the boat. Width also has an effect on hull speed. A wide hull takes more power to drive through the water than a narrow hull of the same length. A long, narrow boat is easier to push through the water, but cruising in a boat shaped like a rowing shell isn't very comfortable since it will have limited space for accommodations.

Although a displacement hull has limited speed, the upside is that this type of boat can be loaded with cargo—such as fuel, water, and cruising gear—without degrading the boat's performance. With its capacities and economies of operation, a displacement hull is a good choice for a cruising boat—but it's not the right choice for thrill seekers.

PLANING HULLS

Planing hulls are designed to be light. They rise out of the water quickly and *plane*, or skim, over the surface, thus reducing drag. A flat-bottomed skiff is a good example. A typical jonboat requires little horsepower to begin planing, and once on plane, the boat can maintain this attitude even if the power is reduced. But if you add a couple of fishing buddies and a cooler full of refreshments, the boat may not be able to get on plane even if the engine is running wide open.

The weight of the planing boat is critical— to get on plane with available horsepower a boat can't be overloaded. As a result, fuel and water capacities are smaller on planing-hull cruisers than on displacement and semi-displacement hulls. You can operate a planing hull at slow speeds to increase range, but you can't easily increase the payload capacity without affecting performance.

Sea state can greatly affect planing-hull boats. For example, the flat bottom of the skiff or jonboat makes an efficient hull shape to skim over smooth water, but a one-foot chop is enough to shake your fillings loose. To overcome the rough ride, most cruising planing hulls incorporate some form of V-shape forward with a flatter section aft. Most have a *hard chine*—a sharp, angular transition from the bottom to the sides of the hull.

Whatever its shape, the planing hull's ability to rise out of the water lessens the friction between water and hull, so the relationship between boat length and speed is broken.

There are 35-foot and larger planing cruisers that can cruise at speeds of more than 30 knots. At these speeds their range is limited, but they get to their destination fast. Slow down and—as with all other hull types—they use less fuel and increase their range.

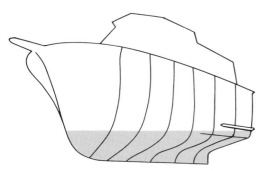

A typical displacement hull—featuring rounded transitions between the bottom and the sides, and a relatively deep draft—goes solidly through the water with an easy motion. (Illustration by Bruce Alderson.)

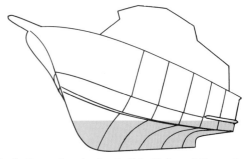

The bottom of a planing hull is V-shaped forward and flatter aft, with sharp transitions between the bottom and sides. This shape allows the hull to rise out of the water and plane on the surface at high speeds. (Illustration by Bruce Alderson.)

SEMI-DISPLACEMENT HULLS

A semi-displacement hull incorporates most of the attributes of a displacement hull into the shape of a planing hull. The hard chines and flatter stern sections of a planing hull are mated with the full, rounded shapes of a displacement hull in its forward third. The hull shape at the center of the boat resembles a champagne glass rather than the wineglass shape of a full displacement hull. This is a compromise, but with careful design most of the best characteristics of both hull types are preserved. The boat can be driven at higher speeds than a pure displacement hull, but it takes more power to reach those speeds.

With a few exceptions, most 30–60-foot pleasure boats have semi-displacement hulls. Among the exceptions are trawler yachts, which are still mostly of the full-displacement variety, although some newer ones are built with semi-displacement hulls.

The hull's cruising speed will depend on the horsepower you select. It's not essential to run semi-displacement hulls fast—they cruise at displacement speeds very economically. Higher speeds mean much higher fuel bills. Today most manufacturers offer cruising boats with several engine options.

A semi-displacement hull is a good choice for cruisers who don't want to be limited by the speed of a displacement hull but want to carry higher loads. Semi-displacement hulls require ever-increasing power to go faster, but the hull shape allows even a fully loaded boat to rise out of the water onto what can be considered a plane. This turn of speed can be awfully handy when a storm threatens and you want to get back to shore.

CRUISING BOAT STYLES

A boat's shape and function can be categorized in the same way that a house is recognized by its architectural style. A Cape Cod has a shape that can be recognized no matter where it is situated, and so it is with boats. The following categories are the most popular boat styles for cruising, but bear in mind that these styles often overlap, and a boat's design may borrow characteristics from more than one category.

PILOTHOUSE

Pilothouse boats are so called because they have a dedicated *pilothouse*, where the *helm station* (steering wheel and engine controls) and navigation equipment are located, separate from the accommodations. In other designs the helm station is most often located in a dedicated forward portion of the main *saloon*, the nautical equivalent of a living room. It is also often incorrectly called a *salon*.

These boats may or may not have a flying bridge (usually a relatively open upper-level helm station that provides better visibility, often abbreviated to flybridge, though traditionalists hate the term). One advantage of this layout is that major navigation equipment like radar, depth-sounder, and GPS can

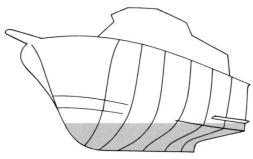

A semi-displacement hull has a displacement hull's full, round shape forward, with flat stern sections that help the hull rise onto the water's surface, partly on plane. (Illustration by Bruce Alderson.)

The Symbol 45 is a pilothouse design with a spacious interior forward of the wheelhouse, which has inside access to the bridge, saloon, and exterior.

be centralized in the pilothouse with only minimal equipment at the flying bridge helm for fair-weather use.

A true (ship's) pilothouse is usually a helm and navigation station only, though many yacht pilothouses also include a settee and perhaps even a small dining table so the owner/skipper need not be totally isolated from other people onboard. The combination of helm and nav station only (with no additional comforts) is often found on yachts large enough to be handled primarily by professional crew.

Many larger boats have a raised pilothouse, which allows accommodations to be placed below it. On these boats an additional passageway from the saloon to the forward cabins may be provided under the pilothouse. Pilothouse designs are available for all types of hulls.

TRAWLER

The fishing boats upon which many trawler yachts are modeled are true displacement boats. Today the trawler style has been expanded to encompass a wide variety of boats. Most are built on displacement hulls that operate in the 7–10-knot range, while many newer ones have semi-displacement hulls that can cruise between 15 and 20 knots, or even faster.

Some trawlers have a dedicated pilothouse. Many also feature an aft cabin. But in all cases it is the overall design—large, traditionally styled deckhouse, shippy-looking hull (even if it is semi-displacement below the waterline); and solid workboat-based appearance—that gives a trawler its name.

A raised pilothouse design like this custom trawler features living quarters below the pilothouse.

There are many popular tugboat-style trawlers; here's an example of a custom design.

SEDAN

A rather small aft cockpit, a large main saloon and, traditionally, a flying bridge are the main features of the sedan. The large saloon opens to the cockpit, which may be partially or completely covered by a hardtop extension of the main *coach roof* (the cabin top). The saloon and cockpit *soles* (floors) are usually at or near the same level, so at the most there's only a slight step down into the cockpit.

The layout has a lot of living space, all on one level, and often features a convertible dinette that makes up into a double bunk. The cockpit may be enclosed with screens or clear vinyl to increase the all-weather living space. Access to the flying bridge may be by ladder or stairs.

Traditionally, sedans featured two helms: one on the flying bridge, and one below, forward in the main saloon. The upper helm was intended primarily for fair-weather use. But as builders discovered that more and more owners were rarely using the lower, inside station (especially in warm-weather boating areas such as Florida), they started offering sedans with a flying bridge helm only. These are now very popular. And, of course, without the lower helm, more living space is available.

This Sabre 34 sedan has an open cockpit with a custom canvas extension to expand its cockpit.

AFT-CABIN MOTOR YACHT

Placing a cabin, rather than a cockpit, in the rear of a boat has many advantages (though some designs offer both an aft cabin and a cockpit, which may then become a sort of patio for the occupants of the aft cabin). Locating the sleeping accommodations in the bow and stern, separated by the main saloon, provides maximum privacy. Many designs extend the aft cabin the full width of the hull, creating a large and spacious master stateroom. If the main deck is extended over the aft cabin it creates an expansive rear deck area, which may be enclosed or left open.

We would call many aft-cabin designs split-level if they were homes. The saloon is elevated above the engine compartment. Down and forward from the saloon there are one or two sleeping areas. Down and aft there is the aft cabin. The bridge level, though not quite as elevated as a flying bridge, is above the saloon. Some designs do add a small flying bridge above the main bridge deck for even better visibility. Most of these aft-cabin designs make very comfortable cruising boats.

The aft-cabin design of this Sea Ray 390 design is made possible by moving the engines to the center of the hull, creating space for an expansive master stateroom.

SPORTFISHERMEN AND CONVERTIBLES

The sport fishing style covers a wide range of boats, including some called convertibles. It is characterized by a large aft cockpit for working the fishing gear and a flying bridge set well aft so that the skipper can observe the action and play the boat to the fish. Some even have an aluminum *tuna tower*, with yet another limited helm to provide a higher vantage point when looking for fish. Most examples of this style, often called a *sportfish*, are built on a planing hull and are designed to run fast offshore.

While a sportfisherman's primary design is geared to fishing, those of 35 feet and longer have the accommodations to take you fishing and cruising in comfort. In this respect, sportfishermen are much like the sedans they resemble.

A convertible generally has a smaller saloon than a sedan, and a larger cockpit, usually set at a much lower level (three to six steps down) than the saloon. Some convertibles have a limited galley/dining area forward of the main saloon arrangement, but unless there is a convertible sofa in the saloon, all sleeping accommodations will be below the large, uncluttered foredeck (which is where the dinghy will be carried if the boat has one).

EXPRESS CRUISER

In general, express cruisers are designed for sun seekers who like to go fast in warm waters. This type of boat has an open helm and large cockpit. Some incorporate a hard top over the helm, while others cover the area with a canvas *bimini*. The open design trades some accommodation space for deck space, but there's usually still enough for cruising comfort, especially in larger models.

Most express cruisers have at least one fully private double cabin in the bow and a smaller but usable *midcabin* under the slightly raised helm area. In those of about 40 feet in length and up, two *heads* (toilets) with showers are not unusual. Most also have convertible sofas in the saloon/dining area to give a total sleeping capacity of at least six—though they rarely have enough stowage to accommodate this many for a cruise of much duration.

These boats usually have large engines installed in their planing hulls, so their fuel

A sportfishing boat like this Luhrs 44 convertible features a huge, uncluttered foredeck, a flying bridge that overlooks the rear cockpit, and a hull designed to go fast in rough seas.

The design of the Albin Tournament Express combines comfortable cruising accommodations with speed and maneuverability.

economy is not always the greatest. But most of them, when throttled back to more reasonable speeds, will do quite well for longer cruises if you're not in too much of a hurry.

DOWNEAST CRUISER

Styled after the traditional New England lobster boat—with its large open cockpit and small-workboat appearance—the downeast cruiser is also called a *lobster yacht*. Many of these cruisers have small cabins forward, with limited sleeping and cooking accommodations. As this style of boat reaches 35 to 40 feet in length, enough room for cruising accommodations can be obtained by taking space from the open cockpit to make a longer forward cabin.

The helm is covered by a hard top, which can be extended to cover portions of the open cockpit. The cockpit is often enclosed with canvas to provide additional all-weather living space. These cruisers are built on a semi-displacement hull, and depending on the engine, can easily cruise at 10 knots or more.

POWER CATAMARAN

Sailing catamarans, with their twin hulls, have been popular with cruisers for years. The powered cat is becoming a popular cruiser too. The twin-hull configuration makes a very stable platform and this hull shape is easily driven through the water in the 10 to 15 knot range (or even higher), so it's economical to operate.

Catamarans may have either planing or displacement hulls. Smaller cruising cats, those under about 35 feet in length, have planing hulls, built light to get up on plane. Larger designs, more than 40 feet in length, are usually displacement hulls and exploit the fact that the twin hulls are very narrow and easily driven through the water. Their *shoal draft* (shallow depth) makes them a popular choice for cruising in regions such as the Bahamas or Florida Keys, where shoal—shallow—waters are the norm.

Since the main cabin is above the twin hulls and extends across the boat's full width, the saloon and other main deck accommodations such as the galley and dining area can be quite spacious. Of course, the narrow-beamed hulls mean that the sleeping areas are tighter and more sailboat-like than most

The Hinckley Picnic EP has an extended pilothouse roof, which creates more space for an L-shaped settee and pedestal table.

The twin hulls of a power cat create double the space for creature comforts with powerful engines and a shallow draft.

powerboating people are used to, but they are generally quite comfortable nonetheless.

A catamaran's wide beam provides a stable ride but can also produce a quick roll in rough conditions. This is less evident in heavier displacement models whose stability more closely resembles that of displacement *monohulls* (single-hulled boats). Also on the plus side, the wide separation between propellers allows some rather spectacular *twin screw* maneuvering if the skipper knows what he or she is doing. The wide beam can't be accommodated at some marinas, but this doesn't seem to be a problem since we see catamarans cruising everywhere.

A houseboat features outdoor and indoor living space with large decks forward and aft and mobile-home living below.

HOUSEBOAT

Often compared to boxy recreational vehicles, houseboats feature expansive living space both inside and out. Their square-top shape provides a large interior and their (usually) shallow draft allows for some very interesting gunkholing in otherwise seldom-visited areas. Houseboats are built on a variety of hulls, including pontoons. Planing hulls, with their low freeboard, make good platforms to swim or fish from.

This design is ideally suited to, and most popular in, protected inland waterways and on lakes, bays, and rivers. Houseboats are generally not seaworthy enough for cruising in exposed waters.

CHAPTER 2
Interiors

The writer Ernest Gann, author of the classic novel *The High and the Mighty*, cruised the Pacific Northwest aboard the Jay Benford-designed *Strumpet*, a salty 35-foot trawler. This boat has always been one of our favorite designs and we were thrilled to see it at a classic boat event at the Chesapeake Bay Maritime Museum in our home port, St. Michaels, Maryland. Gann had said the layout of *Strumpet* was designed to provide space as follows: drinks for six, feed four, and sleep two. That formula has always made a lot of sense to us, because over the years that's exactly how we've used our boat—no matter how spacious or cramped the accommodations.

The interior layout is an important ingredient for any coastal cruiser. If you use your boat as a weekend retreat, it becomes a second home; comfortable seating and sleeping accommodations, and sufficient stowage for all your gear are essential. The importance of galley features and design depends on whether you mostly cook aboard or eat out.

If you prefer to anchor out and be independent of land services, interior creature comforts may be particularly important. You'll need space for relaxing, a convenient and usable galley, and a good-sized *head* (toilet compartment) with shower.

The weather conditions where you cruise are another element that may influence your choice of interior layout. If you do most of your cruising in good weather and moderate climates, you may spend most of your time underway on the flying bridge. If that's the case, then perhaps a simple lower helm station (or even none at all) will suffice, freeing up more interior living space. But consider the consequences: if you *are* underway in bad weather, a minimal interior helm station, or an exposed one on the flying bridge, may be far from ideal. If you operate your boat in the cooler weather of late fall and early spring, a full helm in the main cabin or a pilothouse might be more practical.

The only way to really get a feel for a boat is to go aboard and move about. This isn't always easy at a boat show, where hundreds of other folks have the same idea. If you're looking at used boats with a broker, or boat shopping at a dealer, you have more time to get a feel for the features, space, and layout of many different designs.

BASIC LAYOUTS

Over the years we've seen interior spaces evolve. At every boat show we attend, we discover a boat with a new twist to its interior layout. Some of these ideas are quite clever, others seem to defy logic. There are many ways to arrange the accommodations inside the confines of a boat's hull, and they all involve compromise.

The shape of the boat and the location of the engines can dictate the placement of accommodations, but sometimes designers develop an interior plan first. Here's our take on the advantages and disadvantages of each of the basic arrangements.

SEDAN

The sedan layout places the communal living space or saloon in the center and aft section of the boat. The private areas—sleeping quarters and the head or heads—are usually located down and forward. In some variations the galley is on the same level as the saloon; in others it's a few steps below and forward. Having the saloon and cockpit soles at the same or nearly the same level expands the available living area. The saloon opens directly to the aft cockpit, which becomes a "back porch," though in mosquito- or gnat-

prone areas you'll have to enclose the porch with screens if you actually want to *use* it.

This arrangement provides a spacious common area, but doesn't provide a great deal of privacy if there are two *staterooms* (sleeping cabins) up forward. The *bulkheads* (walls) separating them are usually quite thin. Also, in rough weather, especially a head sea, the motion in the bow can make sleeping difficult.

TRI-CABIN OR AFT-CABIN

A tri-cabin layout divides a boat into three sections, creating two private staterooms, usually each with a head, one in the bow and one in stern. The third cabin, the saloon, is situated between the sleeping areas. The galley is located in the saloon on the same level, or a few steps below in a *galley down* configuration.

This arrangement provides the most privacy by separating the staterooms, but since a large portion of the boat's interior is devoted to sleeping accommodations, the saloon tends to be smaller than in other designs.

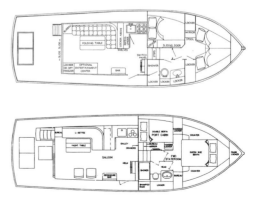

The layout of this Grand Banks Europa 42 sedan features main accommodations on one level and forward cabins a few steps below the main level.

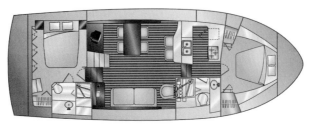

Three separate cabins characterize this Mainship 430, a tri-cabin style with a main salon that separates forward and aft cabins.

WIDE BODY

Traditionally, cabin cruisers and motor yachts have had side decks, or at least walkways, that extend from the foredeck to an aft deck, a cockpit, or both. Several years ago, boatbuilders discovered that many people considered these side decks wasted space, because they were so seldom used. The builders' response was to extend saloons the full *beam* (width) of the boat, creating the wide-body style of motor yacht. The advantage, of course, is more usable interior space, particu-

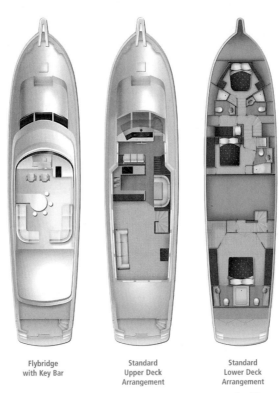

Flybridge
with Key Bar

Standard
Upper Deck
Arrangement

Standard
Lower Deck
Arrangement

The layout of this 75-foot Hatteras Motor Yacht illustrates the expansive space of a wide-body arrangement with no side decks.

larly in the saloon. The disadvantage is that anyone going aft must walk through the saloon, creating more through traffic.

Some wide-body designs have steps leading from the foredeck up to a bridge deck above the saloon. This feature allows you to go aft by climbing to the bridge deck and then down to the aft deck or cockpit. Not all wide-body yachts have this arrangement, and even with those that do, you have to consider if everyone's knees are going to appreciate all the climbing up and down.

POWER CATAMARAN

The extreme beam of a twin-hulled power cat offers spacious room on the main deck level, which usually spans the full width of the boat. Space below deck is generally ample as well, though individual compartments within the two sleek hulls tend to be on the narrow side.

The large main cabin usually houses a spacious, comfortable saloon and quite often a helm station forward and center (though some models are only fitted with a helm on the flying bridge). The galley and dining areas are also most often included within this huge cabin space, with the sleeping and head facilities located down in the hulls. On larger cats (60 feet and up) there is often also a day head (toilet and vanity only) on the main

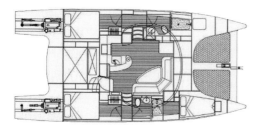

Catamarans lend themselves to interiors with huge, centrally located public areas, and relatively small stateroom cabins in the hulls. (Illustration courtesy Manta Catamarans.)

deck, easily accessible from the saloon or lower helm.

INTERIOR FEATURES TO CONSIDER

What are the key interior features that will make a boat comfortable and convenient for you? To answer that question you'll need to consider how and where you will cruise and create your own list, but here are the features we think are important.

BERTHS

We always laugh when we see advertisements for a 36-foot cruiser that "sleeps eight comfortably." Yes, if everyone is lying still in their bunk and barely breathing. Maybe converting a settee, rearranging a table, and unfolding a hidden panel can create eight bunks, but these maneuvers are neither easy nor convenient. Many cruising families we know say they opt to put kids in sleeping bags on the bridge or on deck in good weather rather than dismantle the boat's interior. Just because it's possible doesn't mean it's desirable to confine eight people on board a 36-footer; four would be far more comfortable.

Well-separated sleeping accommodations offer the most privacy. When the only partition between sleeping compartments or heads is a thin bulkhead, everyone can hear bedroom and bathroom noises.

When you're looking at boats, don't be embarrassed to lie down and test the mattresses. Some forward V-berths may look ideal, but often they are built high above the cabin *sole* (floor) and are difficult to climb into. And if you're a restless sleeper who moves around a lot, you'd better see if there's enough shoulder room for you to toss and turn.

Many folks prefer a queen-size bunk that's centered in a forward or aft cabin so two peo-

The v-berth in a 36-foot trawler.

ple can get in and out with ease. Usually called *island berths*, they are often as spacious and comfortable as your bed at home. They do, however, require a large cabin, and even then can dominate the space, leaving little

This Cabo 35 Express makes the most out of a small guest stateroom, with a one-on-top-of-another bunk bed.

room for anything else, especially in the bow. Island berths in forward cabins are often even higher off the sole than V-berths, as a result of the shape of the bow. There simply isn't enough width for a queen mattress until it's placed far enough up the taper of the hull. A forward island berth often has a complex shape that requires specially fitted bedding and is actually queen width (60") only at its widest point.

A double bunk that's built along one side of a bulkhead is very comfortable for a large person. For two people, however, the person sleeping on the inside may have to crawl over his or her partner on the outside to get out of bed.

Twin berths are used in many layouts, especially in the bow, where they are joined at the bow (the foot of the bed) forming a V. Other arrangements place the V-berths on different levels, so that the foot of one berth passes under the foot of the other. Yet another arrangement places the upper and lower berths on one side of the stateroom, leaving the other side free for built-in drawers and lockers. Either arrangement makes for larger bunks than allowed by a basic V, though

An island queen bed that you can walk around is often a feature in the master cabin of large cruising boats, like this Silverton 39.

access to the upper berth can be difficult, due to its height. In all these arrangements, it can be very convenient and comforting to have a bulkhead to wedge yourself against, especially if the wake of a passing boat rolls you.

HEADROOM AND PASSAGEWAYS

Even though a boat's interior space is limited, you shouldn't find your activity limited by the bulkheads or *overhead* (ceiling). You should be able to move about without having to stoop down to fit into a *companionway* (passageway or entry) or stand sideways to pass through an opening. But if this is your first time looking at cruising boats, what may seem like cramped quarters compared to landside accommodations may seem spacious to someone who is cruising on a smaller boat.

You won't find 7-foot headroom on many 35-foot boats. Some cruisers are advertised

CUSTOM-MADE MATTRESSES

If you're in the market for a new boat mattress, look in the back of any boating magazine and you'll find advertisements for custom-made boat mattresses. On the Internet go to boatbeds.com.

You may have to cut up the old mattress to get it out of the cabin, but a new one that's designed to be folded and tied in half assures easy maneuvering around corners and into tight cabins.

with more than 6 feet of headroom, but that's only at the companionway or in the main cabin. It's considerably less almost everywhere else. Headroom is also an issue when sitting—it's important to be comfortable when you're seated at a settee that's tucked in a corner.

Two feet is pretty much the standard width for companionways but you might notice that these dimensions narrow as you go forward or aft to other cabins—especially if there's a sliding door. A boat's brochure may indicate overall dimensions, but there's no substitute for a walk-through wearing a heavy parka to see how easy it is to maneuver. If you are hitting your head on the overhead or bumping your shoulders in a tight companionway, it might not be the boat for you.

Getting your footing aboard any boat for the first time always takes some adjustment. Steep, winding stairs leading to the lower cabins can be especially awkward to navigate at first. Try backing down the stairs and using the wider, outer part of the tread. Unusually steep stairs can be difficult and dangerous to negotiate.

The number and height of stairs can be a real concern if you or your crew members suffer from aching knee joints. We met one cruising couple who chose a tugboat-type trawler because their agility was an issue, and the low height of the stairs leading from the pilothouse was easy on their knees. We met another couple who were trading their convertible fishing boat for a trawler because they wanted a one-level boat. They weren't having trouble with the steep stairs—their two aging Labradors were.

LIGHTING

Any interior designer will tell you how important good lighting is a room, and the same is true for comfort, aesthetics, and safety in-

side a boat. Many older boats come equipped with standard bulkhead-mounted one-bulb fixtures. More recent models pay greater attention to the lighting detail, but that doesn't mean it can't be improved by fitting more directed lighting. A stroll through the pages of any marine supply catalog or website will reveal a plentiful array of light fixtures, usually of chrome or brass and many trimmed in teak.

One of the challenges of boat lighting is that an area often has multiple uses. Dining tables, for example, are often used as desks, chart tables, or for reading and relaxing. In our trawler, the overhead light was adequate for dining, but we had to add a bulkhead light for reading. On your boat, if you like to read in bed you may need to add a bulkhead fixture or two in the stateroom at the head of your berth.

Sometimes the lighting design in a boat is good, but the location of the fixtures or switches makes them difficult to use. New fixtures can be added, but the challenge lies in running the wires so they're not exposed. The prospect of cutting a permanent hole in the joinery, bulkheads, or built-in furniture is daunting. The job is made easier if there's a wire chase or flexible conduit snaking its way behind the headliner and bulkheads. Either will hold all the wires together for easy access and servicing.

If you're contemplating purchasing a particular boat, find out if you can go aboard at night. You'll see if the illumination is adequate, and you'll quickly learn if the switches are easy to find in the dark. And check out the courtesy lighting of stairs and passageways—this is an important safety feature.

HEADS

Head is the nautical term for a toilet and also the compartment in which it is contained.

Most boats have one or two heads, usually located next to the sleeping quarters, but some have an additional *day head* (toilet and vanity only, no shower) located near the helm station so the captain and crew don't have to traipse through the boat to answer nature's call. While a head is usually the smallest space on a boat, it can be one of the most frequently used. Some heads are plain and basic. Others have fixtures and amenities that rival a home bathroom, with solid surface countertops, wooden cabinetry, and elaborate faucets.

A head that's easy to use and to keep clean makes cruising more enjoyable (and sanitary). You haven't been in boating long if you haven't been humbled by a malfunction, clog, or overflow in a marine toilet. It's not pretty.

SHOWERS

A head with a separate shower or bathtub is the ultimate luxury for many boaters. Two toilets divided by a shower compartment are particularly handy when they are located between two cabins.

A step down from the separate shower is a head design that incorporates a showerhead and faucets in the same compartment as the toilet. Most often it has a grated floor with a drain below, and it becomes a shower stall by using a shower curtain to contain the spray and protect the bulkheads. A pump removes the shower water that collects in the sump below the grated floor. The downside of this arrangement is that even though a shower curtain protects the interior, moisture can still get into storage compartments. It also often means a wet and uninviting toilet seat. On a windy day a wet shower space will dry quickly, but on a muggy, windless day it may take several hours to air. Even so, if your boat isn't big enough to accommodate a separate

shower stall, a combined shower/head is the next best thing.

If you're looking at a boat with a combined shower and head, stand right in it and note the height of the telephone-style showerhead mount. Is it at the right height—neither too high nor too low—to leave the showerhead mounted on the bulkhead, or will you always have to take it in hand? If so, is the handgrip comfortable to hold? Can you reach both the faucets and the showerhead without going through contortions? If you do have to hand hold the showerhead, is there room for you to

A granite countertop, wood cabinetry, and a walk-in shower make the head aboard the Meridian 341 a pleasure to use.

conveniently spray yourself all over without bumping your elbow into the bulkheads in the process? And is the ventilation good enough to remove excess moisture?

We consider a shower of some sort to be an essential item of cruising equipment, even if it's only a shower at the transom meant primarily for rinsing off after swimming. Our current boat, *High Life* (a Grand Banks 36), has two combined shower/head arrangements. The shower curtains are well laid out to contain most of the water.

For short-term cruising, a head that's minimally comfortable and reliable will do just fine, but don't skimp on quality and durability. In Chapter 5 we discuss the mechanical aspects of the plumbing systems and choosing a marine head and holding tank.

The head-shower combination on this Sea Ray 360 Sundancer makes good use of space. The design also features seamless surfaces.

GALLEY

Gene has always said that if sailboat designers had to change the engine oil they'd do a much better job of designing the engine space. The same could be said for whoever designs the galley. For cruisers who love to cook, the design and layout of the galley are major factors. At the minimum, a galley should provide features for convenient food storage and preparation and to keep provisions cold or frozen.

As you look at more and more boats you'll find some with expansive galley space, layout, and equipment, while others keep galley features to a minimum. When appraising a boat's galley space and design, consider how and what you cook and where you will store cooking utensils and food. Try to imagine how well it would suit your cooking style, or if you could adapt your style to the space. Some galleys are short on storage and counter space but feature an entire cabinet for storing liquor and glasses. Others have volumes of storage space that's accessible only by getting down on your hands and knees.

Most galleys are equipped with a small refrigerator that runs on both 12-volt DC battery power and 120-volt AC shore power, a cooktop with or without an oven and/or a microwave oven, and a sink. A galley may consist of a few feet of counter and cabinets, range, and refrigerator all in a line, but a wide U-shape configuration is more convenient. In larger boats, with more room to spread out, the galley can be made more chef-friendly by incorporating a triangular work zone with cooktop, refrigerator, and sink arranged in the most efficient manner. The size of the sink is largely determined by the size of the boat and the space allocated for food preparation. Some galley sinks are too small to soak a dinner plate, while others are large enough for a roasting pan. We have a friend who bought

Built-in appliances and smooth curved walls and cabinetry make an inviting galley on this Regal 3860 Sport Yacht.

9-inch square dinner plates because they were the only size plates that fit into the sink.

Boaters have definite opinions about the location and layout of the galley, with one key issue: should the galley be up or down? That is, should the galley be an extension of the main saloon (up), or have its own separate space, located a few steps forward and below the main cabin (down)? A food preparation area that's part of the main saloon creates a more casual atmosphere, but a separate one defines the space more clearly. Advocates of the galley-down location say they prefer the privacy of being below and having a place to stack dirty dishes away from the main saloon.

There's another consideration: some galleys are quite adequate for preparing elegant meals at dockside or in a peaceful anchorage, when the boat isn't moving around very much. But underway? Without adjustable sea rails or holders to keep pots and pans from sliding around on the stove, *fiddles* (raised edges or sea rails) to keep plates and bowls from sliding off countertops, and hand rails for the cook to hold onto, a galley is totally inadequate.

Of course, if you don't plan to cook underway, none of this matters. There is no right answer to what a galley *should* be. It all depends on how you intend to use it.

CHART TABLES AND NAV STATION

On any size boat it's important to have a space where you can spread out a chart or open the pages of a cruising guide. In most boats that's possible at the helm station where a flat sur-

The galley on this Cabo 35 Express features Corian countertops and sink, side-by-side refrigerator-freezer, and a built-in microwave. (Photo by Forest Johnson)

face may be concealing a storage compartment where you can store the charts or cruising guides. In a pilothouse boat there is usually a large drawer to accommodate a chart book or charts nearby the electronic equipment. Sometimes a flying bridge has a console where material can be opened and remain accessible.

CHAPTER 3
Engines, Drive Systems, Steering, and Stabilizers

Of all the many features that combine to make a cruising boat work, one of the most important is the propulsion system. The whole system includes the engine, transmission, propeller, steering gear, rudder, and—where fitted—stabilizers (which run off the main engine and contribute to the efficient operation of the boat). A failure in any of these components will quickly take the fun out of a cruise, no matter how enchanting it might otherwise be.

When considering the relative merits of a cruising boat, pay critical attention to the reliability of the engine and drivetrain. If you decide to change any part of this system after you've purchased a boat you will be faced with technical difficulties and the work will run into serious dollars.

Designers match the power train to the boat, so it's important to consider how you plan to operate the boat and the cruising style you plan to adopt. The speed and range of a boat can be affected by the choice of power plant. A 40-foot express cruiser may have a turbocharged diesel engine large enough to push it to a cruising speed of 15–25 knots. A displacement trawler will more likely have a power plant designed to push her at 7–10 knots. The trawler isn't designed to go 25 knots and the express cruiser is not designed to cruise at 7 knots day after day.

MARINE ENGINES AND TRANSMISSIONS

Marine engines work hard. It's common to continuously operate your unit at 70 to 90 percent of its maximum rated horsepower. That's like constantly running your car at 90 miles an hour uphill. Both gas and diesel marine engines are designed to stand up to this workload, but a diesel engine will certainly have a longer life expectancy. We know cruisers who make extended voyages with both types of engines; however, today we see fewer 35- to 40-foot cruisers fitted out with gas engines.

DIESEL ENGINES

Diesel technology has made great advances in the last decade. Today's diesel engines are lighter than their predecessors and approach the power-to-weight ratio of modern gas engines. We saw a beautiful 1950s Chris Craft, almost fully restored, at a United States Power Squadrons get-together. The owner had been able to replace the original V8 gas engines with smaller, more powerful diesel engines that weighed hundreds of pounds less.

Diesel engines are more expensive than gas engines, so your investment in a diesel-powered vessel will be greater, but it is money well spent if you plan to drive your boat for more than a couple of hundred hours a year; you save on fuel costs and you can expect longer engine life. A single cruise down the Intracoastal Waterway, or a trip through the Inland Passage from Seattle to Southern Alaska, would put this much time on your engine.

Diesels are also more reliable than gas engines because they have no ignition system (spark plugs, coil, and so on) and once started, they require no electrical system to keep them running. The new computer-controlled diesels do have electrical elements, but they still don't have an ignition system and can't be stopped or slowed by fouled spark plugs.

All a diesel engine needs to run is clean fuel and air. The only time our diesel engine ever stopped underway was the time Gene's rear end accidentally turned off the fuel valve when he was checking the oil. Diesel engines burn fuel more efficiently than gas engines, and diesel fuel is usually less expensive (though the gap is steadily closing).

If you are looking for a boat more than 35 feet in length to take on extended cruises, you should seriously consider one that's diesel powered.

GAS ENGINES

Despite its advantages, diesel power is not the best choice for every boat. If most of your cruising consists of weekend trips on a smaller boat in local waters, then a gas engine will serve you well. Even if you are planning an extended cruise, gas power will get you there.

Gas engines provide a lot of power for their weight and are a good choice to power a small-to-midsize planing boat. The initial cost of a gas engine is less than a diesel of comparable horsepower. Most marine gas engines are conversions of car or truck engines, so their useful lives are shorter than diesels. A well-maintained gas engine can last 1,500 to 2,000 hours before a major overhaul or replacement is needed, compared to 4,000 to 10,000 hours for a well-maintained diesel engine. Despite this shorter life expectancy, you could repower the boat with a new or rebuilt gas engine with the money you saved initially if you chose gas rather than diesel.

There is another consideration: gasoline is more volatile, and thus it ignites and

(Photo courtesy Crusader.)

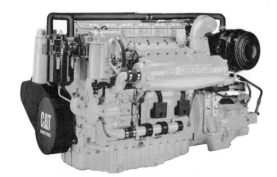

(Photo courtesy Caterpillar.)

explodes more easily than diesel fuel. This means that gas-powered boats have a greater potential for fire and explosion. If you spend a lot of time aboard—as you will when cruising—the peace of mind that diesel engines provide can be well worth their added cost. But good boatkeeping and operating practices will make a gas-powered boat just as safe.

TRANSMISSIONS

To make a boat move, the engine's power has to be transmitted to the propeller. That's the function of the transmission. It connects the engine to the propeller shaft and also provides a means of disengaging the two so that the engine can run without turning the propeller. The transmission can also reverse the rotation of the propeller shaft so the boat can back up.

Most marine engines operate in the 1,500–3,500 rpm range, so a direct connection would require a small, fast-turning prop. Large diameter propellers, however, are more efficient than small props. To reduce the prop revolutions per minute (rpm) most transmissions incorporate a reduction gear. Reduction ratios from 1.5:1 to 3:1 are common on cruising boats. The higher the reduction ratio, the larger the propeller an engine can turn. Typically, a trawler may have a 24-inch diameter prop that turns at about 600 rpm when run through a 3:1 reduction gear with the engine operating at 1800 rpm.

Inboard Transmissions

Marine transmissions come in several configurations. The most common is the *in-line* transmission, in which the engine and transmission are mounted so that the crankshaft aligns with the propeller shaft, with little or no change of angle. But depending on the design of the transmission and reduction gear the propeller coupling may be offset from the centerline of the crankshaft. Boats with engines located midships usually use an in-line arrangement.

A *V-drive* transmission changes the direction of the drive so that the propeller shaft passes back under the engine (which is mounted back to front compared to an in-line drive). A V-drive allows the engine to be mounted level and closer to the stern of the boat. This arrangement can save space, but it's more expensive and requires more maintenance than an in-line drive.

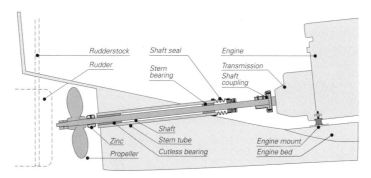

A standard in-line installation has the engine, transmission, and propeller shaft all in a line. (Illustration by Charlie Wing.)

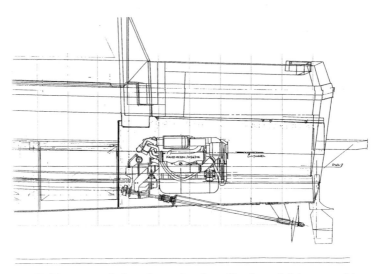

In a V-drive transmission, the engine faces "backwards" (compared to a standard in-line installation), the transmission reverses the drive direction, and the propeller shaft passes beneath the engine. (Illustration by John Kiley.)

Stern Drives

A popular engine configuration for mid-size cruisers is the stern drive, which mates an engine and transmission to an external drive unit. The external drive unit, or *outdrive*, can be raised and trimmed like an outboard engine, so the configuration combines the advantages of an inboard engine with the flexibility of an outboard drive.

Most units have a single propeller, but some have dual counter-rotating props, mounted one directly in front of the other on concentric shafts. The two propellers turn in opposite directions and work together to better transfer the engine power to the water, but the mechanism is more complex. The diameter of the propeller that can be fitted on a stern drive limits its application on larger cruising boats.

The engine is usually mounted in the stern against the transom, but some configurations use a jackshaft to connect engine and stern drive, allowing the engine to be mounted well forward of the transom. This lets the boat's designer provide more spacious accommodations aft, or improve the boat's fore-and-aft weight distribution.

Stern drives are available with mid-range diesel and large, high-powered gas engines. They have the muscle to push a mid-sized, semi-displacement cruising boat, but are best teamed with a planing-type hull.

Stern drives provide efficient power transfer. This model has twin counter-rotating props—a feature that reduces prop walk. (Photo courtesy Volvo Penta.)

PROPELLERS

When a propeller turns, it interacts with the water to create thrust that pushes the boat forward or backward, depending on its direction of rotation. The propeller is like a wood screw. Its diameter is the circle described by the blade tips as they revolve. In cruising boats, large-diameter, slow-turning propellers are more efficient than small-diameter, fast-turning props. A large-diameter prop requires a high-ratio reduction gear to allow the engine to turn at its rated rpm, while allowing the prop to turn at a much slower rate.

A prop's pitch is the distance it would travel forward through the water in a single revolution—as if it were actually a wood screw turning into wood. The pitch of a propeller is only a theoretical number, because one revolution of the propeller does not push the boat the full distance indicated by its pitch. The difference between the distance a boat is actually pushed in one revolution of the prop and its nominal pitch is called *slip*. The amount of slip a prop develops is one indication of its efficiency.

The diameter of the prop is limited by its clearance from the bottom of the hull—or the propeller aperture at the end of the keel on a single-screw boat. To reduce draft, some manufacturers locate the propellers in "tun-nels." These tunnels are indentations in the underside of the hull slightly larger than the diameter of the propellers. The top portion of the propeller rotates in the depression so only the lower portion of the prop extends below the bottom of the boat. The tunnels also reduce the angle of the propeller shaft.

The more blades a propeller has, the less vibration it produces. Higher-speed cruising boats use three or four blade props. Larger, full-displacement cruisers may have five-bladed props. Very fast boats with high-powered engines may use props with six or more blades. When properly sized, any type works.

The amount of horsepower needed to turn the propeller at any given rpm depends upon the diameter and pitch of the propeller and its number of blades. It takes more horse-power to turn the propeller faster, less to turn it slower. And of course the boat's speed varies according to the prop's rpm. The accepted practice is that a correct match-up of engine and propeller is achieved when a propeller allows the engine to reach its maximum rated rpm at full throttle.

Engine manufacturers publish this data for their engines. For example, our boat's 120 hp Ford Lehman engine develops its maximum continuous horsepower at 2,500 rpm. This means that, when the hull bottom is clean and with a medium load of fuel and water on board, the engine should be able to reach 2,500 rpm at full throttle.

If the engine can't reach its maximum-rated rpm at full throttle you can usually assume the prop is overloading the engine. This can happen if the boat is *over-propped*, which means it is fitted with a propeller that is either too large in diameter or has too much pitch. Greater pitch equals greater speed at the same rpm, until it reaches the point of overloading the engine. Similarly, a larger diameter means more thrust, which

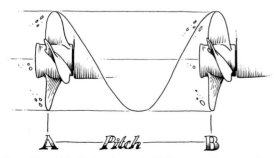

Propeller pitch is the theoretical distance the propeller will travel through the water in one full revolution. (Illustration by Christopher Hoyt.)

can also improve performance, until it over-loads the engine. So an increase in diameter or pitch is not necessarily bad. Over-propping is usually a result of taking the idea too far. The answer to over-propping, of course, is to go back to either a smaller diameter prop or one with less pitch, or perhaps one that is smaller in both dimensions.

Prop selection can be a complicated process. It involves enough interdependent variables so that it is a job best left to experts. If the designer has done his work properly, there should be no need for the boatowner to worry about changing props.

JET DRIVES

Some cruisers don't have props. They are equipped with a jet drive system, which is basically a large water pump. The engine drives the pump, which draws water in from under the boat and discharges it through a nozzle at the stern to propel the boat forward. A jet drive allows for a shallow draft since there is no propeller protruding from the bottom of the boat. It also does away with the rudder, since the jet's discharge nozzle can be turned to control the direction of the water stream and thus the direction it pushes the boat.

There's also no need for a transmission to provide reverse because the pump always runs in the same direction. The nozzle has a bucket that drops in place when you shift the boat into reverse. This redirects the jet's thrust toward the front of the boat, which pushes the boat backwards.

STEERING SYSTEMS

The turning propeller produces thrust to move the boat, but in order to steer the boat, the direction of the thrust must be controlled. This is the job of the steering system.

Boats with a conventional drive employ a rudder. Most cruising powerboats control the rudder with cables or hydraulic motors coupled to steering wheels.

Additional devices are available to help the helmsman steer the boat. The autopilot is used to control the rudder, especially on long passages. It does a fair amount of steering on the average cruising boat. And bow thrusters have become standard equipment on many new cruisers.

RUDDERS

There are two important facts about rudders you should always keep in mind.

First, the rudder will only work if water is flowing past it. Whatever type of boat you have, if it isn't moving through the water or if the prop is not turning, the rudder can't turn the boat. Remember too that if the boat is only moving because it is being pushed by a current, the rudder will have no effect.

Second, the faster the boat is moving, the smaller the rudder needs to be. In fact, a large rudder tends to slow a boat down, so most boats designed to go fast have small rudders.

When a fast boat slows down and the engine is put in neutral, the prop stops pushing water past the small rudder, which becomes less effective. This is why the steering on most planing or fast semi-displacement boats often becomes sluggish at slow speeds, especially when in neutral.

The opposite is true for slow-moving boats. A large rudder is needed to create a turning force, since the water passes by the rudder slowly—especially on single-screw trawlers. But even a large rudder will only turn the boat if water is moving past it. That's why the rudder is placed directly behind the propeller: the water pushed backwards by the propeller, the *prop wash*, passes over the rudder.

When backing the boat, the prop wash does not flow over the rudder, so it is not effective until the boat begins to gain *sternway* (moves backwards). The larger the rudder, the sooner it becomes effective. To back a twin-screw boat with small rudders, it is often more effective to steer with the engines rather than the rudders. (See Chapter 16, Boat Handling, for details.)

Larger single-screw boats usually have a single large rudder that extends vertically from the underside of the hull to an extension of the keel. This arrangement provides two points of support for the rudder. The keel extension, sometimes called the *rudder shoe*, also provides some rudder protection if the boat runs aground.

Twin-screw boats mostly have two rudders, one behind each prop. On fast boats these are usually attached to *rudderposts* leading from the bottom of the hull. Some twin-screw trawlers have *skegs*. Like the single-screw rudder shoe, a skeg runs under the propellers and rudders to protect them. But unlike a rudder shoe, a skeg is not connected to the keel (if there is one). Instead it is attached to the hull just forward of the point where the shaft exits and then extends aft beneath the prop to attach to the foot of the rudderpost. It is also connected to the bottom of the shaft strut that's mounted just forward of the prop. On boats without skegs, the props are totally exposed and more prone to damage from grounding and floating debris.

When rudders (as well as the boats they were attached to) were built mostly of wood, they would often have an engineered *shaft hole*, which the propeller shaft could pass through for removal from the boat: without it, some boats required the rudder to be removed before the shaft could be extracted. You will still see a shaft hole on some boats with thick, heavy rudders. The hole causes drag on a fast boat, and many rudders are constructed with a continuous rudderpost that is in the location of the traditional prop shaft hole. Dropping the smaller rudders of a twin screw cruiser is not a big project, but most single screw cruisers with large rudders must be lifted high enough for the rudder to be dropped out of the boat after removing the rudder shoe.

Boats with stern drives don't have rudders, since the outdrive and propeller pivot together. Even at slow speeds, a stern-drive boat answers well to the helm. As long as the propeller is turning, the boat is easy to steer. And when you shift into neutral and the prop stops turning, the whole outdrive acts like a rudder.

STEERING GEAR

Designers use one of two different systems—cable or hydraulic steering—to turn the boat's rudder, stern drive, or jet. Both systems have their advantages and disadvantages. Smaller boats, and some older boats like the Grand Banks, use cable steering. Large cruisers, stern drive boats, and most jet boats usually have hydraulic steering.

Cable Steering

There are essentially two types of cable systems. For lack of a better description, these may be called *open* and *closed*. A closed cable system is also known as *push-pull* since it involves a single, semi-stiff cable within a flexible tube, like those employed in mechanical throttle and shift systems. The steering wheel drives a rack and pinion: the pinion is attached to the wheel and the rack to the end of the cable. Turning the wheel turns the pinion, which causes the rack to push or pull the cable. The other end of the cable is attached to the rudder arm (or its equivalent in either a stern drive or jet). This in turn pivots to deliver either the left or right rudder movement that steers the boat.

Push-pull systems are usually installed only on boats up to 30 feet or so. The longer the run, the more difficult it is to push the cable. Maintenance is simple, and primarily involves keeping the rack and pinion and the cable itself properly lubricated. Most units have standard *zerk* fittings for easy lubrication with a grease gun.

An open cable system is simpler and, if properly maintained, will remain trouble-free for the life of the boat. In this arrangement, there is a drum behind the wheel. The cable, usually a very flexible plastic-covered wire rope, is wrapped tightly around the drum and each end extends back along its respective side of the boat to attach to the rudder arm(s) or its (their) equivalent at the stern. On larger vessels, there's more often a chain wrapped around a toothed gear behind the wheel, with its ends attached to the port and starboard cables.

When you turn the wheel, the drum pulls on the cable on one side and takes up the resulting slack on the other. If you turn the wheel to *port* (left), for example, the cable will pull the rudder arm to *starboard* (right), which moves the rudder to port. The rudder arm always moves in exactly the opposite direction to the rudder movement, just like a tiller on a sailboat.

Cable systems develop a mechanical advantage by keeping the rate of turn of the rudder small compared to the number of turns of the wheel. The size of the advantage depends on the size of the drum (or gear) behind the wheel. On *High Life* we have cable steering and must turn the wheel four full revolutions to move from full left rudder to full right rudder. That's a lot of wheel spinning while backing a single-screw boat.

The big drawback with an open cable system is the number of pulleys that require greasing. There's a pulley at every point where the cable changes direction as it runs from helm to rudder and back, and the cable wears quickly if any one of these pulleys freezes up and won't turn. The cable also requires space that's clear of any obstructions all the way from helm to rudder or rudders. This is most easily achieved in small, open boats, but open cable systems are installed in vessels of all sizes, even large commercial craft.

Another minor disadvantage of open cable systems is that they are subject to feedback from the rudder. This means that the boat can easily wander off course if you don't keep a steady hand on the wheel, and in many seas you'll even have to fight the wheel to counter the water's force against the rudder.

Hydraulic Steering

In a hydraulic steering system, the wheel is connected to a rotary hydraulic pump. When you turn the wheel, the pump moves fluid through tubing to a ram—an enclosed cylinder with a piston. The free end of the piston is connected to the rudder arm (or its equivalent on stern drives or jets). Hydraulic fluid in the ram moves the piston back and forth, its direction of movement depending on which way you turn the steering wheel.

This system is the best choice for large boats with multiple helm stations for several reasons. First, it uses small diameter hydraulic tubing that can easily be routed through the boat from each helm station to the rudder(s). Second, each wheel has its own pump, which operates independently so that, when you turn the wheel at one helm, wheels at the other helms remain stationary. (In contrast, cable-based systems are connected together mechanically, and anything that might interfere with a wheel's freedom of motion at an unmanned helm station, such as a tight canvas cover on a flying bridge console, can cause serious problems for the system as a whole.) Third, it is easy to incorporate an autopilot into a hydraulic system. The hydraulic lines are cut and an additional hydraulic motor, controlled by the autopilot, is inserted. With this type of setup, *no* steering wheel turns. (When autopilots are connected to cable or mechanical systems, all wheels are usually still active.) Last, no matter how large the boat or rudder, there is no feedback to the wheel. Even when steering manually, you don't need to keep constant tension on the wheel to hold the rudder at a constant angle.

Hydraulic systems are easy to maintain—a periodic check for fluid level and leaks is usually all that is necessary to keep one working. Some types rely on a small reservoir of air to keep the system pressurized, but there's usually a gauge and fitting, like the one on an auto tire, so proper pressure can easily be restored with a bicycle pump. If you plan on cruising to more remote locations, you should carry spare parts and extra hydraulic fluid aboard.

Autopilot Systems

Until you've been on an extended cruise you won't really appreciate the value of an autopilot. Steering the boat is fun for a while, but it becomes a chore if you have to do it for ten hours straight. Our autopilot allows us to supervise the steering while not having to concentrate the whole time on staying on course. When we are on watch we can look out over the water, scan the horizon with binoculars, look at the radar, check the GPS, or read the chart—without the extra burden of constantly checking the compass and adjusting the helm. An autopilot does *not*, however, allow the person on watch to read a book or watch television. On watch means *on watch*.

In its simplest form an autopilot has a built-in compass (so it knows the direction the boat is heading) and a means of controlling the rudder. More sophisticated autopilots use a remotely mounted compass—these days it is usually of the fluxgate variety, which uses a wire coil rather than a magnetic needle to sense the earth's magnetic field. A remote compass can be mounted anywhere on the boat, in any area relatively free of interference from onboard magnetic influences that cause errors (known as *deviation*) in the displayed compass heading. Since most fluxgate-autopilot interfaces are now digital, total accuracy is possible by programming these systems to account for any remaining deviation. Most modern autopilots also allow you to choose between following the built-in compass to stay on the heading you select, or to ignore the compass and take a course toward a waypoint programmed into your GPS. Once the autopilot is set on a particular course, it will steer the boat along that heading with little off-course error. When the water gets rough, built-in computers help it anticipate and react to the sea conditions. The more sophisticated the autopilot, the better it can maintain a course in all types of seas. Most autopilots have a steering control (often called a *dodger*) that allows you to override the unit's basic heading command in order to deviate from the programmed course. In many cases this control is a remote unit connected to the main control head with a long extension cord. The remote unit allows you to steer the boat while you are away from the helm, a handy feature if you cruise in areas full of crab or lobster pots.

The autopilot controls the rudder with a drive unit, and the type of unit you need usually depends on your steering system. Boats with cable steering often use an electric motor drive to operate the cables. Boats with hydraulic steering usually employ a hydraulic pump that's installed directly into the steering system to activate the main steering ram. Other systems employ a hydraulic linear drive, with the hydraulic pump and ram in a single unit attached directly to the rudder arm.

There are other drives as well, each a little different. The best way to find out exactly what drive unit your autopilot uses (as well as how it is integrated into the steering system) is to study your owner's manual. Drive systems that *appear* similar on the outside can have important differences, and the manual will usually clarify what type of system you have. You should also follow the manual's advice on routine maintenance if you want to keep your autopilot functioning dependably.

It's always important to properly match the drive unit to the displacement and type of boat. Heavy displacement boats with large rudders require much sturdier drive units than similar-sized semi-displacement or planing-hull boats with smaller rudders. When shopping, choose an autopilot with the most robust drive unit you can afford. The drive unit is the most important component of the system since it controls the rudder. Whatever bells and whistles the control unit may have, it's the drive unit that actually steers the boat.

If your boat is not already equipped with an autopilot, we suggest you seriously consider one.

EMERGENCY STEERING

Whatever steering system you have, there should be a way to steer the boat if that system fails. Often, the top of the rudderpost is accessible through a hatch in the cockpit sole, and it will accept an emergency *tiller*. The tiller usually consists of a shaft with one end designed to fit over the rudderpost. At the other end there is a long arm, perpendicular to the shaft, to provide leverage. When you push

MIX AND MATCH OR MIX AND MUDDLE?

One note of caution when buying an autopilot: while newer systems are designed to be integrated with Loran or GPS, getting old equipment to talk to new equipment is rarely easy and probably not worth the effort. When we purchased *High Life,* the autopilot and the Loran set, both of mid-1980s vintage, were interfaced. This setup worked OK, but when we replaced the Loran with GPS, the autopilot would not communicate with the GPS.

The devices used different versions of NMEA 0183, the *interface language* that defines how marine electronics talk to one another. The protocol has evolved as electronics have become more sophisticated, but older units have a hard time understanding the new versions. Just because both units support NMEA 0183, there's no guarantee that they'll talk to one another.

If you have older equipment that is functioning properly and parts are still available, especially for big-ticket items like the autopilot, stick with the older equipment and forgo the integration. But if your systems are old and parts are hard to come by, consider replacing your autopilot and navigation electronics with systems that are designed to work together.

on the emergency tiller it turns the rudder. To steer the boat, open the hatch and slide the tiller over the rudderpost. And remember, the tiller arm faces forward, so you push it the opposite way you wish to turn—to port to turn the bow to starboard and vice versa.

It's a good idea to test the emergency steering to see how it works. You need to know how difficult it is to get out the tiller, attach it to the rudderpost, and whether you need to do anything else to make it function. You also need to know if there's sufficient clearance to swing the tiller far enough to steer effectively. Sometimes you may need to move cockpit furniture or other clutter out of the way.

You also need to know if you can see ahead well enough to steer by yourself, since the emergency system will be way back near the transom. You may need your mate to be your eyes from a different location on board while you provide the muscle.

If you have hydraulic steering, there's most probably a quick-and-easy way to disconnect the rudder from the hydraulic ram. Be sure you know how to accomplish this. And remember, even quick-and-easy often requires tools. In some cases, though not all, you may also have to unhook the autopilot drive unit before the rudder can turn freely, so learn how to do this too.

If your boat doesn't have a backup steering system, think seriously about having one installed; the components should not be expensive. If you have one, make sure it works. It is false security to have a backup system that is inadequate or impossible to deploy.

BOW THRUSTERS

A bow thruster allows you to steer and control the bow of the boat, independent of the main steering system. It is helpful when maneuvering in tight quarters, especially if there is an opposing or crosswind or current, and is becoming standard equipment on many new boats.

The bow thruster consists of a motor connected to a propeller through a right angle drive similar to an outboard motor lower unit. The propeller is mounted in a tube *athwartships* (from side to side) at the bow of the boat. Depending on its rotation, the prop jets water to *port* (moving the bow to starboard) or *starboard* (moving the bow to port). Both electric- and hydraulic-powered units are available in a variety of sizes to fit most cruising boats.

A boat's displacement and its *windage* (the area above its waterline that the wind can push against) determine how powerful the bow thruster should be. When shopping for one, pay careful attention to manufacturers' specifications. We've observed boats maneuvering with bow thrusters in all types of weather, and we've reached one clear conclusion: a boat with an undersized bow thruster is just as hard to maneuver as a boat with no thruster at all.

Electric bow thrusters draw a lot of current and require heavy cabling directly from the main battery bank. Larger boats may require additional batteries installed close to the thruster motor for efficient operation. Electric bow thrusters are not designed for continuous running and have a duty cycle that includes a cooling off period.

If your boat is already equipped with an auxiliary hydraulic system to run an anchor windlass or other device, you can tap into this system to also power a hydraulic thruster. Hydraulic thrusters can be operated for longer periods of time without requiring a rest to cool down.

STABILIZERS

All boats roll, but some roll more than others: this is probably the biggest difference we discovered when going from sail to power. Without a sail to steady it, a powerboat rolls in a *beam sea*, when waves approach from the side. This roll can become so uncomfortable that we often change course simply to lessen the motion.

High Life does pretty well with the waves hitting the hull at an angle off the bow or stern, so we bear off until the waves hit at a 45-degree angle on our *quarter* (the side of the boat between the middle and the stern). We steer that course for a while, then we turn to put the waves on a similar angle at the bow. This takes us on a zigzag course, but the extra distance traveled is a small price to pay to lessen the roll.

There are basically three methods to control it. First, *active* stabilizers, which are movable fins mounted on the underside of the hull. Second, *passive* stabilizers, which are attached to the ends of *outriggers*. And third, riding sails. There is one other option: don't go out in rough weather and you'll only have to endure rolling in your slip or at anchor!

ACTIVE STABILIZERS

These systems employ movable fins that extend downward from each side of the hull at about a 45-degree angle. Electric or hydraulic motors (called *actuators*) change this angle to create forces that counteract the roll. Usually the fins are located in or close to the area where the bottom turns toward the vertical, the area called the turn of the bilge. A sensing mechanism (most often a gyroscope) feels the boat begin to roll and activates the motors so that the fins create an upward force on the descending side and a downward force on the rising side. This cancels out the roll and the boat remains level. At least 90 percent of the roll can be dampened in a moderate beam sea.

Active stabilizers are movable fins mounted on the underside of the hull, maneuvered by electric or hydraulic motors. (Illustration by Bruce Anderson.)

Active stabilizers are mostly designed for boats over 40 feet, though they have been installed on smaller vessels. They are expensive, highly stressed machines that require periodic maintenance, and are best installed while the boat is being built. Placing the fins in the optimum location on a used boat is a challenge that often requires relocating existing equipment to make room for the actuators. The advantages of installing them, however, are so great that many people consider the effort and expense well worthwhile.

PASSIVE STABILIZERS

You'll see these types of stabilizers on commercial fishing boats all around the world. They consist of *paravanes*, generally referred to as *birds*, suspended on cables supported by long booms on each side of the boat. The vanes ride beneath the surface of the water. When the boat rolls, the vane on the ascending side of the boat resists the upward motion, thus reducing the amount of roll.

Paravane systems, often known as *flopper stoppers*, are inexpensive compared to active systems, but on a large boat they can be a handful to launch and even more difficult

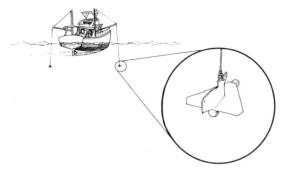

Passive stabilizers or "flopper stoppers" are long booms on each side of the boat with vanes suspended from the booms to keep the boat from rolling. (Illustration by Rob Groves.)

to retrieve, especially in heavy weather. Few coastal cruisers use this system unless they expect to spend a lot of time offshore because it's impractical to constantly deploy and then retrieve the rig. The vanes also require at least 10–15 feet of water depth to prevent them from grounding.

Riding Sails

For centuries fishing boats have used small sails to help reduce roll. To this day, many cruising trawlers are rigged with a mast and boom that can carry a riding sail. Wind pressure against the sail helps dampen the roll of the boat, though it is often only effective if the wind is strong.

A small riding sail is also handy at anchor to keep the boat headed into the wind. If you use it in an anchorage where the tide changes, remember that a boat with a riding sail will stay head to wind longer than a boat without one. And a powerboat reacts to currents differently than a deep-draft sailboat. The powerboat will stay head to wind longer than the sailboat, which usually swings with the tide. If you use a riding sail at anchor where there are other boats, and especially sailboats, be sure to anchor well clear of them or you may have problems when the tide turns.

CHAPTER 4
Electrical Systems and Generators

The electrics aboard many cruising boats are far more complicated than those in a typical house. Most of the complexity arises from having two or three separate systems aboard. All boats have a 12-volt DC (direct current) system that runs off batteries. It is used for starting the engines, much of the lighting, and for operating most marine electronics.

These days, boats 50 feet and over often also employ a 24-volt DC system to operate some equipment and to handle the larger starter motors required by larger engines, which are becoming increasingly common. It's similar to the way cars were once equipped with 6-volt batteries, but changed to 12 volts when engines became more powerful and required greater starting power. The trend, adopted from European builders, is growing.

In addition, most modern cruising boats have a 120-volt AC (alternating current) system, or a dual 240/120-volt system, to charge the batteries, run power-hungry appliances such as a stove or microwave oven, and provide additional lighting (to take some of the load off the batteries). This AC system operates when the boat is tied up at a dock and plugged into the land-based power grid, called *shore power*, or from an onboard generator, or *genset*, while underway or at anchor.

The first time you look at a boat's electrical system it can seem overwhelming, but don't be intimidated. After a shakedown cruise or two you'll get to know what each switch operates, and everything will begin to fall into place. In this chapter we'll take a look at the basic arrangements found on most cruising boats to help you make sense of it all.

HIGH STANDARDS

The American Boat and Yacht Council (ABYC) sets standards for all new boats that include very explicit recommendations for the electrical systems. These standards are *requirements* if the boat is to be certified by the ABYC or National Marine Manufacturers Association (NMMA). Though such certification is not mandatory, quality-minded manufacturers generally follow these standards, and NMMA certification (which indicates compliance with ABYC standards) is becoming more and more common.

Perhaps more importantly, most accredited surveyors use the ABYC standards as guidelines and will give a less than satisfactory report on vessels that don't comply—taking into consideration the age of the boat and the standards prevailing at the time of its construction.

ABYC standards cover all aspects of wiring from the size of wire required in different applications to the way it must be installed. We'll discuss some of these aspects later on. ABYC also has standards for color-coding the wires running through the boat. The color of the wire identifies its function, and it makes the process of troubleshooting much easier when you have an electrical problem. Many older boats, including *High Life*, were not wired using these standards. All our positive 12-volt wires are red and the negative ones black. The 120-volt AC system uses a standard black for hot, white for neutral, and green for ground. Luckily the wires on our boat are tagged at both ends with ID codes so they are not difficult to identify.

In this chapter we'll describe an ABYC compliant system.

12-VOLT SYSTEM

Probably the main reason a boat has a 12-volt system is because that's what's used in cars and trucks. Twelve-volt batteries are readily available, along with circuit breakers, fuses, wire connectors, and all the other components that make up the direct current sys-

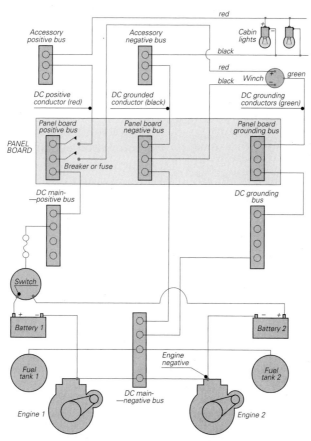

A basic DC electrical system, including proper grounding. (Illustration by Charlie Wing.)

tem. But don't confuse components made for the auto industry with marine-grade components that are corrosion-resistant.

GENERAL LAYOUT

At the heart of the system are the batteries, which store electrical energy. The wiring serves two main functions: it delivers electrical energy from the batteries to start the engine, and it supplies other 12-volt devices such as lights and navigation equipment.

Engine-starting circuits require thick, heavy cables designed to carry high current. The starter motor can draw hundreds of amps when cranking a marine engine: the bigger the engine, the bigger the starter, and the more current it draws. Most of the heavy cable runs between the batteries, the main battery switch, and the engine's starting motor, and starting circuits are protected by high-amp fuses. The battery switch allows you to select which batteries to use to start the engine and to switch the batteries off.

The other 12-volt circuits that feed the lights, electronics, and so on don't draw as much current as the starting system and use much lighter wiring and smaller (lower amperage) circuit breakers. Most of the circuit breaker switches on the main panel service this system.

That's basically it. If you open the back of the main panel, all the wires run from the fuse or circuit breaker to the device and back. They may disappear into the bowels of the boat, but they all have their origin inside this panel.

FUSES, CIRCUIT BREAKERS, AND WIRES

If the current flowing in a wire exceeds the rating of the wire, the wire will get hot and become a fire hazard. The purpose of fuses or circuit breakers is to cut off the supply of electricity before too much current can flow. These over-current devices are rated in amperes (usually abbreviated to amps). A 10-amp circuit breaker will open or trip, stopping the current, if 10 amps or more flows through it. A 10-amp fuse will blow under the same circumstances.

Breakers and fuses are designed to protect the *wiring*, not the *devices* (such as a radio or depth-sounder) connected to it. These individual pieces of equipment usually need smaller capacity fuses to protect their delicate circuitry.

If you add devices to a circuit without proper planning, you may overload it. The fuse will blow or the breaker will open. We know from experience. The engine room of our boat *High Life* seemed a bit dark, so we installed brighter bulbs. It was much brighter for about a minute, then everything went dark as the circuit breaker tripped. The breaker for the engine room lights is rated for 5 amps, and we had replaced all four 1-amp bulbs with 1.2-amp bulbs. Even though the bulbs theoretically drew only 4.8 amps, the circuit was overloaded and the breaker shut them down.

Curious as to why a 5-amp breaker would trip under a 4.8 amp load, we asked an electrician friend for an explanation. He introduced us to the concept of *voltage drop*. Even though wires are conductors, they all have some resistance, and it takes a certain amount of voltage to overcome this resistance, which consumes electricity. As a result, the voltage at the bulb is lower than the voltage at the battery. And when voltage goes down, current goes up.

So if the wiring in our lighting circuit was only adequate for a total load of 4 amps, increasing the current to 4.8 amps, coupled with the increase in current caused by the apparent voltage drop, pushed the total load to more than 5 amps. We had a choice: either replace the breaker or replace one of the new bulbs with an original sized bulb. Of course we chose the bulb since it was easier than replacing the breaker.

Wire size is another important consideration when you're adding equipment to your boat's 12-volt electrical system. A wire's thickness, or *gauge*, and its length both determine resistance and voltage drop. The thinner the wire, the greater the resistance and the resulting voltage drop.

In a 12-volt system, the voltage drop in a long wire can be considerable. At the circuit breaker there may be 12 volts, but at the end of the long wire where the device is located there may actually be only 10 volts under load. In a similar 120-volt circuit, the voltage drop might be insignificant.

For this reason, the ABYC standards for wire size take into account not only the current load it must carry, but also the voltage and distance involved. Our engine-room lights and the breaker panel were not very far apart, and the room was equipped with only 4 amps of lighting, a full 20 percent less than

the breaker's rating, so chances are the builder used a minimum-gauge wire.

Voltage drop is not a big concern for lights because they'll just burn a bit dimmer. But it *is* a big concern for motors, since they draw more current as the voltage drops (to do the same amount of work). Increased current causes further voltage drop and the motor can be overloaded, or at best run hot, which will shorten its life. You should also be aware when installing devices with built-in motors that motors draw more current at startup than when running, so be sure to allow for the extra current draw.

Splicing into existing wiring is not the best idea when you want to install new equipment, even when a fuse or circuit breaker can carry the extra load. Run new wire of the correct size directly from the circuit breaker and ground to the device, and you will experience little voltage drop. ABYC standards also call for the use of *stranded* wire and marine-type crimp-on terminals. The wire and terminals are designed to resist the engine

CONDUCTOR WIRE SIZE (AWG) FOR A 3% VOLTAGE DROP

Amps	Distance from source and back						
	10 ft.	20 ft.	30 ft.	40 ft.	60 ft.	80 ft.	100 ft.
1	18	18	18	18	16	14	14
2	18	18	16	14	14	12	10
5	18	14	12	10	10	8	6
10	14	10	10	8	6	6	4
15	12	10	8	6	6	4	2
20	10	8	6	6	4	2	2
25	10	6	6	4	2	2	0
30	10	6	4	4	2	1	1
40	8	6	4	2	1	0	
50	6	4	2	2	0		

CONDUCTOR WIRE SIZE (AWG) FOR A 10% VOLTAGE DROP							
Amps	Distance from source and back						
	10 ft.	20 ft.	30 ft.	40 ft.	60 ft.	80 ft.	100 ft.
1	18	18	18	18	18	18	18
2	18	18	18	18	18	18	16
5	18	18	16	14	14	14	12
10	18	16	14	14	12	10	10
15	18	14	12	12	10	8	8
20	16	14	12	10	8	8	6
25	16	12	10	10	8	6	6
30	14	12	1	8	6	6	4
40	14	10	8	8	6	4	4
50	12	10	8	6	4	4	2

vibration on a boat. To install them you will need the proper crimping tools.

We mentioned earlier that the fuse or circuit breaker protects the wiring, not the devices connected to it. If there is a short inside the VHF radio it will probably be totally fried before the breaker in the main panel trips. That's why almost all 12-volt navigation and communication equipment comes with a small built-in fuse for self-protection. Many of these fuses are hidden behind the device or are difficult to get to, so it's a good idea to discover their locations *before* they blow. Carry extra fuses for all devices, and keep a list of where the fuses are located.

BATTERIES

The core of the 12-volt system is the battery, which stores electrical energy by converting it to chemical energy. This energy is used to start the engine and to operate the 12-volt house systems—lights, navigation instruments, fans, entertainment systems, and even refrigerators. Once the engine is running, it turns an alternator that generates electrical energy to recharge what has been used to start the engine or to run house systems. As long as the alternator can replace the energy that has been drawn from the battery, everything is peachy.

One measure of the energy taken out of a battery is the amount of current used per hour. An *ampere-hour* (Ah) is the equivalent of 1 amp drawn from the battery for 1 hour. Take, for example, a large car battery that's rated at 80 Ah. Theoretically you could draw 1 amp for 80 hours or 5 amps for 16 hours before the battery is fully discharged. To replace the energy you would need to charge the battery for at least 16 hours with a 5-amp charger. (Batteries do not like to be fully discharged, however, and in practice the battery would be ruined after a few repetitions.)

Three basic battery technologies are suitable for marine use: the traditional wet cell or lead-acid type (now more commonly called *flooded*), gel, and absorbed glass mat (AGM). The differences are largely related to the type of electrolyte, or reacting solution, within the battery. The lead-acid battery is so called, for example, because the plates are lead (and lead dioxide) and the electrolyte is a solution of sulfuric acid in distilled water. The new types of batteries still use essentially a sulfuric acid electrolyte, but take advantage of technologies that allow it to be in nonliquid form. Each type has its advantages and disadvantages.

FLOODED BATTERIES (WET CELL OR LEAD ACID)

Flooded batteries are relatively inexpensive because they are the most widely used type in the automotive, trucking, and marine industries. They have negative plates of lead sponge and positive plates of lead dioxide submerged in sulfuric acid. They require periodic maintenance to keep the fluid level above the battery plates, especially if the battery has been overcharged.

A flooded battery must be installed upright in a spill-proof, vented enclosure, since the charging process produces small amounts of explosive hydrogen gas (and the oxygen it needs to explode). Flooded batteries do not hold their charge over a long period so regular recharging is required.

When you discharge a battery, sulfur leaves the solution and goes over to the lead plates. When it gets there, it gives up electrons—and moving electrons are what we call electricity. When you recharge a battery, you drive that sulfur back into the solution. This change in the amount of sulfur in solution is the reason we can determine a battery's remaining charge by measuring the specific gravity of the electrolyte with an inexpensive hydrometer.

Overcharging batteries on a regular basis causes water to be boiled out of the solution (the process is known as *gassing*). If you need to restore the electrolyte level, which should fully cover the plates at all times, always use *distilled* water. Adding anything other than pure distilled water can introduce impurities that may cause adverse chemical reactions and interfere with the normal functioning of the battery. You should also note that repeatedly overcharging a battery will eventually warp the plates by overheating them.

On the other hand, failure to completely recharge a battery will leave some of the sulfur behind on the plates, creating a condition called *sulfation,* which diminishes the storage capacity of the battery. Sulfation is a leading cause of battery failure.

Most flooded batteries are designed to start the engine and then be quickly recharged, so they are not able to tolerate deep discharges like those that occur when house systems such as lights are left on for several hours. A special category of flooded batteries called *deep-cycle* batteries has been designed for this type of service. These batteries are made with relatively few, thick plates. This allows a small amount of power to be used over a long period of time and requires a slow to moderate recharge rate. These are the best batteries to use in house applications since they can withstand 700–800 deep cycles (or more, depending on size and type) before they need replacing.

Generally speaking, the 6-volt batteries designed to operate golf carts (and other machinery that discharges them on a regular basis) are true deep-cycle batteries. They can withstand many discharge/charging cycles, but they are not very good for use with the brief but heavy loads involved in starting a large engine.

Another type of battery, generally known as *marine deep cycle,* is a hybrid or cross between a cranking battery and a true deep-cycle type. It was originally designed for the marine industry because in many small boats there is only one battery, which has to be used both for cranking the engine and for all the other systems. Marine deep-cycle batteries can withstand around 300–400 deep cycles before they need replacing. They are adequate as house batteries but are not nearly as good or long-lived as the true deep cycle types. Since many newer boats now have separate battery banks for cranking and for house service, there is less need for this type of battery, though they are still available. Your money will be better spent, however, buying true deep-cycle batteries for house applications, and true cranking batteries to start your engines.

Maintenance-free versions of the flooded battery are available, but these are not the wisest choice for a cruising boat. Overcharging a maintenance-free battery will cause it to lose some of its electrolyte, which can't be replaced since the battery is sealed.

GEL BATTERIES

In a gel battery the electrolyte (still essentially sulfuric acid) is mixed with a gel. This allows the case to be completely sealed. Since there is no liquid inside, the battery can be installed in any position and is basically maintenance-free—there is no liquid to boil away or replenish. It must be charged at a slightly lower voltage than a flooded battery, but alternator-regulators and battery chargers are available that can accommodate them.

Gel batteries do not need to be kept upright, so they can be installed in odd-shaped lockers or other unused locations. This characteristic makes these batteries suitable for powering large windlasses and bow thrusters, which often require a dedicated

battery installed close to the unit in a confined area.

AGM (ABSORBED GLASS MAT) BATTERIES

AGM batteries are also lead-acid batteries, but they are sealed rather than vented. The electrolyte is held captive in a fiberglass mat so it can't be spilled. This glass mat also contains pockets that assist in the recombination of the hydrogen and oxygen gases (generated during charging) back into water. The battery does not have to be installed upright and is resistant to vibration. Its big advantage over a flooded battery is that it can be charged at a higher rate. The faster you can recharge the battery, the less time you need to run the generator or main engine.

AGM batteries are more expensive than other types (about twice the cost of flooded batteries) but they have a long life and hold their charge for long periods of time. These batteries have very thick positive plates and belong in the true deep cycle class. They don't *outgas* (boil off electrolyte) unless severely overcharged, and because of this they don't corrode terminals and don't need to have water added. For many owners, the savings in maintenance alone can be worth the extra cost.

Some AGM batteries require a lower charging voltage than standard flooded batteries, so be sure that all your charging sources be set properly. This includes your inverter/charger (or converter), engine alternator, and solar panel system if you have one. Most alternators regulate their output between 13.5 and 14.5 volts while running at normal cruising rpm, so this shouldn't be a big concern. However, high-output alternators, over 100 amps, can damage AGM batteries if not connected to the proper regulator. If possible, though, all alternator regulators should be adjusted to exactly match the battery's charging characteristics.

SIZING THE BATTERY BANK

Most cruising boats now require more 12-volt capacity than a single battery can provide—except for those few boats that rely more heavily on 120-volt appliances and upon the frequent use of a generator to power them. To increase total capacity, several batteries are often combined and are referred to as a battery bank. The battery bank that supplies energy to the boat's house systems is called the house battery, while a separate cranking battery is used to start each engine.

This two-battery arrangement is nowhere near universal, but it is generally better than one-battery systems, because it allows you to use the proper type of battery for each application. It is being used on more and more cruising boats as time goes on.

In many cases the house battery system will be 12-volt, while the cranking batteries will be 24-volt, especially on larger boats with cranking motors that demand lots of power. As voltage increases (from 12 to 24 volts), the same electrical load can be delivered at a lower current. This allows smaller-gauge, less expensive wiring to be used for the starting motor circuit, so it's no surprise that 24-volt starting systems are becoming more common.

BATTERIES: HOW BIG? HOW MANY? WHAT KIND?

Whatever technology you choose for your house battery, it must have sufficient capacity or it will not last. Make a list of all the 12-volt devices on your boat and how much current they draw. (Some list the amperage draw, some list watts. Divide watts by 12 to get the amperage). As a rough estimate on a typical day at anchor aboard *High Life*, we may use 170–200 Ah of 12-volt energy.

To handle this load we installed a house-battery bank made up of four deep cycle 6-volt golf cart batteries. Each battery is rated at 200 Ah and when connected in series to another similar battery makes a 200 Ah 12-volt battery. We wired two of these 12-volt pair in parallel to create one 400 Ah 12-volt battery bank.

This bank replaced a single large battery that weighed more than 100 pounds and was just about impossible to lift without the

ESTIMATED AMP-HOUR USAGE FOR *HIGH LIFE*

Location	Appliance	Amps	Run time (hrs)	Amp-hours
Galley	Refrigerator	4	16	64
	Fan	5	1	5
Lighting	Ceiling	10	6	60
	Reading	3	2	6
	Engine room	6	½	3
	Anchor	1	8	8
Other	CD/Radio	3	3	9
	TV	4	3	12
			Total Ah	167

help of a strong dockhand. Collectively, the bank of 6-volt batteries is heavy, but each of the individual batteries can be lifted easily.

(continued)

Batteries of the same voltage can be connected in *parallel*—with the positive battery terminals of each battery connected together and the negative terminals connected together. When batteries are connected like this they are considered a single battery and the ampere-hour capacity of the bank is the sum of all the batteries in the bank. For example, if you connect two 12-volt, 100 Ah batteries in parallel, you create a 12-volt, 200 Ah battery bank.

If you connect batteries in *series*, with positive to negative terminals, you sum their voltages but not the ampere-hours. Two 6-volt 200 Ah batteries connected in series produce a 12-volt 200 Ah battery bank.

All batteries, whatever their technology, prefer to remain fully charged, and none likes to be fully discharged. To get the longest life from any battery or bank of batteries, it should not be discharged to less than 50 percent of its rated capacity. For example, if your boat's house bank has a 200 Ah capacity you should not use more than 100 Ah before recharging. For this reason, a properly sized house bank should have, as a minimum, twice the capacity of the average daily load.

Of course this is the daily load used at anchor or on a mooring, when the boat is not connected to any power source. If you are connected to shore power, the battery

---

When a battery fails, usually only a few cells have gone bad, killing the entire battery. With a bank of separate 6-volt batteries, when one battery develops a problem it can be replaced instead of the entire bank. We usually replace the batteries in pairs.

We use golf cart batteries because they are designed to deeply discharge and bounce around in the back of a moving cart. They're mass-produced and inexpensive compared to other battery technologies with the same ampere-hour capacity. Six-volt marine batteries are available with a bit more capacity, but they're more expensive and we're not convinced that they will last any longer. However, these are standard flooded batteries and will discharge faster if left unattended, and they can't be charged as fast as gel and AGM batteries using multistage chargers.

Sizing the bank is not an exact science and it is much better to err on the high side. The larger the battery capacity compared to the ampere-hour draw, the better. Of course

we all face space and budget restraints, but if your cruising plans call for extended time away from the dock, it's a wise move to plan your 12-volt system carefully.

High Life's *golf-cart batteries are compact and economical. We can move them in and out of the engine room without Herculean effort.*

charger (not the battery bank) can supply 12-volt current.

BATTERY CHARGING

The success of a boat's 12-volt system depends on its ability to efficiently replace the amps consumed. The engine's alternator is most often the primary source of energy when the boat is underway. Large boats may also run their generator, which allows use of a 120-volt battery charger, just as when on shore power. On any boat the charging capacity must be at least slightly more than the load (it can't be exactly equal because no system is 100 percent efficient)—or the batteries will eventually run down.

ALTERNATORS AND REGULATORS

Depending on the capacity of your alternator, it may take 2–10 hours of running the engine to replace 200 Ah of energy taken from the battery bank. The standard 65-amp alternator found on many engines can at best continuously put out about three-quarters of its rated capacity, or 49 amps. With this output it will take at least 5 hours to charge the batteries. If there are other DC loads on the alternator (as there usually are), charging will take even longer.

The standard alternator has a voltage regulator that is basically designed to charge a starting battery, not the house bank. A starting, or cranking, battery has many, very thin plates, with a large surface area exposed to the electrolyte. This allows the battery to give up a large amount of power in a short period of time, and to be recharged rapidly at a heavy rate. Starting a big engine requires this kind of power, but a cranking battery would be a very poor choice as a house battery as it can only withstand 15 to 30 deep cycles before it needs replacing.

As soon as a standard regulator senses a rise in voltage as the batteries begin to charge, it cuts back on the charge current. There's a very good reason for this. If you try to push more amps into a battery that is fully charged or nearly so, those extra amps will simply split water molecules into hydrogen and oxygen. This is what causes the bubbling known as gassing.

At 80°F all lead-acid batteries begin gassing when the charging current reaches somewhere between 14.1 and 14.4 volts. Gassing causes the battery to heat up, which further lowers the gassing threshold and causes more and more violent boiling. So it is important to taper off the charging current as the batteries reach their gassing threshold.

This gassing threshold changes with the temperature of the battery: it occurs at a lower voltage when the batteries are hotter, and at a higher voltage when the batteries are colder. It is also important to realize that boat batteries may be exposed to widely varying temperatures. Often they tend to get hot because they are commonly located in the engine room. You must allow for the effect of temperature if you need to devise a charging strategy for your boat.

If your charging system doesn't push the batteries to their gassing threshold, sulfur gets left behind on the plates. Thus voltage regulators are designed to let the battery reach its gassing threshold and then cut back on the charging current. While this sequence is essential to battery life, it may actually take 8–9 hours or more to fully recharge the bank. This is OK if you run a boat continuously, but if you cruise in a leisurely manner from anchorage to anchorage, eventually the batteries will run down. It is simple math: amps in must equal amps out.

If your cruising style involves docking at a marina every few days and plugging into shore power, the battery charger will charge the batteries overnight. You may get away with using a small alternator, but this strategy is hard on the batteries.

A better alternative is to increase your charging capacity by installing a high-capacity alternator with an *external* voltage regulator designed to efficiently charge large banks of deep cycle batteries. As a rule of thumb, the alternator should have an output of at least 25 percent of the battery storage capacity, so a 400 Ah house bank should have at least a 100-amp alternator. This is probably the *minimum* size you should install, since the alternator's output may be considerably reduced when it is fully loaded and running hot.

A battery charger like this charges the three types of batteries and has a three-stage charging capacity.

Battery Chargers

Marine battery chargers have come a long way. On our first trawler we had a 50-amp charger that was almost as big as the generator next to it. It contained an enormously heavy transformer that hummed loudly and could charge only flooded batteries.

New charger designs haven't totally cured the hum, but they are certainly smaller and—more importantly—more efficient. And they can be adjusted to charge flooded, gel, or AGM batteries, each of which requires a slightly different approach. For example, AGM batteries don't like to be pushed over 14.4 volts during initial charging and want to be held between 13.2 to 13.4 volts during the reduced-amperage, or *float*, charging period.

Today's chargers usually have three-stage regulators that charge the batteries faster without overcharging. Most also allow an *equalization charge* that can extend the life of the battery. An equalization charge is simply a planned overcharge. Although it is not a good idea to overcharge a battery, neither is allowing sulfate crystals to grow, which hap-

pens when batteries are constantly *under-charged*. Equalization is definitely a lesser evil than sulfation.

Pushing flooded batteries up to 15 or 15.5 volts for three to six hours every six months or so will help knock loose sulfation and allow weaker cells to come up to a full charge. AGM batteries can withstand an occasional short-duration equalization charge also, as long as it is less than 15 volts. But don't overdo it as these batteries can be *forced* to outgas through a tiny vent (which they do not do under normal conditions) and, since they are sealed, there is no way to put water back in.

Large stand-alone battery chargers are expensive, so before you invest in one, consider getting an inverter/charger that we discuss later in this chapter.

Other Options

Solar

Solar technology has also come a long way in a few years, and the cost per watt of energy keeps dropping. An array of three 75-watt solar panels can produce 15 amps when the sun is shining brightly, which would amount to 90 Ah (ampere-hours) per day at the yearly average of 6 hours of sunlight daily. That could be half your daily electrical demand. And if you prefer to rely on a solar panel instead of a generator or engine to keep the batteries charged, you would be surprised at how much energy you can save by using smaller lightbulbs and running the television a little less.

Three of these 2- by 4-foot panels mounted above a hardtop (preferred) or bimini (acceptable) would be in direct sunlight and out of sight. They are silent, have no moving parts, almost unlimited life, and don't use fuel or require oil changes. Solar makes a lot of sense if your cruising plans call for long periods at anchor.

The biggest downside to this technology is that the sun must shine for solar panels to generate current. On a cloudy, gray day the array we talked about may only generate a fraction of its rated output, and then there are the shorter days of winter. For most cruising boats, you should consider solar as merely one part of the boat's total energy generating system.

Wind Power

Another conservation-minded option is a wind generator, though it perhaps makes more sense for a sailboat than a powerboat. Sailboats generally have less superstructure to interfere with a clear flow of wind, and they generally cruise at a lower speed than even the slowest trawlers, so they put less strain on the mechanism. Also, a powerboat has plenty of engine power to charge the batteries while underway. However, a wind generator is worth considering if you anchor a lot for extended periods because it generates electricity efficiently and doesn't use fuel. Most cruising areas have enough wind year-round to power a wind generator, and teamed with a solar panel it can make your boat energy independent. But unlike solar panels, a wind generator has moving parts and requires maintenance.

The sad truth is that most powerboaters don't even begin to consider alternative power sources such as sun and wind. Perhaps we should—both boaters and boat manufacturers. It's tough enough, given the ever-rising costs and finite supply of petroleum, to

Finding an ideal place to mount solar panels is not always easy. The performance of this installation will suffer from being partly shaded. (Photo by Nigel Calder.)

have to use the stuff for propulsion without also depending on it for electricity. Maybe we've gotten so used to burning fuel that we've developed tunnel vision when it comes to other possibilities.

Just imagine, if you equip your boat with solar panels or a wind generator (or both) you could be in the vanguard, changing the way powerboaters think about energy!

120-VOLT SYSTEM

Along with a low-voltage system, most powerboats also have a 240/120-volt (or simply 120-volt) AC electrical system that powers battery chargers, electric stoves, air conditioners, hair dryers, and any other household appliances you may have aboard the boat. The wire used on a boat is subject to vibration and is composed of many small strands, unlike the single stiff wire found in typical household wiring.

SHORE POWER AND SAFETY

The boat is connected to standard 240/120-volt current through a shore-power cable or cord. Almost all marinas have outlets at slips that accept a standard cable with a grounded, three-prong twist-lock male plug. At the boat's end, the cable has a female twist-lock fitting. Boats with large current demands use two 30-amp cords, or one (often more than one) 50-amp cord.

A typical 240/120-volt installation includes over-current protection with a main circuit breaker and a distribution panel with individual breakers for each branch circuit, providing 240 volts to some equipment such as the galley stove, and 120 volts to the rest of the boat.

Household current—120 volts—can be fatal, particularly aboard a boat, because it is in the water, so it's easy for the current to find a path to ground. If you happen to be part of that path you could be seriously injured or killed.

For this reason, ABYC requires that any receptacle installed in a head, galley, machinery space, or on a weather deck be protected by a Type A Ground Fault Circuit Interrupter (GFCI). This device turns off the current in milliseconds if it senses an unsafe situation. The "Type A" designation is equivalent to the Underwriters Laboratory (UL) requirement for a GFCI to trip when there is just 5 mA (milliamps) of current leaking to ground. This isn't particularly dangerous in itself, but by interrupting the current at the slightest hint of a ground fault, you are pro-

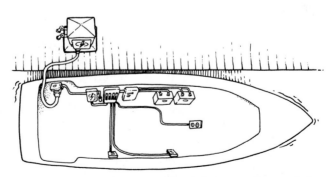

A shore-power system is designed to bring power from a dock outlet to all the AC devices aboard a boat. (Illustration by Christopher Hoyt.)

tected from being shocked by the full current. There's more about GFCIs in Chapter 12, Safety Equipment.

Most older boats don't have these devices, but insurance companies can require them. A GFCI device costs just a few dollars, and it takes 10 minutes to replace a conventional outlet with a GFCI. Any survey will note the lack of GFCI devices, so if your boat is not equipped, make the change for your own protection.

Getting Connected

Most marinas and boatyards have standard 30- or 50-amp service. Not all have both, so you will need to carry adapters for your power cord so you can connect to whatever service is available. There is no problem connecting a 30-amp cord to a 50-amp service, as the circuit breakers on the boat will protect the boat wiring and will open before the cord is damaged.

When you connect a 50-amp cord to a 30-amp service through an adapter you must rely on the circuit breaker on the dock to protect the cord, since the boat's breakers are rated for 50 amps. If you don't limit your electrical use on the boat while connected to the 30-amp shore power, you run the risk of melting the adapter. Boats with dual 30-amp cords can use a Y adapter that connects two 30-amp cords to 50-amp service.

Another handy adapter to carry is one that allows you to plug your boat's power cord into a standard, household-type, 15-amp grounded outlet. This is useful when the boat is hauled out of the water and there isn't a marine-type outlet available in the haulout area. This adapter allows you to run the battery charger and the lights without running down the batteries. We also use the cord for 120-volt power tools.

Generators

Many cruising boats are fitted with all-electric galleys, so a generator is at the heart of their electrical system. The generator supplies standard 60 cycle 240/120V (or sometimes simply 120V) alternating current to operate the major appliances aboard when it's not connected to shore power. On an occasional cruise this works well. But running the generator whenever you're underway for long stretches can become burdensome for all but the largest cruising boats.

Generators are also needed to operate high-load systems like air conditioning and heating when away from the dock. Many cruising folk abhor air conditioning: they say that if they wanted to sit in a refrigerator they'd stay at home—they go boating to enjoy the fresh air. But without an AC unit, many of today's boat designs lack sufficient natural ventilation for the cabins to be truly comfortable in warmer climates, especially when temperatures and humidity are high and breezes are scarce.

The power setup on *High Life* that serves us well works like this. The generator runs the reverse-cycle air conditioning/heating and charges the batteries at anchor. An inverter picks up the slack to run some small 120-volt appliances like the coffeemaker or microwave, so we don't need the generator while underway.

If your boat is not equipped with a generator and you are considering one, keep this in mind: in every discussion we've had with mechanics about generators, the consensus is that most boats have generators that are too large and therefore suffer from being run underloaded. There's little chance that you'll operate every 120-volt appliance on the boat continuously and all at the same time. For example, the AC units cycle on and off and the water heater runs only periodically.

A diesel generator, like this 8 kilowatt Westerbeke 8.0 BTDA, supplies 110-volt power when you're away from the dock.

When running your genset, remember that diesel engines are designed to run with a load. If an 8kW generator is run just to charge the batteries day after day, its engine will suffer. A 100-amp battery charger in the average inverter/charger only draws a little over 20 amps, which puts too light a load on the engine. Lightly loaded diesel engines do not burn the fuel efficiently and soot and other by-products of the fuel combustion contaminate the oil and cause premature wear. The genset is at its happiest when it is at least half loaded. You can increase the load during part of the charging cycle by turning on the hot water heater or some other high-resistance appliance. You will use a bit more fuel, but the engine will run better.

INVERTER/CHARGERS

Inverter/chargers, connected to both the AC and DC systems, are marvelous. The advent of efficient units lets you operate 120-volt appliances without a generator when you're away from shore power, or charge your batteries when you're on the dock—all with a single device. An inverter changes the steady, 12-volt direct current coming out of the batteries into the 120-volt alternating current we're used to at home. A charger changes alternating current to the steady, low-voltage, direct current we need to recharge batteries and run onboard lights and electronics.

Inverter/chargers do whatever's required at the moment. If you plug the boat into shore power, or fire up the generator, the unit will start putting out 12-volt DC power and begin charging your batteries. But if you aren't plugged into shore power and don't have your generator running, turning on a small appliance activates the inverter to supply it with 120-volt AC power. It's almost magic, but it does require a large-capacity battery bank.

Inverters produce their 60-Hertz 120-volt current with either *true sine wave* or *modified sine wave* characteristics. The significance? Household AC current changes polarity, changing from positive to negative 60 times a second, but the change is not instantaneous and follows a smooth sinusoidal wave pattern. Most galley appliances like toasters don't care what the power curve looks like, but some electronic devices like computers do.

Modified sine wave inverters produce current with a waveform that's more of a square wave, though the corners are somewhat rounded. True sine-wave inverters produce current that is close to the characteristic waveform of household power. As you might expect, the circuitry in a true sine-wave inverter costs more. Whether this extra expense is justified depends entirely on what you intend to power. If you consider your needs before you make your purchase, you won't waste your money.

PROTECTING THE BOAT

With all the current flowing through a boat's electrical system, some of it can go astray, causing electrolysis—electrically induced corrosion damage to parts like through-hull fittings, propellers, and rudders. To prevent such corrosion, all the metal parts of the boat are connected together, and sacrificial zincs are installed on key underwater components.

BONDING

It is common practice for all underwater metal parts to be electrically connected to keep them at the same electrical potential and thus prevent galvanic currents from flowing between them. To accomplish this, most boats have a bonding system of #8 wire or copper straps secured to the engine and every piece of metal that penetrates the hull. The bonding system also usually connects to a single common ground (often a specially manufactured *grounding plate*), which provides good continuity to earth ground, via seawater, for any electronic devices that require it.

It's also worth noting that bonding every large piece of metal above the waterline with #6 wire and then connecting them to the ground point helps protect the boat against lightning strikes.

It's important to inspect the bonding system periodically, to preserve the useful life of the underwater running gear. Make sure that everything is actually connected: bonding wires can fall off or get damaged, leaving through-hull fittings exposed to possible corrosion. A good survey will discover faults in the bonding system.

Some engineers believe it's not necessary to bond a boat, particularly if it has a wooden hull. But even they would recommend that, if your boat is bonded, you must maintain the integrity of the system, so never ignore those inspections on the rationale that "it's not necessary, because I really don't need the bonding system anyway." If you choose to bond, bond *everything*, and keep the system intact.

If you have metal fuel tanks, they should also be bonded and connected to the negative terminal of the batteries. This is federal law for gas-powered boats, and an ABYC requirement for all boats.

ZINC ANODES

There's another precaution you must take to protect the underwater metal parts of your boat: attach *sacrificial zincs*, one each to the rudder, drive shaft, and every other piece of exposed underwater metal. The zinc will corrode away instead of whatever it is attached to (which is why the zincs are called sacrificial).

The action is quite simple: zinc is higher on the galvanic scale (less *noble*) than either the bronze, NiBrAl (an alloy of nickel, bronze, and aluminum), or stainless steel used in most underwater hardware. This means that it gives up its electrons—and disintegrates sooner—than the more noble objects it's attached to. Each boat eats its zincs at a different rate, but once the zincs are gone, or nearly so, the other metals will start to dissolve. So it's important to regularly inspect their condition and replace them before they wear away totally.

Galvanic corrosion can occur without the addition of external current. When any dissimilar metals are immersed in an electrolyte like seawater they become, in effect, a battery and generate their own current. But a stray current can accelerate the process and cause the zincs to dissolve more quickly. Such a current can occur if a wire with imperfect insulation is immersed in the bilge water. And the stray current doesn't have to originate aboard your own boat. If the boat next to you at a marina has an electrical problem, it could eat up your zincs in a matter of days.

THE GALVANIC SERIES OF METALS IN SEAWATER

Metals located closer to each other on the scale are more inert in the presence of seawater, and those further apart are most likely to corrode. For example, if you have a type 316 active stainless steel prop shaft protected by a zinc anode, you won't see much corrosion on the zinc. The same zinc, however, would get eaten away more rapidly if you had a silicon bronze shaft. A worse situation would be an aluminum outboard motor near a bronze rudder blade, with no zinc anodes protecting the metals.

Cathodic or Most Noble

Platinum
Gold
Graphite
Silver
Titanium
Hastelloy C
Stainless steel (types 304 and 316, passive)
Iconel (passive)
Nickel (passive)
Monel (400, K-500)
Silicon bronze
Copper
Red brass
Aluminum bronze
Admiralty brass
Yellow brass
Inconel (active)
Nickel (active)
Naval brass
Manganese bronze
Muntz metal
Tin
Lead
Stainless steel (types 304 and 316, active)
50-50 lead-tin solder
Cast iron
Wrought iron
Mild steel
Cadmium
Aluminum alloys
Galvanized steel
Zinc
Magnesium

Anodic or Most Base

Never paint the zinc or the part of the metal that the zinc is attached to. The zinc must be exposed to the water, and there must be an electrical bond between it and the object it protects.

Sacrificial zinc pencils in various parts of the raw-water sides of engine cooling systems serve the same purpose: they protect the essential parts such as heat-exchanger tubing from being eaten away. You must also inspect these zincs regularly to be sure they're still present and working.

If your zincs are dissolving rapidly, get a qualified (preferably ABYC-certified) technician to find the cause and correct it. But don't curse the disappearing zincs: by sacrificing themselves, they are protecting your more costly and more important through-hull fittings. As they say, "Don't shoot the messenger."

ISOLATION TRANSFORMERS

There's another way to avoid corrosion problems and potential grounding problems that not only eliminates much of the concern for the underwater hardware, but also eliminates the need for GFCIs, as well as any concern about major electrical problems on the boat in the next slip.

This solution is expensive, however, as it involves isolating your boat electrically from the rest of the world and its electrical grids by installing a 1:1 ratio transformer between your 240/120-volt AC electrical system and the power supply you plug into on the dock. Isolation transformers, as they are called, tend to be heavy and expensive. They have to be big enough to handle your boat's total AC load without overheating. Finding room

for one where it won't disturb your boat's *trim* (the way it sits in the water) can be a problem, and so can fitting it into your budget.

The benefits, however, can make it well worth the cost. Landside wiring practices call for the 120-volt *neutral leg* to be connected to ground. This is not a problem as long as every boat plugged into shore power has GFCI protection to open any circuits that may be leaking power to ground. But if the boat next to you does not have GFCI protection and it does have current leaks, seawater can conduct this stray current as far as your boat, where your wire connection to ground (through your shore-power cable) provides a path of least resistance. This current flowing to ground by way of your underwater metal can eat away that metal quite rapidly once your zincs have gone.

With an isolation transformer, however, your boat's AC system *floats* above ground, isolated in its own little electrical world where hot lines are hot only to your boat's neutral leg, but not to ground. You have no direct connection to the grounded shore-power system. This means that if you touch a hot wire while standing in water you will no longer receive a shock, and stray currents from the boat next door have to find another path to ground. They will not find such a path through your boat.

In addition to the basic cost of an isolation transformer, installation can sometimes lead to the additional expense of examining your boat's wiring and revising it to eliminate any connections between neutral and ground. But the ability to remain electrically "on your own" while plugged into shore power can have considerable value.

CHAPTER 5
Freshwater Systems, Heads, and Tanks

The plumbing system on a typical cruiser has much in common with the plumbing system in your home, except that it is self-contained, and most of the pipes are much smaller. At home, water is supplied from a water main or well, and waste flows out to a sewer or a septic system. A boat, however, stores its own fresh water (or can produce its own), and generally stores its wastewater too, until it's time to pump out the holding tank—to a dockside pumpout station or overboard, as the situation allows.

ANATOMY OF A SYSTEM

A boat's freshwater plumbing system is made up of the water tank, pressure pump, and the piping that connects the pump to the fixtures. Larger boats will have more fixtures, but even the most complex system has the same basic components.

WATER STORAGE

Once you're aboard, you'll quickly discover that there is never enough fresh water. Sometimes the main reason we stop at a marina is that we need to fill our water tanks. We've never met a cruiser who complained about having too much water aboard.

For years we cruised on sailboats with very small water tanks, but when we switched to a trawler and began to enjoy a daily shower and the advantages of a nice galley, our conserve-water mindset changed. We used to get by with 75 gallons of water a week on the sailboat. Now we go through twice that amount in less than a week.

When cruising in areas like the Bahamas, where water is harder to come by and more expensive, we go back to our miserly ways. *High Life* carries 400 gallons of fuel and 150 gallons of fresh water, and since we're not crossing oceans we would gladly swap 100 gallons of fuel capacity for an additional 100 gallons of water. A watermaker, however, would allow us to indulge our thirst for water and still keep that precious fuel.

PRESSURE SYSTEMS

In the simplest type of installation, a pressure-sensitive pump moves the water directly from the storage tank to the fixtures. Whenever a faucet is turned on the water pressure drops and the pump comes on. The pump then cycles on and off to keep pressure in the system. This constant cycling causes the water pressure to fluctuate rapidly and the pump to wear prematurely.

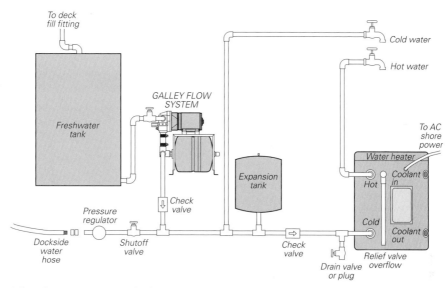

A boat's water system is laid out to provide hot and cold water from a freshwater tank. (Illustration by Charlie Wing.)

To prevent the pump from rapidly cycling, an *expansion tank* should be fitted somewhere in the cold water side of the system. This tank is partially filled with compressed air. When a faucet is opened and the pressure in the pipes drops, the compressed air forces

High Life's *pressure pump distributes fresh water to faucets in the sinks and showers.*

the water out of the tank into the pipes. The air pressure in the tank then drops and the pump comes on—though depending on the water flow at the faucet, it may not come on for a minute or so.

When the pump does come on, it runs for a longer time since it must push water back into the expansion tank and compress the air to restore system pressure. When the tank reaches the cutoff pressure, the pump stops, and the cycle starts again. This longer on-off cycle is easier on the pump and on everyone aboard, since they don't have to listen to the constantly cycling pump. If your water system does not have an expansion tank, it's well worth installing one.

Even the best water pump is going to break down eventually—most likely when you're lathered up in the shower—so be sure to carry spare parts. We use the same type of pump for our anchor washdown and freshwater systems, and we carry one replacement pump and two sets of spare parts.

WATER FILTERS

Keeping the water in the tank fresh and truly potable is another concern. No one wants 150 gallons of foul-tasting or smelly water, so check the quality of the water supply carefully before you bring it aboard. We always run the water for a few minutes to flush the delivery system before we refill our tanks.

The best defense against taking on a load of bad water is to be selective about where you get it. Most municipalities have water that is safe to drink, but it may have a strong smell of chlorine. Some people find this smell unpleasant, but it does prevent bacteria and algae from growing in the water.

If the water doesn't look crystal clear, use a simple sediment filter on the supply hose. It's tempting to run the water through a charcoal filter before it goes into the tanks, but this will remove most of the chlorine—which you need to protect the water even when it's in the tank. In fact, in addition to whatever chlorine the municipal water might contain, we usually add a capful of household bleach to every hundred gallons of water to further prevent bacterial growth.

Filtering on the pressure side of the system is a different story. Here we use a household-type charcoal filter that removes the chlorine taste and smell, and we change it twice a year. This is not the most advanced solution, but while coastal cruising we can generally count on the safety of the water supply. Our biggest water quality issues have been taste and odor.

If you plan to cruise to areas where the water supply may not be as reliable, consider a more complete water treatment and filtration system that will remove just about everything that can cause harm. Most can be adapted for marine use. A combination of sediment filters and charcoal filters will improve the taste and quality of the water. Many cruisers use the Multi-Pure filter system.

Ultraviolet (UV) light can also be used to kill bacteria. By piping water through a chamber that contains a UV light, you can ensure a safe water supply, especially if it's placed after a good set of filters. Sterilight series of UV filters by R-Can Environmental Inc. come in a range of sizes that can be installed on a

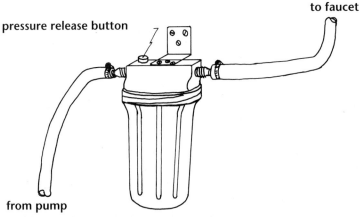

pressure release button

to faucet

from pump

A high-quality filter will remove most of the contaminants from shore-supplied water. (Illustration by Don Casey.)

single faucet or belowdeck to service the entire system.

And if your bank account can stand it, reverse osmosis (RO) watermakers (see below) also produce water that is free from most contaminants.

HOT WATER

We have cruised on boats without hot water, but it was too much like camping. You can make life aboard more enjoyable with a water heater and a pressure water system, although finding room for them on boats less than 30 feet can be a challenge.

Most marine hot-water heaters require electricity, but some also work by heat exchange, circulating hot engine coolant through coils in the heater's tank, which eliminates the need to run the generator while underway. As soon as the engine warms up there is an unlimited supply of *very* hot water. Since the engine operates at 180°F or more, the water in the heater tank can actually become hot enough to scald if you're not careful. Newer water heaters often come with a mixing valve that adds some cold water to moderate the output temperature.

On a fall cruise we find the best time to take a hot shower is after the day's run. The water is still hot, and usually after two showers there is still enough hot water to do the dishes. Of course, if we are at a marina the electric elements in the water heater will keep the water hot. But on a cold morning the first one up usually starts the generator, and in a half-hour the boat is warm and the water is hot. Either way you slice it, a hot shower can't be beat, to either start the day or to cap it.

Another option is to install an on-demand unit that uses shore power or the generator to heat the water. This type of unit can't use the heat from the engine to make hot water since it doesn't have a storage tank, but it does produce ample hot water, almost instantly.

WATERMAKERS

Unless you're running your boat all day at 30 knots, on a cruise you'll go through water faster than fuel. If you can afford a watermaker it can free you from the hassle of frequent stops simply to refill your water tanks. Watermakers make fresh water from seawater by removing the salt. The technology is not new—in fact it's been used on ships since the advent of steam power. But distillation plants are not practical on small cruising boats, so the most appropriate technology is the *reverse osmosis* (RO) process. All marine watermakers available for small- to medium-size cruising boats use RO.

Reverse osmosis works by forcing water under high pressure through a *semi-permeable membrane* with pores so small that only the water molecules can pass through. Salt and almost all other contaminants are left behind. Bacteria and toxins are removed as well. On the downside, RO removes the minerals, leaving the water rather tasteless. Some of those minerals are essential to health as well, so you should consider taking mineral supplements if you're on a steady diet of RO water.

Cruising offshore, the seawater is relatively clean, but in coastal waters it may contain silt and chemicals like gas or oil that will clog or damage the membrane. A good prefilter system is the best way to ensure that an RO unit will have a long life.

An electric pump usually provides the high pressure needed to force the water through the membrane. The energy demand of the pump is roughly proportional to the watermaking capacity of the unit. Smaller

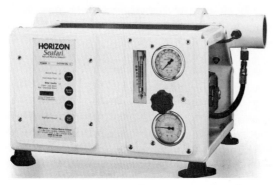

A reverse osmosis watermaker removes salt and contaminants from salt water to produce fresh water.

high-pressure RO pumps run on 12 or 24 volts DC. The more powerful ones require 120 or 240 volts AC. Engine-driven and hydraulic-powered units are also available, though these are usually seen only on large custom yachts.

12- AND 24-VOLT WATERMAKERS

Watermakers designed to run off a battery bank use either 12- or 24-volt motors. Both units use about the same amount of energy if measured in watts, but operating at twice the voltage of a 12-volt unit, a 24-volt unit draws half the current.

Some 12-volt units produce as little as 1.5 gallons per hour (GPH). Others can produce several hundred gallons per day (GPD). The larger units can draw 30 amps, but a large alternator could easily supply this amount of current in addition to whatever is required to run the boat's other 12-volt appliances and charge the batteries while underway.

The main challenge with 12-volt units is supplying the energy they require while at anchor. A larger 12-volt unit rated at 7 to 8 GPH would have to run for at least three to five hours a day to make 20 or 30 gallons of water. If you had a 100 amp alternator you would have to charge the batteries for a few

hours every day just for the watermaker. That's a lot of battery charging.

For boats that anchor a lot without generators these units are the best option, since running a large 120-volt watermaker off an inverter will quickly deplete the batteries. And replacing this energy will take hours of running the engine.

120-VOLT WATERMAKERS

Reverse osmosis units that produce more than 10 GPH are usually driven by 120-volt motors. You'll need to run the generator while you're away from the dock with one of these units. A 20 GPH unit will produce enough water in a couple of hours to satisfy the needs of the average cruising boat. This is not much longer than it takes to charge the batteries. Underway, 120-volt current to run the watermaker can be provided either by the generator or by a 3,000-watt inverter and a high-output alternator on the main propulsion engine.

OTHER OPTIONS

As the capacities of reverse osmosis units increase, so do the power requirements. High-output units have high-pressure pumps that can run directly off the main engine or generator. A hydraulic motor can also be used to drive the pump. Most of these larger installations are custom designed for large yachts.

MARINE HEADS

You can't appreciate the plumbing in your house until you spend a week or more on a boat and become intimately acquainted with the head. Of course there are marine heads . . . and then there are marine heads. Some are barely functional, while others flush reliably at the touch of a button.

THE LAW

It's what happens after you pump the handle or push the button that creates most of the hassles with marine sanitation. In the same way that a boat has a self-contained water system, it has a complete sewage system aboard too. Since the late 1970s, environmental laws have existed that govern the discharge from boats' heads.

Except for the Great Lakes and other inland bodies of water, enforcement of these regulations was initially rather lax, and for a long time most discharge went overboard untreated. That's not the case anymore. If the U.S. Coast Guard boards your boat they will inspect it to see if it conforms to national and regional sanitation requirements. If it doesn't, you're in trouble.

Federal law prohibits the discharge of untreated sewage from vessels within all navigable waters of the United States, including coastal waters (within three miles of shore). Boats with Type I or Type II Marine Sanitation Devices (MSDs) may discharge treated effluent in coastal waters, unless they are in a No Discharge Zone (NDZ). A Type III MSD or *holding tank* is the only type of sanitary device that can be used legally within a No Discharge Zone by boats of any size. This is because Type I and II devices discharge treated sewage overboard, and No Discharge means NO DISCHARGE!

When not in an NDZ, boats under 65 feet may use a Type I or II Marine Sanitation Device. The Type I device is a flow-through treatment system that reduces fecal coliform bacteria to no more than 1,000 parts per 100 mL and discharges no visible floating solids.

Vessels over 65 feet long must use a Type II Marine Sanitation Device. This is also a flow-through treatment system but with higher standards. It must reduce fecal coliform bacteria to no more than 200 parts per 100 mL and discharge no more than 150 mg per liter of suspended solids. Type II MSDs produce a cleaner effluent than Type I MSDs. They also require more space and cost more to install, although they are relatively inexpensive to operate.

For the technically minded, here's a brief rundown on how these MSDs work. The Type I MSD treats waste by breaking up any solids (maceration) and by electrolytic decontamination. A set of electrodes, powered by 12 volts DC from the batteries, is suspended in the treatment tank. When used in salt water, the current flowing between these electrodes chemically turns the water into a diluted, short-lived solution of hypochlorous acid. Small amounts of chlorine are liberated from the seawater as a result of oxidation and act as a disinfectant, killing any pathogens in the treatment tank.

The Type II Marine Sanitation Device is a biological sewage treatment system. Liquid and solid wastes are removed from the water by *aerobic* bacteria (bacteria that require air) that are naturally present in sewage. This type of MSD consists of three treatment stages: aeration, clarification, and disinfection.

In Stage 1, sewage is aerated as soon as it enters the system, and mixes with aerated liquid already in the chamber. The air is needed to sustain bacteria that grow and multiply using the sewage as their food supply. Bacterial activity reduces the quantity of solid matter. Diffusers inject air near the bottom of the aeration chamber to encourage this process of *aerobic decomposition*. The movement created by the injected air also helps mix the sewage solids with the bacterial sludge and prevents them from settling to the bottom. Air discharged from the surface of the liquid is exhausted to the atmosphere through a vent line.

In Stage 2, liquid displaced from the aeration chamber flows into the clarification chamber. Some of the suspended material

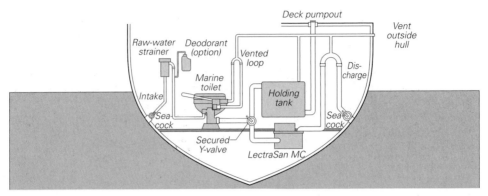

A head and holding tank is the only legal configuration in U.S. coastal waters. (Illustration by Charlie Wing.)

settles out into the chamber below and is returned to the aeration chamber. The liquid flows upward through the *biological filter media*. Bacteria grow on the surface of these media and produce a film that traps small particles of waste. They then consume this trapped waste. By the time the liquid reaches the top of the filter, it has passed by several layers of bacteria that remove the sludge and waste products.

Clear water flowing out of the clarification chamber is collected in the disinfection chamber, Stage 3, where chlorine tablets are located. The water mixes with the chlorine to kill any disease-causing bacteria. The treatment process is now complete and the water is ready for final discharge.

Waste flows through these three stages by direct displacement. When new sewage flows into the aeration chamber, an equal volume flows through the clarification chamber. This volume, in turn, displaces an equal volume from the clarification chamber into the disinfection chamber and, ultimately, overboard. No internal pumps are necessary.

Since overboard discharge of even thoroughly treated sewage is prohibited in an NDZ, many vessels that are equipped with a Type I or Type II MSD can store the final waste in a holding tank, rather than discharging it

overboard. This redundancy allows full compliance in an NDZ as well as freeing the boat from having to carry untreated sewage in the holding tank. Of course, when outside an NDZ, the boat treatment is usually changed back to direct discharge.

All-sized vessels can use holding tanks. They are the *only* devices approved for a No Discharge Zone, so all vessels cruising in an NDZ must be fitted with one.

In sum:

- No discharge of raw sewage is allowed anywhere in U.S. waters.
- A Type III Marine Sanitation Device (holding tank) is the only type that can be used in an NDZ, and all vessels may use Type III devices in all U.S. waters.
- Vessels under 65 feet can also use either a Type I or Type II Marine Sanitation Device, but not in an NDZ.
- Vessels over 65 feet can also use a Type II Marine Sanitation Device, but not in an NDZ.

MANUAL HEADS

The hand-operated marine head is one of the more reliable pieces of equipment on a boat.

All of our boats have had some version of this contraption and they all got the job done. The manual head must be pumped clean using a hand pump, and the easiest heads to operate have a pump handle that moves horizontally rather than up and down. Heads with foot-activated pump levers are also available.

Most manual heads use a single pump that moves raw (flushing) water at one end and sewage at the other. When the piston is moved in one direction it draws clean raw water into the flushing side of the pump, while pushing sewage out of the other. When the piston is moved back the other way, the clean water flows into the bowl, and, at the same time, some of the bowl's contents are pulled into the waste end of the pump.

Check valves on both ends of the toilet discharge plumbing keep the fluids flowing in one direction only. The one on the discharge side is usually all rubber and is often known as a *joker* valve. A worn seal on the piston can cause some sewage to mix with the inflowing water—a sure sign that the unit needs service. This was more prevalent back when seals were usually made of leather, which could dry out and shrink during periods of little or no use. The man-made materials currently used for seals remain flexible and better withstand the wear of sliding back and forth repeatedly, flush after flush.

Manual heads often have a shut off valve on the intake side that allows you to pump the bowl dry, and many also have a valve on the discharge side so that the head may be essentially shut down if it becomes necessary for any reason.

Another type of manual head uses an entirely different principle. The Lavac brand cleverly employs a vacuum to flush and rinse the bowl. Here's how it works: after use, you close the lid, pump the handle a few strokes, and you are done. When you pump the handle, the closed lid seals the system to form a vacuum, which empties the bowl and, at the same time, draws in more rinsing water. This type of head actually originated in the early 1960s, but more and more cruising folk are becoming fond of its simplicity and reliability.

The small toilet seat on the compact heads installed on so many boats can be tolerated for a day or so, but on an extended cruise, when you use the head regularly, it can become annoying. If you have room for a full-size marine toilet it's worth the expense to upgrade. On each of our trawlers we had either a Groco K-H or Wilcox Crittenden Skipper unit, both of which are full-size, expensive heads built to withstand daily use. On both boats they had been in service for more than 15 years when we took over. The only downside to a larger size head is that it uses a lot of water to flush, and fills up the holding tank faster than a small head.

ELECTRIC HEADS

Electric heads are almost as convenient as the home commode—they are certainly easier to use than the manual type. There's a wide variety available, from those that simply use an electric motor to operate the same sort of pump employed in manual heads to those that use a remote vacuum pump. One of the more popular types uses a macerator-pump to both remove the contents from the bowl and break up any solids before the effluent is sent along to the holding tank or other MSD. A number of brands use this technology, and cruisers don't seem to particularly favor one over another.

We've noticed many cruisers switching from seawater to fresh water to flush the head, regardless of the type of unit they have installed. A freshwater flush greatly reduces most of the odor problems associated with salt water, as well as the buildup of mineral deposits inside the hoses. The downside, of course, is that it draws down your freshwater supply, but many new macerating heads use less than a gallon per flush. If you are using a Type I MSD, you need seawater to make the system work. Otherwise, you have a choice.

The vacuum pump system has an enthusiastic following, and employs a remotely mounted vacuum pump and macerator to empty the toilet bowl. Friends of ours have been very satisfied with the VacuFlush system, which uses a partial sphere to seal the bottom of the bowl. The head is operated by a pedal. Lift the pedal and water flows in. Step on it and the semi-sphere rotates, exposing an opening that allows the system's vacuum to pull the contents out of the bowl through a small orifice that also helps in breaking up any solids. When the bowl is clear, take your foot off the pedal, the sphere rotates back to reseal the bowl, and it's ready for action again. These systems are reliable enough that many production builders now install them as standard equipment.

HOLDING TANKS

Since you can't legally discharge untreated waste into United States waters, you normally have two choices: either treat it, or store it. Stored waste can be transferred later to an approved shoreside facility, or dumped when outside territorial waters (beyond the three mile limit). In a No Discharge Zone, you don't have a choice: you must store it. So a holding tank is essential, especially in the Great Lakes and on river systems. We grew up boating on the Great Lakes, so dealing with holding tanks has been a way of life for us. We've had a holding tank on every boat we've owned, and at one time or another it has failed in some way. These tanks either smell outright, or eventually develop an ever-so-small leak with an offensive odor that can permeate the entire boat.

When assessing a boat, don't overlook the holding tank system. Look for one that's properly installed with heavy, vaporproof hoses to ensure an odorless tank. Less than ideal installations will eventually disappoint even if they seem fine at first.

One of High Life's *two 35-gallon fiberglass holding tanks. One is for the forward head, the other for the aft.*

Urine is a highly corrosive liquid and will mercilessly attack steel and aluminum. If your tank is not made of heavy polyethylene, fiberglass, or stainless steel it will eventually corrode and leak. If it has fittings made from any material other than stainless, fiberglass, or plastic, they will corrode.

On *High Life* we have two 35-gallon fiberglass holding tanks, one each for the forward and aft heads. Each tank was originally fitted with an aluminum manifold with the input, output, and vent-pipe fittings welded to a plate secured to the top. While the exterior of the tanks appeared fine, the suction pipe that reaches to the bottom of the tank corroded away on one of the units until it only reached about a quarter of the way into the tank. That meant we could never pump the tank completely empty. This we discovered when Gene was replacing one of the old hoses, and the fill pipe broke off inside the tank and crumbled into white powder. We found the same situation in the other tank and had new manifolds fabricated out of stainless steel for both of them.

ODOR

If operated correctly, a home's septic tank doesn't stink and neither should the holding tank on your boat.

A smelly tank is often the result of anaerobic bacterial activity. Groco's SweetTank holding tank deodorizing system prevents or reduces this activity. The system has a small air pump, similar to those used to aerate fish tanks, connected to the tank with some tubing and a fitting. It pumps air into the holding tank to promote the growth of aerobic bacteria (they don't cause odor) and retard the growth of the stinky anaerobic bacteria. The aerobic bacteria can begin breaking down the waste just like a normal septic system. Since this is similar to the first stage of Type II treatment, it seems like a good idea.

CHAPTER 6
Cooking, Refrigeration, Heating, and Cooling Systems

We're among the many who say, "the best thing we make aboard our boat is dinner reservations." But unlike some cruisers—who don't cook aboard at all and plan their stops for lunch and dinner—we like to have our galley stocked with the makings of easy-to-prepare meals. That way we're free to anchor out or stop when and where we choose. Of course, many times we'll plan a layover in a harbor because there's a favorite restaurant nearby, but after a day on the water we're often content to serve a simple meal aboard, along with a nice bottle of wine. After a day of being underway we tidy up the interior and change it from running mode to dining mode. This involves turning on the stereo, setting the table, and lighting a candle so we can kick back in a comfortable setting before dinner time.

In this chapter we suggest ways to equip a galley to suit your culinary style, as well as ways you can make your boat almost as comfortable as home.

COOKING APPLIANCES

On a chilly October Saturday on Lake Michigan, the first meal we prepared aboard *Gusto* was almost our last.

With all the papers signed and the money transferred, we were proud new owners of a 41-foot sailboat and set sail from Sheboygan, Wisconsin, to Palmer Johnson's Racine yard a few hours south. We had safely cooked with two-burner alcohol stoves on previous boats, but *Gusto* also had an oven. We were happy to use it to heat up garlic bread to serve with our first official dinner aboard— spaghetti and meatballs.

We had cleared the breakwater and were reaching down Lake Michigan when Katie cranked up the alcohol, got two burners going and the oven humming on low. All of a sudden flames shot across the floor. We quickly put out the alcohol fire with the water from the spaghetti pot but for a few seconds things were a little hairy. We later figured out that the oven flame had blown out, and since there was no safety device to stop the flow of alcohol, it had dripped out of the burner onto the floor. The fire was snuffed but our confidence and egos suffered long afterwards. Not surprisingly, we do not recommend alcohol as a fuel for cooking on board a cruising boat.

Other than alcohol fuel, galley stoves and ranges are most often powered either by *liquefied petroleum gas* (LPG, also called propane) or electricity. Some kerosene and *liquefied natural gas* (LNG) stoves are also in use, though they are much less common.

On board High Life, *the propane tank is strapped securely in place, in a seat compartment on the bridge above the galley.*

Perhaps this is partly because, especially in the case of LNG, fuel is not so readily available.

Propane tanks *must* be stored in a special locker to prevent the heavier-than-air gas from collecting in the bilge in case of a leak and creating an explosion hazard. A safe installation is created with a locker that is completely isolated from the interior of the boat, with leak-free connections between the tank, regulator, and solenoid valve. The locker should not be totally sealed. It should have an overboard vent from its base, so that any leaking gas will pass outside to the open air rather than accumulate within the boat.

In addition to the isolated tank storage, there should be some means to turn off the gas between the tank and stove, ideally before the tubing enters the cabin, and preferably via remote control. Most modern boats use an ignition-protected 12-volt solenoid valve located inside the tank locker. A switch is placed close to the stove so the gas

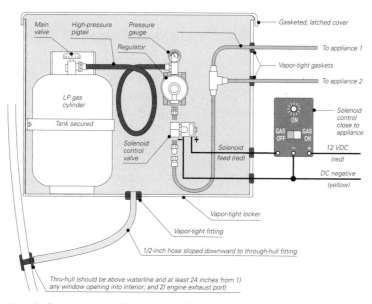

A typical propane installation, supplying galley appliances like a range and oven. (Illustration by Charlie Wing.)

can be turned on when the stove is in use and switched off after cooking.

Electric ranges are also popular on boats. However, unless you have a generator you're limited to cooking only when you're connected to shore power. The galleys on many large boats are totally electric since running the generator when underway or at anchor is standard procedure. The electric stove is easy to operate and does not use a combustible fuel.

You can use many electrical appliances in the galley such as a coffeemaker, toaster, microwave, and blender when you are plugged into shore power or when the generator is running. If you have enough of these small appliances, an inverter is a worthwhile investment so that you can also use them underway without running the generator. With sufficiently large battery banks, these appliances can be powered from the inverter at anchor as well.

In the thirty-odd years that we've been boating we haven't seen any startling innovation in galley stoves, although today's boat ranges are better designed, more efficient, and easier to clean than their predecessors.

GRILLS

We've always liked the option of grilling on the boat because nothing beats the aroma of a sizzling steak or barbecued chicken wafting through the early evening air. And on a hot summer night no one wants to go below and stand in front of a hot oven. A large size marine grill also enables you to use standard-sized pans.

Stainless steel marine grills come in a variety of sizes and shapes, including round kettles, cylinders, and rectangles, and are fueled by propane or charcoal. Smaller grills will hold four large hamburgers or four large pieces of chicken—not much capacity if you

REPLACING A GALLEY STOVE

If you're considering replacing a stove with a new one, before you do anything else, measure both the old and the new stoves and the widths of your companionways and doors. Do as we say, not as we did. When we were replacing an old propane range on our trawler with a new Force 10 range we carefully measured the old stove and the dimensions of the compartment where it was installed. However, we neglected to measure the doorway, and we discovered there was no way to get the old, 22-inch-wide range through the 18-inch-wide opening. We could have squeezed it through the aft cabin companionway, but it wouldn't clear the passage between the aft cabin and the main saloon. With looming thoughts of removing one of the side cabin's windows and all of its interior and exterior trim, we got inspired. We measured the center saloon window and it was a whopping 25 inches square. We removed a hailing horn so the window could open all the way and gingerly eased the old stove out and the new one inside. Lesson learned: some larger appliances and equipment are installed in the boat before construction is complete and may be a real challenge to remove and replace.

A barbecue grill will not heat up the main cabin on a hot night. It also creates mouth-watering aromas.

regularly entertain or travel with a large crew. Large grills can cook a feast, but they present a storage and mounting challenge. We get by with the smaller rectangular Force 10 grill that uses a replaceable propane canister, but we do occasionally pine for a larger one.

Various configurations and mounting systems are available, for installation on round stainless or flat teak rails. If your boat has fishing rod holders there are mounts that slide onto them as well. Some grills can be used as freestanding units either on deck or ashore.

A friend who regularly cruises the East Coast uses a portable grill designed for tailgating at football games. It's a good size and can handle a crowd. And it's portable, so it can be moved around the boat to different locations—a handy feature in a strong wind.

REFRIGERATION SYSTEMS

Even if you never cook aboard, you're likely to want a reliable refrigerator and/or freezer to keep beverages and food cold and fresh. Many marine refrigerators can run on both 12-volt DC battery power and on 120-volt AC shore power, and are as reliable as the one you have at home. For many cruisers a companion icemaker is equally important, although stand-alone icemakers may also be installed in a cockpit or outside the galley.

A marine refrigerator/freezer can be anything from a compact, dorm-sized unit tucked under a counter to a full-sized appliance. One cruiser told us she didn't care what kind of new boat they bought, as long as it had a full-size refrigerator. Her existing, compact refrigerator wasn't large enough for long cruises or entertaining and, while the solution of using an ice chest is an obvious one, it's not as convenient.

Another cruiser told us she replaced the dual-voltage marine refrigerator/freezer that came with the boat with an apartment-size 120-volt AC domestic refrigerator. She bought the fridge at a home center for about half the cost of a marine unit. The boat had an inverter that powered the unit while underway. She turned the refrigerator off overnight at anchor and never had a problem keeping the contents cold and fresh.

While you're underway your engine can produce enough DC power to run a 120-volt refrigerator/freezer through an inverter. But this is not a good option if you plan to anchor out frequently. If time on the hook is an important part of your cruising style, you'll need a generator to power the appliance.

There are other solutions, however, and though they are more common aboard cruising sailboats, there's no reason they can't be used aboard powerboats as well. One option is the strictly 12-volt type of refrigerator, which is slightly less expensive than a dual-voltage unit. You need a good-sized battery bank to run one, but they are generally quite small and not as power hungry as some of the appliances you may run off the inverter.

Perhaps a better solution is engine-driven refrigeration that chills *holding plates*. These plates are effectively man-made ice, but they are totally enclosed and self-contained so there's no melting water to deal with. In fact they can actually get colder than ice. The compressor can be belt driven or connected to a *power take off* (PTO) on your main engine. These holding plates become very, very cold while you're underway. So cold, in fact, that it can take days for them to thaw out completely. If they are installed in a well-insulated compartment, they'll keep food properly refrigerated (and often, even frozen) for two or three days. As long as you are underway for at least one day out of every three or four, you'll have nearly constant refrigeration without having to run a generator.

And, of course, there's always the portable cooler filled with ice. This approach may not be as elegant as built-in mechanical refrigeration, but it works!

CLIMATE CONTROL

Natural ventilation is an important design feature for all boats. Easy-to-operate ports and windows allow fresh air to circulate. Good ventilation and a sea breeze go a long way to keep the boat cool, but on those nights when the wind dies and the humidity and temperature rise, we appreciate the ability to turn on the air conditioner. Then, in the fall, when the air has a bite to it, we find there's nothing more comforting than retreating into a cozy cabin.

Climate control is usually not a big concern for weekend boaters who can pick and choose their weather, but that is not the case on a longer voyage. On an extended cruise you will encounter just about every weather condition imaginable. Some of our most memorable times aboard have been curled up in a comfortable bunk reading while cold rain pelted the windows.

KEEPING COOL

Our boat has three reverse-cycle units that do a nice job of cooling. We're pleased with the system that can heat and cool the same area. It's a small-scale heat pump that works the same way as a refrigerator to transfer heat from the air to water flowing through a heat exchanger. Reverse the cycle and the latent heat in the cooling water is transferred to the air to warm it, although (as we'll explain below) these systems can be far more effective for cooling than for heating.

Another option to permanently installed air conditioning is a drop-in portable unit designed to fit into an open hatch. These units work like a window air conditioner in a house and plug into the boat's power system or shore power. You'll sometimes see boats using roof-mounted air conditioners built for recreational vehicles, but these units are not designed to stand up to the marine environment and are mostly used on boats that seldom leave the dock.

STAYING WARM

Depending on your needs, staying warm can be as simple as toting aboard a small electric heater or as complicated as installing a whole-boat hot-water (*hydronic*) or hot-air heating system that rivals the best units found ashore. Depending on the size of your boat and budget, some of the more elaborate systems may not be practical, but there is an ideal heat source for every boat. These systems can be divided into two major categories: space heaters and central heating systems.

Space Heaters
Portable 120-volt electric heaters designed for the marine environment are a good choice for occasional use while at the dock. These heaters have built-in fans to circulate

the warm air through the boat and can be regulated by a built-in or remotely located thermostat. Built-in electrical units can be flush mounted inside cabinets or under seating. Depending on their heating capacity, some units require as little as 4 inches of clearance inside the cabinet. Units with a ceramic heating element don't get red-hot and pose less of a potential fire hazard. All these units require 120-volt AC current and are only practical to run when dockside since they draw considerable current. A large heater running on high will max out a typical 30-amp service.

There are also flush-mounted heaters that use the hot coolant from the engine as a source of heat. The coolant is pumped first through the hot water heater and then through the heater unit before it returns to the engine. As long as the engine is running you have a "free" source of heat. An external thermostat regulates the temperature by turning a 12-volt fan on or off.

And then there are fuel-burning single-compartment heaters. Many of these designs have the charm of a Franklin stove or fireplace and fit especially well in the saloon of a traditionally styled trawler. Among your choice of fuels are propane, diesel, and charcoal. You may already carry supplies of these fuels aboard for galley, engine, and grill. If you go this route, you will first have to choose which of these fuels is most convenient on *your* boat.

Whole-Boat Heating Systems

Space heaters only warm the cabin in which they are located, so to heat an entire boat you must install several units. The other option is to install a central heating system. There are three basic styles: reverse-cycle AC, diesel-fired hot air, and diesel-fired hot water.

Reverse-Cycle Air

We mentioned earlier that the same unit you use to cool the boat on a hot summer night can also be used to warm it when the weather turns cooler. One drawback to this system is that the efficiency of the heat pump varies with the outside water temperature. If the water temperature falls below 40°F in your regular cruising area, very little heat can be drawn from it, and a reverse-cycle system may not be your best choice for warmth. But as long as the water temperature is 40° or above, these units work quite well.

			HEATING AND COOLING METHODS			
Type of unit	Delivery method	Heat	Cool	2005 costs ($)	Complexity of installation	Electric service required
Marine AC	Forced air	No	Yes	1500–3000	Moderate	120v
Reverse-cycle AC	Forced air	Yes	Yes	2000–5000	Moderate	120v
Mobile AC	Forced air	No	Yes	800–1000	None	120v
Space heater	Forced air	Yes	No	50–100	None	120v
Diesel hot-air heat	Forced air	Yes	No	2000–5000	Moderate	12v
Diesel hydronic heat	Hot water	Yes	No	4500–10000	High	12v

To heat an entire boat, a unit must be installed in every cabin or ducts must be run into each cabin from one central unit. Reverse-cycle air conditioners operate on 120-volt AC current and require a good-sized generator when the boat's away from the dock.

Diesel-Fired Heat

Diesel-fired hot air heaters draw air from outside the boat, heat it in a sealed combustion chamber, and then deliver it throughout the boat via 4-inch diameter air ducts. These compact heaters are available to fit most boats and require only a supply of diesel fuel and 12- or 24-volt DC current (though some are run by 120-volt AC). Installation of the heater itself is straightforward, but running the ducts throughout the boat can be a challenge.

The hoses for a hot-water heating system are easier to run through the boat than the ducts for a hot-air system, but hot-water systems are more complex because they require a circulating pump. Like a household hot-water heating system, these systems circulate hot water through hoses to cabinet-mounted heat exchangers in each cabin. The temperature in each cabin can be varied by a separate thermostat that controls a fan in the heat exchanger.

Diesel-fired marine heating systems usually have a built-in safety cutoff. Any loss of power cuts off the fuel flow and source of ignition, and you have to reset them manually.

CHAPTER 7
Buying the Boat

We once heard someone say that a new boat is wasted on a first-time boater. He reasoned that unless you've owned a boat or two, you don't have any idea what you want, and you can be unduly influenced by the advice of a dealer or broker. That said, we think that cautious first-time buyers who do their homework and get experience on other boats can have a pretty clear idea of what they want, whether it's a new or used boat. On the other hand, an ill-prepared first-time buyer who ends up with a less-than-ideal boat could be stuck with a lot of problems and be turned off boating by the hassle.

A shiny new boat with the exact equipment and features you want is hard to beat, and it comes with a warranty to make things right. But we've also known new boatowners who were woefully disappointed with the lack of service they received from the dealer.

Your budget, and the kind of boat you want, may determine whether you buy a new or used boat. A used boat that's been cared for and has already had all the bells and whistles installed by its previous owner may cost half the price of the new version and seem like a tempting deal. But like buying a used car, buying a used boat demands extra caution. We know of boaters who purchased a boat they thought was in tiptop shape, only to find that the generator ceased to

crank out power or an unsettling sound emerged from the engine room soon after the deal was closed.

In this chapter we hope that, by sharing what we've learned, we can help you select the right boat for your needs.

BUYING AT A BOAT SHOW

We like to go to boat shows any time of year because they have a certain hustle and excitement we don't feel anywhere else. At in-the-water-shows you'll see hundreds of boats bobbing in the water, and indoor shows are a nice way to escape for a few hours from a long winter. Many a time we've driven through cold and snow to a large exhibit hall in the Midwest to climb on boats, look at new equipment, and fantasize with others about the season to come.

When we lived in Chicago we thought nothing of taking vacation time to drive the 700 miles to Annapolis for the October show. Since we now live near Annapolis it's still on our must-do list. We love the excitement in the air, the chaos in the streets, and the brisk fall air. We enjoy seeing cruising friends who work at the show taking tickets or on security detail. It's long been a favorite stopover of southbound cruisers who anchor out, work the show, and then head south.

Be prepared to look at a large selection of boats, equipment, and related paraphernalia when you go to a boat show.

No matter what boat show you attend, wear comfortable clothes and slip-on deck shoes. Why deck shoes that slip on and off easily? Before boarding any boat that's on show you are expected to remove your shoes to protect the cabin sole and carpeting—and it's a chore to keep untying and tying shoelaces.

SEARCH STRATEGIES

Buying at a show can be an "I can't believe I did that" experience or—if you've done your homework and go well armed with information—a well-calculated strategy. If you know the kind of boat, features, and equipment you want, you can take advantage of boat show promotions and special sales. Just make sure you're buying a boat from a dealer in your area, so any warranty work can be easily scheduled. Some boats are clearly boat show specials with "$23,999 cruise away" price tags; for others you have to come right out and ask for a price list.

To get the most for your money, you need to know what boat, or at least what type of boat, you want and the features and equipment that go with it. Before the show, visit a dealer or the manufacturer's website and spend time researching the different models' specifications and available options. Take that information with you to the show so you can refer to it.

Before you go to the show, if you see a boat at a marina that you'd like to know more about, ask the owner. A boater who doesn't like to talk about his or her boat is a rarity, especially if the boat is spanking new. The more preliminary information you can gather, the better prepared you'll be. If you're considering more than one type of boat, do the preliminary work for all of them. If you haven't a clue about what you want in a boat, go aboard as many different models as you can in the size and price range you can afford.

It's one thing to come away from a quick tour of a boat with a brochure, but it's better if you supplement that brochure with notes taken as you walk around the boat. The best bet is to go equipped with a pen and notebook and jot down features you like or don't like. Note your first impressions about the boat: an interior layout that appeals to you, how and where the electronics are installed—any and every observation that strikes you about the boat. Bring a digital camera to document what you see. The photos, brochures, and your notes will make it easy to sort out different boats and their features after a day of traipsing aboard several boats.

Friends of ours recently bought a new Monk 36 trawler after looking at both pre-owned and new boats at boat shows. They were especially pleased with the personal relationship they developed with the Monk broker. They appreciated dealing with one person throughout the process who was always available to listen to their concerns and make recommendations.

Most boat shows have a preview or press day when there are fewer people around, so it's much easier to board boats and talk to exhibitors. If you're seriously looking, spend the extra bucks to take advantage of this opportunity. If you know the dealer you want to buy from, ask if he's giving out complimentary tickets and make an appointment to see the boat. Most dealers accept reserva-

tion by phone or on their website. Also, if you're looking for a dealer, use the boat manufacturer's site to find one. Most have a *Find a Dealer* search based on zip codes.

If you see the boat you like, but the price is way out of line with your budget, don't be discouraged. You wouldn't be the first buyer to come away from a boat show knowing the type and model of a boat you like and then look for a used one.

BOAT CLUBS

If you're not sure about the type of boat you want to buy, consider joining a boat club where you become a shared owner of a boat by paying an annual membership fee and book a boat for when you want to use it. It works like a time-share vacation plan where you buy time on a property but don't actually own it. The experience you gain using different types of boats will help you decide what type to buy. There are also more purely time-share boating options where you actually have a fractional ownership (usually one-eighth) of one particular boat.

Most boat clubs work on a points system, which you use to reserve a boat for the number of days you decide. The cost varies, but the Chesapeake Boat Club, for example, charges $4,000 a year (in 2005) plus an initi-

BOAT SHOPPING: SOLO OR DUO?

It's nice to share the experience of going to a boat show with a partner, but if he or she isn't interested in making detailed inspections and asking lots of questions, make it a two-day event. On day one go alone to scout out the boats you like and narrow the

search to a few of them. On day two bring your partner to see the short list of boats you're considering.

If you and your partner are both enthusiastic, consider yourselves lucky and spend all the time you can shopping together.

ation fee to cruise their fleet of Albin power-boats. The best way to find a boat club in your area is to look for advertisements in a regional boating magazine, or use the Internet to search on *boat clubs*.

For more about boat clubs and fractional ownership, see Chapter 16, Learning Skills.

WHERE TO FIND USED BOATS

There are several ways to find a used boat. The yacht brokerage business, like the real estate business, has been acting as a go-between for buyers and sellers for years. Many new-boat dealers have associated used-boat brokerage businesses, which take in old boats as an incentive for owners to trade up to larger ones. Online boat-listing websites feature thousands of boats on the market. You'll find several in Appendix 1.

If you describe your needs to a good broker, he or she will do much of the research for you and arrange appointments for you to visit the most likely prospects for inspection, especially if they are located nearby. Brokers can also arrange for the inspection of more distant boats, though you will usually have to make your own travel arrangements.

A good broker will also handle all the paperwork involved when you do eventually buy a boat, so using a broker can save you considerable effort all around. A broker's commission (traditionally 6 percent) comes out of the sale price (as we said earlier, brokerage is much like the real estate business), so the seller may hold to a higher price than you might be able to negotiate on a "fisbo" (for sale by owner) deal, but more often the wider experience and extra legwork put in by the broker can make this worthwhile. And in the same way that many real estate buyers now hire a *buyer's agent* to protect their interests, you can also hire a yacht broker (whom you pay directly) to find you the best deal, as well as the best boat.

A large proportion of the pages of national and regional boating magazines is devoted to yacht brokerage and classified ads. The websites of these magazines feature boat listings as well. Free regional marine newspapers are another resource, as are classified sections in local newspapers.

And don't forget word of mouth. Look for a *For Sale by Owner* sign in a boat window or for a card tacked on a marina or marine supply store bulletin board. Also, at some of the large in-the-water boat shows there's an area of pre-owned boats that you can board and inspect.

READING A LISTING SHEET

Brokers and owners create listing sheets for their boats and those sheets become essential reading when you're in the market.

Collect listing sheets. They'll give you a pretty good first glance at a variety of boats, their accommodations, and equipment.

Before you look over these sheets, however, make your own list of the features you'd like on your boat. Be realistic and draw up two columns: *gotta-have* and *nice-to-have*. Use it as you review listing sheets and when you're looking at boats.

When you've narrowed the list, go shopping to see the boats up close and personal for a real evaluation. This can involve a lot of time, travel, and footwork, but you'll spend even more time climbing around boats for sale if you don't know what features and amenities you want.

Despite all this, there's nothing more enjoyable than the hunt for the next boat.

LOOKING AT USED BOATS

Barry Starke of Tred Avon Yacht Sales in Oxford, Maryland, says it's important to

This listing sheet from Yachtworld.com presents a lot of information about the equipment and accommodations of a Mainship 34, one of our favorite designs.

know how you'll use a boat before you shop for one. You don't need a blue-water passage-maker if you're going to be cruising the Chesapeake Bay. He says if the boat is clean and well maintained cosmetically, it's a good bet the engine and systems will be well maintained too. He reminded us that a boat's electronics used to be one of its strong selling points, but with today's ever-changing devices, it's better to buy a good, well-found boat with no electronic systems than a mediocre one loaded with old equipment. You can always add your own electronics later.

Marine surveyor Harry Seemans of Bozman, Maryland, agrees about cleanliness, especially in the engine space. If it's clean and tidy, the engine has most likely been cared for. Jump on the decks as you're climbing around a pre-owned fiberglass boat, he suggests. Pressure with a heavy foot may detect a spongy deck. If the deck feels soft, not solid, it might not be a sound boat. And look for stress marks and spider-web cracks that indicate the deck may have moisture problems.

Whether these minor cracks indicate serious water penetration or are simply cosmetic often requires the services of a surveyor, who will probably use a moisture meter to help determine the condition of the laminate beneath. But the mere existence of such cracks indicates the possibility of water intrusion or that the structure has been flexing considerably. Either of these conditions should be enough to keep you from rushing toward purchase. They don't necessarily rule out buying the boat, but they should raise flags of caution.

If you're seriously looking at a used boat, go prepared. Take along a notebook or clipboard with your list of Gotta-have and Nice-to-have features, a camera, a measuring tape, and a flashlight. Find out how the boat is stored and dress accordingly. It can be a dirty job hunkering down beneath a boat cover or in a shed. And climbing up a shaky ladder if the boat is ashore in a cradle can be a gymnastic challenge, so be careful.

LOOKING FOR *HIGH LIFE*

Our wish list for a boat usually begins on a winter night with a bottle of red wine when we pull out a yellow notepad and write down what we want. These can be features as simple as comfortable seating or more fundamental like a bigger, faster engine. We wait a few days, review our notes, and use it as a starting point for our search.

It took us several months looking at different types of trawlers in the 35–40-foot range close to home to decide that the boat we wanted was a single engine Grand Banks 36. Once we had narrowed the search to that specific boat we were surprised at the many variations we found. We used Yachtworld.com and first looked at several boats close to home, but we didn't find any we liked.

Then we broadened our search and found two on the East Coast within our budget that we wanted to see. In one long weekend we drove from Maryland to Merritt Island, Florida to see one that was out of the water. Then we drove to Charleston, South Carolina to see another one in the water. We chose the Florida boat because we liked its unusual aft cabin arrangement with a custom-built desk on the port side. And it had some of the equipment and gear on our wish list.

We made an offer—subject to survey and sea trial—and returned to Florida to be present when the surveyor inspected the boat out of the water and then ran the boat in the water. The owner was aboard as well, to answer the surveyor's and our questions and to give us an overview of operating the boat and its systems. It was a done deal.

It's OK to be nosey and take a lot of pictures, especially if the boat is a distance away from your home and your first visit may be your only one until you decide to make an offer. Shoot the interior layout and features, the electronic gear, the engine, the decks, and the bridge areas. Open the storage compartments and take shots of everything.

If the boat is out of the water, get shots of the bottom, including close-ups of the shaft, prop, and rudder. A complete set of pix at the end of the day will be your best reference. When you look at them along with the listing sheet you'll have a better way to evaluate the boat.

We've looked at a lot of used boats, always with two mindsets. In one sense we hope the boat is exactly what we want; in another, we want to spot any imperfections that might make it a bad choice. We suggest that the same amount of thought and preparation you would use buying a new boat is what you need when buying a used one.

RED FLAGS

When you look at a used fiberglass boat there's a lot to take in over a short period of time. Your first impression is important. Of course, you'll get the most complete look at a boat if it's out of the water, so you can see the condition of the bottom. Is it riddled with blisters, or does the hull shows signs of crazing?

As with the minor deck cracks that we mentioned earlier, crazed *topsides* (the parts of the hull usually above water) are often cosmetic and can be eliminated by proper refinishing. On the other hand, a deep crack indicates the possibility of more serious problems. Look particularly at joints and bends. Cracks in these locations are almost always serious—signs of unwanted flexing in structures that should be rigid, which

suggests they've been subjected to unusual stress.

You should also examine closely the areas around any mounted hardware such as handrail stanchions. Anything less than total rigidity in the hardware and totally smooth, crack-free fiberglass in the surrounding area is not necessarily all bad, but it should raise some red flags and lead to closer inspection to find out why things are not as solid as they should be.

A boat can be basically clean—no signs of mildew in the head or grease in the galley range—but appear messy because it is filled with books, clothing, and personal belongings. Don't let someone's untidy lifestyle be a turnoff. But when evaluating a boat look for these telltale signs of a boat that's not been cared for:

EXTERIOR

- Dirty, unwaxed hull and exterior trim
- Powdery residue on gel coat, indicating oxidation
- Rust and corrosion around hardware and fittings
- Torn and worn canvas work; crazing in bridge enclosure panels
- Loose stanchions and railings that need rebedding
- Worn, weathered cushions left uncovered or unprotected
- Instruments exposed to the weather without covers

INTERIOR

- Mildew odor
- Holding tank odor
- Stains on bulkheads beneath windows or hatches, indicating leaks
- Dirty seat cushions or mattresses
- Dirty interiors of refrigerator and range
- Out-of-date fire extinguishers

ENGINE ROOM

- Disorderly and unorganized
- Water in the bilge
- Oil in the bilge
- Continually running bilge pump
- Batteries with low electrolyte levels
- Batteries with corroded or frayed cables
- Rusty engine/generator that looks poorly maintained

THE SURVEY: MONEY WELL SPENT

When you find the boat that meets your criteria and you are ready to make a bid, make that bid contingent on an inspection by a marine surveyor. A surveyor spends hours inspecting the boat's structural integrity, electrical systems, propulsion system, fuel system, other machinery, navigation equipment, electronics, any other onboard systems, cosmetic appearance, and overall maintenance. The surveyor will also conduct a sea trial, operating the boat at different speeds and in a variety of conditions.

You may want to run additional tests such as an engine survey, oil analysis, moisture test, carbon monoxide test, galvanic and stray current corrosion test, electrical panel inspections, and ultrasonic test. Some of these terms may be unfamiliar, so here's a quick rundown of what each involves.

An *engine survey* entails as thorough an inspection of the power plant(s) and transmission as the hull surveyor gives to the basic structure of the boat. Engine surveyors are usually well-qualified mechanics who can assess the current state of the engines, determine the care (or lack of care) they've received and, often, spot signs of impending problems.

Oil analysis involves taking samples of the oil in each engine and sending them to a lab that will analyze them for any chemical or mechanical breakdown. All oil inevitably breaks down over time. By comparing its cur-

rent state against that of unused oil, the lab can tell if the engine has internal problems such as water leaks, fuel, or other contaminates like metals in the oil that indicate excessive wear.

The types and amounts of microscopic metal particles in the oil reveal the extent of internal wear and, most often, what parts are wearing. Different parts are made of slightly different alloys, so the exact composition of the metal in the oil indicates where it came from. Some wear is inevitable, but an oil analysis can reveal whether the wear indicated by the metal particles is normal or excessive, which can also reveal impending engine failure.

Moisture testing, as we mentioned earlier, helps the surveyor compare the amount of moisture within various areas of laminate so he can spot potential problems as yet invisible to the eye.

Carbon monoxide tests reveal exhaust system leaks and/or possible ventilation problems in the cabins.

Testing for galvanic corrosion and stray currents is a matter of looking for current where there shouldn't be any (in grounding circuits, for example). The surveyor will use very sensitive instruments that can detect current flow in thousandths of an amp. Such currents may sound miniscule, but they indicate problems that should be sought out and corrected. The situation in a normally no-current wire should be zero current. Anything more indicates a problem.

An *electrical panel inspection* will look for improper wire sizes, or improper breakers for the wire size attached. It will also assess the propriety of the wiring in general, including color-coding if the boat is of more recent vintage. It will look for proper containment or covering of all terminals and, most likely, proper chafe prevention where the wires exit the box.

Ultrasonic testing on boats serves the same purpose it does in the world of medicine. It allows us to "see" what we otherwise cannot. On fiberglass laminations, it allows us to review the internal integrity. Solid laminates and cohesive cored laminates reflect sound differently from panels that have voids or other forms of delamination. With experience, a good surveyor can use ultrasound to spot weak spots that may eventually fail completely.

After making a thorough inspection, the surveyor prepares an in-depth report about the boat's condition. If the boat has flaws or needs repairs, the report will give you leverage in renegotiating the price. If it's in tiptop shape the report will confirm the value of the boat. You'll need to show this report if you are seeking a loan, and to acquire insurance.

In addition to the cost of the survey, which depends on the size of the boat (usually $300–$500 at 2005 prices), you must also pay for any haulout charges.

FINDING THE MONEY

We've left this topic to the last, though in reality it will probably be one of your first considerations when buying a boat. Unless you are in a rarified financial stratosphere, consummating such a large purchase as a yacht in a lump-sum payment is out of the question. And the chances are, even if you had such financial reserves, you wouldn't want to diminish them by the purchase of a boat. So it's almost a given that you will finance the purchase, much as you would a house or car. As we'll reveal in a moment, doing this can have other advantages.

Where and how you acquire your financing are also variables. If you have a strong relationship with a local bank, you might be able to secure a boat loan at a more favorable rate than you can find elsewhere. On the other hand, a lender that specializes in boat loans might be able to do even better.

If you are buying a new boat, you'll find that boat dealers are much like car dealers in many ways. They'll most often try to offer you a package deal with the financing included. You can't blame them: selling loans can be as profitable as selling boats. But the dealer's plan won't always be the best you can do. So it most often pays to shop around as carefully as you did for the boat itself.

It may be "frosting on the cake," but there is a nice tax advantage to consider when you're planning the purchase. Most cruising boats qualify as second homes, which the Internal Revenue Service defines as having "basic living accommodations, such as sleeping space, toilet and cooking facilities," so the interest paid on a boat loan is fully deductible. However, to qualify, the boat loan must be a secured loan, or one where the lending institution holds the boat as collateral. Since most banks or credit firms that finance boats will want to hold a *Preferred Ship's Mortgage* anyway (a lien that takes precedence over all others in case of default), meeting this qualification is rarely a problem.

CHAPTER 8

Where to Keep the Boat

You've bought your boat, or decided what type you would like to buy. Your next critical decision is to find a *slip* (dock space) that will fit your boat and suit your cruising style. In some parts of the country, where marina space is at a premium, wannabe boat-owners are advised to find an available slip *before* investing in a boat. If you don't have a place to keep it, a boat isn't much good. Yacht clubs often have slips or moorings available only on a waiting list basis. In other parts of the country you may be able to pick and choose more freely.

The more time you spend in your slip the more opportunities you have to meet other slipholders. If you're like us, you'll know them and they'll know you by boat name. And that can be very special. We're the *High Life* to a lot of our boating friends, not the Hamiltons.

There are some key issues to consider when you're marina shopping, such as location, cost of dockage, and availability of maintenance services. Here's our take on the subject.

FINDING A SUITABLE SLIP

Some people take marina shopping as seriously as buying a house in a good school district. Others keep a boat in the slip where they bought it to get a feel for the area before relocating. Some boaters go marina shopping by boat. When they find one they like, they use a road map to determine if its location is a convenient drive from where they live.

Marinas situated within a few hours of a large boating population and in prime cruising grounds will demand the most dollars from slipholders. The majority lease slips for a season or a year, but in some areas you have the option of buying a dock or *dockominium*. Marinas in large, populated areas seem to grow and expand with neighboring townhouse developments, restaurants, and marine services clustered around them. Big city marinas often form the anchor for a downtown shopping and housing complex, and offer dockholders all the advantages that go along with such a location while they enjoy their boating.

If a laid-back atmosphere is more to your liking, you'll do better to look for a marina in a remote or rural area. Boaters who drive several hours to such marinas often make their boat and marina friends the centerpiece of their weekend social life.

For boaters who lack the desire or the skills to maintain their boat, a marina offering yard work and service is a good choice. Ma-

The Downtown Marina in Beaufort in South Carolina is home to many Carolina cruisers and a frequent stopover for boats on the Intracoastal Waterway.

rinas that offer "one-stop shopping" for slipholders are particularly popular with busy boaters who want to spend their precious free time using their boat—not working on it. Some marinas are getting out of the service business, but they may be located near a full-service boatyard where slipholders can go for repair and maintenance work, as well as seasonal haulouts and launchings.

SEARCH STRATEGIES

To begin your search for a marina, use a cruising guide of the area to get an idea of your options. Most guides provide details of marina locations and phone numbers, so you can call and ask about availability and costs.

To find the best-priced, best-located home for your boat, visit a lot of marinas, talk to slipholders there, and ask a lot of questions. Then narrow the search and decide on what's right for you. Be prepared with answers to questions about your boat that marina personnel will ask *you*—questions that will determine if they have a slip to accommodate it, such as length, beam, depth, and what type of electrical power your boat requires (30 amp or 50 amp). Then, if the location and price are right and you feel comfortable, it's probably a good choice.

These suggestions and questions will help in your search to find a suitable marina and slip:

• Take a camera when you visit prospective marinas. Visual references are particularly important if you're looking at several marinas. The best time to see a marina is on a mid-summer weekend when it is operating at its peak.

- If you consume a lot of fuel, choose a marina with a fuel dock so you can top off the tanks before leaving. If the marina doesn't sell fuel, look for a fuel dock nearby. It's not a bad idea to ask the same approach questions (depths, currents, and so on) about the fuel dock as you do about the slip itself.

MOORINGS: PROS AND CONS

Many municipal docks, yacht clubs, and marinas offer moorings, which are permanent anchors set in the bottom in relatively shallow waters near shore. They are connected to floating buoys to which you tie up your boat. It's also possible to lay down your own private mooring, either in a designated area within a harbor or in some other out-of-the-channel location. If you are considering putting down your own mooring, be aware that many communities have permitting restrictions and/or annual fees.

Picking up a mooring is, in some ways, easier than coming alongside a pier or backing into a slip. You approach the mooring head on, usually into the wind or current (whichever is stronger), pick up the mooring *pennant* (line) with a boat hook, and secure it to a cleat on the bow of the boat. You are then safely anchored to the bottom.

Only one line is involved, and if you fail to pick it up on the first approach, you simply come around and try again. If anyone happens to be watching—and you'll usually have less of an audience than at dockside—this maneuver can be far less embarrassing than hitting a pier too hard or getting caught on the end of a finger pier because you incorrectly gauged the wind and current.

Still, boaters have distinct views on the pros and cons of being on a mooring as opposed to being in a slip. Some people need to step ashore directly from the boat. They also prefer the camaraderie to be found dockside rather than the isolation of a mooring. But we've enjoyed being on a mooring. It's a quiet, often serenely peaceful setting away from the crowds on shore. It does require the added task of getting yourself and gear to and from the boat, yet this minor inconvenience is more than balanced by the lower cost of a mooring compared to a slip. The difference can be significant.

Often a harbor tender runs a shuttle service (particularly if the mooring belongs to a yacht club) to make the transit relatively easy. Many boaters prefer to use their own dinghy, which is stowed on a storage rack when it's not in use.

If your boat is so power-dependent that you always run your genset underway, moorings are not for you. Running the generator when you sit at anchor is one thing. Running it *all* the time is quite another. But if you can comfortably recharge your batteries without the need to either fire up the genset or plug into shore power, a mooring may be OK. If you enjoy the peace and quiet of a mooring, the solar panels and wind power we discussed in Chapter 4 just might be the answer.

Ultimately, the choice of whether to have a mooring or a slip depends, like so many decisions, on how you plan to use your boat.

- Look at the holding tank pumpout facility and see if it's easy to operate. Ask slipholders if it works efficiently.
- If you fish, look for a cleaning station, and find out if they sell bait and supplies early in the morning.
- If an Internet connection is important, make sure to ask what kind of connectivity the marina offers.
- Ask when slip contracts begin and end and what months the contract covers. This usually depends on the length of the boating season in the area. Find out what type of payment is needed up front and when full payment is required. Also ask when you have to commit for the next season and how much of a down payment is needed to hold the slip.
- If you're considering a particular slip that's available, check it out on a busy weekend to see just how much rock and roll there is from passing boat traffic. Is it protected by a breakwater so that life onboard will be comfortable in strong winds?
- Just to be sure, bring a lead line and check the water depth, especially at low tide.
- Ask about the approach depth to the slip and any strong tides or currents that make docking difficult.
- Does the ramp from the marina head to the slips become impossibly steep at low tide? If so it could cause problems for anyone with a physical disability.
- Check out the construction of the docks and finger piers to ensure that the boards and pilings are strong and there are no protruding nail heads.
- Look at the electrical power boxes on the slips. No loose wires should be exposed, and boats' power cords should not crisscross the dock.
- Is there a water spigot nearby for your hose?
- Are there clearly marked ladders and fire extinguishers on the docks?

- Is there a dock box for each slip or can you bring your own?
- If the marina offers full service for repairs and maintenance, does it prohibit you from working on your own boat? Does it allow outside contract workers to work on your boat?
- Check out the amenities and notice the condition of the washrooms and showers. Are they clean and well tended? Are there enough of them to cope with demand on a busy weekend?
- If you plan to spend most weekends at the boat, look for amenities like a swimming pool, picnic tables, and other diversions—especially if you have kids. If you have a pet, find out if it's allowed and if the marina provides a walking trail.
- Does the property and surrounding area feel safe and secure? Walk around and ask slipholders if they're happy keeping their boat there.
- How far is it from the parking lot to the slip? This is an important consideration when you have to shuttle gear and provisions from car to boat. And how far is it to other facilities you'll frequently use?

BUYING YOUR OWN DOCK

In some boating areas, marinas are being converted to dockominiums that you can buy instead of rent—a much larger commitment of your funds. In 2005, for example, a 30-foot slip in a marina on the Hudson River cost $72,000; a 40-to 50-foot slip in a private marina club was going for $46,000 in Michigan, for $50,000 in North Carolina, and for $168,000 in Florida.

The concept of owning a boat slip is similar to owning a condominium—hence the name—but instead of dry land you hold a deeded title to the basin bottom. In addition to the cost, which you can finance, you pay taxes and a monthly association fee to maintain and insure the complex. Most condominium marinas offer all the amenities of a resort marina: recreation area, pool, clubhouse, and parking near the dock.

While the cost is high, it's a long-term investment if you have the resources to pay for it. On the other hand, owning your slip might be a longer-term commitment than you want to make. And though the sales talk may imply that if you move, leave boating, or buy a boat that's too big for your present slip, you can sell it and get your money back (perhaps with a considerable gain), the whole dockominium concept is too new for anyone to state this conclusively.

In Appendix 1 we list some websites of online brokers selling dockominiums.

YACHT CLUBS

Many yacht clubs have boat slips or moorings for members' use, which can be a key reason for joining. Depending on the club and its fee structure, membership can be a major or minor financial commitment. The only way to find out is to call and ask to talk to the manager or membership chairman. Yacht club membership fees are separate from the annual cost of leasing a boat slip or mooring from the club. Some clubs encourage new members, and run ongoing membership drives. Others accept new members by invitation only, and membership is exclusive.

PART II

Select Gear
for Cruising

CHAPTER 9

Navigation Equipment

When we started sailing on the Great Lakes in the late 1960s, the radio direction finder (RDF) was considered state of the art in marine electronics. Gene enjoys navigation and ended up as navigator on some of the large sailboats racing in the Chicago area. During the Mac Race (Chicago to Mackinaw Island) he spent most of his time listening to rock 'n' roll music on the RDF to get position fixes.

On offshore adventures, a sextant was our primary navigation tool, and reading through our old logbooks we notice many entries with the word "approximate" attached to the navigational fixes. We were happy with accuracy within a few miles. Today, we appreciate the accuracy of a GPS fix that's within feet. How things have changed.

Most of our coastal cruising keeps us relatively close to land, and this requires precise navigation in all weather conditions. We can usually see the aids to navigation we need, so we get to practice our piloting skills. Piloting is the art of navigating a boat using visible (weather permitting) reference points, navigation marks, and water depths. It requires tools like paper charts, a compass, plotting instruments, and a depth-finder. Of course, tools like GPS and radar make piloting easier and coastal cruising safer.

THE BASICS

Navigating a boat isn't difficult, it just takes a little practice. With the availability of modern electronic equipment, it may seem unnecessary to learn basic piloting skills using a paper chart and plotting equipment. But it's important to understand what the electronics are calculating, so that if they stop working, you'll know how to work out where you are and how to safely navigate your way back to port. This is not a problem if you have clear visibility and are familiar with the waters. It becomes more of a challenge if you're looking for a navigational mark to pinpoint your location in unfamiliar waters in bad weather. We will discuss the nuts and bolts of piloting skills in Chapter 21, Piloting and Navigation Basics. Here we'll look at the basic piloting publications and tools that every cruising boat should have.

CHARTS

The National Ocean Service (NOS), a division of the National Ocean and Atmospheric Administration (NOAA), publishes navigational charts for U.S. waters. These charts contain so much information that you could spend an evening studying one for the area you plan to cruise and still miss something.

They show the shape of the land, prominent structures visible from the water, water depth, aids to navigation, and many other features of interest to a navigator.

NOS publishes chart catalogs for the Atlantic Coast, Gulf Coast, Pacific Coast, Alaska, and Great Lakes with a description of each chart and its number. These charts can cover a large area in little detail or cover a specific harbor or region in great detail. The scale of the chart determines the area covered. The most useful scales for the coastal cruiser are:

- 1:50,000 or less, covering a small geographic area like a harbor or inlet with great detail.
- From 1:50,000 to 1:150,000, covering several miles of coastal area, bays, and rivers.
- 1:150,000 to 1:600,000, covering large areas of the coast and usually extending a distance seaward.

Charts with a scale of more than 1:600,000 are used mostly for long ocean passages and show little coastal detail.

OTHER PUBLICATIONS

In addition to charts, NOS also publishes many other books and publications. You'll find a complete listing on its website, which is listed in Appendix 1. Many of these publications can be downloaded from the site as a PDF (portable document format). These publications are bulky, and a full set of coast pilots, tide tables, and light lists will require a foot or more of shelf space. To save space, we download the publications we need and place them on a CD. When planning a cruise, we pull up the publication and read or print out the information we need. The publications are free, and this routine not only gives

us the latest versions, it also saves us a lot of bookshelf space.

Nautical Chart No. 1

One of the most useful publications is *Nautical Chart No. 1, Symbols Abbreviations and Terms*. This is not really a chart, it's an explanation of how to interpret the symbols and abbreviations on the charts.

Coast Pilots

These publications are written to serve merchant ships, but much of the information is also useful to the coastal cruiser. *Coast Pilots* are published in nine volumes, covering the entire United States coastline from Maine on the East Coast to the Pacific and arctic regions on the West Coast, and also the Great Lakes.

These publications include detailed channel descriptions, anchorages, bridge and overhead cable clearances, currents, tide and water levels, prominent features, towage, weather, ice conditions, wharf descriptions, dangers, routes, traffic separation schemes, and small-craft facilities. They also include federal regulations applicable to navigation, and the new Homeland Security regulations. Appendix 1 lists the website address where you can download them.

Light Lists

The U.S. Coast Guard publishes lists of the navigational aids for United States waters. There are seven volumes, each covering a single coast guard district, with a description and location of all aids within that region. Lighthouses and other lighted aids have unique flashing patterns to help distinguish nearby lights from each other.

For example, a ship channel may be marked by several *flashing green* buoys as it progresses from sea to harbor. To help make each buoy more identifiable, one may flash at an interval of every 2.5 seconds, another every 4 seconds. Yet another—especially if it is at a critical turning point—may be *quick flashing*, in a rapid on and off succession quite different from even the relatively short interval of 2.5 seconds. Light lists include these characteristics in the description of each nav aid because it is critical information for all cruisers. Your ability to identify a light by its color and flashing pattern can be key to finding your location.

The website where these publications are available is listed in Appendix 1.

Tide Tables

When cruising in areas with a significant tidal rise and fall (or *range*) that will affect the water depth at any given time, it is vital to know the times of high and low water and the extent of the range. The government used to print tide and current tables, but today NOAA provides this information on the Internet; the address is listed in Appendix 1. There are also many other free tide prediction sites, and you can buy printed versions (along with a lot of other information) in the Nautical Almanacs published by Eldridge and Reeds. These websites and printed volumes contain tidal (and/or current) information for thousands of locations. Most cruising guides also contain tide tables for the area they cover.

THE MAGNETIC COMPASS

The beauty of the compass is that it does not require any source of power, and unless you actually bash it in or place some metal object too close to it, it will point north. Along with a nautical chart, a compass is the most basic tool of navigation.

Main Compass

Unfortunately, the size and quality of the compass installed by many boat manufacturers as standard equipment is proportional to the size of the boat. This doesn't make much sense because an accurate compass is just as essential on a 30-foot cruiser as it is on a 60-footer. Small inexpensive compasses work, but a small *card*, the disc displaying 360 degrees, is not as stable and is much harder to read than its larger brethren. A compass with a card smaller than 4 inches is difficult to read in rough conditions.

A compass with a card marked in 5-degree increments works best for us. A small vessel yaws and pitches so much in any seaway it can be difficult to steer accurately. One-degree markings on the compass card can make it harder to read as the boat yaws back and forth. It's much easier to steer a course of, say, 356 degrees by keeping the center line of the compass, the *lubber line*, aligned just past the 355-degree mark but not quite to the 360-degree mark. Our preference is for a top reading compass card. To read this type card you look into the compass and read the course by aligning the numbers on the forward edge of the card with the lubber line.

For all its simplicity and reliability, a magnetic compass is still subject to basic errors. One we call *variation*. This is the difference between *true north*, the one represented by the north axis of our planet's rotation, and *magnetic north*, the one that results from our earth's magnetic field. The amount of variation depends on where you happen to be, as it differs from place to place around the globe. It also changes slightly from year to year. Navigational charts print the appropriate variation for each chart (or each portion of the chart) and also its annual rate of change in a *compass rose*, which looks like a compass card. A compass rose actually con-

A compass card with detailed markings (on the left) is more difficult to read than one with larger and more readable numbers (on the right).

sists of two roses: an outer one representing true north, and an inner one representing magnetic. Compass roses are placed strategically in several places on each chart.

The second error is called *deviation*, caused by the magnetic influence of the boat's own iron or steel equipment. When it exists, it prevents the compass from aligning properly with the earth's magnetic field so that the north it displays is not magnetic north or true north, but rather a different "north" that we call *compass north*.

Deviation changes with each change in the boat's heading because the boat's relationship to magnetic north changes as it heads in different directions and thus the relative influence of the iron or steel changes also. But there is some good news: we can reduce or often eliminate this error by placing small magnetic objects within or near the compass to counter these onboard influences. For this reason, quality compasses have compensating magnets built into them or their mount.

You can adjust your own compass, but we recommend hiring a professional compass adjuster. Unless the compass is removed from the boat or you make major changes in on-board equipment that influence the compass, the compass adjustment only needs to be done once. Is having your compass adjusted important? Yes! A 3-degree deviation error may not be noticeable when steering short courses between buoys in local cruising grounds. But the same error on a hundred-mile leg of an extended cruise will put you five or six miles off your destination.

On *High Life* we also have several digital fluxgate compass aboard. We'll describe it in the Electronic Aids section below.

Hand Bearing Compass

In addition to the main compass, a hand bearing compass is an essential backup for a coastal navigator. Taking compass bearings on two or more land objects or other aids to navigation and plotting the bearings on the chart provides a *fix*. This is the primary method of finding your position while cruising inland and coastal waters, which we'll discuss more fully in Chapter 21, Piloting and Navigation Basics.

A typical "hockey puck" hand bearing.

We think the best type of hand bearing compass is the small *hockey puck* style. There are several brands, but they all have one feature in common: the card in the compass is light and well damped. A small prism in the compass projects the part of the compass card that will give you the bearing into your line of sight as you look over the compass. To take a bearing, all you have to do is point the compass directly at the object you want to take a bearing on. Then read off the bearing that's visible in the prism.

A hockey puck–type hand bearing compass allows you to look over the compass so you have a full view of your surroundings with your peripheral vision. This is a big advantage if any kind of sea is running, especially at night. It only takes a 3-foot following sea to push a small boat around. If the boat yaws 10 degrees to port and starboard—not uncommon, even with a good autopilot—the relative bearing of a blinking light can move from bow to amidships as the boat yaws. When the light flashes you can see it and take a reading. The light compass card responds almost instantly to your moves and stops spinning fast enough to get an accurate reading.

Don't waste your money on a cheap hand bearing compass. You'll find it frustrating to use in all but the calmest of conditions. Before you buy one be sure to try it out in the store to make sure you can focus on distant objects and still see the compass readout.

Binoculars with a built-in compass are popular with some cruisers, but they suffer from a narrow field of view. This is not a problem during the day, but at night, in rough conditions, a flashing light may not remain on long enough to spot as a boat yaws back and forth. If you like the idea of being able to take a bearing on a distant object through the binoculars, consider a hockey puck–style hand bearing compass as a backup. And that brings us to:

BINOCULARS

In order to relate what you see on the chart to visible landmarks, and for spotting navigation aids, a good set of binoculars is on the "must-have" list of gear. We each have our own set, which we find especially useful when visibility is poor. Many cruisers carry only one set, but it's very convenient to have binocs permanently adjusted to your own eyesight. When you need to pinpoint a landmark in a hurry, you want to do it without fiddling with the focus.

We also use our binocs just for fun because we enjoy scanning the shoreline for wildlife (and to observe what's going on aboard other boats, of course!). And when we go boating on other people's boats, we always bring our own binoculars along.

If you're in the market for marine binoculars there are a few points to consider:

- The lenses in binoculars magnify images. You'll see binocs sold in various sizes. 7×50 and 8×26 are popular sizes for boaters. 7×50 means the object you're seeing is magnified by 7. The 50 refers to the diameter of the objective lenses (the larger end). Larger objectives gather more light and are easier to use in low-light situations, but other things being equal, binoculars with large objectives are bulkier and heavier. Binoculars also have internal prisms to reorient the image so that the binoculars can be made smaller with the same magnification. The better the binocular, the better (and better aligned) the prisms.
- Waterproof binocs can withstand a drop in the water and also prevent fogging by keeping out water vapor.
- Binoculars should feel comfortable to hold. If you use them over a long period of time, a lighter weight will be more comfortable.

- Binocs with a rubber casing will give you a good grip.
- Some binoculars have a center focus mechanism that adjusts both lenses at the same time. Others have lenses that adjust individually.
- A flotation strap will ensure that the binocs won't go straight to the bottom if you drop them overboard. (You may have to buy the strap separately.)

THE TOOLS

Piloting has been practiced for centuries and a wide variety of products has been designed to make it easier and more accurate. No one tool is best, and as you gain experience, you may decide on your own favorites. They all get the job done, but we find that there are several tools we reach for more than all others.

Dividers

No boat should be without a set of dividers, which are used to measure distances on a chart. They come in many shapes, but a good quality heavy brass or stainless single-handed divider is the easiest to use. You can spread the divider with one hand to measure a distance and it will stay in that position while you move it to the distance scale on another part of the chart.

Plotter/Protractor

Parallel rules are traditionally used to plot courses and bearings on a chart. The direction of the course or bearing is transferred from the compass rose by walking the two rules across the chart. They are easy to use since you can account for variation by using the inner compass rose. If your chart table is large enough to accommodate the chart without folding it, the parallel rules work very well. But we always seem to have to fold our charts and the compass rose ends up somewhere in the fold. Also, if you use a chart kit (a collection of charts or chart sections, bound into booklet form), you'll find they don't always print a compass rose on every chart, especially on pages that represent only a section of a chart.

We find the Weems-Zweng Course Protractor solves all these problems. It contains a built-in compass rose that can be used on any chart. It provides correction for varia-

The arms of this type of divider can be spread or closed with a single hand, so it's convenient to use.

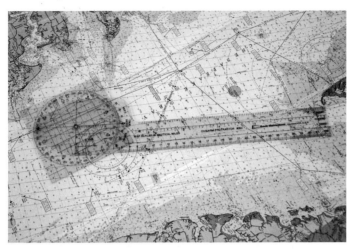

A plotter with a built-in compass rose is easy to use, even on a folded chart in a cramped navigation station.

tion, and you can read the reciprocal of any course directly off the compass rose. There are also distance scales for several of the most popular chart scales along with a latitude/longitude scale. These make plotting information from the GPS onto the chart easier when it's folded and the edges (where the lat and long scales are located) are not visible. Davis Instruments also make a similar one-arm protractor that we have used for years. It's just as functional as the Weems-Zweng plotter and a bit less expensive.

Magnifying Glass

The devil is in the details, they say, and this is especially true on a chart. A magnifying glass is handy for a clearer view of fine details. It doesn't have to be fancy. We like the kind with a plastic handle because metal handles will eventually rust.

MARINE ELECTRONICS

Technology has made communication and navigation easier than it's ever been. Every year, navigation equipment becomes less

expensive, more accurate, smaller, and more user-friendly. Even the smallest cruisers can be fitted with fully functional electronics that are waterproof and use little energy. In a single boating generation, high tech has evolved from the radio direction finder (RDF) to Loran-C to Transit (an early satellite system) to GPS.

Radar sets used to be expensive, large, and bulky and couldn't be exposed to the weather. Now they are sized for just about any boat, and some of the sets with LCD (liquid crystal display) screens are waterproof. Depth-sounders have matured from simple devices with a rotating, flashing neon tube to multifunctional units that not only display the water depth but also tell you if there are fish to catch under the boat.

We use a range of navigation and communication equipment on *High Life*. Here's what we consider essential.

DEPTH-SOUNDERS

We have two depth-sounders, one on the flying bridge and one at the lower helm. Chesapeake Bay—our home cruising grounds—is known for its skinny water, so one of our depth-sounders is always on when we're underway. Both are the recording, fish-finder type. The older one with a CRT (cathode-ray tube) display is at the lower station. Since the unit is shaded from the direct sun and protected from the weather it works just fine. On the bridge we have a unit with an LCD screen, which is readable in direct sunlight. Both units have more features than we actually use since we seldom fish.

Of course, the display is only the visible part of the depth-sounder. More important, perhaps, is the *transducer*, the component that actually makes it work. Though *sounding* is a term that has referred to depth since the earliest days of sail, today's sounding devices actually do use sound. The transducer aims pulses of sound (at a frequency in the neighborhood of 50 or 200 kHz, depending on the depth involved) toward the bottom and then listens for echoes. The device translates the time interval between the transmission of the pulse and its reception into depth information.

Since most depth-sounders display the depth from the transducer down, you need to know how far below the surface it's mounted. Add this depth to the displayed depth to get the total water depth. The transducer should be located as close as possible to the deepest part of the boat, so that the instrument will show you the depth of the water *beneath you* without any need for correction. When the water gets very thin, this can be the most important depth information of all.

Some depth-sounders convert the echoed pulses into a virtual portrait of the bottom, and often do so with considerable detail. Some versions also keep an electronic record of this information so you can refer back to it. This ability to review the depths and other underwater information encountered during a trip can be quite valuable for fishermen, though it has fewer practical applications for cruising.

One feature we particularly like on some of the newer sounder units is that screen retains the bottom contour data when it switches depth scales. For example, if the water deepens and the unit changes from the 0–15-foot scale to the 0–30-foot scale to show the deeper water, the bottom contour is carried over from the previous scale. When the older CRT unit changes scales, the screen goes blank and the sounder starts to record the bottom contour from scratch. It takes a while, depending on the display setting, before the full bottom contour is painted on the screen. This becomes a problem if the unit switches scales several times in a short period. The newer sounders also have a dual-frequency transducer that allows them to switch between 200 kHz for shallow water and 50 kHz for deep water.

On two of our previous boats the transducer was originally mounted *inside* the hull.

Even if you don't fish, it can be useful to have a depth-sounder that displays a digital rendering of the seabed. The bottom contours can be compared to the chart data.

In both cases we were disappointed with the depth-sounder's performance and re-mounted the transducer *through* the hull, which required cutting a hole. This worked well for us, with our slower displacement-type boats. On a high-speed boat, the inside-mounted or stern-mounted transducer (which uses a bracket on the transom to hold the transducer) may be the only choice to avoid a reduction in performance.

ELECTRONIC COMPASS

An electronic, or *fluxgate*, compass senses its relationship to the earth's magnetic field just like a magnetic compass, but it uses an electrical coil, rather than a magnetic needle, to do so. One main advantage is that the electrical output from the coil can be easily converted into a digital readout for display on a liquid crystal or other type of screen. It can be used as a steering compass or connected to other navigational equipment like an autopilot, radar set, or chartplotter.

The coil is as susceptible to magnetic interference as a compass needle, but most fluxgate compasses have separate sensing and display units. The sensor can be located away from magnetic interference to greatly reduce deviation error. Most of these units are also self-compensating once installed and can be adjusted to have zero deviation by following the manufacturer's instructions.

We have two fluxgate compasses on board *High Life*, one that interfaces with the autopilot and the other that we use at the lower helm. The large numbers on the course display are easy to read, even in rough conditions. This compass can also calculate the average course steered, a feature that's especially helpful when we are dodging crab pot bouys and can't steer a steady course. A marker at the top of the display moves to the right or left of the desired course indicating

A digital fluxgate compass supplies heading information to other navigational instruments. Its display panel is highly visible and its features allow you to easily compensate for deviation.

whether our weaving has caused us to steer more to one side of the intended course than to the other.

GPS SYSTEMS

Today, a global positioning system (GPS) receiver is the basic electronic navigation tool on a cruising boat. Even the simplest GPS receiver can give you position data that is accurate to within 25–30 feet. The unit receives signals from several navigational satellites launched and maintained by the U.S. government. It processes the information and calculates your position in an ongoing manner, so you always have a reliable fix. In addition, it can calculate and display your boat's *course over ground* (COG), and *speed over ground* (SOG). All GPS units also calculate the course (bearing) and distance (range) to a distant position, called a *waypoint*, which you enter into the set.

Until May 2000, the U.S. government purposely degraded the inherent accuracy of the GPS system for reasons of national defense, using an application called *selective availability* (SA). Eliminating SA made GPS more accurate, but improvements didn't stop there. To make the service even more accurate, *differential* GPS (DGPS) was developed. In this system, land stations with known locations calculate the difference between their position derived from satellite data and the actual position of the station. This information is broadcast to all DGPS receivers in the area so that they can automatically correct their displays for greater accuracy. DGPS requires that each unit actually has two receivers and two antennas: one for the GPS data from the satellites, the other to receive the land-based differential signal.

Many new GPS units now incorporate the *Wide Area Augmentation System* (WAAS). It works in a similar way to DGPS except that the correction data are sent back to the satellites to be rebroadcast along with the basic GPS information. This allows correctional coverage over a wider area than that attained by land-based transmitters—hence the name. WAAS technology was funded by the Federal Aviation Administration (FAA) as a means of providing better information for instrument-only airplane landings. We boaters get to take advantage of it.

WAAS delivers pinpoint, repeatable accuracy to within three meters of a vessel's actual position. This new technology allows every boater to obtain the accuracy of a differential GPS unit without the additional expense (though the GPS unit must be WAAS-capable for the system to work).

Choosing a GPS can be a daunting task and comparing features against price can keep you awake at night. We have used several different types of GPS receivers, and these are the features we consider essential.

- 12-channel WAAS-capable receiver
- An easily readable, high-contrast screen. We would opt for a small color screen over a larger grayscale unit

- The ability to store at least 500 waypoints and 25 reversible routes
- Easy-to-use software to manage waypoints and routes and allow basic trip planning
- Output of at least basic NMEA 0183 data—like speed, course, and crosstrack error—to interface with other navigational equipment. Units using the NMEA 2000 protocol are even better.
- A handheld GPS should have the ability to plug into a power source on board the boat

The main function of the GPS is to provide accurate position data. All other features are merely added value—nice, but not necessary. Prices have plummeted, and features once offered only on top-of-the-line units have migrated to the less expensive models.

A basic GPS will display the bearing and range of the line that runs from your position to the waypoint you are steering toward. This line is generally known as a *rhumb line*, the navigational term for any line of constant bearing. Whenever you tell the GPS to *Go To* a waypoint or give it a *Route* to follow, the unit calculates the rhumb line to the

A GPS receiver, like this chartplotter, provides highly accurate navigation information.

waypoint and remembers it. If the boat moves off course, to the right or left of the rhumb line, the GPS calculates the distance and direction of this *crosstrack error* and displays it. To save space, the display will usually use an acronym for crosstrack error such as XTE or XTK.

Interfacing a GPS with Other Equipment

If you already have other navigation electronics aboard, like a radar set or chartplotter, and you plan to integrate a GPS with them, check the specification of the GPS carefully before you purchase it. Most units output data in what is called the NMEA 0183 format. Through the years this specification has been enhanced and several versions now exist along with custom protocols unique to each GPS manufacturer.

In our experience, getting NMEA 0183-compliant electronics to talk to one another is not always a "plug and play" event. Finding the proper cable to connect the units can also be a challenge. Do your homework before buying, especially if the manufacturer of the device you want to interface with is not the same as the GPS and the unit is more than a few years old. For example, our Garmin 182c GPS talks to a new Furuno 1832 radar, but will not talk to the older Robertson autopilot that only communicates with an earlier version of NMEA 0183.

And, as if this confusion weren't enough, the National Marine Electronics Association (NMEA) has introduced the long-awaited NMEA 2000 interface standard, which establishes the requirements of a *serial data communications network* to interconnect marine electronic equipment. Equipment designed to this standard will be able to share data, including commands and status, with other compatible equipment, over a single channel. It certainly appears that NMEA 2000 is an improvement. It's also certain that it will

in time totally replace NMEA 0183 on all marine electronics, most probably in the not too distant future.

When NMEA 2000 is the only protocol, interfacing should become easier. But what if you still have a lot of NMEA 0183 equipment? According to most reports, during the transition period there are ways of getting 0183 devices to talk to the newer 2000 models and vice versa. However, given our lack of success in getting NMEA 0183 devices to work together, we think it's safe to say the transition period may not be as hassle-free as the marine electronics industry may hope.

Antenna Placement

Placement of the GPS antenna requires some consideration. The height of the antenna is not important, but it should not be mounted in the direct path of a radar set. Most GPS antennas come equipped with a base that screws onto a standard 1-inch antenna mount and can be mounted on an antenna extension to raise it above the radar beam. Our GPS antennas are mounted at least five feet from the VHF antennas and we have not noticed any degradation in the GPS performance when transmitting on either radio.

If you have a handheld GPS receiver it will have a built-in antenna, so this talk about antenna location may be unnecessary, but handhelds often have the provision for connection to a permanently mounted antenna.

CHARTPLOTTERS

A plotter is part of an electronic charting system that creates a video display of the same features you'll see on a paper chart. It also pinpoints a boat's location on the screen. The image is generated by software that uses stored digital data to create the chart and input from a GPS to track the boat's position. The plotter continually updates the position on the chart as the boat moves through the water. Many GPS receivers now incorporate a chartplotter, and most stand-alone chartplotters interface with Loran or GPS receivers that output NMEA-compliant data.

As boaters become more familiar with electronic systems, they become less dependent on paper charts. But that doesn't mean a chartplotter can totally replace the traditional paper chart. If the electronic systems should fail, it's important to have a paper chart as a backup. It's also important to recognize that a number of unavoidable errors in the system can lead to errors in the position shown for your boat: it's close, but a little bit off. As long as you are aware of this and don't take your shown position as absolute gospel, you're safe. But if you start thinking that your chartplotter gives you a 100 percent accurate *you are here* image, you can be in serious trouble.

The cost of chartplotters has followed the path of most electronics—they are now affordable and compact enough for even the smallest cruising boats. The biggest advance in plotters and other navigational devices that use LCD screens has been the increase in

brightness, resolution, and contrast. This makes them easier to view in sunlight, when on a flying bridge or other open helm. Most units are also now waterproof, which also make them suitable for an open helm station.

When we decided to update our GPS to a chartplotter, the Garmin 182c fit the bill. We installed one unit on the bridge and used our old handheld GPS at the lower helm. The 182c worked so well we decided to install a second unit at the lower helm station. They are easy to use. The screen is bright enough to see during the day but can be dimmed at night. These units were reasonably priced, so having two was not out of reach, and it adds redundancy to our primary navigation system.

Many GPS receivers have a feature called an anchor watch alarm. When set, the alarm alerts you if the boat begins to drag anchor and drift out of position (See Chapter 19, Anchoring). We used this feature all the time on our sailboats since the GPS was in the main cabin, but rarely used it on *High Life* when the GPS was up on the bridge. Now, with the new GPS at the lower helm, we would not think of hitting the sack before activating the alarm function.

Buying the plotter is just the beginning. You also have to buy and update the electronic charts you need. Whatever brand of chartplotter you are considering, don't forget to check out the cost of the charts for the area you plan to cruise. The charts required to cover an extended cruise can cost almost as much as the plotter itself. Competition among the companies that produce these charts has caused the cost to drop, but differences remain.

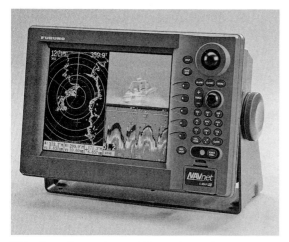

This chartplotter also provides radar and depth information. (Photo courtesy Furuno.)

INTEGRATED SYSTEMS

Integrated navigational systems that include a depth-sounder, GPS, chartplotter, and radar are available from many manufacturers. These units solve the space problem of where to install all the individual units. The split screen shows several functions at once and the radar image can be combined with the chartplotter map—a great feature. We suspect integration will continue, as manufacturers continue to develop expanded networked systems that combine even more types of data into a single display.

We've cruised on several boats that have integrated systems, and they are impressive. About the only downside might be the reliance on a single display for all your information. A failure of this unit puts you totally out of business, although redundant displays, which are also becoming common, take care of this problem. We also noticed that the split-screen functions are more usable if the unit has a large screen. Sets with small screens are more difficult to read when split into multiple functions. Their screens are easier to read when they display functions like the chartplotter or radar in full-screen mode. Still, having a single unit to deal with instead of an array of equipment spread out over the helm certainly cuts down the clutter. If we were starting from scratch we'd certainly consider an integrated (networked) navigation system.

PC-Based Systems

PC-based navigation software is mature and very powerful. This technology is a viable alternative to traditional marine electronics for larger boats that have the room to install a dedicated system. Input from the depthsounder, GPS, and radar can be integrated through a network link. Daylight-viewable screens display the data at the bridge or anywhere the screens are placed throughout the boat. Input from video cameras and engine status can be integrated into the system.

While there are other means of networking various data and navigation systems, bringing everything into a PC, where communications, system controls, and other automated operations can be added to the mix, certainly makes sense.

Laptops

Laptops work well on sailboats or in a pilothouse type of powerboat where the navigation station is protected from the weather and can be shaded from direct sunlight. A laptop computer-based system is not the best choice as the primary navigation system on a powerboat if it must be taken outside. Few laptop computers have daylight-readable screens that are designed for mounting outside on a flying bridge or outside helm, although these screens are available. They are expensive and though you could connect one to the laptop as a remote display, this would defeat the purpose of using a laptop: to have everything in one compact, portable unit.

We can connect our Garmin GPS set to our laptop, and it displays real-time tracking on digital charts. We thought this would be a great feature but it's turned out to be impractical. We've used the laptop at the lower helm several times when steering below in foul weather. As long as the sky was overcast the screen was viewable, but when the sun came out we couldn't see the screen. Running at night we couldn't dim the laptop's screen enough to prevent it from hampering our night vision. There may be laptops with brighter screens, but these computers are not watertight and are difficult to use from the bridge.

We find a laptop ideal for planning a cruise, making routes, and setting waypoints, but not as a primary navigation system. It allows us to do considerable planning regardless of where we are. Either on the boat or ashore, we can plan the trip—down to such specific details as waypoints linked into a continuous route—and then transfer the data to our permanently installed nav system once we get aboard. So, even if laptops are not so good for a primary nav system, they can be extremely useful nonetheless.

Handheld Computers

Handheld computers are able to connect to GPS units and provide real-time navigation. One example is Garmin's handheld GPS computer. Other units that operate on either the Palm or PocketPC operating system (PDAs) can accept input from a GPS receiver. These units can display charts and provide basic navigation information. Many free programs that calculate tides and currents and keep track of all types of ship's data are available to download from the Internet. Of course, these programs can be run on laptops or other computers, too; the PDA is just so much more portable.

We should also mention that several manufacturers now make PCs specifically designed for installation on a boat. The CPU, hard drive, and other sensitive internal elements (such as a CD-ROM drive and a proprietary drive to read the electronic chart cartridges) are mounted in relatively dry and protected locations. The only portions exposed to the elements are the display (or displays), and most probably a keyboard (with perhaps a built-in trackball to eliminate the need for a mouse). This may be where marine electronics are headed. The future looks interesting, indeed.

ELECTRONIC CHARTS

Electronic (digital) charts have been used by commercial vessels for many years, and with the falling prices of chartplotters, PC-based navigation software, and GPS receivers with built-in chartplotters, electronic charts are beginning to supplement and, in many cases, replace paper charts on recreational boats as well.

Digital chart technology is changing rapidly, so be aware of the chart-usage policies of the plotter manufacturer and the company that produces the charts, if they are different. Even if plotter and chart come from the same company, check the license that comes with the chart. Garmin, for example, allows its charts to be used on only two different Garmin units. If we were to change one of our GPS units, we would have to purchase a new set of digital charts, since the new device would have a different serial number and the old charts would not work.

Plotters display electronic charts in two basic formats: *raster* or *vector*. The format of the charts used in a particular plotter is dictated by the plotter's manufacturer. Each has its advantages and disadvantages.

Raster Charts

Raster charts are basically digital photographs of an original paper chart. As a result, they look exactly like the paper charts when displayed by a chartplotter or navigation software on a personal computer. They are stored as graphic images, so this format requires very large computer files. Also, since the resolution of the image depends entirely on the number of pixels per inch in the original copy, you'll often find that when you use the software's zoom function to look at details closely, the individual pixels begin to show and the images become rough and ragged.

Vector Charts

Vector charts also look exactly like the paper charts, but when they are displayed on a chartplotter or with navigation software on a personal computer, much more information is available. Rather than being just a photo of a paper chart, vector charts have groups of related chart data stored in a digital database. Data usually requires smaller files than graphics, which means that much more information can be contained in fewer bytes of storage. As vector charts require less computer disk space than raster charts, you can load a larger area of chart into your plotter at one time.

To view the chart, a *rendering engine* in the navigation software reads the database and constructs a picture of the chart on a computer or plotter screen, using the stored data to tell it what goes where. The structured nature of this data allows for flexibility in its display. Separate elements of the chart can be turned on and off simply by calling up or *not* calling up certain classes of data.

Our plotter, for example, allows us to display several different levels of chart detail, which helps de-clutter the chart of information we are not interested in at the time. With our small-screen plotter, this is handy. Further, since the image is created entirely by software, not from a stored graphic file, when you zoom in you still get the clear picture you get at wider views, because every image is a freshly constructed, brand new chart, not a photo of a paper chart.

NOAA Charts

The companies that produce electronic charts used to use only public domain government charts as a basis. This is not strictly true anymore. Some very good, privately published electronic charts of popular cruising grounds based on private GPS surveys are now becoming available.

NOAA is also beginning production of vector-based charts, which are available in the S-57 international exchange format and free for download from their website. These charts won't work with most commercially available chartplotters as yet, but some PC-based navigation programs are able to display this format. There are links on the NOAA website to several companies that make free or inexpensive software that can display this format. If you have a PC-based nav system, this is good news. If you use a plotter that requires proprietary charts, you'll just have to wait until they come around—if, indeed, they ever do.

Chart Accuracy

One word of caution when using a chartplotter (especially in foreign waters like the Bahamas or the Caribbean): many of the digital charts are based on old paper charts that were created before very precise positioning methods were available. Your GPS can be telling the chartplotter your exact position, but if the objects on the chart are not positioned correctly the chartplotter will display false information.

Even taking latitude and longitude readings of objects off the paper charts and creating waypoints for the GPS to steer to can lead to trouble if the paper charts have errors. Before you purchase digital charts, check their source and consult cruising guides for the area you plan to visit. Most guides give accurate waypoints for key destinations, gathered by on-the-spot GPS recording.

RADAR

We place radar near the top of the list of essential navigational equipment. A compass, paper charts, and basic piloting skills can replace the GPS, but only radar can see through rain and fog. Most manufacturers offer compact sets that won't break the budget.

When we talk radar with other cruisers they inevitably ask what's the maximum

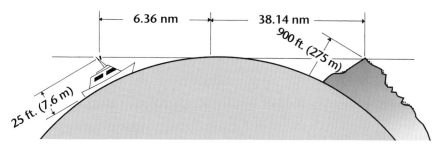

6.36 nm — 38.14 nm

900 ft. (275 m)

25 ft. (7.6 m)

In most cases, it is the height of the antenna that limits a the effective range of a radar unit, not the transmitter power. This is due to the earth's curvature. (Illustration by Bruce Alderson.)

range of our set. While range is important, the power of the transmitter and the height and size of the antenna do more to determine the performance of the set than maximum range.

For example, our radar antenna is only 20 feet off the water and due to the curvature of the earth it can only see about five miles out. If the superstructure of a ship is 30 feet off the water, then the radar can begin to see that ship at about 12 miles as it begins to rise above the radar's horizon. If the radar isn't mounted high enough, it doesn't matter what the potential range of your radar is. Even if its range is 72 miles, it will not detect a ship any sooner than a unit with a 36-mile potential if the antennas are mounted at the same height.

The real advantage of longer-range sets is their transmitter power. In clear weather, low transmitter power works fine, but when rain or fog rolls in, it may not. The thicker the fog and heavier the rain, the more radar energy it absorbs and the weaker the returned signal. A 1.5-kW, 16-mile radar set will not return as strong a signal in rain or fog as a 4 kW, 36-mile set. Most radars work OK to their max range in clear weather, but that's not what you have radar for.

Most of the time we operate our radar in the 2–6-mile range. In the 6-mile range the radar can see stationary objects that are at

least half an hour away. As we approach a nav aid or some other object we are looking for, we switch to the shorter scales.

About the only time we use the maximum range is to look for rain. We were cruising up the Chesapeake Bay in mid-April one year when the weather turned cold and the forecast called for possible snow flurries. We turned the radar to its maximum range, turned up the gain and watched for any precipitation to appear on the screen. About noon a wall of green—that's the color of targets on our radar—began to appear across the top of the screen. That gave us enough warning to duck into a marina at Windmill Point and get tied up before the snow started.

Most of the time we use our radar in the 2–6 mile range. This gives us the best overall picture.

The other major factor affecting radar performance is the size of the antenna or array. The larger the antenna the more accurate the radar. For example, a typical 24-inch radar dome has a horizontal beam width of about four or five degrees. A larger 4-foot open array antenna has a horizontal beam of less than two degrees. This narrower beam allows the radar to separate and display individual objects at greater distances. At 5 miles, the 2-foot antenna may show a tug pulling a barge as a single object on the screen where the 4-foot antenna may display them as separate images.

Picture the radar beam as a searchlight beam. If it rotates clockwise the front edge of the beam hits a target and begins to return and continues until the trailing edge of the beam leaves the target. The wider the beam the longer the target is in the light and the wider the blip on the screen. This is why targets painted on the radar's screen grow in width the farther they are from the center of the set.

Most radar sets can be interfaced with the GPS or digital compass to allow the set to display a picture that can be orientated to heads up, course up, or north up. The heads up mode is the default on most sets and orients the top of the screen to what is directly ahead of the boat. The course up mode imposes the boat's course on the top of the radar display, and all bearings taken with the *electronic bearing line* (EBL) are relative to the boat's course. North up mode orients north to the top of the screen to match the paper chart. Position, course, and speed data from the GPS can also be displayed on the radar screen along with the next GPS waypoint. Having the waypoint displayed on the screen can be especially handy in a crowded harbor with multiple navigation aids.

Radar can create a false sense of security unless you know how to use it. Practice. Go out in your boat and use it in good weather, so you'll know how it works. When you can compare what you see on the screen with what you see around you, you'll know what those blips represent when you can't see them. (See Chapter 21, Piloting and Navigation Basics.)

RADAR REFLECTORS

For radar to display a target on the screen, radio energy transmitted from the antenna must reflect off the target and bounce back. The stronger the reflected energy, the brighter the target will appear on the screen. Fiberglass cruising boats produce poor targets on a radar screen, so to compensate, a per-

The sausage-shaped canister at the top of the mast is a radar reflector. It is mounted as high as possible for best effect. The disc-shaped unit below it is the radar antenna itself.

manently mounted radar reflector should be considered basic safety equipment.

The idea is to make your boat look as large and imposing as possible on other boaters' radar sets. A weak target that fades in and out on the scope may not get the attention it deserves.

We have a Firdell Blipper radar reflector mounted at the top of *High Life*'s mast. Tests have shown the larger the reflector and the higher it is mounted, the better its performance. This unit looks more like a boat fender than a radar reflector and is filled with radio-reflective material. Besides helping other vessels see us on their radar screen, the distinctive shape of the reflector makes it easy to find our boat in a sea of masts in a large marina.

On other boats we have used a Davis Echomaster reflector made of three slotted circular pieces of aluminum that fit together at right angles, forming pockets that reflect radar energy. Hung from our mast, it seemed to keep us from being run down by other vessels. Another unit called the Tri-Lens also gets good reviews.

If you outfit your boat so it's clearly visible by other boats using radar, you only need to hope that they're standing watch and monitoring the screen.

CHAPTER 10
Communications Equipment

Every cruising boat should be equipped with at least one VHF (very high frequency) radio, so it can communicate with the Coast Guard in case of an emergency or with a towing service if the boat breaks down. It's also useful for talking to bridge and lock tenders, marina operators, and other boaters.

The more ambitious your cruising plans, the more thought you should give to keeping in touch—unless, of course, a long cruise is just the excuse to cut loose from an ever-ringing phone or a barrage of e-mails. Boaters can choose from a variety of wireless communication devices in addition to VHF sets. Here's a rundown on some of the equipment that's available.

VHF RADIO

Other than life jackets, the VHF (156–162 MHz) radio, designed to provide reliable short-range communication, is the most important piece of safety equipment you can have aboard. Depending on the height and type of the antenna and the power of the transmitter, this radio can have a range up to about 25 miles in open water, which is basically line-of-sight communication. The radio's limited range is a disadvantage at times, but it allows many more boaters to use the same frequencies or channels at the same time.

Unless you operate a very large yacht, use your boat commercially, or plan to cruise in foreign waters like the Bahamas, you are not required to have a radio station or operator's license. If you will be traveling in foreign waters and communicating with foreign vessels you should have a *Restricted Radiotelephone Operator Permit* and a *station license* from the Federal Communications Commission (FCC), whose website is listed in Appendix 1.

VHF radios operate on preset frequencies or channels. These channels have been assigned different functions. Channel 16 is reserved for emergency calls and hailing. Federal regulations require all boaters to monitor channel 16 when the radio is turned on. After initial contact you *must* switch to a *working* channel. Bridge-to-bridge communication is conducted on channel 13. Commercial vessels are required to monitor both channels 16 and 13.

Even the most basic VHF radios are really loaded with features and functions, but we find that we rarely use half of them. The radio at the lower helm of *High Life* is an Icom set with all the bells and whistles, and

VHF Channels

DISTRESS, SAFETY, AND CALLING—Use this channel to get the attention of another station (calling) or in an emergency (distress and safety).	16
INTERSHIP SAFETY—Use this channel for ship-to-ship safety messages and for search and rescue messages and ships and aircraft of the Coast Guard.	6
COAST GUARD LIAISON—Use this channel to talk to the Coast Guard (but first make contact on Channel 16).	22
NONCOMMERCIAL—Working channels for voluntary boats. Messages must be about the needs of the ship. Typical uses include fishing reports, rendezvous, scheduling repairs, and berthing information. Use Channels 67 and 72 only for ship-to-ship messages.	9, 67, 68, 69, 71, 72, 78
COMMERCIAL—Working channels for working ships only. Messages must be about business or the needs of the ship. Use channels 8, 67, 72, and 88 only for ship-to-ship messages.	7, 8, 9, 10, 11, 18, 19, 67, 72, 79, 80, 88
PUBLIC CORRESPONDENCE (MARINE OPERATOR)—Use these channels to call the marine operator at a public coast station. By contacting a public coast station, you can make and receive calls from telephones on shore. Except for distress calls, public coast stations usually charge for this service.	24, 25, 26, 27, 28, 84, 85, 86, 87
PORT OPERATIONS—These channels are used in directing the movement of ships in or near ports, locks, or waterways. Messages must be about the operational handling movement and safety of ships. Use channel 20 only for ship-to-coast messages. Channel 77 is limited to intership communications to and from pilots.	12, 14, 20, 65, 66, 73, 74, 77
NAVIGATIONAL—(Also known as the bridge-to-bridge channel.) This channel is available to all ships. Messages must be about ship navigation, for example, passing or meeting other ships. You must keep your messages short. Your power output must not be more than one watt. This is also the main working channel at most locks and drawbridges.	13, 67
MARITIME CONTROL—This channel may be used to talk to ships and coast stations operated by state or local governments. Messages must pertain to regulation and control, boating activities, or assistance to ships.	17
DIGITAL SELECTIVE CALLING—Use this channel for distress and safety calling and for general purpose calling using only digital selective calling techniques.	70
WEATHER—On these channels you may receive weather broadcasts of the National Oceanic and Atmospheric Administration. These channels are only for receiving. You cannot transmit on them.	Wx-1 Wx-2 Wx-3 Wx-4 Wx-5 Wx-6 Wx-7

Source: FCC Web site, wireless.fcc.gov/marine/vhfchanl.html

on the bridge there's a basic model by Standard. Both were installed when we purchased her. Over the years we find we prefer some of the controls and functions on each of the sets better than others.

Before you can transmit a distress call you have to turn the radio on, so for any radio, it *should* be obvious how to do so. Unfortunately, this is not always the case. One of our radios turns on and off by turning the volume control: turn the volume down and click, off goes the radio. The other set also turns on and off with the volume control, but you must push the control in to toggle the radio on and off. This allows the volume control to stay set at a preset level—but it baffles almost everyone who tries to switch the set on.

One radio uses a knob to change channels and we think this is easier to use than up/down function keys. Both radios have multichannel scanning modes, which we usually use to scan channels 16, 13, and 9. Channel 9 is now the preferred hailing channel for pleasure boats, to help reduce traffic on channel 16. The radio at the lower helm has a loud hailer and foghorn; we have used the foghorn, but can't remember ever using the hailer.

The receiver of a VHF radio is more sophisticated than most people realize. It needs to be sensitive enough to pick up weak signals, and more importantly, it should be able to reject all other signals and noise. This is vital, because if most of your cruising is done in populated waters, there will be a lot of radio traffic. The radio's ability to reject interference is published in the manufacturer's sales brochure.

For the technically minded, the higher the decibel (dB) rating for adjacent channel rejection, spurious response, and intermodulation rejection (three critical performance elements), the better. Figures of at least 75 dB rejection or better will indicate a radio with a good quality receiver, which should make it capable of clear reception in crowded areas with high radio traffic.

DSC

Most new fixed-mount VHF radios come equipped with a feature called *digital selective calling* (DSC). The government has required this feature in all radios manufactured after June 17, 1999. Radios made before this date can still be sold, so some non-DSC radios may still be available, though they are becoming rare.

A VHF radio equipped with DSC can, at the push of a button, transmit a distress signal including the identity of the vessel. If the radio is interfaced with a GPS or Loran set, it will transmit the boat's location as well. To use DSC, each radio must be registered with the FCC and receive a *Maritime Mobile Service Identity* (MMSI), much like a phone number. The MMSI for your boat is stored in a government database and is accessed when the distress signal is sent out to identify the boat in distress.

This new technology has prompted the USCG to deploy a new system called *Rescue 21* to listen for the automated distress signal. Because of budgetary restraints the USCG will phase in this new system over several years. However, the new regulations require all boats equipped with a DSC VHS radio that receive a DSC distress call to relay the call to the coast guard. Soon there will be thousands of DSC-equipped radios installed on boats, automatically listening for a distress call. This will provide a much safer situation for any boat in harm's way than trying to get through to the coast guard through the clutter on channel 16.

Another feature of DSC is the ability to call another boat also fitted with a DSC radio

All new VHF radios incorporate a safety feature called digital select calling. At the touch of a button, the radio will send out a distress call that identifies your boat and its location. (Photo courtesy ICOM.)

directly. It's more like making a telephone call. When you enter the MMSI of the other boat you want to call into your radio, the radio on the boat you are calling will recognize it is being called and respond. Both radios can be programmed to automatically switch to a working channel so you can communicate. If the radios are interfaced with Loran or GPS the position of the boats will be displayed on each other's radios. The ability to share positions between boats with DSC radios is not fully implemented by all radio manufacturers, but as the Rescue 21 program is deployed, more radios will undoubtedly offer this feature.

HANDHELD VHF

The handheld VHF radio is a great adjunct to the fixed-mount radio and it's handy to take along in a dinghy. The same criteria and features of a fixed unit apply to a handheld unit. Most are waterproof, and don't consider buying one if it's not. The ability to operate with standard alkaline batteries is also important. Our handheld has run out of juice when

the charger wasn't available. Its proprietary rechargeable batteries have a limited life and eventually fail to hold a charge. We think it would be handy to have the option of popping in standard batteries to keep it working.

ANTENNAS

The radio communication gear on a boat relies on a good quality antenna to function. It is probably the most critical element of a successful radio installation. A top-quality radio hooked to an old, poorly functioning antenna will not perform nearly as well as a run-of-the-mill radio teamed with a properly installed quality antenna. If you plan to replace your radio, definitely replace the antenna if it's more than five years old. And give careful thought to the placement. Due to the earth's curvature, line-of-sight distances increase with the antenna's elevation. Ashore, mounting an antenna on a tower can provide considerably more range than just mounting it on the roof. The same principle applies to boat antennas, though tests have shown that unless you can mount the antenna *very* high, like at the *truck* (top) of a sailboat's mast or on the tuna tower of a sportfisherman, a few feet of height one way or the other will not greatly affect the range of the set.

Radio antennas, especially if tuned to the same frequency, do affect one another, so if you have more that one VHF radio antenna on your boat, mount the antennas as far apart as possible. They should be separated by a horizontal distance of three to four feet and installed vertically, not at an angle, for the best range and efficiency.

It is important to secure the antenna with a good quality mount and solid, through-bolted fasteners so it can withstand the whipping it will receive when the going gets rough.

VHF antennas should be spaced as far as possible from one another to prevent interference between them.

The transmitting pattern of the antenna is also an important factor to consider. Antennas are rated by what is called antenna *gain*, which is a measurement of their *effective radiated power* (ERP). A standard 4-foot VHF antenna is rated at 3 dB gain, which means that a radio connected to this antenna will have twice the ERP it would have with a zero-gain antenna—it will sound twice as powerful. The radio can only transmit a maximum 25 watts, but the antenna concentrates this output by directing toward the horizon the energy that would otherwise be directed skyward. As the antenna gain increases, the radiation pattern becomes more concentrated in a horizontal band. A 14-foot antenna rated at 9 dB concentrates even more energy toward the horizon and creates a narrower horizontal radiation pattern.

This works fine as long as the boat is in calm waters, but if it begins to roll in a seaway, the concentrated horizontal radiation pattern is directed at the sky on one side of the boat and at the water on the other. As a result the receiving station will hear the transmission fade in and out.

If you are considering replacing your radio because it just does not perform like it used to, look to the antenna before you replace the old set. If you are replacing the set for a new feature like DSC, make an antenna upgrade as part of the package.

KEEPING IN TOUCH

VHF radio is an essential communication tool for the boater but it won't help you call

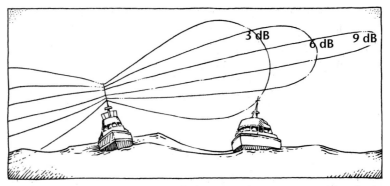

The radiation pattern of a VHF radio becomes more concentrated in a horizontal band as the output power increases. But lower-power antennas perform better in some sea conditions. In this example, the boat on the right would reliably pick up a 3 dB signal from the other boat, but a 9 dB signal might fade in and out as the boat rolls and the direction of its signal shifts. (Illustration by Christopher Hoyt.)

CALL HOME OPTIONS			
Miles from shore	Voice	Mail	Internet
5	Digital cell phone	Digital cell phone	Digital cell phone
10–40	Analog cell phone	Analog cell phone	Analog cell phone
Unlimited	SSB radio, Satellite Services	SSB radio, Satellite Services	Satellite Services

home. Fortunately, many other options are available to keep you in the know while cruising. The equipment and services break down into two basic categories. The first and easiest to use are communication systems designed for land use—like cell phones—but which function just as well on a boat. The other category involves specialized hardware and services that are specifically designed for offshore marine use and can keep you in touch from just about any place on earth. Basically, the farther from land you cruise the more sophisticated the equipment you need.

THE INTERNET AND E-MAIL

Using e-mail to communicate while cruising is becoming easier as more and more marinas provide at least a phone line to connect with your Internet service provider (ISP). Most cruising guides now list whether or not marinas offer Internet connection.

Some marinas offer wireless high-speed connections: some charge a fee, and others provide it for free. We consider the $40 we spent on a wireless networking card a good investment. Many new laptops have built-in wireless capabilities so if you're in the market for a new computer, consider this a must-have feature.

Cell phones and single-sideband radio links can also provide e-mail connections, and both of these technologies are keeping boaters in touch. Wide-ranging cruisers may wish to take advantage of satellite telephone systems or other satellite-based communications gear that, like other electronics, are steadily becoming more reasonably priced.

CELL PHONES

A cell phone is the easiest device to use for both voice and e-mail communication. There are many places where it can't connect from the water, but overall, cell phones have proven to be a reliable and convenient way to keep in touch.

The cellular system is designed to carry thousands of calls simultaneously. To do this over a finite number of radio frequencies, the transmission range of each phone is limited. To make up for the short range, cellular transceivers must be placed on towers that are close together so the phone can connect to one tower as it moves out of range from another. As the number of users increases, more transceivers are installed but each transceiver's power is turned down. A single transceiver on high power may have extended coverage five to ten miles offshore. With an increased number of users, its power may be reduced so reception may only extend three to five miles offshore.

The cellular companies are constantly expanding services and functionality of their phone systems. Connection speeds keep increasing and the areas where higher speed data connections are available are expanding.

Top on our list of personal improvements was installing a marine cellular antenna to increase the range of our phone's reception. In addition to a cellular antenna there's a cellular amplifier that boosts the signal and extends the range of either an analog or digital phone.

When we want to make a reservation at a marina or contact a boatyard we think a cell phone is much more reliable than using the VHF radio. Someone usually answers the phone, but they may not always monitor the VHF. And as a safety device a cell phone is not a replacement for a VHF radio, but it makes a good backup, especially in coastal waters.

You can also use a cell phone to call a local Internet service provider, for a slow but adequate e-mail connection. If your phone has a software package—usually available from the service carrier where you purchased the phone—you can most likely get e-mail. The software allows the phone to communicate with your computer. When the phone dials the number of your ISP it acts as a modem, or if a digital connection is available the phone can connect directly with the ISP. Multimode phones that can switch between analog and digital service are the best. Your ISP must also allow slow speed connections. At best the phone can connect at 14 kbs (kilobits per second), which today is considered slow.

SINGLE-SIDEBAND RADIOS

Except for a quick dash across the Gulf Stream to the Bahamas our coastal cruising keeps us within VHF radio range. We do, however, have a single-sideband (SSB) high frequency (HF) marine radio on *High Life* plus a ham (amateur radio) set that is also fully functional for listening on the marine SSB channels (though it is illegal to use ham radios to transmit on marine). We use ours to stay in touch with cruising friends who regularly use their SSB radio for e-mail and weather information. You need a marine station license to legally transmit on marine bands, but this is a matter of filling out a form and writing a check as opposed to taking an exam, so it's no big deal.

For ham radio, it is the *operator* who is licensed, while for marine SSB, both the *station* and *operator* must be licensed. In addition to the marine station license a *restricted radiotelephone operator permit* is all you need as operator of noncommercial vessels, and no test is required. In many cases you will not be acknowledged on ham-radio bands unless you are licensed and have a call sign. In ham radio, there are several license levels that give either partial or full access to frequencies. A general class license, for example, is required for access to maritime mobile nets in the 15-, 20-, and 40-meter bands. To get a ham license, there's an examination in Morse code, radio theory, and rules and regulations with respect to operations. It is often a fear of technical matters and theory, as well as the Morse code exam, that frightens many would-be radio amateurs. And yet, with a little study, the exam is easy. The ham operator must have a license appropriate to the frequency band being worked while using an SSB radio on the ham bands.

MARINE SSB AND HAM RADIO: DO YOU NEED BOTH?

While they operate in the same high frequency portion of the radio spectrum, there are distinct differences between these types of service, and the answer would be a resounding "*yes*, if it's at all possible." Marine

A single-sideband radio can communicate over thousands of miles. It's the primary long-range communication tool for long-distance cruisers. (Photo courtesy ICOM.)

SSB sets are generally easier to operate for nontechnical people, and with the automatic tuning that's now most common, it is extremely simple to punch in a channel number and talk. Antenna tuning, which also used to be a big SSB bugaboo, is now mostly automatic as well. Additionally, marine SSBs have automatic emergency channel selection.

And, most important, they are type-approved for marine communications.

While using a ham set to transmit on marine channels is forbidden, you are allowed to operate a marine SSB radio on amateur frequencies if you have a ham-radio license. There is a disadvantage to using marine SSB on ham-radio frequencies in that marine synthesizers are programmed in 0.10 kHz steps. Ham communications may often take place at frequencies outside these channels, so that marine SSB sets can be marginally off frequency. Also, most marine SSB sets operate in the *upper sideband* (USB) while most ham frequencies below 40 meters are *lower sideband* (LSB).

Access to Global Maritime Distress and Safety System (GMDSS) emergency frequencies is illegal for ham sets except in emergencies, which means an SSB set is needed to contact ships on the high seas. On the other hand, ham radio allows for casual conversation and chitchat, which marine SSB does

Satellite communication and entertainment antenna systems are becoming smaller and can be installed on any boat.

not. Ham allows full access to information-packed nets and a worldwide communications network. Ham radio does not readily allow access to telephone networks, although some stations offer phone patches. So if you have the room for both sets and are willing to get a ham license, having both systems can be the best of both worlds.

In addition to the long-range voice communications capabilities, a marine SSB radio can also be a primary source for high seas text and weather fax information. Software is available for a personal computer that can decode and display this information. Modems and SSB e-mail services are also available that allow the SSB radio to send and receive e-mail from just about anywhere in the world. If you have a ham radio and a special radio-frequency Pactor modem you can send and receive free e-mail all over the world. This is probably the very best HF radio e-mail system available and if you have an HF transceiver, you might want the Pactor modem, also.

SATELLITES

Satellite communications have come of age and like most electronics the equipment has shrunk in size and cost. It is commonplace to receive news reports from the far reaches of the globe delivered over this type of equipment. The large antenna domes that once dominated the superstructure of ships and megayachts have shrunk in size. This technology is constantly changing, with companies emerging and going out of business. The trend is clear: the hardware has reached a point where it can be installed on just about any cruising boat. The key challenge to wide use of satellite communication gear is the high cost of the online time, but as volume goes up, competition will force prices down. Inmarsat, probably the best-known maritime satellite service provider, has many options available, including some that are ideal for the cruising yachtsman in both the features offered and also the price.

CHAPTER 11

Anchors and Related Gear

CHOOSING AN ANCHOR

While the U.S. Coast Guard *recommends* that boats have an anchor and anchor line (which together with associated equipment are known as *ground tackle*) there is no federal regulation that *requires* it. Many state boating laws do require this equipment and we (along with most other experienced cruisers) consider it essential safety gear.

Often you'll find that a boat's anchor equipment is adequate for occasional use, but the anchor may be undersized and the line (usually called the *rode*) may be too lightweight to hold the boat in storm conditions. Additional properly sized anchors, and a combination chain/rope rode, are essential for anchoring in a variety of situations. Even if your cruising style takes you to marinas most of the time, at some point you will need to anchor and rely on your ground tackle.

Of course "properly sized" means different things to different people, so opinions vary in any discussion about ground tackle. There is really no best anchor, but there are several types that are widely used and reliable.

ANCHOR TYPES

The anchor must have been invented about five minutes after the first boat was launched, due to the obvious need to keep the boat in one place occasionally. That very first anchor may have been simply a large rock. But we'll bet it wasn't long before those early boatmen figured out that while they needed weight to take the anchor to the bottom, being able to *grab* the bottom would help them hold better.

And that is why, most likely, anchors started to assume the traditional form that still decorates blazers and captain's hats, even if we rarely use that type of anchor on our boats any more. This design features a *shank*, the backbone that holds everything together, and a *stock* to help it balance properly and assume the proper angle so that the *flukes*—the pointed tips that do the bulk of the work—can dig into the bottom.

Modern lightweight anchors hold by burying themselves in the seabed. In order to stay buried, the pull of the anchor line must run almost parallel to the bottom. As a result, the length and type of anchor line you use will affect the holding power of the anchor, as will the type of bottom you're anchored in.

The type of anchors you choose will usually depend on where you cruise and what type of boat you have. Where you cruise is important because different kinds of anchors hold best in different types of bottom. You need an anchor that will hold well in the most prevalent bottom—sand, mud, clay, or rock—found in your favorite cruising grounds. Rarely does one type suit all.

Here are the most popular types of anchors used on cruising boats.

Single-Fluke or Plow-Type Anchors

The plow-type anchor looks and acts just as its name suggests. It has but one fluke, a one- or two-piece structure that's shaped like a farmer's plow. The sharp point of the fluke digs into the bottom and the pull of the rode buries the anchor. It has less holding power in very soft mud bottoms since it tends to plow its way through the muck rather than bury itself. But in sand or clay, a plow can be superb. It stores easily on a bow anchor roller or pulpit, but is difficult to store on deck.

CQR

This old standby is on the bow of more cruising boats than any other type of anchor and is what many boating people think of when they hear the word *plow*. The anchor is drop-forged from high-tensile steel and holds well in most types of bottom conditions. And since there's a hinge between the shank and the single plowlike fluke, it continues to hold as the boat swings. It's an expensive piece of equipment, but it's a lifetime investment.

Delta Fast-Set Anchor

This anchor is similar to the CQR (and is made by the same manufacturer) but it has a one-piece body—there's no hinge. Its unique shank profile and ballasted tip make the Delta anchor self-launching from a bow roller, which makes it especially well suited to mate with a chain rode and electric windlass, especially if the windlass is remote controlled from the helm. It will hold in most bottoms because the design also allows for quick and easy penetration of sand, mud, and even weeds. Its low center of gravity and self-

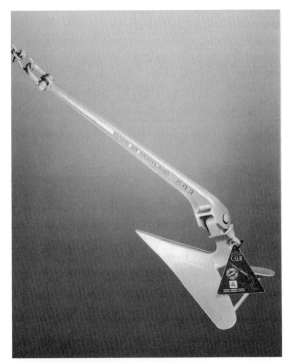

A CQR anchor. (Photo by Jay Stuart.)

righting geometry ensure that the anchor will set almost immediately.

Bruce Anchor

This design (which is not exactly a plow, but has just one fluke and fits this description better than any other) is derived from anchors designed to hold North Sea oil rigs in place. It is a single-piece casting that stores well in a bow roller, but is difficult to store on deck. It sets fast and holds well. It is also usually less expensive than other plow type anchors mentioned above. The humps on either side of the central fluke usually help it to quickly reset if the boat swings on a changing tide. It is also better in rocky bottoms than most other modern anchors because it will hold in rocks but rarely gets stuck—the less prominent point on its single fluke seems to be the advantage.

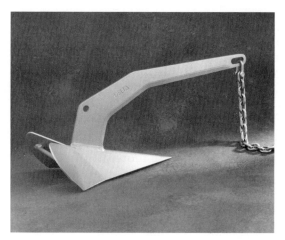

A one piece plow anchor. (Photo by Jay Stuart.)

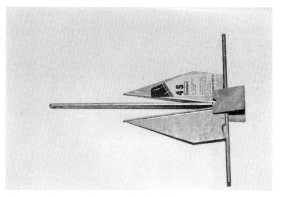

The sturdy Danforth anchor's folding design makes it easy to store. (Photo by Bob Armstrong.)

Two-Fluke Anchors

The old-fashioned design many people think of when they hear the word *anchor* is rarely used anymore. Anchors of this design hold well in rocks, but need to be much heavier than the more modern types we discuss below to hold in other bottoms.

Modern two-fluke anchors, which have been with us since the early days of World War II, bury their flukes into the bottom as a result of the flukes' shape and angle rather than the anchor's weight. Since the flukes can have a hard time penetrating sea grass, hard clay, and rocks, these anchors are most useful in sandy and muddy bottoms.

Danforth

This is the original lightweight anchor, the first to rely on fluke angle and shape rather than weight to gain its penetration and holding power. The Danforth was originally developed for the landing craft used in amphibious invasions in World War II. They are currently available in several grades, of which the Hi-tensile and Deepset II models are the strongest. This anchor folds flat and can be stored on deck or launched from a bow roller.

Fortress

This aluminum version of a lightweight anchor is constructed of an extremely strong aluminum-magnesium alloy that makes it the lightest of all. It is also designed to be taken apart for storage. A Fortress anchor has the most holding power per pound of any anchor currently available.

Several of our cruising sailing friends use the Fortress and swear by it. The anchor's

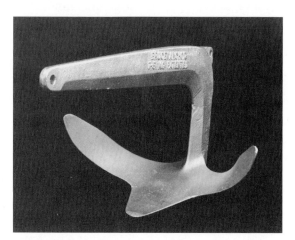

The Bruce is another popular anchor. Coastal cruisers like its holding power, but the ungainly shape makes it difficult to stow. (Photo courtesy Imka Corp.)

The Fortress anchor is similar to the Danforth, but is made of lightweight aluminum alloy. (Photo courtesy Fortress.)

light weight is a big factor for them, though it's less important on a powerboat. But the ability to fold up and store the anchor does make it a good choice as a spare anchor that's relatively easy to handle. Fortress anchors hold well in soft mud but are less advantageous in sand or clay. Also, if you anchor in a strong current, they sometimes have a tough time reaching the bottom, though once they do, everything is fine.

Some other new anchor types are available, and you'll often see them displayed at boat shows. But we don't have any personal experience with any of them, nor do any of our cruising fiends, so we won't cover them here.

ANCHOR SIZE

It doesn't take a rocket scientist to understand that larger anchors have more holding power. So, large boats require larger anchors. While you really can't have too large an anchor, there are some practical limitations. Anchor manufacturers publish tables of anchor sizes recommended for boats of different length. The problem with these tables is that, to keep things simple, they divide boats by length into groups separated by intervals of ten feet or more, and there is usually one table for both sail and powerboats. Boat length alone is not a good measure when sizing an anchor because the displacement, beam, and wind resistance caused by its freeboard and canvas should also be considered.

A powerboat tends to have more beam than a sailboat of the same length. A powerboat also usually has more freeboard, especially at the bow. At anchor, a boat faces into the wind most of the time, so the wider a boat and the higher its freeboard, the more area the wind has to push against. And more wind resistance places more strain on the ground tackle.

In addition, powerboats usually have loads of canvas, at least a bimini and possibly an enclosed flying bridge. In some cases, a typical 40-foot trawler with an enclosed bridge may have two to three times the silhouette of a typical sailboat of comparable length.

The displacement or weight of the boat also affects how much strain a boat puts on the anchor line. In calm water, wind and current are the major forces pushing the boat against the anchor line. If the wind increases, the waves build, and the boat starts to move up and down as each wave passes under the bow. A heavy boat bucking up and down in a choppy anchorage can put additional strain on the anchor line. The heavier the boat the more momentum it generates.

Boat movement can exert tremendous force on the anchor as the boat moves back and forth in the wind and bucks up and down against the wave action.

MAKING THE CHOICE

Taking all these factors into consideration, you can see that choosing an anchor from a table that uses length as the only criterion usually leads to an undersized anchor for a cruising powerboat. We recommend that unless your boat is at the bottom of the length bracket, you choose an anchor size from the next highest boat-length category.

For example, we have a 45-pound CQR anchor on the bow of *High Life*, our 36-foot trawler. On their website, Lewmar, the manufacturer of the anchor, recommends a 35-pound anchor for a 36-foot boat. In our opinion that's correct for a 36-foot sailboat, but too light for our heavy boat with the added windage caused by our high freeboard, wide beam, and canvas. On the other hand, we once had a C&C 35 Mk I sailboat that had low freeboard and rather light displacement, and we always slept well at anchor with a 25-pound CQR.

PROPER ANCHOR INVENTORY

Most of the time we rely solely on our main anchor, but there are times when we find it necessary to use more than one anchor. A crowded anchorage, strong current, and other factors sometimes require different anchoring techniques, so here's our take on having more than one anchor.

Main Anchor

Our preference is a plow anchor weighing at least 35 pounds. We have cruised on boats with CQR anchors, Bruces, and Deltas. They all work as advertised but didn't always set fast and hold consistently. But no anchor is perfect: plows don't hold in a soft bottom.

On High Life *we carry both a Danforth and a plow anchor in a bow roller.*

Sometimes you just have to go elsewhere to anchor.

Second Working Anchor

We think the Danforth and Fortress are the best in this category because they hold well in soft bottoms, set faster than the plows, and make a good second anchor. The 20-pound Danforth and 15-pound Fortress are minimum sizes.

An aluminum anchor does not sound very macho, but after hearing cruisers say they weathered gale-force winds with aluminum anchors we have changed our mind. Even a really large, lightweight Fortress can easily be tucked away, because it comes apart, whereas finding storage space for another type anchor might be impossible.

In addition to the plow-type anchor, we carry two additional fluke-type anchors: a 20-pound Danforth anchor in a roller on the bow, and another large Fortress with its own chain and nylon rode—stored in the lazarette, in case it's needed for a big blow. So far we haven't had to use it, but it's ready if we do.

Small Lunch Hook

We used to carry a small twin-fluke anchor to use as a lunch hook (an anchor used for a short stop, during which at least one person usually remains aboard to be sure that the anchor doesn't drag), but we don't anymore. It was handy on our sailboat since the main anchor was stored on deck, but on the trawler, the main anchor is so easy to launch from the windlass we use it as a lunch hook as well. But it's handy to have a small light-weight anchor in case you run aground. You can use the anchor to pull the boat off.

CHOOSING AN ANCHOR RODE

An anchor is attached to your boat by an anchor line or *rode*. The anchor and rode work together as a system and unless they complement each other, neither will accomplish its mission. Attaching a light anchor line to a hefty anchor is a waste of money since the anchor will hold fast long after the anchor line has parted. Conversely, attaching a heavy anchor line to an undersized anchor can lead to the anchor dragging.

Most large ships and commercial vessels use chain exclusively for an anchor line; many experienced cruisers follow suit. A combination of chain and nylon rope also makes an excellent rode. The ideal anchor rode would be strong enough to take the heaviest load wind and waves can throw at you and resist chafing and damage from rocks, coral, and junk on the bottom. Nylon line is very strong for its weight but falls victim to chafing. Chain resists chafe but is relatively heavy. Here's a more detailed look at the characteristics of each.

Chain

Galvanized steel chain is an essential element of a proper anchor line. Chain is heavy, tough, and resists abrasion. For example, ⅜-inch chain weighs about 1½ lb. a foot. So 50 feet of ⅜-inch chain weighs 75 lb.—more than most anchors. The alternating orientation of the chain links creates a lot of friction as it sits on the bottom, which makes it hard to drag. The sheer weight of the chain also enhances the holding power of the anchor.

Chain suitable for an anchor rode comes in three basic types:

- Proof Coil chain is made from low-carbon steel with long links that are usually not compatible with most windlasses. It can be used as the chain portion of a rope/chain rode if you don't plan to use a windlass.
- BBB chain is also made from low-carbon steel but has short links that will fit most windlasses.
- High-test chain is made from high-carbon steel, is stronger than either Proof Coil or BBB chain, and is also compatible with most windlasses.

All three types are also usually available in stainless steel, but stainless is so much more expensive that it is not a realistic choice for most boaters.

An all-chain rode hangs in a curve (called a *catenary*) between the boat and anchor, due to its weight, creating a built-in shock absorber. When the anchorage is calm, the chain hangs straight down to the bottom, where it makes a right-angle turn and heads toward the anchor. As the boat moves backward it lifts chain off the bottom. In all but the severest conditions, the weight of the chain prevents the rode from coming taut. The pull of the anchor chain remains parallel to the seabed, allowing the anchor to achieve maximum holding power.

Since chain hangs straight down when not under tension it can't tangle with the props or rudder. In contrast, a nylon anchor rode can more easily become entangled, especially in a tidal anchorage where the current changes direction several times a day, and the boat swings randomly during slack tide.

Chain does have its downside. A long heavy chain is difficult to handle without a windlass. Anchoring in 25 feet of water with a 45-pound CQR and ⅜-inch chain will put almost 80 pounds of metal in the water before the anchor hits bottom. That's all dead weight that you have to lift, along with a big ball of mud that's probably stuck to the anchor. Along with the mud clod the chain itself will bring aboard several pails of muck. Before we installed a saltwater washdown hose to clean the chain, Gene would don an old set of foul-weather gear when we weighed anchor. Even buckets of water splashed on the chain links didn't do a complete job of getting the muck off the chain.

On most boats there's a limit to how much weight you can put in the bow without affecting the trim. Heavier displacement boats with fuller bow sections are less affected, but a hundred feet of chain is a big load to add to any boat. In our opinion, an all-chain rode requires a windlass with sufficient room beneath it to store the chain. If you plan to do a lot of anchoring, keep that in mind when you're looking at the design of a boat. We think that ⁵⁄₁₆-inch and ⅜-inch high-test chain is best suited for the anchor rode or at least part of a rope/chain combination for a cruising powerboat.

Nylon Rope

Pound for pound, nylon rope is much stronger than chain. Lightweight ⁷⁄₁₆-inch nylon line has about the same breaking strength as ⅜-inch high-test chain. The difference is that though strong, thin nylon line will chafe through in a short time if not protected. Chain, on the other hand, will probably saw through your bow pulpit if you don't protect it.

Nylon also stretches under load and provides a built-in shock absorber between a bucking boat and anchor. However, since the rope is light it will pull up tight between the boat and anchor. Unless you have enough *scope*—the ratio of rode to water depth (7:1 is the accepted minimum for overnight stops in moderate weather)—the direct pull of the line on the anchor will not be parallel to the seabed and can break the anchor loose. Scope is important no matter what the rode is made of, but an all-chain rode has a catenary action that allows it to hold well with less than the normal (7:1) scope, unless there are storm conditions.

Even on smaller boats we recommend at least a ½-inch nylon 3-strand anchor line. Some cruisers swear by braided nylon line but we have used three-strand line with good results and see no compelling reason to change.

A lightweight anchor line may be more than strong enough, but in a heavy blow a small-diameter line can chafe through before you realize it is in jeopardy. A larger diameter line has much more bulk and resists chafe longer.

In Annapolis for the boat show one year, we set two anchors when it really began to blow. We took turns standing anchor watch and at first light were horrified to find that one of the anchor lines had almost chafed through. Apparently the two lines had gotten twisted and one line, pulled by the other, had been rubbing all night on the stainless stem fitting that ran a foot or so down the bow of the boat. This had never been a problem before, but two of the three strands of the ⅝-inch line had worn completely through. Lighter line, while strong enough, would have parted and the anchor and chain at the end of the chafed line would have probably been lost. Since that episode we've been true believers in heavy line and chafe protection.

Chain and Rope

A combination of chain and nylon produces an anchor rode with the best characteristics of both. When we say a combination of chain and rope we mean a *long* piece of heavy chain, not a 6-foot section sold as an anchor chain. Even a short length of chain is better than none, but to be effective it should be at least 25 feet or longer. A section of ⁵⁄₁₆-inch or ⅜-inch chain at least as long as your boat is a good starter.

When we bought our first trawler, a wooden GB42, she had an adequate 45-pound plow anchor, but only 8 feet of ⁵⁄₁₆-inch chain on a ⅝-inch nylon rode. That might have worked for the previous owners but we had a heck of a time getting the anchor to set.

We rode out a November gale in that trawler in a protected creek in Chesapeake Bay, and even in 10 feet of water we had to let out 200 feet of line to stop the anchor from slowly dragging. We dropped a second anchor to put a stop to that and spent two days watching the geese fly backwards as they tried to make headway into 45–50 knot winds. When we went ashore we went straight to the marine store and bought 50 feet of ⅜-inch chain. The following spring, we met a similar blow and the anchor set and held with a quarter of the scope.

On our current boat, our primary anchor rode is 100 feet of ⅜-inch high-test chain spliced to ⅝-inch 3-strand nylon. We hardly ever get into the nylon line since we cruise in relatively shallow waters. In effect, we anchor on all-chain rode.

Bottom line: get a long section of heavy chain, secure it to your nylon anchor line, and sleep well at night.

Connecting the Rode

There are two ways to connect the chain and rope portions of the rode, either by a shackle or a chain-to-rope splice. We splice the end of the nylon rope to the last link of the chain. This works well and the splice passes smoothly over the *gypsy*, the wheel of the windlass that grips the chain and rope. We frequently check the splice for chafe. If there is any question, we cut off the line and re-splice it.

The best method to secure line to chain, if you are not going to use a chain/rope windlass, is the traditional eye splice over a galvanized thimble, attached to the chain by a shackle. It is probably no stronger than the chain-rope splice, but the shackle between the chain and rope does allow you to separate the line and chain without cutting the anchor line. There is less chafe between line and chain with a galvanized steel thimble than with a chain-to-rope splice.

ANCHOR-HANDLING EQUIPMENT

Large anchors and heavy chain can be hard work. It's important to be able to store, deploy, and retrieve an anchor as easily as possible. You'll be more inclined to anchor out.

Bow Roller

The most significant improvement we made to our first serious cruising boat was to install a robust anchor bow roller. Today, most boats come equipped with some sort of bow roller, but if yours didn't, consider adding one. Even if you plan to handle the anchor by hand, a bow roller makes the job easier and protects the topsides from the anchor and chain. And the roller lets you retrieve the last few feet of line and anchor with a horizontal pull rather than bending over the side and hefting the anchor aboard, as you try to prevent it from banging into the hull.

Washdown

The feature we appreciate most is the pressure washdown system we added to our anchoring rig to clean the chain. Chain can be messy and washing it with a bucket is a real chore, especially in areas with mud or clay bottoms. Drop the bucket in the water, lift it up, and splash the water against the chain a couple of times. Pull in more chain; repeat. Washing thirty or forty feet of chain is bearable and a good morning workout, but if you're using a full chain rode you really need a better way to wash it.

A washdown pump must produce enough pressure for a strong water stream to reach the chain in a stiff wind. Get a pump rated for washdown that can produce 40–50 psi. It should have a nozzle that creates a powerful jet of water to blast the mud from between the links. Don't get a spray nozzle designed for the garden; one that looks like a miniature fire hose is better. Years ago we found one made of brass and it comes with us from boat to boat. They are also available in plastic.

Electric Windlass

On cruising boats over 35 feet, a windlass is almost a necessity. Both of our trawlers have been equipped with an electric windlass.

There are many designs to choose from but basically they fall into two categories: horizontal or vertical. A horizontal windlass has the gypsy orientated horizontally on one side. On the opposite side it has a smooth capstan drum to haul in rope. All the hardware, including the motor and gearbox, is mounted on deck. A vertical windlass has the gypsy and capstan drum oriented in a vertical plane. The drive system is mounted below deck with only the gypsy, drum, and mount showing, so vertical windlasses look sleeker.

Both types are operated by waterproof switches mounted close to the windlass. Some switches are mounted in the deck, others on the windlass itself. When you step on the foot switch the windlass begins to haul in the anchor. Some installations have an additional switch that turns the windlass in the opposite direction for letting the anchor and chain out. Some also have a remote switch at the helm so that the skipper can handle the anchor without any help. Whether this is really practical depends on many factors, including the type of anchor and rode and the anchoring situation itself. Sometimes, the anchor can be neither set nor weighed without someone forward to correct a minor glitch. And often, crew are needed on the foredeck, if only to wash off the mud as the rode reels in.

Both horizontal and vertical windlasses get the job done if properly installed. At least a foot of space or more is needed below the windlass (between the deck and top of the chain pile) for the chain and rope to properly stow itself. The weight of the chain must be sufficient to pull itself into the locker as it comes off the windlass gypsy. This is important for vertical windlasses since the chain and rope wrap a full 180 degrees around the gypsy.

Windlasses draw a lot of current when they are under load and they are located a long way from the battery bank, so they require

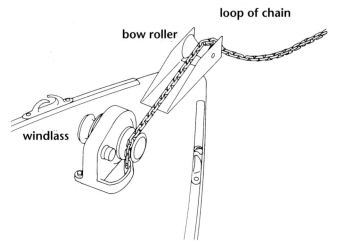

The motor assembly of a horizontal windlass is mounted on deck. (Illustration by Jim Sollers.)

heavy wiring. The windlass may require cables as heavy as the starting circuits used for your engine. Long runs of heavy cable are expensive. If there is room, some windlass installations utilize a dedicated battery located close to the windlass to power it. The cable runs are shorter and lighter wiring can be used. The windlass battery is charged along with the other banks of batteries from the engine. The cables used to bring the charging current don't carry heavy current and can be smaller.

A manual backup system is a very desirable feature for a windlass. On some designs you can insert a handle into the drum and crank in the chain or rope by hand; the handle should be long enough to give adequate leverage. We have a Lofrans Tigress windlass, and it has this feature. Others work in a way similar to the purely manual windlasses (usually the horizontal type) that use a lever and ratchet to turn the gypsy by pushing a lever back and forth. Each pull on the lever brings in some rode. Each push releases the ratchet until the lever is far enough forward

to begin hauling again. Small boats with insufficient battery power (or the space to easily install an electric motor on the bow) often use lever-operated windlasses all the time instead of having an electric model. They require a lot more work than an electric

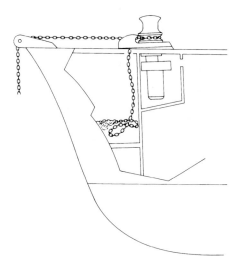

The motor assembly of a vertical windlass is mounted below deck, but the wildcat and drum are located above deck. (Illustration by Jim Sollers.)

windlass, but that still beats hauling in the rode by hand.

A word of caution about windlasses: even the smallest windlass can crush a finger in an instant. Be sure you know how to use the windlass properly; also follow the manufacturer's maintenance instructions. When the windlass is not in use, turn the circuit breaker off to prevent someone from accidentally stepping on the deck switch and starting it.

CHAPTER 12
Safety Equipment

As the owner and operator of a boat, you are responsible for the safety of the boat and its crew. This involves outfitting your boat with safety equipment required by law and with additional, optional safety equipment. Some boats barely carry the basics; others are outfitted to the hilt.

The best-equipped boats are the ones whose owners invest in quality equipment and know how to use it.

If you've never had man-overboard practice how do you really know what you'd do in such an emergency? Just having a Lifesling aboard doesn't make the crew safe if no one knows how to deploy it. Learn how to use whatever safety gear you have aboard. And make sure everyone on board knows where the life vests are located and how to operate the VHF radio.

Outfitting your cruising boat with safety gear can be a challenge because, while the law requires you to carry some equipment, it's really not enough if you have a real emergency. Should you invest in safety equipment you hope never to use?

We think the reasonable approach to outfitting a boat for safe cruising is to first analyze the type of cruising you plan to do and then decide what additional safety equipment is necessary. We'll discuss the equipment you are obliged to carry by law, and we'll look at additional safety gear you may want to consider.

MANDATORY GEAR

Federal regulations specify the minimum safety gear required aboard every boat operated in United States waters. You must follow these *Federal Requirements for Recreational Boats*.

LIFE JACKETS OR PFDs (PERSONAL FLOTATION DEVICES)

Cost is often what determines the safety equipment that boaters buy. But should you compromise safety to save a few dollars? A $6 Type II life vest and a $40 Type I jacket, for example, both fulfill the regulations, but there's a big difference between them. The Type II vest is required to provide a minimum of 15.5 pounds of buoyancy compared to the Type I jacket's minimum of 22 pounds. Fall overboard in rough conditions and the difference in flotation capacity may determine your survival.

Through the years, we have amassed a dozen or more Type II life vests, the yoke style designed to keep an average person afloat. We carry this stash for when we entertain a group of friends, a vest for everyone aboard. In our

FEDERAL REQUIREMENTS FOR RECREATIONAL BOATS

< 16	Vessel length (in feet) 16 to 26	27 to 40	41 to 65	Equipment	Requirement
X	X	X	X	Life jackets (PFDs)	One Type I, II, III, or V wearable PFD for each person on board (must be USCG approved). Also one Type IV (throwable) PFD.
X				Visual distress signal (VDS)	(a) One electric distress light or three combination (day/night) red flares. Note: only required to be carried on board when operating between sunset and sunrise.
	X	X	X		(b) One orange distress flag and one electric distress light—or three hand-held or floating orange smoke signals and one electric distress light—or three combination (day/night) red flares: hand-held, meteor, or parachute type.
X				Fire extinguishers	(a) One B-I (when enclosed compartment).
	X	X	X		(b) One B-II or two B-I. Note: fixed system equals one B-I.
					(c) One B-II and one B-I or three B-I. Note: fixed system equals one B-I or two B-II.
X	X	X	X	Sound producing devices	(a) A vessel under 39.4 ft must, at a minimum, have some means of making an "efficient" sound signal (i.e. handheld air horn, athletic whistle. Human voice/sound not acceptable).
		X	X		(b) A vessel 39.4 ft or greater must have a sound signaling appliance capable of producing an efficient sound signal, audible for 1/2 mile with a 4 - 6 second duration. In addition, it must carry on board a bell with a clapper (bell size not less than 7.9 inches—based on the diameter of the mouth).
		X	X	Oil pollution placard	Placard must be at least 5 by 8 inches, made of durable material. Placard must be posted in the machinery space or at the bilge station.
		X	X	Garbage placard	Placard must be at least 4 by 9 inches, made of durable material. Displayed in a conspicuous place notifying all on board of the discharge restrictions.
		X	X	Navigation rules (inland only)	The operator of a vessel 39.4 ft or greater must have on board a copy of these rules.

Source: USCG http://www.uscgboating.org/safety/fed_reqs/equ_refchart.htm

COAST GUARD LIFE VEST TYPES				
Type I	Type II	Type III	Type IV	Type V
Life preservers (off-shore life jacket)	Buoyant vest (near-shore)	Marine buoyant devices #1* (flotation aid)	Commercial life ring buoys	Work suits and thermal coveralls
Inflatable PFDs (recreational)	Inflatable PFDs (recreational)	Inflatable PFDs (recreational)	Recreational life ring buoys	Commercial whitewater rafting vests
Hybrid PFDs	Hybrid PFDs	Hybrid PFDs	Buoyant cushions	Sailboard harness PFDs (Special-use devices)
Inflatable lifejackets (commercial)			Horseshoe buoys (Throwable devices)	Inflatable PFDs (recreational)
				Hybrid PFDs

*#1 Marine buoyant devices are Type III PFDs and any Type II, IV, or V device which does not comply with the construction and material requirements of its corresponding specification subpart for the standard device.

home waters that means cruising up the Miles River for a few miles to watch log-canoe races or anchoring in a protected cove for dinner. We don't normally entertain in bad weather, and when we do, we are never more than a couple of hundred yards from land, so this collection of life jackets fits the bill. We store them in a couple of mesh bags on the bridge.

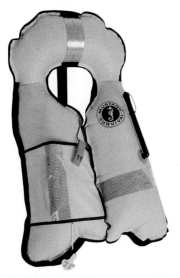

An inflatable life jacket. (Photo courtesy Mustang.)

We also carry four commercial Type I life jackets equipped with a whistle. If we cruise offshore, to the Bahamas for example, we'll add a personal strobe on each jacket, just to be on the safe side.

An adult life jacket is too large for a small child so if you have kids aboard, be sure to have correctly sized vests that *fit* them. If you have grandchildren or guests with kids, insist that they bring their own life jackets so you can be assured of their safety.

The U.S. Coast Guard suggests these criteria when choosing a PFD:

- Select a properly sized, USCG-approved PFD.
- Try on the PFD to see if it fits. It should be comfortably snug.
- Ensure that all straps, zippers, and ties are fastened.
- Raise your arms over your head to see if it's comfortable.
- Have someone lift your PFD straight up by the shoulders to see that it stays in place. If the zipper touches your nose or the PFD almost comes off, it's too loose.

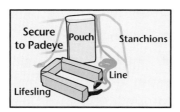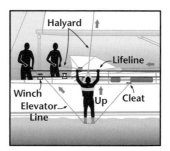

The Lifesling method for rescuing crew overboard. (Illustration by Paul Mirto.)

THROWABLE DEVICES

The coast guard requires that every boat over 16 feet LOA (length overall) have at least one throwable lifesaving device. A standard USCG approved seat cushion meets this requirement, and we have several aboard. When you purchase a cushion check the label to be sure it is an approved Type IV device.

In addition to throwable cushions we carry the Lifesling system, a throwable device that's easy to deploy, especially important for our short-handed crew. If someone goes overboard you throw the U-shaped flotation device, attached to the boat by a long tether, toward the person in the water. If the person can't reach it you circle the boat around them and the long tether forms a loop around the person. They then can reach the U-shaped flotation device, put it around their torso, and be hauled to the boat.

Getting a line to the person in the water is only half the battle. Getting a heavy, wet, and possibly injured person aboard is the real challenge. The Lifesling and its companion block and tackle allow you to hoist the person out of the water and into the boat. The

SAFETY HARNESSES

After extensive short-handed cruising on sailboats, we became firm believers of staying on the boat. A quality safety harness is by far the best solution, and we use them often in all but the nicest weather. A harness attaches to your torso and is not at all uncomfortable to wear while outside the cabin (especially when you consider the peace of mind it brings). It has a tether with a snap-shackle on the end that can be clipped over a *jack line*—a fore- and aft-safety line that allows moving about while attached with the harness' tether. Since sailboat deck crews often have both hands full, and can therefore not hold onto a grab rail or lifeline, the harness provides assurance its wearer can't go far overboard. Though the situation is slightly different on a cruising powerboat, the security of the harness can still be quite welcome. The harness with an attached inflatable vest is a good choice. It combines two lifesaving devices in one unit that's easy to put on.

5:1 purchase of the tackle makes it possible for a single person to lift aboard someone weighed down in heavy, wet clothes.

Packaged throw-rope kits are also on the market. These consist of a self-contained small float and line, often enclosed in a bag for neatness and convenience. The float at the end of the line is lighter than a typical Type IV PFD (though it is still weighted for easier heaving), and the line is fairly long (usually about 50 feet), so you can toss this rescue device farther and easier than any approved PFD. Though a throw rope is not mandated by law, it's not a bad idea to have one on the flying bridge where it can be quickly grabbed in any *man overboard* situation. If your boat has a cockpit, placing one back there might be wise, too.

Visual Distress Signal (VDS)

The USCG requires that at least three flares with *current* dates (less than 3½ years since their date of manufacture) be aboard your boat. USCG-approved hand flares burn for about three minutes, so three flares give you a total signaling power of less than ten minutes. In many locations this may be adequate, if you have requested help on the VHF radio and it's on the way. But if you're in rough water conditions and your radio fails, three flares provide a meager distress call. Buy more of them.

It's a good idea to have a few additional inexpensive items on board like a signaling mirror and a distress flag that has a black square and circle on orange background, to call attention to your plight. Smoke bombs are very good, too, because the orange smoke they produce rises and can be visible over great distances. It also lingers a while and can be visible for longer than a flare (though, depending on wind conditions, the smoke can dissipate quickly). When a search party gets close, you can light off your flares.

SOLAS (Safety of Life at Sea) is an international convention, administered by the IMO (International Marine Organization) that sets standards for safety devices used on the high seas. They are higher than the USCG standards. Look for flares manufactured to SOLAS standards. They will cost more, but SOLAS aerial flares burn brighter, for a longer time, and reach a higher altitude than standard USCG-approved flares.

We carry a 25 mm flare gun, assorted meteor and parachute flares, and handheld flares. As the flares go out of date we replace them but hold onto the old ones. As the parachute flares go out of date we replace them with SOLAS approved flares because it's a small additional price to pay if you're ever in a real emergency. The phrase "more bang for the buck" comes to mind.

If you have some really old flares that you don't want to throw away, contact your local Coast Guard station; they may take the flares and use them in their training exercises.

Fire Extinguishers

A fire aboard any boat is a major event because there's plenty to burn: fuel, oil, and the boat itself. Extinguishing the fire immediately is the first priority in saving the ship, so all but the smallest boats with outboard motors are required to carry at least one marine type fire extinguisher.

Extinguishers are classified as either B-I or B-II, depending on the amount of extinguishing agent they contain. To be most effective, they should be mounted in an accessible position so they can be reached as soon as there is a sign of a fire. The following chart shows the number of extinguishers that are required, based on the overall length of the boat.

USCG CLASS FIRE EXTINGUISHER RATING

Classes	Foam (gals)	CO_2 (lbs)	Dry Chemical (lb.)	Halon (lb.)
*B-I (Type B, Size I)	1.25	4	2	2.5
*B-I (Type B, Size II)	2.5	15	10	10

*Type B devices are designed to extinguish fires fueled by flammable liquids such as gasoline, oil, and grease.

Always remember, the coast guard requirements are minimums. It stands to reason the larger the boat, the more extinguishers it should have. We have an extinguisher in all compartments except the heads. We have a B-II extinguisher in the main cabin and engine room, and B-I units in the forward and aft cabins and on the underside of the hatch in the lazarette. If a fire should start inside the boat, we can open the lazarette hatch, grab the extinguisher, and we're armed before we enter the boat. The extinguishers in the main and aft cabins are installed near the doors and we can reach them without fully entering the cabin.

SOUND-PRODUCING DEVICES

All boats are required to have a means of sound-signaling another boat, and usually carry a horn of some type. In addition to signaling your intent in crossing or passing situations or in poor visibility (see Chapter 17, Rules of the Road), the horn is used to signal drawbridge operators and to signal for help.

We have a permanently installed air horn on *High Life*, as well as a portable air horn and an assortment of whistles. We take the portable horn in the dinghy, along with a couple of life jackets with whistles attached.

FIRST-AID SUPPLIES AND MEDICINES

With the exception of the Bahamas, most of our coastal cruising has been in areas where help is available for a major medical emergency. However, it may be several hours before help comes, so everyone on board should know how to administer primary first aid.

There are no federal regulations that require a basic first-aid kit, but common sense demands that at least one should be aboard

MINIMUM NUMBER OF HAND-PORTABLE FIRE EXTINGUISHERS REQUIRED

Vessel length (ft)	No fixed system *	With approved fixed systems*
Less than 26	1 B-1	0
26 to less than 40	2 B-1 or 1 B-II	1 B-I
40 to 65	3 B-I or 1 B-1 and 1 B-II	2 B-1 or 1 B-II

*Where a USCG-approved fire extinguishing system is installed for the protection of the engine compartment, the required number of units may be reduced in accordance with the chart.

KEEP YOUR POWDER LOOSE

Dry chemical extinguishers are filled with a fire-suppressing powder. Engine and other vibrations on your boat will cause the powder to settle into a tightly packed cake in the bottom of the extinguisher. To prevent the powder from compacting, shake the extinguisher and turn it upside down several times a season. If you can't feel the powder moving inside the extinguisher, get the unit serviced.

Self-contained, automatically activated extinguishers can be easily mounted in the engine room. These units contain a fire suppressant gas, these days usually FE-241, an environmentally friendly agent. To be most effective, this type of extinguisher should be installed with a system that stops the engine room blower when a fire-fighting agent is dispensed.

Vessels with diesel engines should also have an engine shutdown system that automatically stops the engine(s) when the system discharges. Diesel engines must be shut down immediately, because if diesel engines continue to run, they can deplete enough agent to allow a fire to reflash. In addition to an automatic system, a manually activated system is also available. Most insurance companies offer a discount if either of these systems is installed.

every boat. Specially designed marine first-aid kits are sold at marine stores. The basic advantage of most of them is that they close tightly with rubber seals, and are water resistant, if not actually watertight. This protects the contents from moisture-laden air. Many also provide for easy bulkhead mounting, so you don't even have to open a locker to grab the kit.

Commercially available marine first-aid kits come in many sizes, from the most basic to those designed for world expeditions. The basic kits have bandages and antiseptic ointments, while the large kits may contain blood pressure cuffs and skin staplers. The basic kits assume that help is on the way; the large ones assume that someone on board will be the primary care provider, since professional medical help may be days away.

We have two first-aid kits on board. One is a basic container with bandages, burn ointments, and supplies to deal with dings and skinned knuckles; a larger coastal-rated kit has supplies for more serious injuries.

Be sure to replenish the supplies as you use them. Don't forget that while some items in the kits have a long shelf life, others become outdated, so periodically check the expiration date on any medicine and replace it as needed.

A basic first-aid kit for coastal cruising should contain at least these items:

- 3–4 sterile gauze pads (4 in. × 4 in.)
- 2 rolls of 4 in. wide sterile gauze
- 12 Band-Aids (include a couple of large-sized ones)
- 6 butterfly bandages
- 2 triangular bandages (useful for slings and lashing to improvised splints)
- 1 roll of athletic tape
- 2 wrapped sanitary napkins (for nosebleeds, or to clean up blood from wounds)

- 1 microshield (lightweight mouth shield for giving CPR)
- 1 small bottle of tincture of benzoin (for cleansing wounds)
- 1 tube of Neosporin or povidone-iodine ointment (to dress wounds)
- 1 piece of moleskin (4 in. × 4 in., for blisters)
- 1 elastic wrap (4–6 in. wide)
- 2 safety pins
- Small bottle pain killers (aspirin or Tylenol)
- Small bottle antihistamine tablets
- 5 Pepto-Bismol tablets
- 1 thermometer
- 1 pair of scissors and tweezers (also available on Swiss Army knifes)
- 2 pairs of rubber gloves
- Any prescription medicine you need to carry

In order to put a first-aid kit to use you need the basic knowledge of how to administer first aid. Take a course from the U.S. Power Squadrons, U.S. Coast Guard Auxiliary, or the Red Cross. Keep aboard a book on first-aid basics for boaters to give you confidence if a medical emergency arises. If you can't remember, you can always look it up.

OTHER EMERGENCY GEAR

In addition to required safety gear there are other useful safety items that some consider optional, and others consider essential. The decision is yours.

EPIRBs

In the mid-1970s, when we sailed offshore, we carried an Emergency Position Indicating Radio Beacon (EPIRB) and a life raft. Today, since we seldom venture far offshore, except for a dash to the Bahamas, we don't carry a life raft but we do have an inflatable boat and a 406 MHz EPIRB.

As its name suggests, an EPIRB is a device that you can use to emit a radio signal if you are in distress, so that search and rescue services will be able to locate your boat. The first EPIRB we had transmitted a distress signal on radio frequencies monitored by airplanes, while today's models use a system of satellites that constantly monitor the radio frequency 406.025 MHz. The old style EPIRBs used the same frequency as aircraft Emergency Locator Transmitters (ELTs), so an airplane (or airport control tower) receiving the signal had no way of knowing whether it was from a downed aircraft or a vessel in distress. In addition, if you were way offshore (beyond the range of control towers) you stood the best chance of rescue if your distress occurred under a well-used flight path. The message didn't always get through.

The newer EPIRBs can transmit identification and location data to satellites, which in turn relay it to a ground station. Not only does the coast guard know that it's a vessel in trouble—not a downed aircraft—it also knows where the vessel is. And if the EPIRB has been properly registered, the search and rescue people know which vessel is in distress. As with most electronic gear, the new units are smaller and more sophisticated than the older ones.

Depending on the model, a 406 EPIRB can have a built-in GPS receiver or can be connected to a GPS. Some EPIRBs require manual activation; others are automatically released and activated if the unit is submerged. Personal EPIRBs that can be attached to life jackets are also available.

In order for rescue agencies to identify your boat, you must register the EPIRB with NOAA. Each EPIRB sends out a unique identification code that the coast guard or other rescue services use to search through a world-wide database to find information about your boat. It's surprising how specific the information is. For example, if you paint your boat a different color you should notify NOAA, or the search and rescue operation will be looking for a white boat that you painted navy. If you buy a new boat, or lend an EPIRB to someone to take it on another boat, you have to update the information in case it is activated.

For an EPIRB to be effective it must be readily available, so its mounting location is important. This is a contentious issue aboard *High Life*. Gene wants it out in the open, Katie doesn't like the bright yellow canister hanging in the main cabin, so our solution was to put it in the ditch bag (more on that in a moment). If we're ready to deploy the EPIRB, there's a darn good chance we'll be ready to abandon ship.

LIFE RAFTS

When we were considering buying a life raft for an upcoming cruise to the Bahamas, we asked the advice of some friends who have made several Atlantic crossings in sailboats and have extensive offshore cruising experience. Gene wanted to make the investment, but our friends said they didn't feel we needed one. They reasoned that it's a short trip across the Gulf Stream, and once there, island hopping in well-traveled waters didn't present the same risk as an ocean passage. They carry an (inflated) inflatable dinghy and two sea kayaks that could act as a life raft in the warm Gulf Stream waters. Their thinking changed our mind, and we now feel the same way about cruising in coastal waters where help is not too far away.

The main problem with owning a life raft is that, for reliability's sake, it must be in-

spected and repacked on a regular basis. The water and emergency rations carried aboard also have a limited shelf life. And they need to be replenished when the raft is serviced. Time and again we see boats with life rafts that look like they have not been serviced for years, although that's hard to judge since it's the condition of what's inside the case that counts, not the condition of the case. Investing in a life raft means investing in its maintenance.

If you do decide to invest in a raft, purchase a good quality one that is large enough to accommodate your crew. Look inside and you'll see that a four-man raft is small. On the other hand, if the raft is too large, it will be too lightly loaded and less stable in a sizeable sea. Togetherness is a good thing in cold water. Too much room makes it harder for the occupants to stay warm.

Rafts are approved by the SOLAS or USGC. United States pleasure boats are not required to have a life raft so you can use either type. The SOLAS rafts are constructed to a slightly higher standard than the USCG approved rafts. Both standards include classifications for coastal, offshore, or ocean use as follows:

- Coastal, for use where there is a high probability of rescue within a day or so.
- Offshore, for use where survival time is expected to extend to four or five days.
- Ocean going, for long-term survival of at least 30 days.

These ratings are based on stability and the extent of the emergency rations, potable water, and other supplies the raft contains. Obviously, the longer the raft must sustain you, the more supplies it must have.

Another option is to rent a life raft for the duration of an open-water passage. This is popular among racing sailors who participate

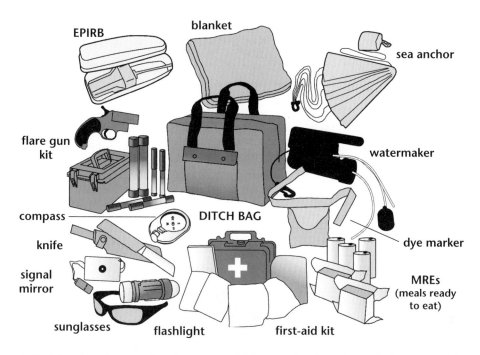

A ditch bag is only as good as its contents. Make sure that batteries and other perishable or time-sensitive items are replaced regularly. (Illustration by Paul Mirto.)

in an occasional ocean race that requires one. Make sure the raft has been serviced by a company certified by the manufacturer before you place it on your boat. Finding a easily accessible but out-of-the-way place to store the raft can be a issue on a smaller cruising power boat with limited deck space. If a permanent location can't be found, the raft can be taken out and temporarily stored in the cockpit while making the passage. When cruising in protected water it can be stowed in a locker or some other out-of-the-way area.

DITCH BAG

The idea of abandoning ship is not appealing, but if you have to do it, make sure you bring the necessities in a ditch bag. And so much the better if the bag floats. We carry a ditch bag that has most of the stuff we may need if we end up floating around in our inflatable.

You can use a canvas bag or knapsack to make up your own ditch kit, but the ready-made bags sold at marine stores have built-in flotation and watertight compartments to keep the gear sorted. Some designs have several external pockets for storage of an EPIRB or handheld VHF radio. If you have a ditch bag aboard, make sure everyone knows where it is.

The following table lists some items we and other cruisers have in our ditch bags. Modify it to fit your needs.

ADDITIONAL SAFETY EQUIPMENT

The USCG compiles statistics about boating accidents, and three preventable dangers

DITCH BAG CONTENTS			
SAFETY	FOOD AND WATER	MEDICAL	PERSONAL
406 manual EPIRB	Can opener/jackknife	Bathroom tissue	Duplicate credit cards
AM/FM radio w/ spare batteries	Fishing gear	First-aid kit and manual	Long-sleeved shirt
12 chemical lightsticks	1-gallon folding jug	Multivitamins	Photocopy of identification (e.g., passport, driver's license)
3 flares, red parachute	Graduated drinking cup	Pencils	Sunglasses
3 flares, red handheld	High-energy food rations, 1 per person	Pocket notebooks (waterproof)	Survival blankets
2 flares, orange handheld smoke	Other food by preference	Seasickness pills	Toothbrush
Hand bearing compass	10 water packets, minimum	Sun block	
Handheld GPS and batteries		Sunburn cream	
Inflatable or raft repair clamp kit		Vaseline	
Sea anchor			
Signal mirror			
Spare air pump			
2 waterproof flashlights w/spare			
Waterproof watch			
Water-resistant handheld VHF			
Whistle or horn			
Zip-locking bags			

stand out. Alternating current (120-volt AC) can be deadly aboard; so can carbon monoxide (CO) fumes; and you'd be surprised how many boating accidents involve an outboard's propeller.

GROUND FAULT CIRCUIT INTERRUPTERS

New boats must have GFCI (ground fault circuit interrupter) 120V outlets with either a GFCI circuit breaker, or an individual GFCI outlet, for any receptacles installed in a head, galley, machinery space, or on a weather deck. These devices protect you against electrocution, so if your boat is not equipped with them, replace the old outlets with GFCI devices.

Most insurance companies require this upgrade if a survey reports that the boat is not so equipped. We upgraded our outlets in an afternoon.

CO DETECTORS

Carbon monoxide (CO) is an odorless lethal gas that is a byproduct of engine function. A properly designed exhaust system vents the gases to the outside. However, malfunctions in the exhaust, or the wind, can blow gases back into your boat. Gasoline engines and generators produce more CO than diesel engines. If you ever need onboard heat, keep in mind that many heating devices also give off CO and must be vented outside the cabin. Even then, CO can accumulate inside if atmospheric conditions are just right.

Just as a smoke detector should be standard equipment in your home, a CO detector should be installed on your boat. The aft cabin is the most vulnerable since a following breeze can blow exhaust gases into it. The danger from CO poisoning is greater when the boat is closed and the gases can accumulate inside.

A stand-alone CO detector that relies on batteries is not expensive, and it's easy to install. There are also 12-volt units that can be wired directly into the boat's electrical system. This is the most reliable arrangement since there are no batteries to replace.

OUTBOARD RING PROPELLER

Several prop guard devices are available for outboards, but they look so cumbersome that

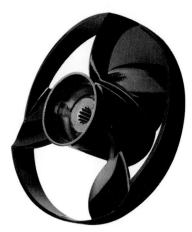

To prevent injury to swimmers, consider a propeller with a built-in prop ring.

we've never considered getting one. When we received a press release on an item called the RingProp we said, "Why didn't someone think of this before?" It's a propeller with a ring around the outside of the blades that prevents anything from getting between the propeller blades—and being cut. If you were hit by a propeller with a safety ring, you might get a nasty abrasion, but that would be preferable to a deep gash.

CHAPTER 13

Dinghies

Some powerboaters get along very well without ever owning a dinghy (the small boat you carry as a tender), but if your main boating activity is cruising you *need* one. This is true even if you mostly cruise from marina to marina. There will always be times you have to sit at anchor, and if you don't have some means of traveling back and forth to shore, you'll be stuck. There may also be times when you need a dinghy to help set an anchor. For a cruising boat of any type, a dinghy is essential equipment.

You have many options when choosing a dinghy, but your first decision is usually whether to go for a hard dink (cruising jargon for dinghy) or an inflatable. As you might expect, there are advantages and disadvantages to each.

HARD DINGHIES

Once upon a time dinghies were wood, period. Your only choice of material was solid plank or plywood. They came in a number of styles, from the boxy plywood *pram* with its squared off bow to the sleek Whitehall skiff with its elegant, classic lines. And, of course, there were many others in between. Wooden dinghies are still available in several types, and owners of wooden boats often want them for many of the same

reasons their main boat is wood. But these days, most hard dinghies are made of fiberglass.

The primary drawback to hard dinks is that they are mostly heavy and *always* take up space, which means that that they are less convenient to carry than inflatables, which can be deflated and rolled up if stowage is a problem. Most hard dinghies also have a tendency to scratch your boat's topsides, even if they have soft rubrails; they are, after all, hard. So you have to be very careful coming alongside and/or use fenders.

In their favor, if you have to climb a boarding ladder to get aboard your cruising boat, a hard dinghy often offers a more stable platform to start from than the traditional inflatable with a canvas only floor. Inflatables with a hard floor however are very stable. Stability can be even more important when you stand to pass gear or groceries aboard. Also, with a hard dinghy, you don't have to worry about sharp objects puncturing the topsides and deflating the tubes.

INFLATABLES

Inflatable dinghy technology has come a long way. A great many today are essentially

A full line of inflatable and rigid dinghies in Annapolis, Maryland, illustrates just how many boats are anchored in this popular harbor.

hybrids known as *rigid inflatable boats* or RIBs, with hard fiberglass bottoms and inflatable topsides. The fiberglass bottom makes an RIB more efficient in the water than the older style inflatables because it can be deep or, more often, a modified V-shape. Pure inflatables have a flat bottom, usually made of the same fabric as the tubes, though it is usually reinforced and stiffened with folding plywood inserts or floorboards that can be removed for stowage.

Flat-bottomed inflatables can plane easily under the right conditions, but they are not so good when the seas get rough. Plus, they are not quite as stiff and rigid as wooden dinghies or RIBs. And though the plywood inserts help, they have never been a perfect answer. An RIB can really be the best of both worlds: the rigid bottom gives it many of the properties, including performance and stability, of a hard dink. And the inflatable topsides are more buoyant than any hard dink; plus, their soft topsides can be kinder to your cruising boat when you come alongside. The only downside with RIBs is that the rigid hull makes them less easy to stow than other inflatables.

PROPULSION

Power cruisers who used to have sailboats often carry a sailing dinghy so they can still get in a little sailing whenever they feel the urge. For others, good old muscle power via oars is the traditional method of moving a dinghy, and rowing is still a viable option if you enjoy the exercise and don't have to go too far.

To cover greater distances without the work, most cruisers use an outboard motor. The size of the dinghy, which should be proportional to the size of your boat but also big enough to fill your needs, will determine the horsepower you can have, which should always be equal to or less than what's specified on the boat's capacity plate. But you should also consider the weight of the motor and fuel tank because they are part of the load you'll have to bring aboard. With an inflatable you will have to remove the motor first, which can be a job in itself, and the greater the horsepower, the heavier the motor.

STOWAGE

What do you do with the dinghy when you're not using it? This can be a huge problem. Sailors most often tow their dinghies simply because there's usually no good place to carry one aboard. Powerboaters most often don't tow, because towing a dinghy behind a fast boat is not good for either—plus, it slows them down! Many slower trawlers tow a dink when they're underway and cruising, though it can get in the way around piers and floats, and especially when backing into a slip.

Powerboaters have traditionally used a pair of small cranes, called *davits*, to lift the dink at the stern so it can be carried, in its normal upright position, just above the transom. Sportfishermen often have a larger single crane up forward, most often powered with hydraulics, to lift the dinghy from the water and set it into chocks on the foredeck.

Many express cruisers have a large swim platform that raises and lowers hydraulically. If the platform is large enough, it can be fitted with chocks or a cradle for either a hard dinghy or an RIB. This method usually works well, and also makes the job of launching and retrieving the dinghy quite easy.

Unfortunately, the design of some powerboats means there's no *good* place to carry a hard dink. Their owners must either suffer through carrying one awkwardly, or resort to constantly inflating the dinghy when they need it (which may not be all that often for many powerboaters), and deflating it to stow away when they don't.

Remember, if you do tow your dinghy, you need a long *painter* (the traditional name for a dinghy's bow line), so that once you are out in open water, you can let it out until the dinghy rides on the second wave behind your transom. Riding back there it will offer less resistance to being pulled, which is easier on the dink itself, the painter, and the hardware to which it is attached. Of course, you must then shorten the line again when you enter more congested areas like harbors, and bring it up *very* short when you come to a marina and need to maneuver around piers or floats.

The *High Life* Solution

Our first cruising boat had a hard dinghy that we stowed in chocks upside down on the cabin house. It was heavy and cumbersome, but it came with the boat, so we used it until it sank.

On *High Life* we carry two dinghies, a hard dink that came with her and an Avon 260 RIB. The hard dinghy couldn't be saltier and it looks terrific on the aft cabin house, but we use it mostly as a deck box. When we do

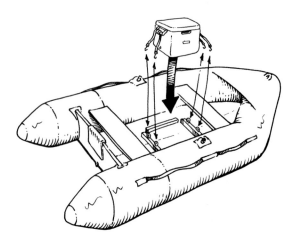

A cooler secured to the flat wooden floor of an inflatable provides a seat and dry, protected storage. (Illustration by Christopher Hoyt.)

launch it, we use a block and tackle system on the mast for raising and lowering.

We use the inflatable daily as our main transportation for cruising around anchorages, visiting other cruisers, exploring, and going ashore. We use two lines tied to the last rungs of the swim platform and looped under the inflatable as it floats next to the platform. A pull on these lines raises the inflatable up on the swim platform and then they are secured

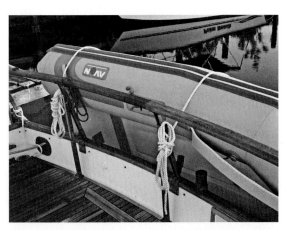

This simple rig uses lines to lift and secure our inflatable on a swim platform. It has worked for us on several boats.

to cleats on the stanchions to hold it securely in place. To lower the dinghy we release the lines, tie the painter to the railing and it's afloat. We know there are other alternatives, but this simple rig works for us.

We've seen boats with elaborate custom-designed stainless steel hydraulic systems. There are also lifting arms attached to the swim platform that hoist a dinghy out of the water and hold it on its side, either on the platform or held away from it. Some trawlers with a mast use a block and tackle to raise and lower a dinghy and store it on deck, with or without its outboard.

Our dinghy conceals the nameboard and hailing port, so to comply with the requirement to display them, we've painted our boat name and hailing port on its bottom. Of course, we realize that this is not in compliance with the letter of the law, which requires that the name and hailing port always be visible *on the boat itself*. But we figure that unless we're boarded by a really hard-nosed, "by the book" officer, our good intentions should satisfy the spirit of the law. It has worked so far.

We power the inflatable with a 3.5 hp Johnson outboard. Though it makes for slow going, the motor is easy to lift and move from its mounting bracket to the inflatable. We've had larger outboards, but we prefer one that's lightweight so that putting it on the inflatable is a one-man job.

All dinghies require gear such as oars, foot pump inflator, life cushions, outboard, and gas tank. We stow ours in the hard dinghy. Other cruisers use a deck box, lazarette, or other compartment to keep it all accessible. A storage bag with big pockets that fits over the seat of the inflatable and keeps things dry inside it was a good investment.

Some friends had a good idea for stowing the battery for their electric outboard: they use a cooler in their RIB as a waterproof battery compartment. Years ago we did something similar by taking the center seat out of our inflatable and replacing it with a cooler that we used as a seat and for stowing our camera gear. To prevent the cooler from sliding we screwed thin strips of wood to the floorboards to act as a brace.

CHAPTER 14

More Essential and Useful Stuff

Squirreling things away must be an inherent part of cruising: even with limited space, the packrat mentality is rampant in the cruising world. What you bring along should make cruising more comfortable, and this depends on your cruising style. We've pared things down in a mission to simplify our life (and boat) and keep stuff to a minimum. We try to adhere to one basic rule: if we bring something new aboard, we have to take something off. Sometimes that's easier said than done. In this chapter we itemize the things that we use and enjoy and have a permanent place in our boat.

CAMERA

From the lowly $10 throwaway to the lofty digital, a camera is a must-have item aboard any boat. There's no excuse anymore for pleading that you can't operate a camera. The cheap ones are goof-proof and the really good ones make a beginner look like a seasoned pro. We use a camera to document our travels, especially if it's an extended cruise. And when we're cruising in local waters and get a good shot of a friend's boat, we give it to them. With today's digital cameras, it's never been easier to take good pictures to share the memories of a great day aboard.

PROTECTION FROM THE SUN

Don't even think about going on a boat without sunblock to protect yourself against sunburn and skin cancer. Sunscreens are rated by their SPF or *sun protection factor*, which indicates their effectiveness at filtering ultraviolet rays. The higher the SPF, the better the protection. Of course, it doesn't do much good unless you apply the lotion to all body parts exposed to the sun. Don't forget the tips of your ears and back of your neck, both sensitive areas that can burn easily.

We keep two containers of SPF 45 sunblock aboard, one in the head, the other on the bridge so we can reapply it every couple of hours.

Two additional tactics we use for sun protection are wearing wide-brimmed hats and sunglasses with a lanyard to keep them around our neck.

VACUUM CLEANERS

We carry two vacuum cleaners aboard regularly. We use a lightweight stick vac that easily converts to a hand vacuum. There's no bag. Instead it collects the debris in a dust cup, which is easy to empty. Its small, collapsible design makes it convenient to stow

TAKING PICTURES

We've switched to a digital camera and haven't looked back. It's easy to use and gives us a full range of shots from close-up people pictures to that best-ever sunset.

Here's what we've learned about taking pictures from a boat, which is not always the most ideal camera platform, what with moving targets, wobbly horizons, and bright sunshine, which can create a nasty glare.

- Capture the essence of a place by shooting living things—a close up of an egret, a child's face, or a cat napping on a coiled line. These personal shots capture the sense of place from the people and things that are there.
- To capture a sunset, shoot about 15 minutes before the sun is on the horizon, then again after sunset.
- When shooting outdoors in bright sunlight, use a flash to fill in the dark shadows and soften the sharp contrasts between bright and dark areas in the image.
- When taking pictures of people, place them off-center in the shot and get close so they really fill up the frame. Off-center figures, with part of them not even in the

picture, seem quite normal to us these days. It's what TV news cameramen do all the time and we've become accustomed to seeing shots framed this way.

- Shooting from a boat requires fast film so you can use a higher shutter speed to freeze movement. Despite this, on-water pictures are often underexposed. This is because the water reflects a lot of light and fools the camera's exposure meter into thinking the subject matter is brighter than it actually is. Try opening up one F-stop above what the light meter calls for. Or, shoot several pictures at F-stops settings both above and below what the meter suggests. This is called *bracketing*, and some cameras can be set to do it automatically, every time you release the shutter.
- If you're not interested in taking beauty and landscape shots when cruising, at least take along a Polaroid camera for instant portraits. They will help you to remember cruising friends and their boats. Note names, boat name, and hailing port on the back of the photo or save them in a scrapbook.

under a stair compartment, so it's ready to use when needed. After we've successfully killed off a bug invasion we use a small battery-operated vacuum that makes quick work of this unpleasant chore.

For major cleanups or when we're in sanding/varnishing mode, we bring aboard a small shop vacuum, but we leave it ashore when we're cruising.

SMALL INVERTER

We call it the brick, because it looks like one. It's the small, portable inverter that converts 12-volt to 120-volt, and it's handy when we're at anchor and need to charge a laptop computer or the handheld VHF. Units with 400 to 500 watt capacity are adequate for these light-duty charging tasks. Installing a full time heavy-duty inverter/charger makes more sense than using one of the large portable units, but if you don't feel like going this route, a *small* portable unit is still worth having.

SCREENING

To keep bugs out and let a cool breeze in, screening is the answer. On various boats we've had wooden-frame screens and custom-made door and hatch screens that matched the boat canvas. The wooden screens look good when they're in use, but their size makes them a nuisance to store. The canvas screens are user-friendlier because they can be rolled up and easily stored.

MORE USEFUL ITEMS

- Fly swatters and spray repellent to defend against pests. You can't have too many swatters aboard because you should arm your guests too.
- Flashlights—minis and standard sizes stowed in the main cabin; a heavy-duty, rubber handled flashlight mounted in a bracket in the engine room; and a good supply of fresh batteries.
- Canvas sacks for carrying ice, groceries, dirty laundry, and anything else you need to transport to and from the boat.
- A wind scoop tied in the forward hatch to bring a cool breeze to the forward cabin.
- 12-volt inflator to inflate large fenders.
- Freshwater handheld shower attachment that fits on an outlet in the deck cockpit (if your boat doesn't have a built-in transom shower; many do today, but not all).
- A small collapsible table for use on the bridge or in the cockpit.
- Folding dock cart for toting groceries or propane tanks that need refilling.
- A lightweight hammock strung on deck for a lazy afternoon.
- Clothespins to dry out swimsuits, towels, and other items.
- Bag of quarters to take ashore to buy newspapers in a street box, a cold drink in a vending machine, and operate a clothes washer and dryer.

CHAPTER 15

Records and Paperwork

It's a good practice to keep boat papers organized and accessible, so they're easy to retrieve when you need them. We categorize them in this way: ownership documents, manuals for the engine and equipment, and ship's records for maintenance and an inventory. And on a daily basis, we keep a ship's log with log sheets we've customized. We also make copies of ownership papers, the insurance policy, and any other material we might need to keep at home.

OWNERSHIP PAPERS

According to the Federal Boating Safety Act of 1972, boatowners are required to register their boat and obtain a certificate of number from the state where the boat is most often used unless they get a federal certificate of documentation. So after you buy a boat, you're required to show proof of ownership with a bill of sale and then pay a fee to register it.

CERTIFICATE OF NUMBER

In addition to a proper bill of sale, the state where you register your boat will also usually require proof that you paid state and local sales taxes when you purchased the boat. Before being issued a certificate, you may have to come up with a check for the state

tax in addition to the cost of the certificate of number (the formal name for a boat registration). The important point here is to keep the receipt as your proof of tax payment.

Unless your boat is federally documented, you are required to display the registration numbers on the forward half of the bow so they can be read from left to right on both sides of the boat. Contact your state office for more information about specific requirements where you live. If you don't know which office handles the registration of boats, start with the Department of Motor Vehicles; in most states they handle boat registrations too. Or call a local boat dealer or yacht broker who should be happy to give you the information.

DOCUMENTATION

Many cruising boats, including *High Life*, are documented by the U.S. Coast Guard, which is now a part of the Department of Homeland Security. This national registration is useful, especially for boaters who cruise extensively and spend time in several states. There's no debate about which is the state of the boat's principal use (but if you spend more than half the year in some states, you still have to register it there, despite your federal documentation; you don't have to display numbers on the bow, though). Also, the documented status is often required by a bank that carries a loan on the boat so they can hold a preferred ship's mortgage.

No documentation numbers are displayed on the exterior of the boat. Instead, the documentation number is permanently marked on a visible interior surface so that any alteration would be noticed. Our numbers are carved into the main beam in the engine room.

You pay some fees when applying for a certificate and every year you must renew the certificate of documentation (no fee required) to keep it current. For more information about documentation, see the contact information in Appendix 1.

INVENTORY

We would never have created an inventory of everything aboard *High Life* unless we had to when our charter agency asked for one. It's not that difficult to do, but it seemed daunting at the time. When we began to open all the hatches and document what was aboard we discovered an amazing assortment of things we'd forgotten we had. The payoff was getting rid of a lot of unused stuff, knowing what we had, and where it was located. And by itemizing the gear and its location on the boat, we were forced to rethink where we stow things and to consider relocating them for easier access. And of course, if we ever have to make an insurance claim, we will have a record of what was actually aboard our boat.

We know people who love this kind of task. They create line art of the layout of their boat by copying an illustration from the boat manufacturer's brochure or website. Sometimes more than one is required if the boat has two or more decks so they can describe what's tucked away under the flying bridge seat or what's stored inside a lower stateroom. Using the boat's layout they itemize what's stored where.

Others use their camera and simply open a cabinet or compartment and photograph what's inside. This they attach to a printout describing the items.

For chartering purposes we were required to come up with a simple list of items. We also created a simple visual guide for quick reference using a line drawing of the boat and indicating where things are stored. It's not nearly as detailed as others we've seen, but it makes us feel smug when we can actually find a seldom-used item.

LOG BOOKS

Marine stores sell any number of different logbooks for the cruising boater; some are lightweight and designed as a diary of a cruise, others are a detailed record of a boat's passage using navigation aids, GPS waypoints, and coordinates. The best log we've seen is *Chapman Boater's Log* by Captain John Wooldridge. While other logs resemble a travel diary and guest list, this one has sections to keep an up-to-date record, and checklists to help you keep track of equipment and maintenance schedules.

Custom Log Sheets

We've been making customized log sheets for years, and it's become a lot easier using word-processing software. Since we print them ourselves, the sheets have been revised, tweaked, and adjusted over the years to fit the boat we have and the type of cruising we do. Here's a look at the two pages of our current log sheet, which is printed on both sides and designed for a 3-ring binder.

When opened up, the left-hand side of the log features the heading "Log of Yacht *High Life*" with the date. Below that the page is divided into two boxes, for morning and afternoon navigational entries: Time, Course,

Log of Yacht **High Life**   Date: _____

Time	Course	Speed	Log	Wind	Helm	Position/Comment
6:00	165	7.5				*leaving anchorage*
6:30	220	7.5				*abeam deadman's cove*
6:50	355	7.5				*turn at waypoint*
10:00	355	7.5				
11:30	355	7.5				

Noon Position:

Time	Course	Speed	Log	Wind	Helm	Position/Comment
1:15	345	7.5				*enter Johnny Bay*

Generator Hours

On	Off	Run Time
1432.2		
Today		
Previous		
Total		
Since Oil Change		

Engine Hours

On	Off	Run Time
800.5	811.1	10.6
Today		10.6
Previous		172.5
Total		183.1
Since Adding Fuel		82.7
Since Oil Change		183.1

Daily Check List

Item	Eng	Gen	Remarks
Coolant			
Engine Oil			
Trans. Oil			
Fuel Filter			
Water Pump			

Distance

Today	85.45
Previous	1232.1
Total	1317.5
This Cruise	1317.5

The left side of our log sheets features the running and operating details of a day's run.

Speed, and so on. And across the bottom of the page are three boxes that summarize engine and generator hours and checks. The small box at the very bottom of the page records a running summary of the distance traveled during the cruise.

At the top of the right-hand page there is space to record departure and arrival locations, followed by plenty of space under the heading Remarks for personal comments, observations, and names and contact information for cruisers we meet along the way. When we find a particularly good anchorage or friendly marina this is where we note it.

At the bottom of some logbooks there's a box to record the condition of the wind and sea and another for tidal information. This information is helpful if you're concerned about shallow water or want to arrive on a rising tide.

Though this loose-leaf format suits us just fine because we have customized our page layout, we can't, in good conscience, recommend it. If you should ever need to present your log in court to defend your position in a lawsuit (either as plaintiff or defendant), loose-leaf logs are generally inadmissible. It's too easy for pages to be modified or even swapped outright after the fact. The only logs usually accepted in court are those written into previously bound books where any tinkering with the pages or the data contained on them would be easily and plainly visible.

Of course we try to operate in such a way that we should never find ourselves in this position, so we prefer to keep our customized log on loose-leaf sheets that have blanks for the specific information we want to be able to recall.

SMART STORAGE SOLUTIONS

It's not enough to designate one drawer for all this paperwork. Better by far to bring order to the chaos by organizing it in a way that makes sense to you. You won't misplace a new state sticker or insurance policy if you have a designated place for it. The same is true for other printed material you want to be able to refer to. Keep similar papers together and avoid stuffing everything into a general folder. Before you know it the folder will be bulging with everything from purchase receipts to your current USCG inspection certificate. You'll never find what you're looking for.

There are a variety of ways to organize and store boat papers. The key issue is to keep them clean, dry, and accessible so they're safe and easy to retrieve. Choose a container or storage system to fit your boat. A larger boat will likely have more space than a small one to accommodate a file box or plastic crate. In tighter quarters it makes sense to use expanding files with accordion sides or a ring binder with transparent sleeves into which you can slip papers and manuals. Don't be tempted to put them in that unused compartment beneath a bunk. If you have to tear the boat apart to reach it, the space is better suited for extra supplies and gear, not important paperwork.

The aft cabin of *High Life* has a built-in desk on the port side with two hinged-top storage compartments below the desktop that are ideal for several large plastic envelopes and binders. The two thickest ones contain manuals. One is a collection of operating manuals for the boat engine and systems; the other is a collection of manuals for all the equipment and gear. Ownership documents we keep in a large binder with transparent sleeves for documentation papers, state boat registration numbers, insurance policy, and other ownership-related papers. The sleeves are particularly handy for small items like the inflatable boat's registration form and the license to operate the single-sideband radio. There's also a *Ship's Record* binder with inventory and maintenance records.

PART III

Use Your Boat

CHAPTER 16
Learning Skills

Cruising is no exception to the saying that life is one long series of learning experiences. Rarely is one day on the water exactly the same as any other, so gaining new knowledge and acquiring new skills are an integral part of boating. Every time you go out on the water you encounter different conditions and circumstances that make cruising as exciting and enjoyable as it is. There's the challenge of operating the boat safely, understanding how to read the weather and its effects, as well as skills like planning a cruise and preparing food aboard. This section of the book takes a look at the many boating and life skills that make cruising enjoyable.

A variety of ways and resources is available to help you gain the skills you need to operate your boat. People have different learning styles, so it makes sense to first ask yourself how you learn best. For most of us, the learning process begins with reading about boating, then watching what other boaters do, and finally by trying it out ourselves. We all learn by doing, but a new set of circumstances will always test how much we've learned. Any seasoned boater will tell you that the sea can humble even the saltiest of skippers.

YOU ARE WHAT YOU READ AND WATCH

If you don't already subscribe to a boating magazine, start. One is better than none, but if you're addicted like us, you'll probably end up with a mailbox full of them. To find the widest selection of magazines, go to a boating retailer. Large bookstores also carry a good assortment.

We've been fans of regional boating magazines for years. Though national magazines are interesting, you can't beat a magazine like *Southern Boating* if you're a Florida boater, *Chesapeake Bay* magazine in the Mid-Atlantic, *Lakeland Boating* for the Great Lakes, or *Sea* if you cruise the West Coast. Buy a selection of magazines, take them home to read and enjoy, then decide which ones you'd like to receive regularly.

As you become more proficient and confident, continue to extend your knowledge with boating books. There are entire books about many of the topics we cover in just this one. Expand your library with specific titles about weather, anchoring, coastal navigation, or whatever subjects interest you most. Eventually you will develop a decent collection that you can refer to time and again.

Boating retailers carry a pretty comprehensive selection of boating videos, about

EXTRA CREDIT READING

You can't become too familiar with your boat and all its systems, but that's not always easy if the manuals are on the boat (where they should be) when you have some free reading time ashore. Get a second copy of these manuals so you can refer to them as time permits. Learn about the electrical system by studying the schematics, and check out the engine manual so when it's time to change the oil filter you'll know where it's located. Your new knowledge won't make sparkling party conversation, but it will give you a thorough understanding of your boat and its systems.

everything from basic skills to cruising areas. And don't forget boating-related television programs, which you'll usually find on cable stations. They're another good source for learning about boating.

EXPERT ADVICE AT BOAT SHOWS, EVENTS, AND SEMINARS

Boat shows are enjoyable places to gather information, ask questions, and learn about the amazing array of boats and equipment that's available. You'll find seminars covering a variety of skills. They are conducted by authors promoting their books and by experts from manufacturing companies explaining how to use their equipment or products. Boat shows are big business and are usually held in large cities across the country, often in the fall and winter months. Some are specific to fishing boats. The larger shows include boats of all sizes and types. It's never been easier to learn about boating directly from the experts and professionals.

Even if you're in the buying phase and don't yet own a boat, consider attending one of these events. The experience is invaluable. In addition to the educational value, you will meet people with the same interests and learn

from their adventures and misadventures. Some of the larger shows have daylong seminars with a schedule of topics ranging from "How to Be Your Own Weather Forecaster" to "Understanding Diesel Engines." Two of our favorite events are:

- TrawlerPort, a popular event sponsored by *Passagemaker* magazine, always draws a large crowd. It's a trawler show within a mainstream boat show, with organized trawler displays, seminars, and social events. The seminars are held in conjunction with large boat shows (Newport, Boston, Annapolis, Seattle, and Miami) and provide a great opportunity to see the latest boats while you learn.
- Trawler Fest is a boat show, seminar, and rendezvous all rolled into one. This three-day event takes place in boating centers across the country (Solomons, Maryland; Stuart, Florida; Puget Sound, Washington; Newport, Rhode Island; and Manitowoc, Wisconsin). The seminars are scheduled around in-the-water and social events. Speakers cover a range of topics such as medical and safety issues, using e-mail aboard, anchoring, and cruising destinations. In-the-water events include docking demonstrations, engine room inspections,

and a host of hands-on presentations. In addition, they offer Trawler Fest University, in-depth programs covering two oft-requested and important topics: diesel engines and weather prediction.

Local Resources

On a local level, you'll find seminars offered at boating retailers, boat and yacht clubs, and maritime museums, usually in the winter months. They attract speakers such as manufacturers, authors, and other experts.

The best place to find information about these events is in the regional boating magazines. All regional magazines feature a calendar section listing events, workshops, and boating courses. They also report the news from boat clubs and include information about any regional rendezvous sponsored by boat manufacturers with dates, locations, and contact information.

Closer to home, you'll find that many boat manufacturers sponsor an annual rendezvous at a popular cruising destination to keep in contact with existing and potential customers. These events provide good opportunities for owners of similar boats to meet and learn from the educational sessions and demonstrations.

Join an Organization

The U.S. Power Squadrons and U.S. Coast Guard Auxiliary are two national boating organizations with a network of local chapters. Join one of them and take their classes. Both organizations have developed instructional programs on basic seamanship and coastal navigation that will give you the knowledge and confidence to operate your boat. You'll also meet classmates who are boaters in your area. The instructors provide useful learning guides and materials as well as practical advice. Classes are usually held in

the evenings or on weekends at local schools or other public meeting places.

There's an extra bonus to learning this way: by attending one of these courses you may be eligible for a lower insurance rate. Many marine insurers give a discount to boaters who have successfully completed these programs.

In addition, these two organizations have joined together to create a home study course for those who can't attend the classroom sessions. It's in the form of a manual and CD-ROM so you can learn at your own pace at home or away, using either a PC or a Mac.

Both organizations have websites where you can learn more about their activities and courses and find details of their local chapters. These websites are listed in Appendix 1. Go to the Power Squadrons site and click on *Locate a Squadron*, or to the Coast Guard Auxiliary site and use their *Flotilla Finder* to find the unit that's nearest your home. These organizations usually have booths at regional boat shows, and you'll also find their brochures at local boating retailers, public libraries, boat clubs, and boating events. It's easy to get connected.

The Marine Traders Owners Association (MTOA) is a popular boating group that sponsors seminars, cruises, and regional meetings all over the country. The organization began with owners of Marine Traders trawler yachts, but today it invites all boaters to join. Members receive a comprehensive newsletter full of ideas and information, and their regional cruising rendezvous offer the opportunity to meet boaters in their home areas.

Women Aboard is a network of women in boating that has local chapter and national meetings at boat shows. It publishes a newsletter that's filled with suggestions, solutions, and good ideas.

Then of course, there's BoatU.S., the Boatowners Association of the United States. This national boaters' advocacy group does a lot of lobbying in Washington, and also has a number of consumer-oriented benefits for its members, including a monthly magazine to keep them informed.

Members also save on everyday boating expenses using their Online Store and receive West Advantage Plus Reward Coupons based on the amount of your purchases.

Members also save money every time they use their membership card at more than 800 cooperating marinas for discounts on fuel, slips, and boat repairs. BoatU.S. also offers on-the-water and on-the-road towing services and insures billions of dollars worth of members' boats at competitive rates.

JOIN A BOAT CLUB

There's an interesting alternative to ownership for newcomers to boating. For an annual fee, members of a boat club enjoy the use of a fleet of different types of boats. Membership usually entitles you to a specific number of days aboard, but with some clubs there's no limit. In many cases it includes several hours of classroom and on-the-water instruction.

For example, the Freedom Boat Club, currently (in 2005) with 34 locations throughout the United States, charges approximately $4,500 annually for unlimited use of its boats for a year. Each time you use a boat, you only pay for the fuel you burn. And membership is recognized at any locations that may open in the future as well as current ones. Other clubs operate in a similar way. For someone who has time constraints, and wants to learn the basics of boat handling, a club membership is an option worth considering.

FRACTIONAL OWNERSHIP

Another possibility for newcomers is fractional ownership. This concept, which like so many boating activities began with sailboats

but has recently crossed into powerboating, is similar to time-sharing in real estate. A number of programs are available, and though they're all different, each works in a similar way. Many agree that, since membership in one of these programs costs about 10 percent of what you'd pay to own a boat, it can be worth every cent. Shared time of fractional ownership is very much in line with the actual usage of an owned boat (where you bear 100 percent of the cost) so it can be a good investment.

This system doesn't offer quite the variety of boats you'll find in most boat clubs, but many of these programs also have swap arrangements, where owners at one location can swap boats with owners from other locations, creating more variety in both boats and cruising grounds. Many of the currently available programs also offer instruction, so that beginning boaters are not left on their own. A number of fractional ownership contacts are listed in Appendix 1.

LEARN BY DOING WITH A BUDDY

Book knowledge is the first step, but to put that knowledge to the test you have to get on board and just do it. And it takes time to learn by doing. If you like to go it alone, go ahead, but we find learning with someone else can be more fruitful.

Find someone who has more experience than you, for example, and ask them to go with you. The more patient the person the better, of course. A stressful afternoon on the water with someone who has a short fuse is no fun, let alone a good learning experience.

We know many women who have learned to handle their boat from a skipper other than their husband. Learning how to dock a boat from a husband can be a negative experience. A skipper swap for the afternoon can be far more beneficial. If you and your part-

BE AN ARTFUL OBSERVER

If you're a member of a boat club, volunteer to help out on the docks and observe how boaters operate their boats in different, sometimes difficult situations. Watching how other skippers maneuver their boats gives you valuable insights for when you're at the helm. And when you see a skipper magically maneuver his boat, don't be afraid to ask, "How'd you get that boat into that tight space?" He'll be pleased that someone noticed.

ner work as a team, then learn together, that's terrific. But you'll be surprised how easy it is to teach or learn from someone who is not your spouse.

Practice, practice, practice, then practice some more, ideally in calm conditions at first. If you're embarrassed to make a mistake in front of people you know, go where nobody knows you or your boat. Practice docking at a different marina by pulling up to the fuel dock or into an empty slip. Practice early in the morning or in the afternoon after most of the boating traffic has died down (but before the day's returning boats start it up again).

When you're feeling confident, venture out in more difficult conditions to experience operating the boat when it's windy or when there are strong currents to deal with.

GO BACK TO SCHOOL

Another way to gain real experience and to learn by doing is to take a vacation and enroll in a formal boating-school program that offers hands-on training. You'll find advertisements in boating magazines for several companies who specialize in power cruising instruction in popular cruising areas. Vic Hansen of Florida Sailing & Cruising School told us that most of the people who attend the school's three- or six-day power courses are not necessarily new to boating. They are boatowners who want to learn how to do it right and gain more confidence in handling their boats. The hands-on lessons combine book learning with in-the-water practice of seamanship, piloting, navigating, and anchoring, under the guidance of a certified licensed captain.

CHAPTER 17

The Rules of the Road

We like to cruise in the late fall and early spring when boat traffic is light and there's less congestion, but it seems that even when there are few boats on the water, sooner or later one of us has to alter course to avoid a collision. Unlike a car that's limited to paved roads and marked traffic lanes, a boat in open water can travel in just about any direction. To clarify who has the right of way on the open water, nations have agreed on a set of navigation rules. The *International Navigation Rules* govern the operation of vessels in international waters; another set, called the *Inland Navigation Rules*, governs the inland waters of the United States. To understand and learn all these rules, we suggest all boaters should take a basic boating course offered by the U.S. Power Squadrons or U.S. Coast Guard Auxiliary. (See Chapter 16, Learning Skills, for more information about the courses.)

In this chapter we suggest safe operating guidelines for what, in our experience, are the most common situations you will encounter while cruising inland and coastal waters. We hope our advice will give you the confidence and knowledge to operate your boat safely and according to the rules.

THE RULES

The navigation rules governing vessels on the high seas are called the *1972 International Regulations for Preventing Collisions at Sea*. With a mouthful like that, it's no wonder they're more commonly known simply as the Collision Regulations, the 72 COLREGS, or, in everyday use, simply the COLREGS. These rules, and the U.S. Inland Navigation Rules, which are very similar to the international rules, are set out in a book: *Navigation Rules International—Inland*. The book is formatted to display the international rule on the left page of each spread and the corresponding inland rule on the right. This makes it very easy to locate a specific rule, as well as note any difference between the international and inland versions. Blank pages are used where there are no corresponding rules.

There has to be some kind of line defining the transition from inland rules to international rules. On coastal charts you will see a magenta line drawn across the entrance to a harbor or sound, labeled *COLREGS Demarcation Line* to clearly show this transition. Seaward of this line, international rules apply.

The Coast Guard requires that the rules book be aboard all boats over 39.4 feet in length, but we think all boats should have a copy to refer to. The rules cover many aspects of operating a boat in the presence of others, including the required sound signals (both in good visibility and in fog—they are not the same), right of way in different situations, and the lights that boats and other types of vessels, including ships, tugs, and barges, are required to display.

Another useful addition to a boater's library is *Chapman Piloting and Seamanship*. This volume, long considered the bible of boating, is as heavy as an anchor, but worth its weight. It covers all the rules in depth and everything else you'll ever want to learn about piloting and seamanship.

SAFE OPERATING GUIDELINES— RIGHT OF WAY

The primary goal of the navigation rules is to provide a framework for the safe operation of your boat. As skipper, one of your primary responsibilities is to avoid a collision with another vessel. When everyone follows the rules, boats can maneuver in any direction, pass, and be passed by one another and all is right with the world.

Knowing and following *all* the rules can help keep you out of trouble, but there are two specific requirements that are especially important. First, the rules demand that you at all times maintain a *lookout* by sight, hearing, and any other means available. This includes radar if your vessel is so equipped. They also state that you must, at all times, maintain a *safe speed*, which is defined as "the speed at which you can take proper action to avoid collision."

Here's a rundown of the basic rules you need to know and follow when operating your boat.

- You must avoid collision at all costs. Even if you have the right of way, it is still your responsibility to do everything you can to avoid a collision. If you hit another vessel, even if you have the right of way, you have violated this rule.
- You must give way to any boat that you are overtaking. You are considered to be overtaking another boat when you are approaching the vessel from astern. This rule is especially important to keep in mind when overtaking another boat in close quarters. At night, if all you see is a boat's stern light, you are overtaking and you must give the boat the right of way.
- You must give way to any vessel approaching from your starboard side that is not overtaking. Any vessel approaching from ahead to just past abeam on the starboard side must be given the right of way. At night, if you see a boat's red sidelight, you must give this boat the right of way.
- Boats under sail, working fishing boats, and boats with restricted maneuverability have the right of way over powerboats. This rule applies under any circumstances. If you are confined to a channel that restricts your ability to maneuver, slow down and allow any of these vessels to pass.

That's it in a nutshell. Keep these four basic concepts in mind and you will avoid 99 percent of all right-of-way issues.

SOUND SIGNALS IN GOOD VISIBILITY

To avoid a collision, boats must be able to communicate, so a system of sound signals (generally known as *whistle signals*) was developed long before we had such conveniences as VHF radio. That's why today, most boats are required to have a means of signaling another boat as part of their legally mandated equipment. On vessels over 39.4 feet, the horn or whistle must be mechanically operated, while a mouth-operated type is allowed on smaller vessels, as long as it can be heard at a distance of one-half mile.

Over time, whistle signals have mostly been replaced by direct radio communication, so except between commercial vessels the actual signals are rarely heard any more. But this is certainly not a valid excuse for not learning them. Sound signals are called for under the rules, and sometimes you'll still hear them, so you should know what they mean.

Under the inland rules:

- One short blast (1 second) means I intend to leave you on my port (left) side
- Two short blasts mean I intend to leave you on my starboard (right) side
- Three short blasts mean I am backing up
- Five (or more) short blasts signal danger or disagreement
- A prolonged blast (4–6 seconds) means I am leaving my berth or approaching a bend or other blind spot on a waterway

Since the most frequently used inland signals are signals of intent, they require an assenting response from the other vessel in any situation where there's the possibility of a collision. An assenting response, which is an exact repetition of the signal given by the other boat, says in effect, "what you intend to do is OK with me." If it isn't OK, never answer with anything but the danger signal of five or more short blasts.

Sound signals for international rules are similar, but indicate action rather than intent. For this reason, no response is required under international rules unless both vessels are changing course.

Under the international rules:

- One short blast (1 second) means I am turning to starboard (right)
- Two short blasts mean I am turning to port (left)

- Three short blasts mean I am backing up
- Five (or more) short blasts signal danger

SPECIFIC SITUATIONS

Here are three scenarios that deal with boats approaching each other head on, boats on converging or crossing courses, and boats overtaking from behind.

MEETING HEAD ON

When two boats are approaching each other head on (or nearly so), neither boat has the right of way. Meeting port side to port side is the standard (and recommended) practice. This situation usually arises in channels, where everyone is supposed to keep to the right, or when boats are steering a course between navigational marks. It's like car traffic, where you keep to the right on all United States roads.

When you are in a head-to-head situation, as soon as you determine that a course change is required, make the change large enough to be readily apparent to the other skipper. A swing of at least ten degrees to starboard will make it clear that you intend to pass port-to-port. If you do this early, and make a course change large enough that your intent is obvious, there is usually no need to communicate with the converging boat. When it's apparent that you will pass safely, you may resume your previous course.

If there is any question as to the intent of either skipper, one short blast of the horn from one boat answered with one short blast from the other will signal a port-to-port meeting (inland rules only, where they are signals of intent and consent; under international rules, there would be a short blast only from the vessel changing course to starboard). Two short blasts signal a starboard-to-starboard meeting, which is acceptable if you are already

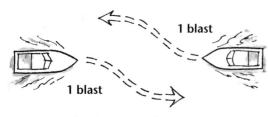

leaving a vessel to port

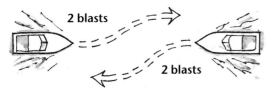

leaving a vessel to starboard

Under the inland rules, one boat approaching another head on should signal its intention with one horn blast if passing to port. The other boat should answer with one blast if that's OK. If, for some reason, that arrangement is not acceptable, the other boat should answer with five short horn blasts. (Illustration by Elayne Sears.)

starboard-to-starboard or if other aspects of the situation suggest it (as we'll explain shortly). Though a port-to-port meeting is preferred, there's no point in crossing in front of another boat to do so.

Communicating Bridge-to-Bridge via VHF

To confirm a meeting situation with another vessel, particularly a larger commercial one, use the VHF. Here's what an exchange on VHF channel 13 (which is the bridge-to-bridge frequency that commercial vessels constantly monitor) might sound like.

> "Tug and barge approaching marker 36, this is the white trawler *High Life* off your bow calling on 13. How would you like to take us? Over."

> "*High Life*, this is *Big John*, we will see you on one whistle. Over."

"OK, *Big John*, we will meet port to port, thanks. *High Life* out."

Under inland rules, if the skipper of either vessel does not agree with the signal of the other vessel, he replies with five or more short blasts of the horn to indicate that there is danger, and in this case the skippers should establish communication from bridge to bridge immediately.

In some cases it may be safer to pass starboard to starboard. One example of this would be when both vessels are already so far to their respective left sides of the channel that there would be a greater risk of collision if one or the other crossed over for a port-to-port meeting.

Another example would be when a larger vessel must swing wide around a bend in a river or channel to stay in deep water (the deeper water is usually on the outer side of a bend). Passing starboard-to-starboard would allow the larger vessel to slide wide over to its left side of the channel and thus into "your" side, without the danger of forcing you out of the navigable water, as might happen if you tried to meet port-to-port.

In this case, the large vessel must signal two short blasts on its horn, indicating it intends to show you its starboard side. If you think you can safely slide over to your left side and still have enough water as the larger vessel takes the outside of the bend, you answer with two blasts, indicating you agree to a starboard-to-starboard meeting. If you don't agree, answer with the five short blasts that indicate danger. Of course, the larger boat may be *forced* to swing wide, simply due to the maneuvering room and depth it requires. If this is so, and especially if it is bound downstream, in which case it has the right of way regardless of size, your only choice is to stay out of the bend until the large vessel has completed its turn and gone back to its "own side." Here again, bridge-to-bridge communication on channel 13 might go a long way toward avoiding potential trouble.

CROSSING SITUATIONS

When two boats approach each other from the side they are considered to be crossing. You must give way to all boats that approach from your starboard unless they are overtaking and passing you. Generally, the safest course of action (and the one we usually take) is to make a course change to starboard that allows us to pass astern of the crossing boat. Make your avoiding turn clear. In fact, it's actually better to exaggerate the turn, so the other skipper knows for sure which way you are turning, instead of gradually altering course to pass clear astern, which might leave your intentions in doubt.

If you have the right of way, the rules require you to hold your course so the other skipper knows what you plan to do. The most important point to remember in a crossing situation is that you must avoid a collision no matter who has the right of way. Many boaters don't know the rules or choose to ignore them, so if another skipper does not appear to alter course to give you the right of way, you should take avoiding action. If it's unclear what the other skipper intends, or the other boat makes several course changes but none that will avoid a collision, slow down or even stop, especially if the other boat is traveling at high speed. A wrong move by either skipper, like a last minute turn to port by one and a turn to starboard by the other, could mean that trying to avoid a collision may actually cause one.

Risk of collision is clearly evident when another boat's relative bearing (the direction

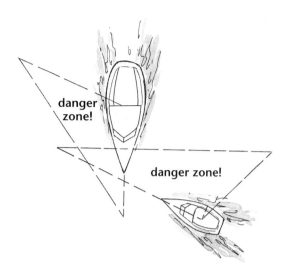

Give way to a boat that approaches from the starboard unless it is overtaking and passing you. Alter course toward the stern of the boat. Make your course change obvious. (Illustration by Elayne Sears.)

in which it appears to be located, relative to your boat, for example, just in front of your starboard windshield post) doesn't change, yet the boat keeps coming closer. In navigational terms, this is known as *constant bearing, closing range,* and it is a sure sign of impending collision. Your best option once again is to turn to starboard, so you change the potentially dangerous crossing situation into a safe port-to-port meeting.

OVERTAKING

Any boat overtaking another must yield the right of way. The boat you pass has the right to maneuver and you must keep clear, so it's generally a good idea to ask for permission from the skipper of the boat you intend to pass. This alerts the skipper that you are passing and what your intentions are.

Under the inland rules, one short blast of your horn indicates you plan to leave the other boat to your port, which means you will pass on its starboard side; two blasts indicates you'll leave the other boat to starboard, which means you'll overtake it on its port side. The boat ahead should answer with the same signal if your intentions are OK, or with the five or more short blast danger signal if they are not.

The signals for overtaking under international rules are much more complex than those we just described for inland situations. But there's generally enough room in the open waters covered by international rules that an overtaking situation involving a pleasure boat should never occur. So knowing those signals is really unnecessary for the skipper of a typical cruising boat. If you encounter another vessel in open water, you don't need to signal; just give it a very wide berth.

While the sound signals alone are meant to suffice, not all skippers know them. So we think the VHF radio is the best tool to use when overtaking boats in confined channels or waterways. Use channel 16, as this is the one channel that everyone is supposed to be monitoring. A conversation usually goes something like this:

> "*Full Sails*, this is *High Life*, the northbound trawler off your stern. We'd like to come by you on your starboard side. Over."

> "*High Life*, this is *Full Sails*, roger that, come on ahead. Over."

> "Thanks, *Full Sails*, if you slow a bit we will give you a slow pass. *High Life* standing by 16 and 13. Out."

Unfortunately, it's also true that many boaters don't monitor their radio, so a horn signal may be the only way to get their attention. Many times we've given a short blast of the horn and had the skipper of the boat ahead leap into action. Sometimes they give us a hand signal to come on by, other times they answer the horn or call us on the radio.

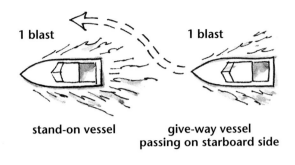

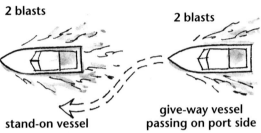

Using inland rules, you would signal you wish to pass a vessel to port by giving two short blast of your horn, to pass to starboard give one short blasts. (Illustration by Elayne Sears.)

It's good practice to occasionally look behind and scan for approaching traffic so that an overtaking boat does not surprise you, especially if you are in a busy channel.

OTHER CIRCUMSTANCES

On a river or in a restricted channel, boats traveling with the current (usually downstream on a river) have less maneuvering ability than those traveling against the current, and thus boats traveling downstream have the right of way. Also, commercial boats, such as ferries, have the right of way when crossing a river, though all noncommercial crossing traffic is supposed to yield to vessels running up- and downstream.

Boats traveling with the current also have the right to pass through a bridge before boats coming in the opposite direction. However, don't assume other boaters will know and follow the rule, especially small boats. We have seen many situations where a boat facing the current lines up right in front of an opening bridge so that it's first through when the bridge opens.

MIGHT MAKES RIGHT

Skippers of commercial vessels know the Rules of the Road and practice them, but even if we have the right of way, we usually wait and follow their lead. They don't have the maneuverability of a small boat. A large container ship steaming at full speed on the high seas takes more than a mile to stop—much longer if the current and/or wind aren't favorable. A large vessel or tug towing barges has to maintain speed in order to have steerage, so it can't easily hesitate or slow down. Since we travel quite slowly, at 7½ knots, our philosophy is to get out of the way of a passing ship. If we're in doubt about a large vessel's intentions, we stop, or even reverse course, to keep out of the way until it has passed by. Using the VHF (on either 16 or 13) to ask what they are planning to do is also a good idea, though we've found that if we pause for a while to assess what's happening, their intentions will often become clear.

SOUND SIGNALS IN RESTRICTED VISIBILITY

It's important to remember that the signals and situations described above will apply only when vessels can see each other. When there's restricted visibility, which doesn't mean the darkness of night, but rather any time there's fog, heavy rain, smoke, or some other atmospheric condition that limits visibility, you have to use different signals. And what you use depends on whether or not you are under-

way. We'll quote directly from Rule 35, Sound Signals in Restricted Visibility:

UNDERWAY

In or near an area of restricted visibility, whether by day or night, the signals prescribed in this Rule shall be used as follows:

(a) A power-driven vessel making way through the water shall sound at intervals of not more than 2 minutes one prolonged blast.

(b) A power-driven vessel underway, but stopped and making no way through the water, shall sound at intervals of not more than 2 minutes two prolonged blasts in succession with an interval of about 2 seconds between them.

(c) A vessel not under command; a vessel restricted in her ability to maneuver, whether underway or at anchor; a sailing vessel; a vessel engaged in fishing, whether underway or at anchor; and a vessel engaged in towing or pushing another vessel shall, instead of the signals prescribed in paragraphs (a) or (b) of this Rule, sound at intervals of not more than 2 minutes, three blasts in succession; namely, one prolonged followed by two short blasts.

(d) A vessel towed or, if more than one vessel is towed, the last vessel of the tow if manned, shall at intervals of not more than 2 minutes sound four blasts in succession; namely, one prolonged followed by three short blasts. When practicable, this signal shall be made immediately after the signal made by the towing vessel.

(e) When a pushing vessel and a vessel being pushed ahead are rigidly connected in a composite unit they shall be regarded as a power-driven vessel and shall give the signals prescribed in paragraphs (a) or (b) of this Rule.

AT ANCHOR

(f) A vessel at anchor shall, at intervals of not more than 1 minute, ring the bell rapidly for about 5 seconds. In a vessel of 100 meters or more in length the bell shall be sounded in the forepart of the vessel and immediately after the ringing of the bell the gong shall be sounded rapidly for about 5 seconds in the after part of the vessel. A vessel at anchor may, in addition, sound three blasts in succession; namely, one short, one prolonged and one short blast, to give warning of her position and of the possibility of collision to an approaching vessel.

(g) A vessel aground shall give the bell signal and, if required, the gong signal prescribed in paragraph (f) of this Rule, and shall, in addition, give three separate and distinct strokes on the bell immediately before and after the rapid ringing of the bell. A vessel aground may, in addition, sound an appropriate whistle signal.

(h) A vessel of less than 12 meters in length shall not be obliged to give the above-mentioned signals but, if she does not, shall make some other efficient sound signal at intervals of not more than 2 minutes.

Obviously, you are not going to use most of these signals when operating a cruising yacht. But since you may hear any of them, and should really know what they mean when you do, we've included them all. Which brings up another important point: if you hear the fog signal of another vessel apparently forward of your beam, you must reduce speed to *steerageway* (just enough speed that you can still steer effectively) until you're sure there's no risk of collision. Of course, you should be going slowly to begin with, so that you can stop in half the distance of the visibility.

LIGHTS AND SHAPES

The navigation rules spell out the type of navigation lights required to allow safe travel between sunset and sunrise. The rules affecting pleasure boats operating under power fall into three categories: small boats and dinghies less than 23 feet, vessels under 39.4 feet, and vessels under 164 feet. Whatever the size of your boat, in times of reduced visibility it's a good idea to turn on your navigation lights.

RUNNING LIGHTS

When it's dark, it's difficult to determine the location of another boat and the direction that it is traveling, so specific lights are required by the rules. All boats except dinghies must have a system of running lights: a red light on the port side, a green light on the starboard side, and white lights on a forward masthead and at the stern. These are described in Rule 23.

Depending on which lights are visible, you can determine if a boat is heading toward or away from you, or if it will cross ahead or astern of you. For example, if the red and green sidelights and the white masthead light are all visible, it is coming directly

Type of Light	Color	Viewable
Masthead	White	225°
Side	Red (port), green (starboard)	112.5°
Stern	White	135°
Anchor	White	360°

at you. If only the red sidelight and white masthead light are visible, then you are looking at the port side of the boat, and it is moving from right to left. If you see only the white stern light then the boat is moving away.

It is the position of the approaching boat *relative* to your boat that determines which running lights you see. For example, if a boat is approaching from directly behind you, but a good distance astern, you will see both red and green sidelights and the white masthead light. As the boat gets closer and begins to pass to starboard you will see only the red sidelight and white masthead light; the green sidelight on the other side of the boat will no longer be visible. The masthead light and sidelights are only visible from the bow to slightly past amidships (112.5 degrees from dead ahead, to be precise), so when the overtaking boat pulls ahead of you the red sidelight and white masthead light will no longer be visible. As the boat pulls away the stern light becomes visible. By noting how the running lights of another boat appear to shift, you can determine the relative course of another boat as it maneuvers in the dark.

For this reason, the bigger and brighter the running lights the better. In real life, big ships have large, bright running lights, and little boats have small, dim running lights. If we could fit the running lights of an aircraft carrier on *High Life* we would. Of course that's impossible—but you get the idea. If you have large, bright running lights other boats will take note.

Small Boats

Under the international rules, boats of less than 23 feet that do not go more than 7 knots are not required to have running lights. Most dinghies fall into this category. When underway they are required to show a single white light visible from all directions (360°). Under the inland rules, however, all vessels less than 39.4 feet may show an all-around white light instead of the separate masthead and stern lights, but must show red and green sidelights also (the combination red/green bow light is allowed).

Small boats that do go more than 7 knots are required to have red and green sidelights in addition to the all around white light. Or they can be fitted with the standard set of running lights that includes a masthead and stern light.

Mid-Sized Boats

Boats more than 39.4 feet but less than 65.6 feet in length are required to have a masthead light that is visible for at least 2.5 miles, and sidelights and stern lights visible for at least a mile.

Large Vessels

Larger vessels, over 65.6 feet but less than 164 feet in length, are required to have a masthead light that is visible for at least five miles. The sidelights and stern light must be visible for at least two miles. She may also display an additional masthead light behind and higher than the forward masthead light, both must be visible for at least five miles.

Large ships over 164 feet LOA must have this second masthead. This allows the forward and aft masthead light to act as range lights to help identify the vessel's direction.

Other Lights You May See

The lights we've described so far should more than cover any powerboat in which you may be cruising, but it's also important for you to recognize other types of watercraft you may encounter at night. For instance:

Sailing Vessels

A sailboat will most often exhibit nearly the same lights as a similar sized powerboat with

Lights for Power-Driven Vessels Under Way

Deciphering Lights at Night

starboard side view   bow   stern

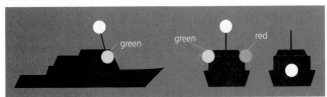

Under 164 ft. (50 m), masthead light, sidelights, and sternlight.

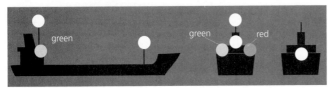

Over 164 ft. (50 m).

Lights When Towing

Under 164 ft. (50 m), two white steaming lights and towing light aft (yellow over white).

Vessel being towed shows sidelights and sternlight.

If tow is over 657 ft. (200 m), three steaming lights.

Lights When Pushing

In inland waters only, the lights are as shown, with the yellow bow light flashing. In international waters, there is no yellow bow light, and the two yellow stern lights are replaced by a white stern light.

(Illustration by Jim Sollers.)

If you see this at night . . .

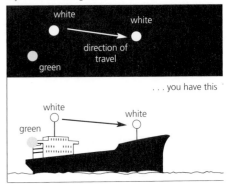

. . . you have this

If you see this at night . . .

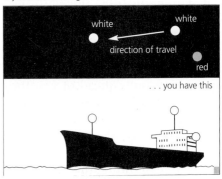

. . . you have this

If the two white lights are aligned . . .

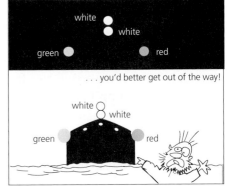

. . . you'd better get out of the way!

one important difference. A boat operating exclusively under sail does *not* display the white masthead light required of all vessels under power. Of course, if an auxiliary sailboat uses its engine as well as its sails, the masthead light should be lit to show that the vessel is under power as well.

Sailboats *heel* (lean to the side) while underway, and their large foresails can mask parts of the hull or deck at certain angles. For both these reasons, sailboats are also allowed (though not required) to display colored lights at the tops of their masts to ensure better visibility. These lights come in two varieties. Sailboats of less than 65.6 feet may display—*instead of* separate sidelights and stern light—red, green, and white lights combined into a single fixture. Sailing vessels of all sizes may also display—*in addition to* sidelights and stern light—two all-around (360°) lights at the top of the main mast, the upper light being red and the one beneath it green. Either of these arrangements is acceptable under both the international and inland rules.

The basic *running* lights we have so far described are the ones you will see most frequently on vessels of all sizes. But in or near ports, and along the coastal runs between them (as well as on the Intracoastal Waterway), you'll also encounter a great number of tugboats with barges in tow. Since these tug and barge combinations are most often quite large and far less maneuverable than most other craft, the rules prescribe the lights they must exhibit to show us the specific arrangements involved.

Whether you plan to cruise at night or not, at some time or another you'll be forced into it by circumstances you can't avoid. So it's best that you learn what these lights mean. When you are sharing the water with a tug and tow, you need to know what you're dealing with so you can stay out of the way (or at the very least, communicate with the tug on VHF channel 13, as we discussed earlier).

Tugs with Tows

When you encounter a tug and tow with the tow being pulled astern, you'll see almost the same lights as on any power-driven vessel underway. The difference is that from ahead or alongside, anywhere you'd see the white masthead light and one or both sidelights of another power vessel, you'll see *two* white masthead lights, one directly above the other. And if the length of the tow (as measured from the stern of the tug to the very end of the last barge or whatever is being towed) is more than 656 feet, the tug will display *three* white masthead lights mounted vertically on the same mast.

When viewed from astern, you'll see the tug's usual white stern light and above it a similar yellow light, known as a *towing light*, that lets you know the tug has something in tow.

The barge(s) or object(s) being towed should display red and green sidelights at its (their) forward end and a stern light. These lighting arrangements apply under both international and inland rules.

Keep in mind that the tow is most often well behind the tug, and since the heavy towing line, or *hawser*, sinks below the surface, you may not see any connection whatsoever between the tug and the "other thing" that seems to be following way behind, even in broad daylight. They may look like two totally independent vessels that just happen to be on the same course. But if you try to cross between them, you'll quickly discover just how firmly they are connected! More than one pleasure boat skipper has discovered that running into a towing hawser can wreck a vessel and seriously injure (or kill) everyone aboard. *Never* try to pass between a tug and its tow.

Tugs Pushing

Tugboats pushing barges fall into one of three categories: tug and barge locked together as a composite unit; tug pushing the barge ahead; and tug pushing the barge from alongside (*on the hip* in tugboat parlance). A composite unit is regarded as a single vessel under both sets of rules and will be lighted as such according to its overall length.

The lighting requirements are different for a tug pushing a barge ahead and a tug towing on the hip. The lighting requirements of both the tug and the barge are also different for tows on international waters and those operating primarily on inland waters.

Under international rules, the tug will display two white masthead lights in a vertical line, red and green sidelights, and a white stern light. The vessel being pushed ahead will also display red and green sidelights at its forward end, and if the tugboat is alongside, a white stern light as well.

Under inland rules, the tug and barge will display similar lights with two notable exceptions. First, instead of a single white stern light, the pushing tug will display, in a vertical line, two yellow towing lights. And the barge, in addition to its red and green sidelights up forward, will also have at front and center a special flashing light, which is similar in size, shape, and brilliance to the flashing yellow lights you see on highway barricades.

Fishing Boats

Whenever they have gear in the water at night, boats fishing are required to display, in addition to their appropriate running lights, two all around lights, green over white, as high as possible above the superstructure. Whenever you see these lights, give the vessel a wide berth, particularly at its stern. You have no way of telling how far their gear may extend.

Anchor Lights

Whenever a boat is at anchor, the rules require it to display a white all-around (360°) light from its masthead, or as high as possible. The anchor light is not required in a designated special anchorage area or in a mooring field.

SHAPES

In addition to lights, the navigation rules prescribe a combination of ball, cone, and diamond shapes to be used during the day to signal the specific activity of a ship. For example, a vessel with a single black ball shape hoisted aloft is at anchor.

These shapes can be combined to indicate a wide range of activities, from fishing to towing, and are used almost exclusively by commercial vessels. The *Navigation Rules* has a complete listing, along with a picture of the shapes on the vessel.

One shape that's handy to know is the diamond displayed by a tug and tow. In daylight when a tug and tow measures more than 656 feet (from the stern of the tug to the very end of the last barge or whatever is being towed), both the tug and the barge should display a diamond shape where it can best be seen.

Another set of shapes we have found useful is the one used by dredges. A dredge that is working to deepen a channel will hoist a diamond shape with a ball shape above and below it to indicate that it's in operation. It also hoists two ball shapes on the side of the dredge where the dredging operation is working and two diamond shapes on the side that is safe to pass. If you travel on inland waterways or the river system, you are sure to encounter many dredges so it's worth becoming familiar with these shapes.

BRIDGE LIGHTING

The U.S. Coast Guard prescribes certain combinations of fixed lights for bridges and structures extending over waterways. These lights are not described in the COLREGS, but the patterns are simple, so we'll outline them here. Not *all* bridges you encounter are lighted according to coast guard specifications, but the majority are, so it pays to know the system.

In general, red lights are used to mark piers and supports at the sides of the navigable channel through most bridges, and green lights mark the centerline through a fixed bridge. If there is more than one channel through the bridge, the preferred route is marked by three white lights placed verti-

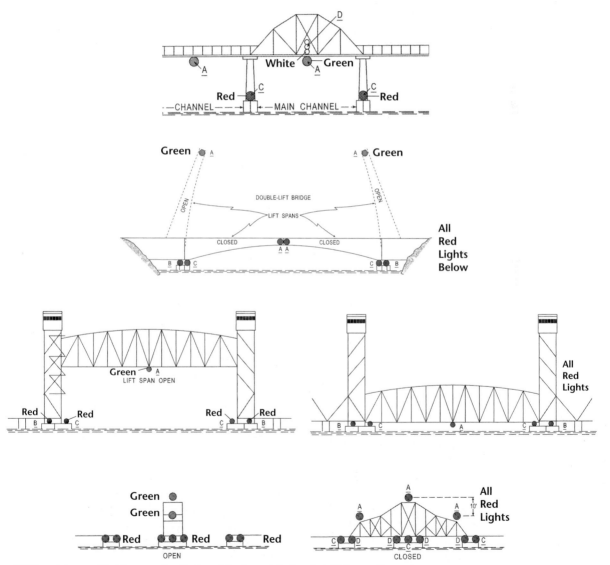

Different types of bridges can be distinguished at night by their light configurations.

cally. Red lights are also used on some lift bridges and drawbridges to indicate that the span is closed, and green lights to indicate that it is open to vessel traffic. These lights are used in addition to the red lights on the piers and fender boards.

Double-opening swing bridges are lighted with three lanterns on top of the span structure so that when viewed from an approaching vessel, the swing span when closed will display three red lights, and when open for navigation will display two green lights, indicating that it is safe to pass through the bridge.

CLEARANCE GAUGE

The vertical clearance between a bridge structure and the water at *mean high tide* is published (you'll usually see it on charts and in the *Coast Pilot* books published by NOAA) and is probably the least clearance you are likely to find. At other stages of the tide the clearance under the bridge is more or, in the case of extremely high tides, less than the published clearance.

A clearance gauge is often installed on the fenders of bridges, particularly if the bridge crosses a major waterway. It looks like a giant yardstick. The exposed portion of the gauge shows the clearance under the bridge in feet. One problem with some clearance gauges is that marine growth can sometimes obscure the lower portion of the gauge and make reading the numbers difficult. If you can't read the gauge, call the bridge tender and ask what the clearance is.

Many bridges show the clearance as measured from the lowest part of the bridge. If the bridge arches upward there may be several feet more clearance in the center. If so, this information is usually stated on a sign on the bridge near the clearance gauge. On some bridges, however, the clearance indi-

In tidal waters, the minimum clearance under a bridge is indicated by a clearance gauge.

cated is for the centerline of the channel, and there will be less clearance at the sides.

A good indication of which situation exists is a sign stating something like: *5 Feet Additional Clearance at Center* or perhaps *Low Clearance*. In the absence of a sign, your best bet is to assume the *minimum* clearance is also the *maximum*, and plan accordingly. If the clearance looks close, it doesn't hurt to ask the bridge operator (by VHF) where the clearance is measured. Fortunately, most newer bridges show the clearance between the lowest part of the bridge and the water and the clearance at the highest point, usually in the center of the span. But you can't always count on it.

CHAPTER 18
Boat Handling

The responsibilities of running *High Life* are pretty well divided evenly, but Katie would just as soon leave the docking to Gene. Even experienced skippers admit to a slight rise in blood pressure anytime they bring their boat near a dock, a bridge, or other boats in crowded conditions. That's probably why boat-talk so often eventually touches on hairy docking stories.

One of our most hair-raising misadventures involved a close encounter with a piling. We were traveling from Chicago to the Bahamas and were feeling pretty good, with more than 700 miles under our keel, when we pulled into the Grosse Point Yacht Club, north of Detroit, on Lake St. Clair. It was a blustery day and blowing like stink as we entered the basin, passed through the small drawbridge, and proceeded to our assigned slip—or at least tried to. We had to make a 180-degree turn to get into the slip, and we were aboard our Rhodes 41 sloop, *Gusto*, a boat with a large bow pulpit that extended well beyond the stem.

To make a long story short, we came up a bit short on the turn into the slip and on the second attempt a large swell lifted our boat so high that the pulpit hooked itself over the outer piling. The boat was firmly stuck. A crowd soon gathered, of course, and being a Sunday afternoon, it seemed like the entire club was witness to our arrival. It took five people standing on the stern, half a case of beer, and another large swell to raise the bow high enough to unhook our pulpit.

Handling a boat is one skill that's impossible to master without practical experience. You can learn to plot a course at your dining-room table, but you can only master boat handling onboard. Over time you develop a feel for your boat, and know how it will react to the helm and throttle in different situations. Every boat is unique, but the same laws of physics govern them all. If you're new to boating, an understanding of what is happening under your boat can help explain the moves you have to make to get it to go where you want. Some of these moves may seem counterintuitive. Even if you have boat-handling experience, a basic understanding of these forces can shed some light on why at times your boat seems to have a will of its own.

Docking is not the only tricky maneuver a cruising skipper performs. Other challenges include navigating through locks and under bridges, and dealing with currents. In this chapter we'll make suggestions and share what we've learned about handling a boat in these situations.

WHY SHE DOESN'T WANT TO BACK IN A STRAIGHT LINE

A boat's propeller doesn't only produce forward or reverse thrust. It also creates a side thrust, often called *prop walk*. A *right-hand* (clockwise turning) propeller in forward gear produces side forces that push the stern to the right (starboard).

Exactly why this happens has been debated for years. Some say it's a result of shaft angle, others that it's a result of greater push from the prop as it moves down into deeper, denser water, which gives it more thrust on its starboard side. Yet others say it's a matter of torque—the spinning force of the clockwise turning propeller "walks" it to starboard, and the boat's stern goes with it.

There probably isn't one single explanation of prop walk, so each of these theories may be at least partially right. The main point to remember is that regardless of why it happens, prop walk most certainly does exist. If you push the throttle full ahead on a single-screw boat, its stern will swing to starboard before the boat picks up speed. Of course, in reverse, the propeller turns in the opposite direction, so prop walk pushes the stern to port. Most twin-screw boats have props that rotate in opposite directions, so that the prop walk from one prop counter-

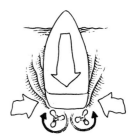

The props on most twin-screw boats rotate in opposite directions. Therefore, prop walk from one prop is counteracted by the other. (Illustration by Christopher Hoyt.)

acts the prop walk from the other. As long as both props are pushing the boat forward or backwards, the boat moves basically in a straight line.

The size and location of the rudder also affect the handling characteristics of a boat. Single-screw displacement boats most often have large rudders that steer the boat effectively even when the propeller is not turning (as long as the boat is moving faster than the current). High-speed boats have smaller rudders that are not as effective when the propellers don't push water past them.

Differences in prop walk and rudder efficiency explain the different handling characteristics of single-screw and twin-screw boats. Of course hull shape, windage, and other factors make each boat unique, but we have found that most single-screw boats share similar basic handling characteristics, as do twin-screw boats. Keep in mind how prop walk affects which way your boat wants to turn, especially in reverse, and pretty soon you will be able to anticipate its movements.

CLOSE-QUARTER MANEUVERING— DOCKING

Most of our white-knuckle experiences have occurred close to land. In fact, a bit too close. Handling the boat around docks and in other close-quarter situations can be a real test of

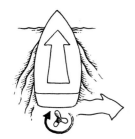

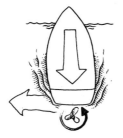

Prop walk is an important issue on single-screw boats. A right-hand prop will push the stern to starboard when going forward and to port when backing. (Illustration by Christopher Hoyt.)

seamanship. Twin-screw, single-screw, large or small—sooner or later all boats must be docked.

HANDLING A SINGLE-SCREW BOAT

Our trawler has a clockwise turning, or right-hand propeller. If you're not sure what type of prop you have, look at the rotation of the propeller shaft. If it turns clockwise when viewed from astern as the boat is moving forward, you have a right-hand prop; if not, it's a lefty. This discussion assumes a right-hand prop, but if you have a lefty, you should be able to figure out what to do.

Starting and Stopping

Prop walk may or may not have a great influence on how a boat behaves, depending on its displacement and hull shape. A lightweight, shallow-draft boat, for example, will have a strong tendency to swing to starboard when the throttle is opened, but a heavy, deep-draft boat will be affected less.

You need to experiment a little to discover how your boat will behave, and it's best to do this in open water. Come to a stop, and center the rudder. Then shift into forward and open the throttle about half way. Take a look at the wake, and note if the stern swings a little to starboard. If it does, keep this in mind every time you pull away from a dock. You'll notice that prop walk has the greatest effect on the boat before it starts moving forward. Once a boat gains headway, the rudder takes control and counteracts much of the side force created by the propeller.

Try shifting into reverse to stop the boat at different speeds and observe what happens. If you are traveling forward at more than a knot or so, you may hear a rumble when you shift into reverse. This is the propeller *ventilating* or *cavitating*. The prop is either sucking air from above (ventilating), or the pressure

between the prop and water is so high that small bubbles form at the tips of the propeller blades (cavitating). In either case the prop becomes much less effective. Remember this the next time you come into a marina at 4 knots: a boat does not have brakes like a car. The only way you can stop is to shift into reverse, but if the boat is moving too fast, reversing will not stop it in its tracks.

If you know what your boat will do when you put her in forward or reverse you can anticipate what will happen. You have to work *with* your boat, not against it.

Backing Up

Figuring out how to get a single-screw boat to back in a straight line can be one of life's great mysteries. Most of the boats we've owned could be steered once they were underway. The challenge is getting the boat to *start* backing in the right direction. When you shift into reverse, the prop walk will push the stern to port and as the boat picks up speed, the rudder will become effective. This is where finesse comes in. You must apply just enough starboard rudder to overcome the prop walk. Too much and the stern swings to starboard; not enough and it keeps backing to port.

While the boat is backing, the helm will have a different feel, since the water is now flowing against what is normally the rudder's trailing edge. The force of the water tends to push the rudder to port or starboard instead of straightening it out, as it does when flowing against the rudder's leading edge while going forward. (On *High Life*, with her cable steering, we can feel the rudder pressure through the wheel. If we let go of the helm, the rudder will move full port or starboard. There is less tendency for this to happen with hydraulic steering.)

Once the boat has gained *sternway* (moving in reverse), if it starts to veer off course to port, shift into neutral to stop the prop walk

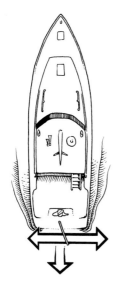

A boat with a single right-hand prop can be backed in a straight line by applying starboard rudder. As the boat gathers sternway, less starboard rudder is needed. (Illustration by Christopher Hoyt.)

and allow the rudder to steer the boat to starboard. If the boat continues to port, then turn the rudder to port and shift into forward to kick the stern to starboard. But if the boat starts to back to starboard, don't shift into forward until you have applied some starboard rudder, then give a quick burst of power. The prop wash hitting the rudder will push the stern to port.

Pushing the rudder to starboard will move the stern to port? Yes. When the boat is moving forward, a starboard rudder turns the bow to starboard and pushes the stern to port. Just remember that prop walk has the most effect before the boat begins to back—after that the rudder becomes effective.

Turning Around

Our 8-foot tender can turn in a complete circle while staying in the same spot, but *High Life* takes three or four boat lengths to complete a circle. In close quarters around docks and congested marinas, few cruising boats

have a small enough turning radius to make a 180-degree turn without some maneuvering. It's essential to master the skill of turning around in a confined area. Sooner or later you'll find yourself in a situation where you have to turn around and head back out the way you came in. Of course you can back up, but turning around is much easier. Take our word for it.

Once again, prop walk is the name of the game. Remember a right-hand prop pushes the stern to port in reverse and to starboard in forward. You can use this piece of knowledge to turn your single-screw boat around in its own length. Consider this scenario: you entered the wrong aisle in a marina by mistake and now you must turn around. The aisle is 75-feet wide and your boat is 36-feet long. What do you do? Put the helm over hard to starboard. As the boat begins to turn, it's obvious that you won't complete the turn before you hit the shiny cruiser on the starboard side of the aisle. Relax, shift into reverse, and apply some throttle, leaving the wheel turned hard to starboard. The boat will stop but prop walk will help swing the stern to port, just the direction you want it to go. As the boat gains sternway, shift back into forward and give another burst of throttle. This will kick the stern over before the boat gathers forward motion. The moment the boat begins to move forward, shift into reverse and do it all again. Once you have turned fully around, you can straighten the rudder and proceed forward. (Of course, if your boat has a left-hand prop, make the turn to port.) Using this technique we can usually make a 180-degree turn in three or maybe four cycles, depending on the width of the area.

A few warnings are in order. Most important, pull the throttle all the way back and pause in neutral for a moment as you go between forward and reverse, or your transmission will take a beating. Wind and cur-

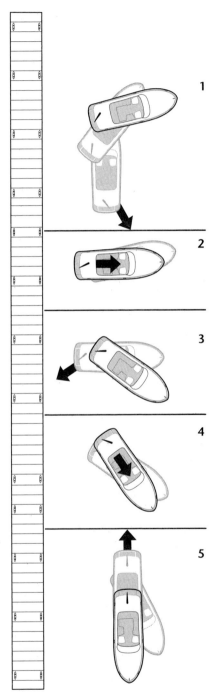

To make a U-turn in a single-screw boat with a right-hand prop put the helm over hard to starboard and alternate several times between forward and reverse. Each arrow indicates the direction of the prop wash. (Illustration by Joe Comeau.)

rent, especially a strong current, will also affect this maneuver, so you most often will not turn exactly on the spot. You *can* also make this a turn to port with a right-hand prop if you must, but it is much harder, as you have to work against the boat instead of with it. This means constantly turning the wheel hard to starboard every time you shift from forward to reverse and then back hard to port when you again go forward. As a result, you will not be able to make as tight a turn, and it will probably take longer. You can do it, but we don't recommend it.

Approaching a Dock

Plan your approach to compensate for the wind or current, heading into the current, if possible, and adjusting your approach angle to minimize the action of the wind. Assuming there is plenty of room along the dock, approach slowly into the prevailing current at a 20- to 30-degree angle. If there is a crosswind blowing you onto the dock, use a shallower angle. If a crosswind is blowing you off the dock, use a steeper angle. We usually put the boat in neutral well before we get close to the dock, and with our large rudder, the boat slowly responds to the helm. If you need more maneuvering power, shift into forward for a short time to push some water past the rudder and make it more effective. When you get close to where you want to tie up, put the helm over to bring the boat parallel to the dock and shift into reverse to stop it.

If the dock is on your port side, prop walk is a help, as shifting into reverse to stop the boat also swings the stern into the dock (with a right-hand prop). It's not so helpful for a starboard approach where hard stopping will swing the stern away from the dock. In this case, approach at a slower speed so you require less reverse power and produce less prop walk. Just as you shift into reverse, turn the helm hard to port to counteract the prop walk and swing the stern. If the stern is still too far from the dock, shift into forward and give a short burst of throttle to kick the stern in. But do so with care: you don't want the boat to move forward, or the stern to swing in so rapidly that it smashes into the dock.

Later in this chapter we'll describe how you can make docking less of a hassle by using docklines to your advantage.

Approaching a Slip

Before we approach a strange slip, we talk to the dockmaster, who gives us directions about where the slip is located. Usually Katie talks to him on a handheld VHF radio, and always asks if there is any current. She also asks if someone will be at the slip to catch our lines, and whether our port or starboard side will be lying on the finger pier. All this information gives us a better idea of the slip we're entering.

We put out six docklines: a bow line, midship spring, and stern line on both the port and starboard sides. We seldom need all of them, but we'd rather be prepared, instead of scurrying about at the last minute to change docklines from one side of the boat to the other because our slip assignment or the conditions change.

Unlike approaching a dock, you should approach a slip straight on, with the boat lined up with the slip. This isn't always easy, since you might have to contend with the wind or current. In most marinas the slips are laid out with aisles between the docks. As we turn down the aisle to the slip, we assess the wind and current and decide—before we turn into the slip—which lines should go on first. If we have crew, we make sure everyone knows what we plan to do. You have plenty of time to secure the boat in the slip on a calm day and no current, but if it's blowing, or there is a cross current, you have limited time to tie the boat down before it begins to drift, possibly into trouble.

When we start down the aisle and approach the slip, we stay close to the opposite side of the aisle to give us the most room to turn the boat into the slip and get it lined up. This can be tricky if the current is flowing in the same direction as the boat, in which case we stay closer to the middle, knowing that the current will push us toward our desired turning spot. Once the boat is lined up with the slip, we turn and go straight in.

Since most slips have a pair of pilings beyond the end of the dock or finger pier, as we enter the slip we place the *windward* (upwind or up-current) stern line over the piling. We've learned not to pull all the way into a slip until the stern line is secured on the piling, though we usually leave it slack so we can maneuver. Most of the time there is some help with the bow lines, but if the stern line is not in place and the boat is all the way in the slip, the stern can drift over toward a neighboring boat.

If you keep the stern of the boat outside the slip, the worst it can do is drift down and rest against the downwind piling. You can then concentrate on getting the bow secured. If you have problems securing the bow you can back out. But if the stern has drifted into the other slip you can't back out without hitting the piling, and things can get really interesting. That's usually when the door of the neighboring boat opens and the owners make a grab for their boat hook.

Backing into a Slip

The main reason we back into a slip is because it's easier to get on and off the boat at the stern, where our boarding gates are located. Many slips have finger piers that don't extend the full length of the slip, and on *High Life* the high bow and handrails make getting off the boat difficult from up forward. But there are times, mostly weather related, when backing into the slip with a single screw doesn't make sense. We would rather face the hassle of climbing over the bow than try to back into a slip in a blow.

That said, we should add that with a little practice, it's not all that difficult to back into a slip under moderate conditions if you keep in mind which way prop walk will push the boat. Remember, prop walk on a boat with a right-hand prop (clockwise rotation) pushes the stern to port, so if you're making a port-side approach you can use it to your advantage. That's the situation we'll describe now.

In our single-screw trawler it works like this. We slowly move down the aisle and don't get too close to the side of the aisle that the slip

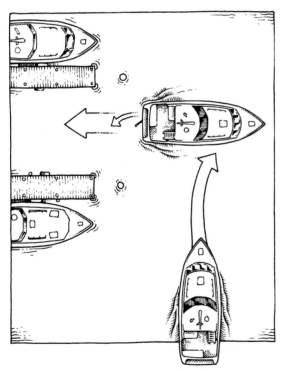

When backing a single-screw boat into a slip with a right-hand prop, apply right rudder to compensate for the prop walk that pulls the stern to port. If the boat backs to starboard, shift into forward to kick the stern to port. (Illustration by Christopher Hoyt.)

is on (port side, in this case). If we can, we allow at least a boat length or more between our boat and the bows of the other boats protruding out of nearby slips. Of course, we have to be careful not to get too close to the boats on the other side of the aisle either and, as we noted above, we must also consider the current.

We proceed slowly by using neutral as much as possible to keep our speed down, but also engaging forward often enough to maintain control. (The right balance of being in and out of gear is one of the things you learn with practice.) Every boat is unique, so you will have to work out your own correct approach speed and the right distance from the slip to initiate your turn.

On our boat, when the bow is about half a boat length from the first piling of the slip, we shift into neutral, put the helm hard over to starboard and shift into forward again. Turning the wheel while in neutral and then applying forward power *after* the rudder is hard over will guarantee a sharper turn, as the prop wash will work against an already-turned rudder. Halfway through the turn, we shift into reverse (after pausing for a moment in neutral to protect our transmission) and open the throttle slightly to stop the boat and swing the stern to port, but we leave the helm over to starboard.

If we've timed everything correctly, the boat will start backing into the slip. But if we are badly out of alignment, we simply abandon the maneuver and try again. It's never a good idea to try and make corrections once you've messed up in mid-approach. It's much easier to start over from scratch, so we simply circle around and make another pass.

If the boat is fairly well aligned with the slip, we proceed in reverse and the boat will tend to back to port until it gains sternway, when it will start to follow the rudder and move to starboard. Without moving the rudder we let the boat gain some sternway and then shift into forward and give a brief shot of power. The hard right rudder will swing the stern to port. A shift back into reverse lets the prop walk continue to push the stern to port, and as the boat picks up speed, the rudder steers it to starboard. When this happens, we shift into forward to straighten the boat.

Leaving the rudder hard to starboard may not seem logical since it causes the boat to move to starboard, but you can easily correct this by shifting into forward. It is much easier to have only two controls to work rather than trying to move the helm back and forth at the same time as shifting and working the throttle. Actually, with practice we've learned how and when to make the fine adjustments of throttle, reverse, forward, and neutral that usually allow us to back almost straight into the slip. Practice with your boat can work the same for you.

Of course if you're backing into starboard, everything will be just the opposite. And since you won't have the boat's natural tendency to swing to port in reverse to help you,

it will also be much more difficult. But if your slip is initially to starboard as you enter the aisle, and the aisle is wide enough, we recommend that you go past the slip, execute the 180-degree turnaround we described earlier, and approach it as you are heading out of the aisle. The slip will now be on your port side as you back into it. This requires a little more work to begin with, but it makes the backing in easier.

Handling a Twin-Screw Boat

Close-quarters maneuvering is easier in a twin-screw boat, but there is not too much difference once the boat gets underway. The rudders are generally smaller on this type boat and they are less responsive at slow speeds, especially when both engines are in neutral. *Old Grand Dad* had twins and we found it easier to steer the boat with the engines than with the rudders when going very slow. The main difference is that the opposite turning propellers cancel each other's prop walk forces when they are both turning forward or both are in reverse.

BOW THRUSTERS

Maneuvering any boat in adverse conditions is a challenge. Over a thirty-plus year period we've operated both sail and powerboats with single and twin screws, and so far we have only had a few close docking encounters where a bow thruster may have saved our bacon. There have been many times when a bow thruster would have made maneuvering *easier*. Bow thrusters make controlling even a twin-screw boat easier.

We put a bow thruster on a nice-to-have list. Would we like one? Sure. Will we have one installed on our 36-footer? Probably not.

As cruising boats get larger but are still operated with short-handed crews, a bow thruster can be a very important tool for maneuvering. Fending off a large boat is just about impossible for even the beefiest of crew. The extra control a bow thruster provides when working a large boat into its berth is a big help.

Going Straight, Backing Up, and Stopping

Twin-screw boats tend to start and stop in a straight line as long as both propellers are used for the maneuver. If both engines are not given the same amount of throttle when starting, the boat will veer away from the side of the faster-running engine. As with any boat, take her out in open water and get to know how she responds to the helm and throttles.

Backing is much easier with two engines than with one. If the engines are turning at the same rpm, the boat usually goes backwards in a straight line. The small rudders, however, are less effective at slow speeds, so it is usually easier to steer the boat with the shift levers. Once the boat has started to make sternway, shifting either of the engines into forward will cause the stern to move toward that side. In other words, if you shift the port engine into forward, the stern moves to port. When you shift it back into reverse, the boat will continue straight back in the new direction.

Approaching a Dock

Docking a twin-screw boat is not much different from docking a single-screw boat, but it *is* different. We use the engines to steer, as they're more effective than the small rudders at slow speeds.

Let's make an approach to a pier on our starboard. Our initial approach should be with both engines in gear at idle and, as with the single-screw trawler, at an angle of 20 to 30 degrees off the pier, depending on the wind. As we near the dock, we put both engines in neutral. This is partly to slow down a little, partly to confirm that our rudders are, indeed, centered. If they are, our direction shouldn't change appreciably when we go into neutral.

Now we have several options. If we put only the port engine in forward we will add a little speed, and the bow will swing toward the dock. If we put only the starboard engine in forward we will also add speed, but the bow will swing away from the dock. If we alternate between engines, putting only one engine in forward at a time, we will stay more or less straight while applying less power than using both engines. This could be useful if we have misjudged our speed and need more thrust to approach the dock.

When we're close to the dock, putting the port engine in forward will keep us moving toward the dock and bring the bow closer. Putting the port engine in reverse will help us stop and swing the stern in. If we are near the pier but want to move farther forward without bringing the bow any closer, we can put the starboard engine in forward (with the port in neutral). This will also help bring the stern in as the bow turns to port and straightens us out. Generally, putting the port engine in reverse will be enough to stop the boat and swing the stern in. But if we need more stopping power, and/or if the stern is swinging too much, also putting the starboard engine into reverse will usually make things right. When we have arrived, we put both engines in neutral and secure the lines.

Backing into a Slip

Backing into a slip with the added maneuverability of twin engines is considerably easier than with a single-screw boat. The boat can usually be aligned with the slip and then backed straight into it.

Assuming the slip is to starboard, come abeam of the slip and put both engines in neutral. Leaving the rudders amidships, shift the port engine into reverse and the starboard engine into forward. Swing the boat until it is almost aligned with the slip, then shift both engines into reverse and start backing into the slip. Use the propellers to steer the boat. For example, if the boat gets

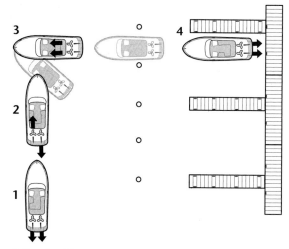

When backing a twin-screw boat into a slip, put the rudder amidships and steer the boat with the props by shifting the starboard or port engines as needed. (Illustration by Joe Comeau.)

together or separately, as necessary to keep the boat backing straight in and not hitting anything. When you are all the way into the slip, put both engines momentarily into forward. You'll stop in place.

USING DOCKLINES TO ADVANTAGE

A discussion of docklines may seem out of place in a chapter on boat handling, but experienced boaters know that a simple dockline used to advantage can solve 90 percent of boat docking hassles. How many times have you passed a bow line ashore and by the time it is secured the stern has drifted away from the dock? If you cruise with a small crew, securing both the bow and stern lines can easily turn chaotic.

too close to a piling on the port stern as you back in, shift the port engine into forward and the stern will move away from the piling. Then, once you are realigned, put the port engine into reverse again and continue backing in. Repeated use of neutral will allow you to approach more slowly. Just keep putting the engines back into gear,

AMIDSHIPS SPRING

We've had our fair share of docking fiascoes, especially when the wind was blowing the boat away from the dock. After one particularly landlubberly docking maneuver, we noted the uneventful arrival of another boat. No fuss, no hurry, no help needed, all because of a single well-placed line.

FENDERS AND LINES

For our 36-footer we carry six 8×26-inch fenders, three for each side of the boat. We prefer fenders with a rope tube end-to-end so a line can be passed through the center, rather than those with eyelet holes on both ends. A fender with a rope tube can be hung horizontally or vertically depending on where it's needed. In addition we carry two 15-inch round fenders that we use when we go through a lock, at a raft-up with other boats, or any other time we need additional protection for the hull. We also carry two fender boards, which we place over a couple of fenders to bear against pilings. Underway we carry six ¾-inch 35-foot double-braid docklines. We leave six similar docklines attached to the dock and pilings in our slip, so they're easy to retrieve when we return.

The line, of course, was an after-bow (or amidships) spring, a line secured to a cleat located between the bow and the stern (though usually closer to the bow), and led aft to a cleat on the dock. Once the spring was in place, the skipper put the helm hard over (away from the pier) to pin the boat against the dock and left the engine in forward gear. The boat stayed in place against the dock until the bow and stern lines were secured.

After witnessing this effortless maneuver we became converts to spring lines. Our boat has a large amidships cleat that makes this process easy, but a spring line can also be rigged from a bow cleat, though it won't work nearly as well. You may have to protect the boat from the dock if it doesn't rest comfortably while the lines are made fast. Our trawler has a hefty rubrail, so unless the dock is in very poor shape, positioning the fenders can wait.

There is always some discussion about whether to secure the end of a line to the dock and adjust it from the boat or secure it on the cleat and adjust the line from the dock. If there is someone to help with the lines on the dock, we pass the end of the line to that person. If it is a spring line, we also make it clear that it is *not* a bow or stern line and tell them where we would like it secured (forward or aft of the point we hand it to them). The person ashore then secures the line and we adjust it from the boat. If there is no help on the dock, then one of us goes ashore with the line already secured to the boat, wraps it around the dock cleat and adjusts it as needed from the dock.

Either way, powering slowly ahead with the helm turned away from the dock brings the boat against the dock. Then the bow and stern lines can be made fast, and a forward amidships spring rigged as well.

Putting out a forward bow (or amidships) spring (one that leads from the amidships

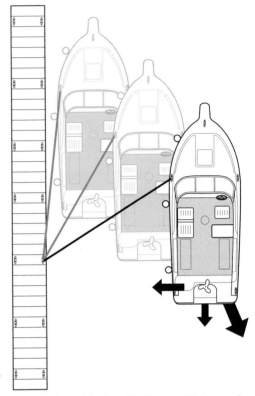

When docking with the aid of an amidships spring line, shifting the idling engine into forward with the helm turned away from the dock will move the boat against the dock and hold it there, as long as it remains in forward gear. (Illustration by Joe Comeau.)

cleat forward toward a piling or dock cleat) can also be an advantage when backing into a slip, as it will help prevent backing in too far. As when coming alongside, this spring will also hold the boat in place until all the other lines are rigged.

STERN SPRING

A spring line led forward from the stern (technically known as a *forward quarter spring*) can help when steering a boat back into a slip when it's windy or there's an adverse current. It can also be helpful for backing a single-screw boat against its natural prop walk ten-

DOCKING ESSENTIALS

Here's a recap of the docking procedure that usually works for us.

- Decide where to place the fenders as you approach the dock.
- Bring the boat close to the dock and put the boat in neutral to allow a crew member to hand off the spring line to a dockhand. If there's no one on the dock, someone steps off the boat with a spring line and secures it. If you use an after bow (or amidships) spring—a spring line that leads aft from a cleat that's closer to the bow than the stern—the rest of the maneuver will be almost automatic.

- The helmsman again places the boat in forward for a short time to put tension on the spring, with the helm hard over so the bow is heading away from the dock. This brings the boat against the dock. If the wind or current pushes the boat away from the dock the engine is left idling in forward.
- Stern lines are attached to pilings and then bow lines are secured ashore and on the boat.
- Fenders are secured.
- Engine is turned off.

---

dencies, or when a twin-screw boat has one engine down. (In this illustration it would be the starboard engine that's down. Without help from the spring line, backing on only the port engine would swing the stern to starboard, rather than into the slip.)

The maneuver goes like this. Have a spring line ready. As you begin the turn to align the boat with the slip, try to position the upwind—or up-current—side of the stern close to the first piling so that the crew can place a line on the piling. The crew then lets the spring line pay out from the stern cleat as you back the boat into the slip. When the boat is as far back as it can go without hitting anything—that is, just far enough to be able to clear the other piling—the crew secures the spring line. The stern is then pulled around as the boat pivots on the line. The crew may have to slacken the line to allow the boat to go back into the slip, but some tension must be main-

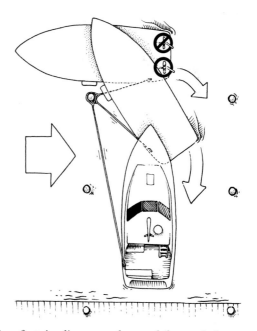

An aft spring line secured around the upwind or up-current piling will help pivot the stern into the slip. Once docked, move the line forward and reattach it to a bow cleat. (Illustration by Christopher Hoyt.)

USING LINES AND KEEPING THEM IN ORDER

Sometimes the most basic skills of line tending can be intimidating. When you need to secure a boat to a dock you often need to do so in a hurry, so it's important to know the best way to use a dockline. Also, storing all the lines aboard a boat in an orderly manner can be a challenge. If they're left loosely coiled in a locker, they uncoil and often become entangled with other items, making matters worse.

The skills required to use lines effectively and keep them organized aboard are easily learned. Here we've pulled together the basics that you need to know.

Look at the illustrations and read the steps to learn these knots, but more importantly, practice making them. You don't need to be on your boat; you can practice tying a bowline with a piece of string while you're watching television. Or practice coiling a piece of rope out in the garage. Practice until it becomes second nature. Then you'll feel competent and confident when you secure your boat to a dock or when another boater throws you a line.

Securing a line to a cleat

To secure a line to a cleat, put one complete wrap of the line around the base of the cleat to keep the line from slipping. Then make a figure-eight around the cleat and finish with a hitch by twisting the final turn so the tail emerges from underneath the line. (Illustration by Paul Mirto.)

Bowline

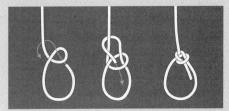

The bowline (rhymes with stolen) knot forms a loop at the end of a line. It is both secure and easy to untie, and the loop doesn't tighten under load, so it's useful for throwing over pilings to secure the boat. We think of the "rabbit hole" image when we tie this knot. Make a rabbit hole as shown in the first illustration. Picture the rabbit as the end of the line. It comes up through the hole, around the tree (or the other end of the line), then back down into the hole. That's it. (Illustration by Paul Mirto.)

tained throughout the maneuver to keep the stern from swinging the other way. When the boat is in the slip, the crew moves the spring to the bow and secures it as the bow line.

This technique accomplishes two things at once. The spring helps to pivot the boat into

the slip, and we also have the windward bow line already in place simply by moving the spring line forward, once the boat is in place. This maneuver takes a bit of practice, but it makes it possible to back into a slip when there's a crosswind, cross current, or other adverse condition.

Two half hitches

Two half hitches is a useful knot for securing a boat to a piling that's too tall to throw a loop over. Make two loops around the piling from the direction you want to pull the line. Then tie two overhand knots on the line leading to the boat. (Illustration by Paul Mirto.)

Clove hitch

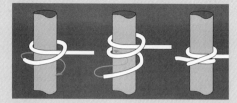

The clove hitch makes a good temporary hitch around a piling. It's quick and easy to tie to secure the boat while you adjust other lines, but don't use it for a long-term tie-up. It's also popular for tying up a dinghy. Make a loop around a piling with the tail passing under the line leading from the boat. Then make a second loop that crosses over the first loop. Pass the tail under the second loop and pull both ends of the line to tighten the knot. We use a clove hitch to secure fender lines to the hand railings. (Illustration by Paul Mirto.)

Rolling hitch

A rolling hitch is similar to a clove hitch with another twist or two. It's used to transfer a load from one line to another. With the free line, make two loops around the line that's already bearing a load. Pass the tail across the two loops and make a third loop, then pull the tail under this third loop to make a hitch. (Illustration by Paul Mirto.)

Coiling a line

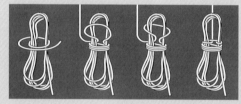

Keep lines properly coiled when not in use to prevent tangling. And coil up the loose ends of docklines to keep them out of the way. Hold the end of the line in one hand and begin coiling by making a loop about 18–20 inches long. Coil the line loosely in a loop and stop when about 4–5 feet remain uncoiled. Wrap three or four loops of this remaining part around the coil creating a "throat" at one end. To finish and secure the coil, loop the tail through the throat and over the top of the coil. (Illustration by Paul Mirto.)

WIND AND CURRENT

Under almost all circumstances, it's easier to maneuver a boat when you face into the wind or current. Unless it's blowing a gale, consider the effect of the current first. Water is a lot denser than air and even a tame ¼-knot current has more effect on a boat than 10 knots of wind. Of course there are exceptions. Wind may have more effect than a weak current on a cruiser with a draft of less than four feet, a high flying bridge, and a lot of canvas. *High Life* draws four feet and doesn't have a lot of canvas on the bridge, so in most circumstances the current rules our maneuvering decisions. But no matter what type of boat you have, remember that with a ½-knot following current, your boat must be going ½ knot through the water in reverse to be stationary over the bottom.

Before you attempt a landing, check the current carefully by looking at navigation marks or pilings and note on which side there is a current wake. If a strong wind is blowing counter to the current, stop the boat and see which force is greater. It takes a strong wind to push our boat up-current. Respect the strength of the current no matter what type of boat you have.

Maneuvering in a Current

The key to understanding how current affects a boat is to visualize where the current will take the boat if it's not moving through the water. Let's say there's a current moving at a speed of 1 knot. A boat with no way on (that is, stopped in the water) will drift at one knot in the same direction as the current.

Now if you put the boat into forward and steer into the current at a speed of 1 knot through the water what happens? The current is moving the boat backward at 1 knot and the boat is going forward at 1 knot, so it's really not moving over the bottom. But turn the boat around and all of a sudden it is going over the bottom at 2 knots.

This example is easy to understand. It gets a little more difficult when the boat is traveling *across* the current, but the principle is the same. See Chapter 21, Piloting and Navigation Basics, for an explanation of how to compensate for current when plotting a course.

Motoring into the current or traveling with it affects the speed of a boat, but a cross current affects both the speed and the direction it travels over the bottom. Holding a boat in position in a channel with a strong cross current can be a challenge. The best way to judge how the cross current is affecting your boat is to look behind you.

Channels usually have several markers placed along the edges but it's hard to tell if the current is pushing a boat sideways by only looking at the markers ahead. The boat can be pushed out of the channel even as you steer toward the next marker. But by looking back at the markers you just passed, if the boat is in the channel, the marker you are heading for and the marker you just passed will be aligned. You steer the boat down an imaginary line between the front and back marker. To put it another way: if you pass a marker on your starboard side, it should stay off your starboard quarter as you progress. But if it appears to be moving more directly behind you, you are drifting out of the channel and need to correct your heading to allow for the

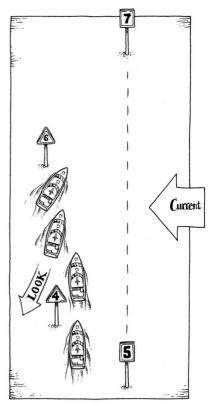

Don't forget to look behind the boat to see if a cross current is pushing you out of the channel. (Illustration by Christopher Hoyt.)

current by steering into it. In this case you would adjust your course slightly to port.

Remember it's the course that the boat makes *over the bottom* that determines where you go, and this is not necessarily the heading shown by your compass, which indicates the way your bow is pointed. This process of steering into the current (or wind) so that some other spot near the bow, rather than the bow itself, becomes the boat's point of forward progress is called *crabbing*, probably because a crab can move sideways while facing forward. If you could look at the boat from above, it would be going straight, but the bow would be pointed a bit up-current. In most cases, any time you're faced with a cross current and/or crosswind, you have to crab to stay on your intended course.

PASSING AND BEING PASSED

Sooner or later you are going to be passed by another boat or you will have to pass one. That can be either a pleasant or disruptive experience, depending on how each skipper handles the situation. In Chapter 17, Rules of the Road, we talked about the proper signals and who has the right of way. In open water this isn't a big deal, but in a channel, both boats will be close together, and proper technique makes all the difference. The most important point to remember when you are being passed is to slow right down, because unless you decrease speed, it's impossible for an overtaking boat to pass without creating a wake.

If you run at 10 knots and slow down to 5 knots to allow another boat to pass, a large displacement boat can often overtake you without creating much of a wake. Large planing boats may or may not create a wake, depending on the speed at which they pass. If they're going slow enough the wake will be mild, though still greater perhaps than that from a large displacement boat. Small planing boats, however, quite often create a nasty wake because they have to *plow* to attain a good passing speed that's slower than their planing speed.

Plowing occurs when a planing boat is no longer in displacement mode but not yet up on plane. Due to its high running angle, the boat creates a disproportionate wake. So if a smaller fast boat wants to pass, you have to slow way down unless it can go by on plane, which will depend on how much room there is and if there are any speed restrictions. If you slow to idle and the boat still passes with a big wake there is not much you can do about it, but at least you are not *forcing* the boat to pass with a wake.

Don't slow down until the passing boat is close astern. Then cut the throttle and let your boat come to idle speed. After the other boat passes, steer your boat to get behind the passing boat to avoid the big wake it may create as it accelerates away. This move cuts down the rocking and rolling on your boat. Be cautious and remember that a large boat can create a *huge* wake as it accelerates to get up on plane.

When a passing boat is close astern, throttle back to idle speed.

Once the passing boat is safely ahead, move behind it while the wake is still small.

When passing another boat, you should go as slow as the other boat's speed allows. You don't have to slow down until you are close to it, since your wake trails your boat. The actual distance will vary since each boat slows down at a different rate. We have to slow to 5 knots or less before *High Life's* wake lies down. If the boat you pass doesn't move behind you after the pass, then move your boat in front of it as soon as you are safely clear before you accelerate to cruising speed.

Stay behind the passing boat to avoid the large wake it will create as it accelerates to cruising speed.

HANDLING THE BOAT AROUND BRIDGES AND LOCKS

Extended cruising will bring you face to face with both bridges and locks, especially on the East Coast. With the increase of both boat and car traffic, many older bridges are being replaced with high, fixed bridges, but there are still plenty of old low drawbridges spanning rivers and waterways that must open to let boats through. Boats tend to pile up at bridges and locks waiting for passage, so you may be in for some close maneuvering.

Negotiating Bridges

Today most bridge tenders answer the VHF radio, and they monitor either channel 9 or 13. A call to the bridge will almost always raise a response from a bridge tender who is courteous and professional. If you disagree with a tender about an opening, remember you'll never win the argument. He or she has ultimate control and decides when to open the bridge. A polite "We'd like to request your next opening," gets the best results.

Several years ago on a return trip from the Bahamas we decided to come into the waterway at Cape Kennedy and continue north. When we approached the Bridge of Lions at St. Augustine, we knew it was restricted between 7:00 A.M. and 9:00 A.M. so we got there before 7:00 A.M. and blew the horn (today we would use the VHF radio), and nothing happened. Finally after circling and tooting and circling and tooting, we called the bridge tender and asked why the bridge didn't open, since it was 6:15 A.M. and there were no opening restrictions until 7:00 A.M. He answered in a cool southern drawl saying, "Be informed the local time is 7:15 A.M. and the bridge will not open until 9:00 A.M." Of course, everyone in the United States except us had reset their clocks to Daylight Saving Time so we sheepishly thanked the bridge tender, dropped the anchor, and enjoyed a leisurely breakfast.

If you can't establish contact via VHF, the standard sound signal is one prolonged blast followed by one short. This is also the signal the bridge tender will sound just before he or she opens the bridge. Please remember that if a bridge is on a restricted schedule, a tender may not respond to either the VHF call or a whistle signal until it is almost time for the bridge to open (though many will be courteous enough to inform you of the length of your wait).

Unless your boat requires less than 10 feet of overhead clearance, no matter where you cruise sooner or later you will probably have to wait for a bridge to open. Whenever our trip brings us toward a bridge with restricted hours, we have to decide if we should continue at cruise speed and get to the bridge early and wait, or slow down and arrive shortly before it is scheduled to open. Speeding up is usually not an option since we cruise at less than 8 knots with a top speed under 9 knots.

The advantage of arriving early at a bridge with restricted openings is the possibility that the bridge will open for a commercial

Wait for the bridge to open fully. Then approach cautiously; stay mindful of overhead clearance.

vessel. The passage of such vessels is not restricted. When it happens, we give a cheer to the vessel and scurry behind it under the open bridge. Otherwise we sit at the bridge and wait for it to open.

While waiting for a bridge to open, you have to make a decision. You can drop the anchor and wait it out or maneuver in idle, maintaining position head to current by matching boat speed and current speed. With a following current, turn around, face the current and move slowly away from the bridge. Don't allow the boat to drift close to the bridge; the current gets stronger as it runs under the bridge.

If there are boats waiting on both sides, some bridge operators will direct traffic and announce which group should go first. If the bridge tender doesn't do this, then the inland rules (See Chapter 17, Rules of the Road) apply and give boats traveling with the current the right of way. However, don't count on other boaters knowing and abiding by the rules.

If you're waiting for oncoming traffic to clear a bridge opening, don't proceed without looking for late arrivals. Several times we've waited for all the circling boats on the up-current side of the bridge to clear only to find a straggler coming at us full speed trying to make the opening. If you can't make it through the bridge with the waiting boats, ask the bridge tender to hold the bridge and let the boats on the other side pass before you go through. Don't barge in, even if you have the right of way.

Another point to remember—and we learned this from years of cruising in a slow sailboat—is to let the faster boats move to the front of the line and go through the bridge first. We still can't figure out why some sailboats or slow powerboats go to the front of the line to be the first to go through the bridge, and then complain when a string of powerboats passes them. Go figure!

Negotiating Locks

Many of the popular cruising areas of the country are linked together by rivers and manmade canals. Where the canals were constructed with sections at different elevations (determined by the contours of the landscape), they have locks that allow vessels to go from one level to another.

At both ends of a conventional lock there are watertight doors that close and seal the lock chamber. To *lock up* (go to a higher level), the gates at the lower end of the lock are opened, and boats enter and tie off using their fenders to protect the boat from the sides of the lock wall. The lock tender will instruct the entering boats and direct them to the lock walls, where lines usually hang for crew members to hold on to. In some locks, boaters use their own lines by running one end through or around the rung of a ladder in the wall. The accumulated exhaust from several boats can be overwhelming in an enclosed lock chamber, so you're required to shut your engines down until the locking process is finished.

When all the boats in the lock are secured, the lower gates are closed. Valves at the upper level of the lock are opened so that water from this level floods into the lock, raising all the boats inside it until the water level in the lock chamber matches the level outside the upper gates. As the water rises, crews on the boats in the lock chamber adjust the lines. When the gates at the upper end are opened, soon after the water levels match, the lock tender instructs the boaters to drop the lines and proceed out of the chamber.

For a down cycle, the process is the reverse. Note, however, that when locking down, you will be entering the chamber with the current behind you. If you are not really careful in approaching the wall, especially if you are in a single-screw trawler, it is very easy for the current to catch your stern and swing you around 180 degrees. One way to avoid this is to approach the wall at a very shallow angle. But if it happens, go with it. Then use the 180-degree turnaround maneuver we described earlier to get you headed in the right direction as you leave the chamber after locking down.

The actual process of locking through is straightforward. As you approach a lock you first encounter an *arrival point*, usually with instructions to wait for a green light to proceed into the lock. When the lock is in use, boat traffic has to wait for it to fill or empty, so there is a designated holding area at each side of the lock. When you get to the arrival point, call the lock on VHF channel 13 and request to lock through. Ask on which side the lockmaster wants you to tie up, so you can hang fenders. Sometimes you're allocated a side, sometimes you can choose. Then wait until the lock tender tells you to proceed into the lock or you see the green light.

The good thing about locks is that they are all pretty much the same. Some are larger than others, but they operate in much the same way whether the rise is a few feet or many. There are exceptions, for example, the Big Chute Marine Railway on the Trent-Severn Waterway linking Lake Ontario to Georgian Bay, Canada. This engineering marvel is not technically a lock, but it takes boats from one water level to another by transporting them over a 57-foot rise or fall in a giant carriage between the Gloucester Pool and the Upper Severn River.

The Trent-Severn Waterway also employs hydraulic lift locks that operate more like conventional locks but use less water. A lift lock is a self-powered machine that is used in place of conventional locks where there's a great difference in level within a short distance. There are two such locks on the Trent-Severn system: the Peterborough hydraulic lift lock, with a lift of 65 feet, the highest of

When you enter a lock, make sure your fenders are down and your crew is ready to work the docklines. (Photo by Migael Scherer.)

its kind in the world, and the Kirkfield lock, with a lift of 49 feet.

In these locks, there are two identical movable chambers: one at the high level, one at the lower. As one chamber moves up, the other moves down. These chambers are basically large watertight boxes, each end of which is closed by a gate. There's also a gate at the end of the canal. A boat enters one of the chambers; both chamber and canal gates are closed. This leaves the chamber independent of the canal channel, and free to move vertically. The raising of the lower chamber is achieved by filling the upper one with about a foot more water than is in the lower, thus making it heavier. As it descends, it pushes the other chamber up when the valve connecting the two is opened. The system is amazingly efficient.

The entire chamber, with the boat and water in it, is then raised or lowered to the other level of the canal. By opening the gate at the other end of the chamber, and the gate at that end of the canal, the boat can again pass out into the canal.

CHAPTER 19
Anchoring

Anyone who tells you they've never dragged anchor is either bending the truth or doesn't anchor very often. Simply getting the hook to set is the first challenge, and it can be an exasperating task if you have to deal with changing tides and currents.

We had a humiliating experience the first time we anchored our new (to us) trawler in Mile Hammock Bay, North Carolina, one of our favorite anchorages on the Intracoastal Waterway. On previous visits to this anchorage we had never had a problem anchoring our sailboat, and we rode through the nights safe and snug. On the trawler, however, we had a heck of a time getting the anchor to set, under the watchful eyes of neighboring boats that we knew were enjoying our drill. Eventually we got it set, and then it dawned on us that we had forgotten to increase the scope to compensate for the extra height of the powerboat's bow. When we let out more rode the anchor held.

CHOOSING AN ANCHORAGE

Choosing an anchorage is more of an art than a science. The ideal anchorage should have a good holding bottom and provide shelter from wind and waves from all directions. It should be deep enough to keep the boat afloat at low tide, but not so deep that you have to let out an excessive amount of anchor rode. Of course there are few places that exactly meet these conditions, so most anchorages are a compromise at best.

Every cruising area presents unique challenges. In some parts of the country, like the Pacific Northwest or the Florida Keys, water depth is a major factor. Areas with many coves and islands that would otherwise offer good protection from the sea and wind are sometimes either too deep or too shallow. The lower cays of the Bahamas offer protection from the sea but very little from the wind.

The first thing we do when deciding where to anchor is to listen to the weather forecast—both the current conditions and the forecast for the next couple of days. We've found that the NOAA weather forecasts are generally right on in telling us what weather to expect, though they're sometimes off target about when these events will actually happen. So if the forecast sounds good for the night, but a weather change is on the way, we look for an anchorage that will be good for both the current and the upcoming forecast conditions, in case the change arrives early. You know the situation: a forecast predicting a sunny day and light south winds today and a weather change tomorrow afternoon, but at 4:30 A.M. it's blowing 15–20 knots from the northeast, and there's not a star in sight.

Of course an anchorage that provides good protection from Mother Nature's wind and waves is our first choice. But it's also important to find one that provides protection from the wave action created by other boats. A spot on the chart that looks like a great place to spend the night but is open to the wake of passing boats can make for very uncomfortable sleeping. If we don't have an alternative we'll tough it out, anchor where there's boat traffic, and hope it falls off after sunset. But many a time we've been awakened in the dead of night by a lumbering tug and barge passing by. Shrimp boats seem to take special pleasure at rocking an anchored boat. But the shrimper goes by this point every working day, and we are anchored in his channel, so we are the intruders, not him. Before you anchor in what may seem like a quiet branch of a creek check the chart to see if there is a shrimp or fishing dock just around the bend.

You can also be anchored in what appears to be sheltered water and still get wave action that reflects off a nearby island. If you're in the lee of a small island or close to the end of a large one, waves may bend around the island. You may get protection from the wind, but the waves swinging around the island can make the anchorage almost unbearable. In this situation, the boat will lie head to wind but roll like crazy as the swells come in broadside.

We try to avoid an anchorage with depths of more than 25 feet when the weather is predicted to turn sour. In some parts of the country, that isn't considered deep, but we prefer an anchorage with 10 feet at low tide. That's deep enough to prevent our boat from hitting the bottom in a large swell, but shallow enough so we don't need to let out hundreds of feet of anchor line to allow for a storm surge that can add several feet to the normal high tide.

In addition to protection, there must be room for the boat to swing should the wind or tidal current shift. If you have let out 100 feet of anchor rode, the boat will swing in a circle with nearly a 200-foot diameter. Make certain that the water is deep enough inside this area and that your boat will not interfere with others at anchor.

Finally, we have to find a bottom with good holding. All of the other characteristics don't matter much if the anchor drags. Our CQR or Danforth can set in most bottoms, but we have trouble in sea grass and rocky conditions. The Danforth might set, but it can have trouble resetting if the wind changes. The CQR tends to be better in grass, but neither is very good in rocks. However, for mud, clay, or sand they are our first choice.

PROPER SCOPE

Scope refers to the ratio of the length of anchor line—from the ship's bow to the anchor—and water depth. In our earlier discussion on anchors we mentioned that they produce most holding force when the pull on the anchor rode is parallel to the seabed. The greater the scope, the more horizontal the pull on the rode. That sounds simple, but many cruisers forget to take into consideration the height of the bow when they are working out how much scope they need. This is not a big factor on smaller powerboats, since a couple of feet won't matter in any but the worst of conditions. It's a different case with mid- to large-size powerboats. In each of the following examples, for instance, we add 6 feet to the water depth because that's how far *High Life*'s bow stands above the surface of the water.

In normal conditions, a scope ratio of 7:1 is considered adequate for a rope/chain anchor rode and 5:1 for all chain. In 10 feet of water we basically use all chain (the first 100 feet

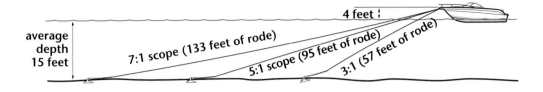

15 feet of water + 4 feet of freeboard = 19 feet
7:1 scope means 7 x 19 = 133 feet of rode

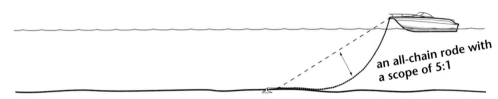

A scope ratio of 7:1 is usually adequate for a rope/chain anchor line and 5:1 for all chain. Don't forget to allow for the height of your bow above the water. (Illustration by Joe Comeau.)

of our rode is chain), so we'd let out at least 80 feet of chain—(10 + 6) × 5 = 80. If our anchor line consisted of 30 feet of chain and the rest rope, we'd let out at least 112 feet of anchor line—(10 + 6) × 7 = 112. As wind and chop build, more scope may be needed, and in storm conditions, the more scope the better.

TIDE

In tidal waters, the depth in an anchorage changes with the state of the tide. In areas with a small tidal range of a couple of feet or so, the depth change is really not significant. But remember that for every foot of increase in depth, 7 feet of anchor line (5 feet of chain) should be added to the total. If there's a tidal range of 7 feet, and the depth of the water is 8 feet at low tide, it will be 15 feet deep at high tide, which would require more than 100 feet of line or chain. Of course if you enter at high tide, the line you let out will be adequate when the tide goes out. Just be sure that you aren't sitting on the bottom at low tide.

DROPPING THE HOOK

Having the proper ground tackle is only half the battle. If you don't set your anchor properly it won't hold. After watching the anchor drill of many cruisers, we've concluded that the single biggest mistake most seem to make is deploying the anchor and line before the boat has begun to back down. If you do this there's a good chance the anchor, chain, and line will end up in a pile on the bottom.

To prevent this, and to ensure that the line does not tangle around the anchor, the boat should face the wind or current, whichever is stronger, and be stopped dead in the water before you drop the hook. It's not easy to tell when you've stopped moving through the water. One way to check is to lower the anchor until it just touches the water; if the anchor does not make a wake, you are stopped. Then it's a matter of lowering the anchor until it hits the bottom. A chain rode often wants to run free as soon as it's released, so this can get tricky. Only let out enough chain or rope until the anchor rests on the bottom. Then

MARK YOUR ANCHOR LINE AND LINE CHAIN

Mark your anchor line so you can easily estimate the length of line you've let out. In twisted line, insert inexpensive colored plastic labels at intervals of 30 feet. On chain, use spray paint. We have two marks on our chain, one at 50 feet and the other at 75 feet, because we rarely use less than 50 feet of chain even in shallow water, and we try to avoid anchoring in more than 15 feet of water.

when the boat starts to back (as it usually will by the natural action of the wind or current, though we always help matters by putting the boat in reverse at idle), let the chain or rope out a little at a time, keeping slight pressure on the line.

We used to pull into an anchorage, select our spot, stop, drop the anchor, gradually back up until the proper scope was out, then secure the anchor line to stop the boat and set the anchor. After that we'd reverse the engine to test the holding. This worked OK with our sailboats, but it's not adequate for a powerboat with its added weight and windage. Now we apply more power in reverse and wait. We run the engine at 1,000 rpm and wait, then at 1,200 rpm and wait. At 1,200 rpm the pull is equivalent to about 5 knots of boat speed and it puts a real strain on the anchor. If bad weather is forecast, we rev up even more. We'd prefer to pull the anchor out before we settle in for the night than to find that it's dragging at 2:00 A.M. during a squall.

Most times the anchor digs in and we are set for the night, no matter what the weather. At other times, even after the anchor seems to be set, we begin to slowly drag. It may reset and really dig in or not. If it doesn't, we pull it up and try another place. We've found that the trick to getting the anchor set deep is to be sure we've let out enough scope before really powering up. If the anchorage is crowded and we're satisfied that the anchor is set, we pull in some chain to reduce the radius of our swing, but we know the anchor is set deep and secure.

HOW TO PREVENT CHAFE

As wind increases, so does the strain on an anchor line. Nylon line under tension will chafe if it is allowed to rub against a rough object. Under severe strain, the line can rub so hard that it actually starts to melt. Protecting the anchor line from chafe, even during calm conditions, will lengthen its life and ensure that your anchor system performs well.

The standard rubber chafe guards sold at most marine supply stores work well. It's important to use one that fits your line. If the guard is too small for the size of rope it won't fully close over the line. When it's bent over the edge of a deck or a dock, the edges will separate, exposing the line to chafe.

Let the anchor line out to the proper scope and set the anchor before you apply the chafe guard. After you are satisfied the anchor is set, fit the guard about a foot or so back from the point where the line passes over the roller or through the chock. After the guard is secure, let the line out just far enough so that only the first third of the guard passes over the roller or chock. Then it will protect the line even when it stretches under strain.

CHAIN HOOKS AND SNUBBERS

An all-chain rode does not need to be protected from chafe, but a chain rattling back and forth over the roller can be annoying. In rough conditions the chain may pull tight between the boat and anchor resulting in a loud thud and extra strain on the anchor and chain. A chain hook spliced to a length of nylon line, called a *chain snubber,* can solve this problem. When you've set the anchor, attach the hook to the chain just forward of the bow roller or chock, make the line fast, then let out more chain until the snubber goes taut as it takes the strain. The stretchy nylon acts as a shock absorber for the chain, and line moving over the bow roller is quieter than chain.

A chain snubber is easy to make. Most marine suppliers sell chain hooks. They are made to fit a particular chain size, so check your chain before you purchase one. The nylon line should be long enough to reach the water from the bow of the boat, or longer. We made ours longer than necessary, about 30 feet, so that if the wind pipes up

A snubber, made up of stretchy nylon line, can be attached to the chain with a chain hook. It absorbs the shock of the boat bobbing up and down in rough conditions.

and we feel it's necessary to let out a bit more anchor chain, we can easily let out the snubber line. With a short snubber you have to pull up the chain until you can reach the snubber, remove the hook, then let out the extra chain and replace the snubber.

Another type of snubber is in the form of a bridle. Attach two snubber lines to either a chain hook or a stainless plate with a slot in it to engage the chain. Lead the lines through the chocks on either side of the bow. Boaters who use this type of rig say it reduces the tendency of the boat to tack back and forth at anchor.

USING A SENTINEL

For ages, mariners have used a heavy weight on the anchor line, a *sentinel,* to make it sag and to help keep the line running parallel to the bottom. This is an effective device, but we use what we call a mini-sentinel for an entirely different reason. We place a small weight of a pound or so—right now it's an old zinc—on the rope part of our anchor line to make sure it hangs downward when it's not under tension. The idea is to make sure the nylon line doesn't get tangled on anything under our boat. This is always more of a concern on a boat with exposed props and rudders.

Frequently we use two anchors set off the bow when we're anchored in a current. Depending on tide and wind conditions, one of the anchor lines is often not under tension. Nylon will sink, but in a current it can stream out behind the boat, making it possible for a swinging boat to get tangled up with the slack anchor line. But with a mini-sentinel, the line is pulled directly to the bottom and cannot cause a problem.

The mini-sentinel has its own line, and when we've placed the weight on the anchor rode we let out enough of the line until the weight hits the bottom. The light weight doesn't do much to reduce the angle of the line, but it keeps the rope on the bottom. Of course, a chain anchor rode hangs straight down when not under strain.

WEIGHING ANCHOR

Pulling the anchor up is usually straightforward, but there are ways to minimize the strain on back muscles and windlass. Here's how we do it.

First of all, we start the engine. Our windlass draws a lot of current, so we want the engine running before we engage it. Then, unless it is dead calm, we use short bursts of forward engine to move the boat slowly toward the anchor. Using engine power takes the strain off our windlass, but we also move slowly because the anchor chain needs to be washed before it goes below.

We pull in the chain until the muddy section is almost to the bow roller, then we hose it off. Then we raise more chain and hose that off. In calm conditions, the weight of the chain is often enough to pull the boat forward until we are over the anchor. In a blow, one of us will continue to put the boat in forward occasionally to lessen the load on the windlass. When the rode is straight up and down, we power ahead to break the anchor out, clean everything off, and stow the anchor in the roller.

To pull in a nylon line, we motor ahead slowly and pull in the line by hand. When we get to the chain, we secure the line and clean the chain section by section. After the anchor is secured in the roller, we stuff the line and chain below. Without a very good *hawsepipe*, a tube that allows the rope to run below freely, it takes too much time to stuff the line below while pulling it in. The boat loses momentum and begins to back down on the anchor line before we can get it below.

USING A TRIP LINE

In areas where there are a lot of snags on the bottom for the anchor to get caught on, we use a trip line. The line is secured to the body of the anchor so that it can be pulled at a direction different from that of the anchor rode. A float tied to the other end of the trip line keeps it on the surface of the water. If an anchor gets caught on an obstruction or snags while you're weighing anchor, a pull on the trip line will hopefully release it. If the anchor won't budge, the trip line lets you know where the anchor is so you or a diver can find it later. If you're in tidal waters,

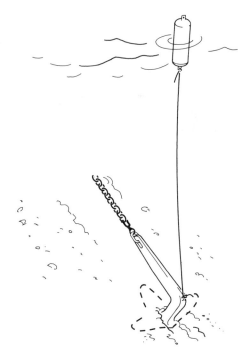

A trip line attached to the base of the anchor will allow you to pull it backward to free its flukes from obstructions on the bottom. (Illustration by Jim Sollers.)

make sure the trip line is long enough to stay on the surface when the tide comes in.

ANCHOR TECHNIQUES TO MEET SPECIAL NEEDS

There are many ways to set an anchor or combination of anchors, but we rely basically on three techniques: a single anchor off the bow, two anchors set at 180 degrees to each other in a *Bahamian moor*, or two anchors off the bow set at about 90 degrees to each other. An anchor can also be used to pull the boat off the bottom if you run aground.

SINGLE ANCHOR OFF THE BOW

Most of the time we swing to a single hook, our trusty CQR, even if the wind shifts or the current changes. No magic here, just good ground tackle.

BAHAMIAN MOOR

When anchoring in a narrow creek or an area with strong currents, we use the Bahamian mooring technique. This two-anchor arrangement reduces the swinging radius of the boat as currents shift, but still allows it to pivot 180 degrees to face the current. And you don't have to worry about the anchor breaking out when the tide changes.

First we set the upwind or up-current anchor and then drift away from the anchor by paying out twice the scope we need. Next, we drop the second hook and pull the boat back toward the first anchor until the boat is centered between the two anchors. Then we set the second anchor by pulling the anchor line tight. (The first anchor has already been well set, so it prevents the boat from moving back.) Then let out about 20 feet of extra line for each anchor so the boat has some room to move. We drop the CQR first since it takes

longer to set. The Danforth anchor sets faster, with less pulling, and makes a good second drop.

The Bahamian moor is also a good technique when there's a chance of a strong wind blowing against a strong current. With a single anchor, the wind can blow the boat forward past the anchor and break it out. One blustery night we were anchored in a Georgia river, and went out to check the anchor after the wind picked up. We were surprised to see the main anchor line slack. The wind was just strong enough to push the boat forward through the water against the current, but not strong enough the turn it head to wind. The second anchor prevented the boat from riding up over the other anchor and breaking it out.

Note that both anchor lines are run from the bow of the boat in a Bahamian moor. We

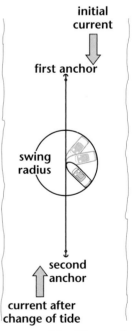

A Bahamian moor consists of two anchors, one up-current and one down-current. It allows the boat to face the changing current with a small radius of swing. (Illustration by Joe Comeau.)

don't think that an anchor secured to the stern is a good idea. For one thing, the shape of the bow is better suited to taking any seas that may build up while we're at anchor. In fact, a small boat anchored by the stern alone may have so little freeboard aft that waves can break over the transom and flood the boat if conditions turn really nasty. Larger boats may not have this problem, but they ride more comfortably with the bow to the weather, so it's best to let the boat come head to wind or current and anchor from the bow.

We do, however, tie off to trees and other objects ashore at times and drop a stern anchor if we pull up to a beach with a steep slope. But only, of course, when the weather is good.

TWO ANCHORS SET FROM THE BOW

When a storm is predicted, or when a single anchor won't hold, we use two anchors off the bow, ideally set about 90 degrees apart. Usually they end up 60 or 70 degrees apart, since there is seldom that much room in the typical crowded anchorage.

We usually drop the first anchor to one side of where we want to finally lie, pay out the anchor line and set it. Then we power ahead and away from the first anchor. That keeps the anchor line from fouling the prop and gives us an idea where the first anchor is. When the first anchor line runs out abeam we drop the second anchor and fall back. We check that the first anchor line can't foul the prop, then we back down on the second anchor.

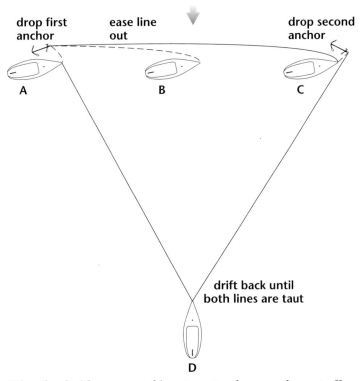

When faced with an approaching storm, two heavy anchors set off the bow at about a 60 to 70-degree angle will increase the holding power. (Illustration by Affinity Design Group.)

KEDGING OFF

When we were discussing anchors in Chapter 11, we mentioned that it's handy to have a small lightweight anchor in case you run aground. You can use the anchor to pull the boat off.

This process is known as *kedging*, most likely since one of the early forms of anchor was known as a kedge, and the old term lives on. A smaller anchor is easier to place in the dinghy than the heavy primary anchor. Here's what you do. Assuming the water is calm and it's safe to be in a dinghy, lower the anchor, chain, and line into the dinghy and head for deeper water. Make sure you have enough scope to reach the area where you want to set the anchor. It's easier to pay the anchor line out from the dingy as you move away from the boat than drag the anchor line from the boat. Lower the anchor into the water and have the crew on board the boat haul on the line. Once the anchor is set, use this anchor and rode to pull the boat free of the bottom. If the boat won't budge, the anchor will at least keep it from moving further aground, especially if the tide or wind is pushing the boat toward the shoal.

HOW TO GET A GOOD NIGHT'S SLEEP AT ANCHOR

Anchoring is one of our favorite aspects of cruising, but we're always concerned when we rely on a hunk of iron to keep us safe. Many a night we have tossed in our bunks and listened to the wind howl as the boat tacked back and forth on the anchor line. When it was choppy we moved from the forward cabin to the bunks in the center of the boat, where there was less motion. Those were long nights and, at times, some days were not much better. But even during the worst, we had confidence in our ground tackle and took positive action to see that we were not dragging anchor.

The knowledge that you have not moved from the spot where you anchored goes a long way toward lowering anxiety, even in the foulest weather conditions. It can be a terrifying feeling in the middle of the night in a crowded anchorage when the wind picks up. You go out on deck to check the anchor line and all the boats, including yours, are tacking back and forth on their anchors. In those conditions it's difficult to tell if you or others are dragging. Here are a few techniques we use to check that we have not moved.

HAND BEARING COMPASS

We use a hand bearing compass to take the bearing of at least two, preferably three, landmarks. We plot them on the chart and record the bearings in the log. To verify our location later, we take new bearings on the same objects, and if they stay within a few degrees of the original observations, we know the boat has not moved from its original position. At dusk, we pick out a new set of landmarks, usually lights on a dock or streetlights that we hope will stay on all night for later reference, and again take bearings.

If the wind shifts or the tide changes, the relative position of everything around the boat changes. A 180-degree shift means that everything that was on the port side is now on starboard. If we have 100 feet of rode out the boat will have moved nearly 200 feet downwind or current from its original position, even though the anchor (we hope) is still doing its job. Again, we have to take new bearings, plot them on the chart, and check if our change of position has put us in an area where the boat can swing safely.

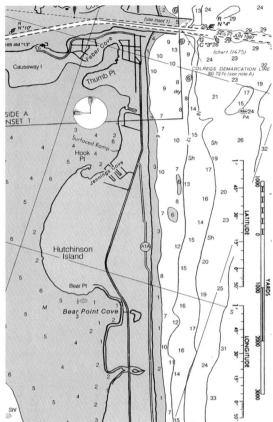

When choosing an anchorage, remember that a boat at anchor will move to face the wind or current. It will swing in a circle with a diameter twice the length of the anchor line.

RADAR AND GPS

Technology such as radar and GPS make fixing a boat's location easy. Radar can be used to take bearings on landmarks for later reference. Radar sets have either electronic or physical *bearing markers* that measure the relative bearings of contacts displayed on-screen. By setting the bearing marker on several identifiable landmarks you can obtain a fix. If you leave your radar set on standby during a blow, you can check it periodically to see if the bearings to the objects have changed. Radar sets with two EBLs (*elec-*

tronic bearing lines) can be set up and the bearing lines left on the landmarks. A quick look at the radar will show the bearing lines still pointing to the landmarks if the boat has not moved.

Most GPS sets have an *anchor watch* feature that sounds an alarm when a boat moves beyond a specific zone or area. This *alarm zone* is a useful and reliable sentry to ensure a good night's sleep. When we were anchored off Great Sale Cay in the Bahamas—not known for its good holding ground—a squall came through in the middle of the night, blowing hard from the south. Unfortunately, we were on the south side of the cay so we had no protection. When the GPS alarm went off at 2:00 A.M. we were rousted out of our bunks. We checked our new position with the bearings we had logged on arrival, and this confirmed that we had dragged at least 50 yards. The track on our GPS/plotter clearly showed our progress out of the alarm zone. We reset the anchor and launched a second one.

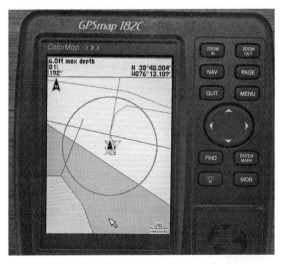

Many GPS receivers have an anchor watch alarm. Don't set the size of the alarm zone too small or the alarm will sound with every wind shift or change of tide.

You can adjust the size of the alarm zone to allow for the length of the anchor line. We usually set the alarm soon after anchoring with a value of 50 feet. If there's enough swing to keep setting the alarm off, we increase the value. Or, you can keep the value low so that the alarm feature will also act as a wind indicator: when there is a big wind shift the alarm will go off. This is can be useful information for the skipper. In tidal waters, where you will experience a 180-degree shift in current, you need to increase the alarm zone setting. It must be at least double the length of the anchor line. If you have 100 feet of anchor line out, set the alarm for 200 feet. The boat will move almost that far from its original position when it swings around to face the other way as the tide changes.

ANCHOR WATCH

If the wind really blows and we are worried about the anchor not holding or other boats dragging onto us, we take turns standing anchor watch. One of us stays awake during the night so the other can sleep.

MINDING YOUR MANNERS AT ANCHOR

When we ask cruising friends how other boaters in an anchorage annoy them, their answers primarily concern noise. Barking dogs, boisterous partying, loud generators, blaring television sets or music—all offensive noises that are amplified on the water. Other annoyances include boaters who anchor too close, boaters whose poor anchoring allows their boat to drag, and boaters who leave their vessels unattended during a storm (when there's a good chance they'll drag). It should go without saying that common sense and common courtesies make for an enjoyable and safe anchoring community.

USE AN ANCHOR LIGHT

Inland and international rules state that any boat at anchor must exhibit a white 360-degree light so that it is clearly visible. Many boats come equipped with such a masthead light, which is powered by the boat's battery.

This light should be displayed from sundown until sunrise when at anchor. The only exception is when you are anchored in a designated anchorage, but even then it's not a bad idea to display this light.

Our biggest challenge is to remember to turn the light off in the morning. Many a time we have arrived at an anchorage and went to turn the anchor light on only to find it was already lit. There are anchor light assemblies that have a built-in light sensor that turns itself off when the sun comes up. That sounds like a great idea but then the light will come on when we are docked. We're still working on this situation; feel free to give us a call on the VHF if you notice a trawler happily cruising along with their anchor light on.

CHAPTER 20

Weather

Boaters who cruise the coastal waters of the United States are seldom cut off from a source of weather information.

One of the best sources for boaters is VHF radio. There are few areas of the country where you can't pick up a marine weather forecast on VHF. Local radio, television and cable television also offer forecasts continually, or so it seems. And the Internet is bristling with weather data collected by the government and other sources. With all this information at our fingertips, there is no reason to be surprised by changing conditions.

Forecast predictions are usually correct, but their timing isn't always precise. Even with supercomputers at their disposal, meteorologists must live with the reality that weather forecasting is not a precise science.

In this chapter we'll concentrate on a few basic weather concepts, and then we'll take a look at sources of free information, new forecasting technology, and commercial marine weather forecasters.

FRONTS AND OTHER EVENTS

Most of the weather events that a coastal cruiser deals with are caused by *frontal passages* created when air masses with different temperatures meet. Heavy, cold air creates high pressure, and lighter warm air creates low pressure, but air temperature is relative. What's considered warm air in the winter may be cold air in the summer. It's the *difference* in temperature between the two air masses that creates weather along the front. Air flows from areas of high pressure to areas of low pressure. The greater the difference in pressure, the faster the airflow, or wind.

COLD FRONTS

A cold front is a line along which cold air replaces warm air. As lighter warm air is displaced by heavier cold air, it rises over the cold air and, if the warm air contains enough moisture, clouds and precipitation form. The passage of the front is associated with a shift in wind direction and a noticeable temperature change.

Depending on the temperature difference between the colliding air masses, the front can produce little rain and mild winds or violent thunderstorms with heavy winds. The larger the pressure difference between the air masses, the stronger the winds the front will produce as it passes.

WARM FRONTS

At a warm front, lighter warm air replaces heavier cold air. It's basically the same process that takes place at a cold front, but in order for the warm air to displace cold air, the heavier cold air must recede. The warm air travels faster than the receding cold air and overruns it, essentially climbing up over it. As the warm air mass rises, it loses heat to the cooler air below, and moisture within the warmer air condenses. As a result, clouds and precipitation form.

PRESSURE GRADIENT

A pressure gradient reflects a difference in barometric pressure between cold and warm air masses. The greater the difference, the stronger the winds and, generally, the worse the weather. When a cold front arrives—as may happen when a cold air mass with temperatures in the mid-60s approaches after a

INCHES OF MERCURY OR MILLIBARS?

Why both? And what's the difference? Well, in the 17th century a scientist named Blaise Pascal showed that the height of a column of mercury varied with changes in atmospheric pressure. So the initial unit of pressure became the height of that column, expressed as millimeters of mercury (mm Hg) in the metric system and inches of mercury (in. Hg) in the Imperial system.

But since pressure is correctly defined as a force acting over a unit area (pounds per square inch or psi is a perfect example), some years back the scientific community adopted a pressure unit called the *bar* for standard use in international weather observations. Average sea-level atmospheric pressure is 1.01325 bars, which is also 29.92 inches of mercury.

For ease of plotting and analyzing weather maps, the millibar (or one-thousandth of a bar, abbreviated as mb) became the standard for everyday use. Thus, 1013.25 mb denotes one standard, sea-level atmosphere of pressure. Although the millibar is common elsewhere, the United States has been slow in adopting this terminology, and we've continued to use inches of mercury as the publicly

reported pressure measurement for many years. We have slowly come around for certain applications.

As if the confusion between inches of mercury and millibars weren't enough, in recent years the scientific community has also taken to renaming certain measurements in honor of the men involved in their discovery and development. The name for the standard unit for pressure has changed as the bar was replaced by the *Pascal* (Pa). One sea-level atmosphere of pressure, or 1013.25 mb, became 101,325 Pa.

This basic unit is too clumsy for general use in meteorology, so atmospheric pressure was initially measured as the *kilopascal* (kPa), which has evolved further to the *hectopascal* (hPa). Fortunately, perhaps, 1 hectopascal is exactly the same as 1 millibar, and 1013.25 hPa is the same as 1013.25 mb.

Though scientists now prefer the term hectopascal, it is still less commonly used than millibars in U.S. meteorological reports, and our TV weathercasters are still inclined to state the atmospheric pressure in inches of mercury.

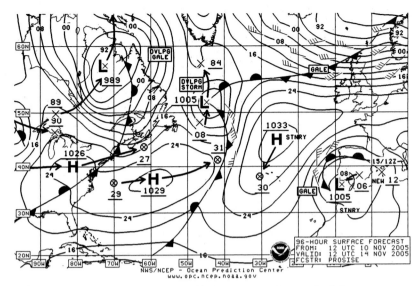

Isobars on a weather map look like depth contours of a nautical chart.

week of hot weather in the high 90s—it has the potential to create hazardous boating conditions.

To display this information, meteorologists plot points of known pressure, measured in millibars (mb), on a weather map and then connect them to form lines of equal pressure called *isobars*. Your ship's barometer is usually calibrated in mb, inches of mercury, or possibly both.

Isobars are like the depth contour lines on a nautical chart. When they are close together they signify a steep change in pressure (a high pressure gradient). The faster the pressure changes, the faster the air flows from high pressure to low, and therefore the higher the wind speed.

HIGHS AND LOWS

Areas of low and high pressure are usually associated with fronts as they develop. In the Northern Hemisphere, air circulates in a clockwise direction around a high-pressure area and counterclockwise around a low. The spacing between the isobars shows the strength of the high or low. Tightly spaced lines indicate a fast change in pressure that signifies an intense area with high winds. Widely spaced isobars, especially around a high, indicate moderate to light winds. Closely spaced isobars anywhere on a weather chart indicate strong winds. Adjacent pressure systems can combine to create areas of very high winds where the isobars are compressed between the pressure systems.

The main point to remember is that it is the rate of change in the atmospheric pressure that makes high winds. A gradually changing barometer signals changing weather, but a rapidly falling or even rising barometer indicates a rapid pressure change and possible high winds. It can be very windy even on a clear day.

FOG

On any extended cruise, especially in the summer and fall, you can expect to encounter fog. When you are underway, you must deal with low visibility, but if you're in port, you have a choice. It could be a good time to roll over in your bunk, go back to sleep, and plan a day ashore. Or you can decide to bite the bullet and get underway. Fog is elusive and some types burn off as the sun rises, others don't. Here's the rundown.

ADVECTION FOG

This type of fog occurs when warm, moist air flows over colder land or water and is cooled to near or below its *dew point temperature*. When the air temperature falls below this point the moisture in the air turns to fog. With light winds, the fog near the ground or on the water can become thick and reduce visibility to zero. You can't count on this type of fog to burn off with the rising sun. It may last all day or for several days.

RADIATION FOG

A chilly night may allow the ground or water to cool enough so that water vapor in the warmer air above it condenses, forming what is often called *ground fog*, because it hugs the surface. You may be in clear visibility on the flying bridge, while the rest of the boat is blanketed by fog. Radiation fog will normally disappear soon after sunrise as the sun warms the air and evaporates the moisture.

SEA SMOKE

This kind of fog forms over cold seas when cold, dry air blows over seas that are actually warmer than the air. Some of the water evaporates into the lower layers of the air. As the air warmed by the water rises, it mixes with colder air above. The mixing cools the moist air enough to begin condensing some of the water vapor back into tiny droplets, causing fog.

WEATHER INFORMATION

When it comes to weather data, we have certainly entered the information age. Free data is available on the Internet—via a laptop, cell phone, or personal digital assistant (PDA)—and from broadcasts over VHF and SSB radios and fax receivers. Voice, text, and graphical forecasts are available for all coastal waters of the United States and the high seas. Most of this data is gathered for either military or commercial use.

The challenge in making a list of the primary sources of weather data is that it's constantly changing. The U.S. government is the prime source of weather data, but others are taking the raw data and making it available in more user-friendly forms that can be displayed in navigation programs. The Canadian government is also a provider of weather data for the Great Lakes and Canadian coastal waters. And there are several private weather forecasting companies that supply free basic services.

Ten VHF channels are dedicated to weather broadcasts, but in coastal regions, NOAA is currently using mostly channels WX1 (162.55 MHz), WX2 (162.4 MHz), and WX3 (162.475 MHz). You don't really have to know which one applies to your present location because each station has a short range (about 35 miles or so). The strongest signal you can receive will probably be the one you want. Listen for a while and the station will eventually identify its location and coverage area. If you do happen to get the wrong station, try again. But even a different station will be close by, so any information it gives may still be valid.

Many cruising guides list the channels that apply to the areas they cover. If you want to be really thorough, NOAA lists all available stations at http://weather.gov/nwr/listcov.htm.

NOAA

The National Oceanic and Atmospheric Administration (NOAA) collects weather and climate data gathered by the National Weather Service, military services, Federal Aviation Administration, and Coast Guard. The agency prepares marine forecasts for U.S. coastal waters and the high seas, and all these products are available on its vast website.

NOAA also prepares and distributes many of these forecasts by voice over VHF and SSB radios. Its weather maps are available by high frequency radio fax. The map images can also be downloaded by any device capable of accessing the Internet, which includes cell phones and satellite phones.

Bay and Coastal Marine Forecasts

Virtually the same coastal forecasts you receive over the VHF radio are available in text format at the NOAA site (www.nws.noaa.gov/om/marine/zone/usamz.htm). This page is a map of the coastal waters, which makes it easy to choose the local forecast area you want. It's best to use the text-only interface (www.nws.noaa.gov/om/marine/wxibay.htm) if you're downloading the information over a cell phone.

Regional Surface Forecast Weather Maps

NOAA transmits weather maps to weather fax receivers worldwide over HF (high frequency) radio. Many cruising boats carry these receivers, which print out the maps as they are received, though as we'll explain in a moment, they are not absolutely necessary.

NOAA also transmits text forecasts and essential weather information for mariners, known as NAVTEX, which can be received and printed by dedicated NAVTEX receivers. Most weather fax machines can also receive and print NAVTEX.

```
FZUS54 KLIX 111522
CWFLIX

COASTAL WATERS FORECAST
NATIONAL WEATHER SERVICE NEW ORLEANS LA
922 AM CST FRI NOV 11 2005

PASCAGOULA TO ATCHAFALAYA RIVER OUT 60 NM

GMZ555-575-120030-
/O.ROU.KLIX.MA.F.0000.000000T0000Z-000000T0000Z/
COASTAL WATERS FROM PASCAGOULA MS TO THE SOUTHWEST PASS OF THE
MISSISSIPPI RIVER OUT 20 NM-
COASTAL WATERS FROM PASCAGOULA MS TO THE SOUTHWEST PASS OF THE
MISSISSIPPI RIVER FROM 20 TO 60 NM-
922 AM CST FRI NOV 11 2005

THIS AFTERNOON
NORTHEAST WINDS 10 TO 15 KNOTS. SEAS 2 TO 4
FEET. PROTECTED WATERS A LIGHT TO MODERATE CHOP.

TONIGHT
EAST WINDS 10 TO 15 KNOTS. SEAS 2 TO 4 FEET. PROTECTED
WATERS A LIGHT TO MODERATE CHOP.

SATURDAY
SOUTHEAST WINDS 10 TO 15 KNOTS. SEAS 2 TO 4 FEET.
PROTECTED WATERS A LIGHT TO MODERATE CHOP.

SATURDAY NIGHT
SOUTHEAST WINDS 10 TO 15 KNOTS. SEAS 3 TO
4 FEET. PROTECTED WATERS A LIGHT TO MODERATE CHOP.

SUNDAY
SOUTHEAST WINDS 10 TO 15 KNOTS BECOMING SOUTH 5 TO
10 KNOTS IN THE LATE MORNING AND AFTERNOON. SEAS 1 TO 3 FEET.
PROTECTED WATERS A LIGHT TO MODERATE CHOP. ISOLATED SHOWERS AND
THUNDERSTORMS.

SUNDAY NIGHT
SOUTH WINDS 5 TO 10 KNOTS. SEAS 2 TO 3 FEET.
PROTECTED WATERS A LIGHT CHOP. SCATTERED SHOWERS AND
THUNDERSTORMS IN THE EVENING...THEN ISOLATED SHOWERS AND
THUNDERSTORMS AFTER MIDNIGHT.

MONDAY
SOUTH WINDS 5 TO 10 KNOTS. SEAS 1 TO 3 FEET. PROTECTED
WATERS A LIGHT CHOP. ISOLATED SHOWERS AND THUNDERSTORMS.

TUESDAY
NORTH WINDS AROUND 20 KNOTS. SEAS 3 TO 5 FEET.
PROTECTED WATERS ROUGH. SCATTERED SHOWERS AND THUNDERSTORMS.
```

National Weather Service
Generated 1557 UTC, Friday, Nov 11, 2005
Document URL http://weather.noaa.gov/cgi-bin/fmtbltn.pl?file=forecasts/marine/coastal/gm/gmz555.txt

The National Weather Service provides up-to-the-minute forecasts on its website (weather.noaa.gov).

Weather maps can be downloaded at www.opc.ncep.noaa.gov. The fax and NAVTEX broadcast can also be picked up by an SSB receiver and displayed on a PC with the right software and interfacing.

A 24-hour regional surface forecast can be downloaded from the NOAA website as a black-and-white GIF file that is best displayed on a PC screen. NOAA describes this map as a surface forecast that covers adjacent and offshore waters of the eastern and western United States. Using computer graphic workstations, these surface forecasts, showing high and low centers, are prepared twice daily.

They show surface pressure with a 4-millibar contour interval and the direction and speed of air movement in knots for the next 12 hours. The forecast map includes the location of fronts, troughs, ridges, areas of fog, and likely areas of freezing spray, when applicable.

The 24-hour regional wind and wave forecast can also be downloaded from the NOAA website. The accompanying example shows the Pacific coast, but maps are also available for the Atlantic coast. These charts are based on the regional surface forecast and depict forecast winds (in knots) and significant wave heights (in feet).

The 48-hour surface forecast map is generated twice each day for each ocean: at 0000Z (midnight UTC, or Coordinated Universal Time—also known as Greenwich Mean Time); and at 1200Z (noon, UTC). It is based on computer modeling, with input from the U.S. Navy's Operational Global Atmospheric Prediction System (NOGAPS) and also input from foreign sources, such as the Canadian Regional Model.

The maps show surface isobars or lines of equal pressure every 4 mb, with labeling of two digits like 32 instead of 3200 mb. The cen-

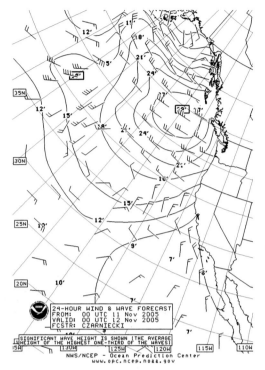

Regional wind and wave forecasts are published for both the east and west coast and offshore waters.

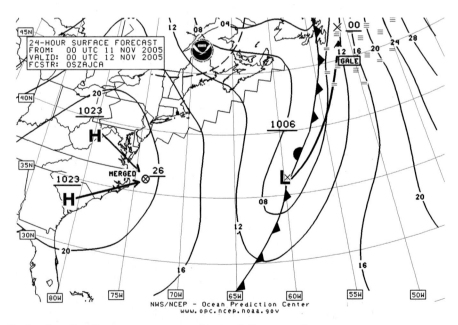

Regional surface forecasts are generated twice daily on weather.noaa.gov.

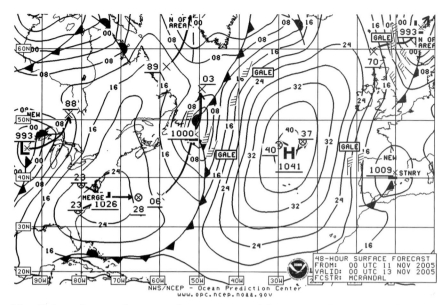

The 48-hour forecast shows weather patterns and their expected movements for the next 2 days.

tral pressure value, in millibars, of lows and highs are shown in bold and underlined displaying the first three or four significant digits, adjacent to or under the "L" or "H." The expected movement of the system for the next 72-hour forecast is shown by a vector line with an arrow indicating the direction of its movement. The new position is drawn as an "X" for low centers and a "circled X" for high centers.

The 48-hour surface forecast depicts surface wind speeds in knots. They use *wind barbs*, the featherlike projections at the end of wind indicators. Each full barb indicates 10 knots, each half barb indicates 5. The direction of the indicator stem (the other end from the barbs) shows the wind direction. Significant systems have labels depicting whether they are expected to have *gale* or *storm* conditions. If 72-hour forecast gale or storm conditions are expected, the appropriate area has the label *developing gale* or *developing storm*.

All NOAA weather maps use the same symbols. A complete guide to all its maps and reports is available for download at www.opc.ncep.noaa.gov/UGbegin.shtml. This guide is available as a text-only version or an Adobe Acrobat file.

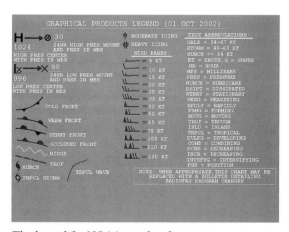

The legend for NOAA weather forecasts.

METEOROLOGICAL SERVICES OF CANADA

The Canadian government operates a weather site that provides forecasts for Canadian inland and coastal waters, with regional and offshore marine forecasts and buoy reports for any region in Canada. The website includes public and marine weather warnings, hurricane information, satellite imagery, 5-day weather, and other climate data.

Cruisers operating on the Great Lakes or planning a cruise there will find the *Tide & Current Tables* maintained by the Canadian Hydrographic Service a useful resource. Information on tides, currents, and water levels are available for 700 Canadian locations (at www. waterlevels.gc.ca/english/Canada.shtml). High and low tides, as well as hourly height values, are presented in graphical, tabular, and text format for seven-day periods up to a year in advance and within the past year.

INTELLICAST

Intellicast.com is a large website that specializes in weather reports designed to help you plan all outdoor and weather sensitive activities, whether golfing, boating, hiking, or skiing. The service provides radar and satellite images and an extensive set of weather maps.

The site is graphics-heavy, so it's time consuming to access it by cell phone.

THE WEATHER CHANNEL AND ACCUWEATHER

These websites have up-to-the-minute weather information, including water surface temperatures, wind conditions, and buoy reports. Both sites require that you enter the zip code of the area of interest, which is easy enough to find on the U.S. Postal Service's website (http://www.usps.com). These are useful sources for major storm updates and long-range forecasts.

SOUTH BOUND II ON SINGLE SIDEBAND RADIO

Herb Hilgenberg provides a daily ship-routing/weather forecasting service, as a hobby, on marine HF/SSB frequency 12359.0 kHz, from 2000 UTC to 2200 UTC or until completion of traffic. He uses 8294.0 and 16531.0 kHz as alternate frequencies from time to time, subject to radio propagation conditions. Herb started doing these forecasts while living in Bermuda and has continued since retiring to his native Canada. The idea came about in 1982 when Herb and his family were heading

FREE WEATHER SOURCES	
Name	Website
National Weather Service (NOAA)	www.nws.noaa.gov
Meteorological Services of Canada	www.weather.ec.gc.ca/marine
Intellicast.com	www.intellicast.com
Weather Channel	www.weather.com
Accuweather	www.accuweather.com

south aboard their boat *South Bound II* (hence the name of his service) when they encountered weather far worse than, and quite different from, the conditions that the weather services were calling for. Herb's services have grown over the years, and he now communicates with an average of 50 vessels per day (it can peak to 80 in prime season), seven days a week, from his home in Burlington, Ontario.

EMERGING WEATHER TECHNOLOGY

Most graphic weather maps are actually computer pictures, primarily in the GIF format. Even though these files are compressed, they still need to be quite large to hold enough detail to be useful.

An emerging format called GRIB, which is short for *Gridded Binary*, is a unique form of weather and ocean data. Instead of an actual picture, the file contains a database of points and symbols that describe the weather map. Software on the client computer uses the GRIB data to create the weather map in a manner similar to the plotting programs that read vector chart data and construct a visual image from it.

GRIB data is special because of its size, information content, and versatility. Generated by weather and ocean models operating on regional, national, and sometimes global scales, GRIB files associate an environmental variable with a geographic position. The resulting file consists of just a collection of these points, is extremely small, and readily transferred over bandwidth-limited satellite phones, cell phones, and other wireless devices.

Some commercial weather services have developed software to decode and display GRIB data files. NOAA is beginning to experiment with this format and has GRIB data files available for download. Nobeltec and

Raymarine have released navigational software that can display GRIB data as an overlay on their chart displays.

Global Marine Networks (GMN) is now offering forecasts as a public service via its GRIB Mail Robot. The forecasts are generated daily for every region of the world. GRIB forecasts are based on the National Weather Service Wave Watch III model, yielding highly accurate forecasts every six hours for up to seven days into the future. All GRIB forecasts are delivered via e-mail and optimized specifically for low-bandwidth wireless connections. E-mail gmngrib@globalmarinenet.net for information on how to receive free GRIB forecasts.

COMMERCIAL WEATHER SERVICES

Commercial weather forecasters have served aviation, trucking, shipping, and marine industries for years. Some have developed products to service the cruising boater and many specialize in providing high-seas weather information. Some, however, have developed products that can be useful to the coastal cruiser. Here is a short rundown on the popular services.

ROUTING SERVICES

These services will prepare a customized weather prediction package for a specific voyage. Most also offer general weather data and predictions.

Applied Weather Technologies

This professional weather routing service will prepare a customized weather package and provide updated information for a particular voyage. It has also developed software for real-time weather analysis that is updated over a wireless device.

Jenifer Clark Gulf Stream Analysis

Jenifer Clark offers unparalleled insights into the dynamic nature of the Gulf Stream. Racing sailors use these analyses to help navigate the intricacies of the stream. They are also available on the WeatherNet, a product offered by OCENS (see below).

Commanders Weather Corp.

This professional weather routing service for cruisers and commercial yacht delivery skippers provides suggested date of departure, routes, and updates en route.

Locus Weather

This service provides custom forecasts for ocean voyages and yacht races, and general marine weather forecasts.

Weather Window

Bob Rice's Weather Window provides weather route forecasting for racing sailboats, and detailed delivery and cruising forecasts for sail and powerboat voyages.

Weatherguy.com

This service specializes in route planning and supplying detailed weather forecasts and tactical weather routing for yacht racers.

Yachtweather.com

Fleetweather Ocean Services provide voyage-planning support between any locations in the world.

GENERAL WEATHER SERVICES

These weather services offer more general products, which may include worldwide weather, and can be accessed by most devices with wireless connections like cell phones, Globalstar satellite phones, Iridium, Inmarsat M/F, SSB/HF Pactor III, Geosat Solutions, and generic Internet connection (dial-up, DSL, ISDN, broadband).

OCENS

This service provides real-time weather updates and software using a wireless or satellite phone connection. The software receives weather faxes, charts, and satellite images over wireless devices and the service has developed a GRIB viewer. Its WeatherNet database also supports the GRIB format.

BuoyWeather

This service can provide more than 500,000 unique forecast points based on NOAA's WAVEWATCH III, GFS, and ETA weather models. You can get an instant marine or weather forecast for any point on earth. The forecasts are identified by latitude/longitude rather than named locations. You can use the Web interface and click on a preset location to generate a forecast, or create virtual buoys with the tools provided on the site. The Buoy-Weather system then compiles a custom weather forecast for the position of the virtual buoy.

BuoyWeather also provides marine weather e-mail services designed for low-bandwidth HF and satellite e-mail systems. By sending a specially formatted e-mail message to their server, you are able to get seven-day wind/wave forecasts; set up automatic daily forecasts; and receive NOAA buoy reports, official text forecasts, and five-day passage outlooks.

Skymate

This service provides satellite equipment to send and receive e-mail, get weather faxes,

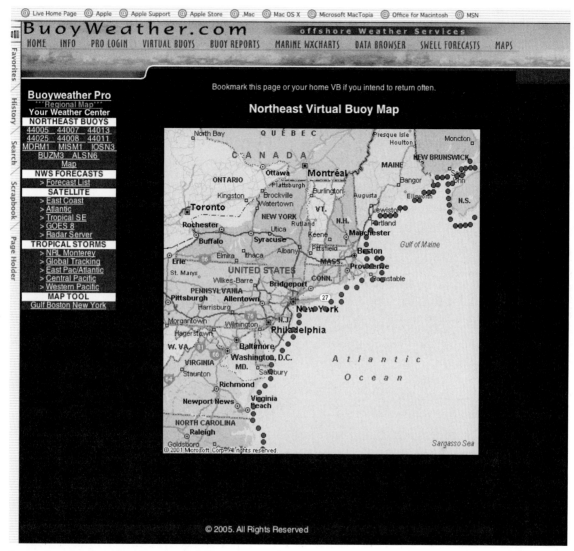

A page from the BuoyWeather.com website.

and report your position on a regular basis. The weather reports are based on your current position.

WSI
Weather Channel Marine delivers personalized and up-to-the-minute marine weather and forecast information by satellite broad-cast. The same type of graphics available on the Weather Channel website are overlaid on charts. The service requires a satellite receiver and software.

The Caribbean Weather Center
This service provides forecasting services for the cruising community with daily SSB

COMMERCIAL WEATHER SERVICES

Name	Website	Telephone
Applied Weather Technologies	www.appliedweather.com	408-523-8000
Jenifer Clark	www.erols.com/gulfstrm	410-286-5370
Commanders Weather Corp.	www.commandersweather.com	603-882-6789
Locus Weather	www.locusweather.com	207-236-3935
Weather Window	www.powercruising.com/ricewxwin.html	603-569-4700
Weatherguy.com	www.weatherguy.com	808-291-9949
Yachtweather.com	www.yachtweather.com	800-343-4567
OCENS	www.ocens.com	206-878-8270
BuoyWeather	www.buoyweather.com	
Skymate	www.skymatewireless.com	866-759-6283
WSI	www.wsi.com/solutions/marine	978-262-0735
The Caribbean Weather Center	www.caribwx.com	

WeatherNet, daily e-mail forecast, offshore single-passage weather routing, and phone-in routing and consultation.

All these services provide information above and beyond what NOAA supplies on its VHF weather channels. That said, we have to admit that while this extra data can be extremely valuable for sailing or offshore cruising, it is perhaps way more than you need for coastal cruising. We love weather, and enjoy really digging into it. If, like us, you want a detailed picture of the weather that lies ahead when getting underway, any of these sources can be quite useful.

CHAPTER 21
Piloting and Navigation Basics

Except for an occasional run offshore, most coastal cruising takes place within sight of land and requires only basic piloting skills. Even with the most sophisticated electronics aboard, every skipper should have a grasp of these techniques and concepts, and feel confident enough to use them if the GPS and radar fail to work. They are easy to learn, and the tools are inexpensive.

This chapter is by no means a course on navigation; it's a synopsis of the techniques we use most often when underway. In Chapter 9 we discussed navigation equipment. Here we will show you how to put it to use with both a low-tech and a high-tech approach.

CHARTS AND NAVIGATION AIDS

Even with the most elaborate navigation system, no boat should depart on a cruise without a basic supply of paper charts. Chart kits, spiral-bound books that include all of the necessary charts for a given area, are probably the most economical solution. There are kits for most cruising areas, arranged logically in regions, like *Norfolk VA to Florida including the Atlantic Intracoastal Waterway*; *Block Island RI to the Canadian Border*; *Chesa-* *peake and Delaware Bays*; *Florida East Coast and the Keys*; *The Bahamas*; and others. There are also kits for most river and canal systems.

These chart kits cost far less than what you'd pay for the individual charts they contain, but they still add up rather quickly on an extended cruise. Add this to the cost of the electronic versions, if you use them, and you can easily invest hundreds of dollars. You don't need every chart of every scale, but don't skimp. An up-to-date paper chart won't malfunction or crash, and it doesn't need batteries or any other source of power that can fail just when you need it most, so paper charts may be your best investment.

When planning a cruise, get the charts you need before you depart because they're an invaluable planning tool. Don't wait to buy charts when you get to your destination. Local charts are often the most popular and may be sold out.

A paper chart displays information that is not always immediately available on the corresponding electronic chart. To access all of the information on an electronic chart, you may have to do some clicking. But on a paper chart, all the information you need is right in front of you. Here's how to understand its basic features.

CRUISING THE GREAT WHITE NORTH

Cruisers planning to enter into Canadian waters can obtain charts for these areas from most navigation equipment stores and many nautical book stores. The charts are very similar but be sure to purchase *Chart #1* and study it because there are differences in U.S. and Canadian charts. For example Canadian charts use Lowest Normal Tide for their sounding datum while U.S. charts use Mean Lower Low Water.

THE LEGEND

Charts are produced in many different scales, and it's important to know what units of measurement are used. This basic information is printed in the legend that identifies the chart by name and number. The legend includes additional details, like the chart's scale, whether the soundings (water depths) are in feet, fathoms (an ancient nautical measure that equals six feet), or meters.

Scales showing *longitude* are printed along the chart's top and bottom edges. Longitude is the imaginary north-south lines that run from pole to pole and are measured in degrees east and west from longitude zero that runs through Greenwich, England. Scales showing *latitude* are printed along the chart's sides. Parallels of latitude are imaginary lines that run east-west, parallel to the equator, and measure our distance north or south. Distance scales are printed on the chart also, usually in nautical miles and yards. Some charts, especially those for inland waters, are also scaled in statute miles. The latitude scale can also be used as a distance scale since one minute of latitude equals one nautical mile.

DEPTH AND BOTTOM CONDITIONS

The water depths, or soundings, are printed all over the chart. In areas where the depth is constant, fewer soundings are indicated (though be aware that charts based on old surveys, which you may encounter from time to time, especially for cruising areas outside the United States, may show few soundings because few were taken). Some charts will show areas marked "wire dragged to __ feet." This means the entire area so designated will be at least as deep as the wire drag depth. Even with many close-together soundings, there can still be spots that are shallower but not shown on the chart because they didn't get sounded. A wire drag eliminates any such surprises within the dragged area.

The bottom contour is shown on the chart by connecting like soundings with a line. For example, by drawing a line through the 10-foot soundings along the shore, it is easier to see where the water depth varies by looking at the contour line rather than trying to read each individual sounding. All water seaward of the 10-foot contour line is generally at least 10 feet deep. Gradually sloping bottoms have widely spaced contour lines; steep changes in the bottom are marked by closely spaced contour lines.

Charts also show the makeup of the bottom. The abbreviations for these conditions are covered in *Chart No. 1*. Rocky (*rky*), hard (*hrd*), and soft (*sft*) are the bottom conditions most commonly found.

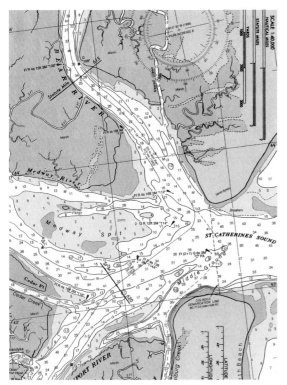

The chart shows the nature of the bottom as well as water depths.

UNDERSTANDING THE BUOY SYSTEM

You have to admire the skill of the first explorers who navigated the world of uncharted waters. And we can thank the British Admiralty, who realized the value of having charts so that its warships, and the country's merchant vessels, could safely sail around the world. The chart itself is useful, but it's the aids to navigation printed on the charts that are perhaps most helpful to the boater. In the United States, a uniform system of aids to navigation has been developed, consisting of major aids like lighthouses and large lighted buoys, backed up by a system of smaller aids. In most cruising waters, navigation aids are maintained by the U.S. Coast Guard.

Most navigation buoys conform to a system of uniform shapes and colors. Green buoys, called *cans*, have a cylindrical shape and a flat top and are always odd-numbered; red buoys, called *nuns*, have a tapered, cone-shaped top and are always even-numbered. Lighted green buoys have green lights, and red buoys have red lights. Fixed aids, the markers on pilings at the edges of shallower channels (often called *daymarks*), are similar, with square greens and triangular reds. These marks are coated with reflective paint so they are easier to see at night. They may also be lit with a corresponding green or red light. Daymarks are numbered the same as buoys: odd on green, even on red.

You'll also occasionally encounter markers that are both red *and* green, divided horizontally. These will be found at junctions, where a side channel splits off from the main channel. The overall shape and top color will apply to the main channel, the bottom color to the side channel. For example, a triangle with red over green should be taken as a red marker for the main channel and kept to starboard if you are *returning* (see below). The same marker should be considered green and kept to port if you head up the side channel. While green or red buoys or markers are always numbered for reference, red/green or green/red marks are not. They may carry an identifying letter, such as A, but not always.

At the entrances of major channels that lead in from the ocean you'll find mid-channel aids. Often called *sea buoys*, these vertically striped red and white buoys may be taken on either side, but since the rules say we should keep to the right, common practice is to leave sea buoys to port. Sea buoys most often have identifying letters that relate directly to where the channel leads. For example, the sea buoy off Port Everglades, Florida, is identified by the letters PE. Sea buoys are most often lighted and display a white light that repeatedly flashes the Morse code letter A (two flashes: one short and one long).

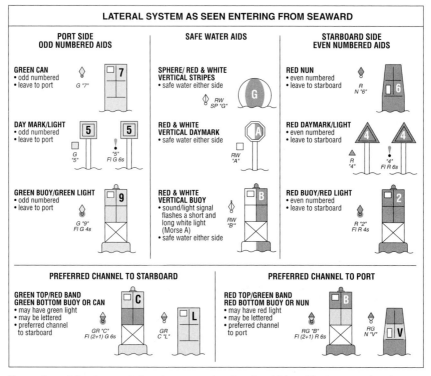

For safe cruising in coastal waters, every boater should be able to recognize these basic navigational markers.

DECIPHERING NAVIGATION AIDS

The purpose of coloring aids to navigation red or green and giving them distinctive shapes is to signal to the navigator on which side he can pass to remain in safe water (hence the name *lateral* system). When entering a harbor, red marks are usually kept to the right—the mark will be on the starboard side of the boat as you pass it. Green marks are kept to the left—-the mark will be on the port side of the boat as you pass it. Remember the saying "red right returning" when you're entering a harbor to help you recall which side to take them on. If you are leaving a harbor or going down a channel toward the sea it's the reverse: the red aids are on the left and the green are on the right.

Using marks can sometimes be confusing, depending on where they're located. For example, the Atlantic Intracoastal Waterway (ICW) runs parallel to the Atlantic Ocean, so while traveling in this waterway you may never be actually returning from or going to sea. In this case, the red aids have been placed on the mainland side of the waterway for the whole length of the system. They are on the right of the waterway as you go south along the Atlantic coast. They remain on the right as you go north up the west coast of Florida and across the Gulf Coast to the Mexican border.

But when the Intracoastal Waterway enters or crosses other bodies of water, the buoys for that particular system take precedence, and the red and green aids may be reversed from an ICW viewpoint. For example, heading south on the ICW where it enters the Cape Fear River in North Carolina, the red marks are on the left side of the river channel because you are traveling toward the sea and the river is marked for vessels entering from the sea. Of course, as soon as you leave the river to reenter the waterway, the reds are back on the right.

To help in straightening out this confusion, all ICW aids to navigation have small yellow indicators: a triangle on the red marks, a square on the green. Wherever the channel markers agree—that is, when red marks are on the right side of the ICW—the yellow triangles will be on red marks, the yellow squares on green. But when the markers disagree, as on the Cape Fear River, the yellow triangles will be on green buoys and the yellow squares on red for that portion of the river where the main channel and ICW overlap but are essentially marked in opposite ways. On the ICW, *yellow rules.*

The only drawback is that these yellow indicators are very small and almost impossible to see until you're up quite close. Your best bet is to personalize the chart and circle

The symbols on this chart of Cape Fear River illustrate a variety of navigational aids that a cruiser must be able to recognize.

the area of confusion, adding the notation, *colors reversed.* This will give you advance warning to be on your toes while cruising in this area.

USE COMMON SENSE

If you come to a point where you don't know which side of a navigation mark to pass, refer to the chart. Except for mid-channel aids that you can safely pass on either side, all other aids are placed to warn you of a danger. Find the aid on the chart and it should be clear on which side to pass.

This is where the numbers are useful. By comparing the number on the aid with the number shown on the chart, you can be reasonably sure of where you are and where you should go in relation to the mark. The only drawback is that there are many lone red markers numbered 2. If you are looking at a lone aid, look also for easily identified landmarks and compare them to the chart so you can be sure which red 2 you're considering.

RANGES

A range exists whenever you can line up two clearly visible landmarks, one behind the other. As long as the objects are in line as seen from your boat, your boat is on an extension of the line that connects them. This is one of the most reliable of all *lines of position* (LOP), the name we give to any line on which your boat may be located. Remember this term; we'll be using it again soon.

Most charts will show a number of natural ranges, but, in addition to these, the U.S. Coast Guard has installed navigation aids to form manmade ranges in many critical narrow channels that may have a cross current. These consist of front and rear markers placed so that if the boat is in the channel, the markers will be aligned as seen from the boat. The rear range marker is taller than the front marker and they are usually both painted with matching vertical stripes that make alignment easier.

If the range markers stay in perfect alignment, all is well and the boat is in the center of the channel. But if the rear range marker appears to move to the right, the boat is drifting to the right of the channel, and vice versa. The farther out of alignment, the farther you've drifted, so you should take corrective action as soon as the rear marker appears to move even slightly off center.

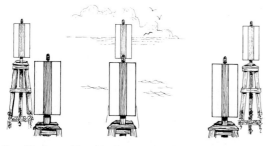

By aligning tall vertical range markers, you can stay on course even in a strong current. (Illustration by Rob Groves.)

With a strong cross current, you will have to steer slightly to the left or right of the front range marker to keep the boat on course. You most often have to crab your way along the range. We talk more about ranges below and in Chapter 18, Boat Handling.

THE COMPASS

The magnetic compass has been the primary tool of navigators for centuries. Since the compass relies on the earth's magnetic field to sense direction, and this field is not uniform, the compass does not always point directly to true north. In order to relate the information read off the compass card, some adjustments are needed. The key to relating the compass to the chart is the compass rose.

COMPASS VARIATION

Unless otherwise indicated, charts are oriented so true north is at the top. Since magnetic north is not aligned with true north in most parts of the world, each compass rose on the chart has two rings. The outer ring is aligned with the longitude lines of the chart and points to true north. An inner ring is aligned with magnetic north and shows the variation from true north. Depending on the area covered by the chart, the variation can be either east or west, and as little as 1 degree or as much as 20 degrees (or more).

You can use the compass rose to plot courses and bearings on the chart. If you use the outer ring, you'll be plotting in reference to true north and you have to allow for variation in order to get the correct course to steer. In our home waters of the Chesapeake Bay, for example, the variation is 11 degrees west. To travel north we must steer a compass course of 11 degrees.

Depending on where you are, you must either add west variation or subtract east vari-

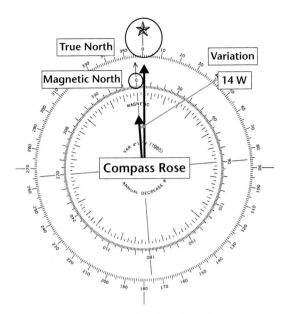

The compass rose printed on the chart shows true north on the outer ring and magnetic north on the inner one.

ation to determine the correct course to steer. In most places along the East Coast the variation is west, and on the West Coast the variation is east. The Great Lakes have less variation both to the east and west, and the variation becomes less the farther south you travel. How do remember that you're supposed to *add* west and *subtract* east? The U.S. Power Squadrons teach this mnemonic device: *East is least, West is best.*

Since the inner compass rose on the chart has already accounted for variation, it is much easier to use this ring and simply plot magnetic courses.

COMPASS DEVIATION

In addition to regional variation, which equally affects all compasses within that region, each boat's compass is affected by magnetic influences on the boat. This individual boat error is called deviation. In most

cases, however, the compass can be *compensated* so that the error is greatly reduced or eliminated.

The easiest way to check your compass for deviation is to steer the boat toward or away from a series of ranges. On the chart, find landmarks like lighthouses, church steeples, or piers that you can align with one another or with other nav aids to form such a series. By connecting the landmarks to one another with a line, you can determine the magnetic bearing between the objects. When out on the water, align the aids, steer your boat toward them, and then check your compass course. Of course, you must do this when the current is slack or there are no high winds to push the boat off course. Like variation, deviation can be either east or west.

For example, if you select a range on the chart, say, of a lighthouse and a daymark that should bear 260° (magnetic) from your boat's position, your compass should read 260° when you align the two objects and steer toward them. If your compass reads 255°, its deviation is 5° east. If it reads 265°, its deviation is 5° west.

If possible, find several ranges, and include ones heading toward the four *cardinal points* of the compass (N, E, S, and W). This will give you a pretty good idea of how accurate your compass is. It is necessary because deviation not only differs from boat to boat, it also changes with the boat's heading.

On most fiberglass boats, compass deviation can be reduced to zero (or nearly so) on all headings. If, for some reason, you can't eliminate deviation error on your boat, you'll need to develop a *deviation card* that shows you the deviation and required correction for various headings. By correcting for deviation, you'll know what course you need to steer—the course the compass should show—to follow the magnetic course you've plotted on your chart. The process of determining

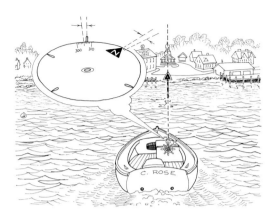

To check the accuracy of your boat's compass, find navigation aids and landmarks that align to create ranges. Steer toward a range and compare the compass reading with the range bearing that you can determine from the chart. (Illustration by Rob Groves.)

compass error in all directions is known as *swinging ship*.

The number of different headings you need to use depends on how close you can get to zero deviation on the cardinals. If you can get zero deviation on N, E, S, and W by adjusting the internal compensating magnets, you'll most probably also see no deviation on the *intercardinals*: NE, SE, SW, and NW. If you have more than a degree of deviation on any of these headings, you should probably swing ship to note and record the deviation at intervals of 30 degrees all around (000, 030, 060, and so on up to 330 degrees).

If you can't eliminate deviation altogether, you must apply the error when you convert courses from magnetic to compass. Follow the rules we outlined above for variation: add for west, and subtract for east.

You'll find some useful tips on compensating a compass at www.ritchenavigation.com.

DEAD RECKONING

Dead reckoning is an age-old navigation method. It provides approximate positions based on the assumption that traveling in a known direction at a known speed for a given length of time produces predictable results. For example, if you head southeast at 7.5 knots, after half an hour you'll be about 3.75 nautical miles (NM) southeast of where you started. After an hour you'll be 7.5 NM along the same line; after two hours you'll be 15 NM along, and so on.

The first step is to plot the course you plan to steer on the chart. In its simplest form, the course is a line drawn on the chart between two points. After you start a voyage, you should monitor the compass, clock, and knotmeter or log at set intervals, calculate your progress, and note it on the chart.

Many factors, such as current and wind, can alter your progress and keep your boat from following the exact course you've drawn, and unfortunately dead reckoning does not account for them. At best, dead reckoning will give you only an approximate position. This is better than not knowing your position at all, but it must be constantly checked against observed progress because the farther you travel from your starting point, the less accurate dead reckoning becomes.

There are several ways to check your progress. If the boat passes close to an aid to navigation of known position, you can compare this position to the dead-reckoning (DR) plot. You can take compass bearings of known aids to navigation or landmarks and plot them on the chart to produce a *fix* and compare it to the DR plot. Or compare the reading from the depth-sounder to the depths shown on the chart to reaffirm your position. These simple methods form the backbone of piloting.

PLOTTING A COURSE

Piloting has been practiced for centuries, so there are many tools available to plot a course on the chart. The chart's compass rose can make the correction for variation for you (if you use its inner, magnetic ring), and tools like parallel rules allow you to transfer a course you want to follow, or the bearing of a prominent landmark, to or from the compass rose. We like a course protractor, which has a circular base plate with its own compass rose and a single movable arm. The arm is long enough to use as a straightedge to draw the DR track on the chart.

To plot a course between two objects on the chart with the course protractor, first draw a line on the chart between the objects. Then place the center of the circular base over the first point. Align the grid lines embossed on the base with a latitude or longitude line on the chart so the compass rose points north. Then swing the arm into alignment with the course line on the chart. Read the true bearing of the course line off the compass. A scale for correcting variation is printed on the movable arm. This correction will give you the magnetic bearing.

To learn the basics, let's plot a course on the chart for a short trip from Annapolis Maryland out into the Chesapeake Bay and back (see illustration). We want the first leg of the trip to take us from mark "A" on the chart to mark R "92." To plot this leg, draw a line from the starting point, "A," to R "92." Then draw lines from R "92" to "B," and from "B" to "A."

You can use any sharp pencil, but we prefer a mechanical pencil with .05 lead. Thin lead makes a fine line on the chart and it is easy to erase. (We also found that an art gum eraser is by far the best tool to clean up a chart.)

Now we can find out the course we will need to steer. We place the center of the protractor over the end of the line near "A" and move the arm so it aligns with the line you just drew. Align the plotter's compass with a latitude or longitude line on the chart so it

points north and then read the true bearing, 073° from the compass rose.

There's a variation of 11° west around Annapolis, so add 11 to the true bearing to get the magnetic course: 084°. Because we've recently checked our compass for deviation and found none, we can label the course line C 084 M to indicate the compass course to steer on that leg (by convention, we always label compass headings or bearings with three digits so we'll know at a glance they represent directions). Of course, if we had deviation to contend with, we would have to allow for it here to arrive at the proper course to steer, which would not be the same as the magnetic course.

Use dividers to measure the distance from "A" to red "92." Spread the dividers to span the distance. Then, without changing the spread, bring the dividers over to the latitude scale adjacent to this part of the chart. Put one point on a convenient starting mark, such as a

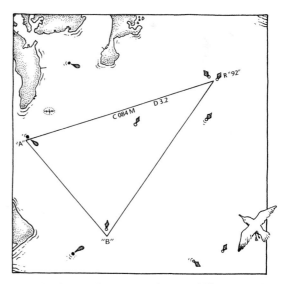

Knowing how to keep a DR plot is a skill every cruiser should have. You should be able to plot a boat's course and speed on the chart and then update its progress. (Illustration by Christopher Hoyt.)

zero or 10, and see where the other point falls. In this case, it spans about 3.2 minutes of latitude; because 1 minute of latitude equals 1 nautical mile (NM), this equals a distance of 3.2 NM (tenths of a mile are as accurate as we can handle, even if the distance is a little more or a little less than 3.2). Under your course line, label the distance D 3.2.

Use the same process to measure and label the other two legs and you will have the DR plot for the trip. Knowing the speed of your boat, you can keep track of your position on the chart. If you depart point "A" at 9:00 A.M. and travel at 6 knots on a compass course of 084°, every 10 minutes you will move one mile down the plot line.

PLOTTING A FIX

Dead reckoning techniques provide approximate positions that we label DR on the chart to remind us that they are based solely on compass and clock. If we have some idea of how wind and current may be affecting our course, either from past experience or by observation, we can also plot an *estimated position* (EP) near the DR to better reflect actual conditions. Many factors, such as an inaccurate estimation of current, can also cause an EP to be incorrect. But unless our observations are way off, an EP will still probably be closer to our actual position than the DR position we plot. An EP is marked on the chart as a square.

But we can do even better. By observing known landmarks, you can find out where the boat is actually located (or at least, with *much* more accuracy than either the DR or EP). For example, you know exactly where your boat is whenever it passes close to an aid to navigation. Any known position is called a *fix*. By comparing the EP to the position of the fix, you know the accuracy of your estimates of wind, current, and so on.

Another method of obtaining a fix is to take compass bearings of two or more known landmarks or aids to navigation and plot them on a chart. This method works extremely well for all but very fast-moving boats that cover too much ground between bearings and tend to bounce too much for even the individual bearing lines to be very accurate. You can also use radar, if you have it, to take a bearing on a known object and then transfer the bearing to the chart.

The first step in taking a fix is to positively identify the objects you are going to take bearings on. Smokestacks, church steeples, water tanks, and many other prominent and easily identified landmarks are printed on charts. Double-check the chart to be positive that it shows the objects you plan to use.

When you have identified and located the objects on the chart, use a hand bearing compass (See Chapter 9, Navigation Equipment) to take bearings and record them. If one of the objects you have chosen is a navigation aid close to abeam, take its bearing last, because that bearing will change faster than those of objects ahead or behind the boat. Let's say, for this example, the last bearing you took was 170°.

Since you don't yet know the exact position of your boat on the chart, you must plot the bearing from the object to your boat, which is the reciprocal of the bearing you have taken (bearing plus or minus 180°).

The compass rose can save you time here, because the bearing and its reciprocal will be opposite each other on the rose.

But even handier in this instance is a course protractor. First, place the center of the course protractor on the charted object on which you had taken your bearing of 170°. Next, you'll need to align the plotter's compass dial with north. To facilitate this,

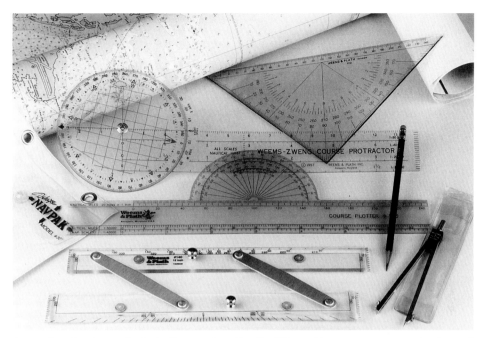

A set of navigation tools, including our favorite: the Weems-Zweng course protractor (second from top). Another popular navigation tool is a set of parallel rules (bottom).

the dial has a grid made of parallel lines running north to south and lines running east to west. Adjust the dial until the north arrow faces the top of the chart and one of the north-south or east-west lines on the dial aligns with a latitude or longitude line on the chart. The next step is to plot the line between the object at 170° and your boat. To do this, you need to find your bearing relative to the charted object, or the reciprocal of 170°. The plotter arm intersects the protractor dial at two points. These points are reciprocal to each other. The short end of the arm has an arrow printed on it. Align the arrow with 170° and the long end of the plotter's arm will be aligned to its reciprocal, or 350°.

Draw a line along the edge of the plotter arm from the object to, and beyond, your estimated course line and you have the bearing line for that object. Then repeat this process for the other bearings you had taken. The point where your bearing lines intersect is your fix. A fix is marked on the chart as a circle.

A single bearing line is another example of a line of position (LOP) because your boat's position will lie somewhere along it. If you happen to know the distance between the boat and the object—as you might by using a radar screen's *variable range marker* (VRM)—then you can mark the distance on the bearing line to produce a fix.

The illustration on page 227 shows the DR plot for the trip we discussed earlier, along with several fixes. The first fix was taken with bearings on the lighted red marker, "2W," north of the boat and the green can "1" just off the bow to the east. The hand bearing compass gave us a reading of 100° to the green mark and 006° to the red. If we want to plot the bearings on the chart as true, we need to find the reciprocals of the compass bearings and adjust them for variation. The reciprocal of 100° is 280°, and when adjusted for a variation of 11 degrees west, the true bearing from green "1" to the boat works out at 269° (100 + 180 − 11). Apply the same math to the second bearing and you get 175° true (006 + 180 − 11).

While courses and bearings are often plotted as true, we've used magnetic bearings for our course lines, so it makes sense to plot our compass bearings as magnetic also, using the inner compass rose. This eliminates the need for considering variation or figuring the reciprocal. We just line up the parallel rules on 100/280, for example, and then transfer the line to mark "1" and draw it toward our course line and beyond. We do the same with the lighted red, setting the rules on 006/186, and then transferring them to the mark and drawing the line from the mark in the direction of our boat, to and beyond our course line.

To remind ourselves at a later time just why we drew these lines, we label bearing lines with the time above the line (in four-digit 24-hour time) and with the three digits of the bearing under the line.

Incidentally, because any bearing you take from a moving vessel will always include some error (a result of vessel motion), the fix you get from crossing two bearing lines is not 100 percent accurate. (Though it is much better than not having a clue where you are!) You can improve the accuracy by crossing a bearing LOP with the LOP from a natural range. Unfortunately, this is not always possible. It's one of those things navigators always hope for and take advantage of whenever they can, but don't hold your breath.

In the illustration, the fix we plotted at

0910 shows that the boat is on course and pretty close to the DR plot, but slightly behind and a little south. Later, at 0930, another fix shows the boat has drifted even farther south of the DR plot and has fallen farther behind the EP. It is obvious that as the boat moved out into the bay, the current slowed its progress and set it south. Of course, in this example, red "92" will be in sight for the whole trip, so it would be easy to make the minor course correction required by eye.

On a longer trip you would need to alter course about 5° north (from 084° to 079°) to compensate for the set of the current. To see if your correction was right, you would then check your progress at the next available opportunity to get a good fix. If you have any way of anticipating the current, either from charts or published tables, you can make course corrections in advance. We'll describe the method shortly.

Practice taking compass bearings and plotting them on the chart. If you have a fast boat, you must take bearings quickly to get accurate fixes. With practice, you can take several in a minute or so. When you plot the fix, remember that it represents the location of the boat when you took the bearings, not your current position. This is why it is a good idea to write the time along each bearing line and note the time of the resulting fix.

Practice makes perfect. If you have a GPS aboard, compare the fixes you plot from your hand bearing compass against the GPS to see how accurate they are. In no time you will have mastered this basic skill. Do it often enough to keep in practice; then, the day your GPS quits you will still be able to plot a reliable fix.

Even if you can't take bearings on two objects at nearly the same time to get an accurate fix, a single bearing is still useful. The point at which that lone LOP crosses

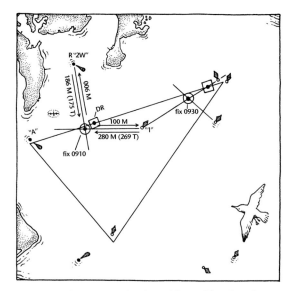

Bearings taken on navigation aids and landmarks allow you to plot a fix. This can be used to correct your DR position. (Illustration by Christopher Hoyt.)

your DR track can provide another EP. You know you are definitely somewhere along the LOP, and since you are trying to follow your intended track, this EP will be better than a simple DR. And if the bearing is nearly abeam—at ninety degrees to your course line—it is a very close approximation of your forward progress, but your actual position may be to either the left or the right of your intended track.

You can also use a single LOP to start what is called a *running fix*. Let's say you take a bearing to a daymark, plot it, name it LOP1, and note the time. Later in the day, you take a bearing to a distant lighthouse and plot a new line called LOP2. When you look behind the boat toward the daymark, you see that it has slipped beneath the horizon. No problem. As long as you have been steering the same course and speed since you plotted LOP1, you can use dead reckoning and a set

of parallel rules to transfer LOP1 to a point that represents the approximate distance you have traveled. The point at which the transferred LOP1 and LOP2 intersect is your new EP. This running fix is not as good as a true fix, but it's much better than a DR.

NAVIGATING IN CURRENT

As demonstrated by the example we plotted in the illustration, current is most often the cause of the difference between a DR plot and the boat's actual position. Knowing how to adjust your course to compensate for current is an essential skill. There are several ways to do this, but drawing the situation on a chart is the easiest.

To cruise from Florida to the Bahamas you must cross the Gulf Stream. The stream flows north at about 2.5–3 knots or more, and presents the classic current correction problem. If a slow boat doesn't correct its course for the Gulf Stream current, the current will push it far north of its destination. To arrive where you wish to go, you have to correct for this current in advance. Fortunately, many of the charts of the Florida Straits show the direction of the Gulf Stream's flow, which provides the information you need to determine its effect on your crossing.

Our trawler, for example, can make 7.5 knots in just about any conditions; a little faster when the seas are calm. The distance from Lake Worth Inlet (Palm Beach, FL) to West End, Bahamas is about 55 nautical miles. We can make the run in 7½–8 hours. The rhumb line course is 095° true, 100° magnetic. During that 7½-hour run, the Gulf Stream current carries the boat north at 2.5 knots. After 7½ hours, the current would set the boat about 20 miles north of the rhumb line. Obviously, we must steer a different course to compensate for the current set.

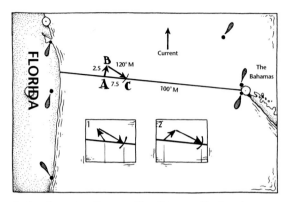

A simple vector diagram like this can display the effect current has on your boat's course and speed as it travels from one point to another. (Illustration by Christopher Hoyt.)

To determine a more accurate course to steer, we use a *vector diagram* (see illustration above). That term might sound scary to a beginner, but it's really very simple, so don't let it throw you. We start with the rhumb line course from Palm Beach to West End—100° magnetic. Now we need to allow for current. And we do it with vectors. The best way to think of a vector is as a line that represents both direction and speed. A boat in motion has a direction and speed. Current also has a direction and speed. A vector's direction is indicated by an arrowhead. A vector's speed is indicated by line length.

Here's how it works: to keep things simple let's assume average speeds and directions for both the boat and the current. That way we can use just a representative one-hour segment of the passage, to draw our vectors on the chart.

In this example, our boat moves 7.5 miles east through the water in one hour, and the current moves it 2.5 miles north. (To determine the speed [*drift*] of the current and its direction [*set*], we can consult charts and guidebooks or current tables, diagrams, or perhaps our own log entries from previous trips through this area.) Anywhere along the rhumb line, at an arbitrary point A, we use dividers and a pencil to draw a 2.5 mile-long vector in the direction of the current flow. We label the end of this vector B. Then we spread our dividers to 7.5 nautical miles, which represents our boatspeed through the water. With one point at B, we swing the dividers toward our destination down across the rhumb line and mark the point of intersection C. We can then draw a vector from B to C. This represents our *course to steer* to overcome the current.

In this illustration, the course is about 120° magnetic. To figure our speed over the ground during the crossing, we can measure the vector from A to C. The current is almost 90° to our rhumb line, so our speed is affected very little; it's still almost 7.5 knots. However, if the current were more on our bow, B would be farther back, and vector AC would be shorter, representing a slower pace (see insert panel 1). And of course, if the current were more behind us, B would be farther ahead and vector AC would be longer, indicating a greater speed over the bottom (see panel 2). One of the elegant aspects of this method is that it gives us course to steer and a predicted speed over ground (SOG) in one easy visual solution.

In reality, the current will be nowhere near constant and will vary from almost zero to way above average during our passage. As a result, our course over the ground will not be a straight line, but rather a lazy "S" because we'll wander to either side of the charted rhumb line as the current increases and wanes during our crossing. This also means that, since we will not be following our rhumb line, cross-checking our position by referring to a GPS display will rarely show us where we're supposed to be. But the method works, and as we near the end of the crossing, GPS, visual bearings, and the chart should all agree as we approach our destination right on the mark.

You can also use the GPS display of *course over ground* (COG) to follow the rhumb line, but this isn't always the best idea. For one thing, if you rely solely on your GPS, you'll be lost (quite literally!) when it fails. And you can be sure that at some time it will fail, so you should know how to navigate without it. But there's another reason. As we saw in the above illustration, a current at nearly right angles to our course line has little effect on our speed over ground. So by making the correction for current in our course to steer, we'll arrive at our destination just a little later than if there were no current. But if we use the GPS to keep us on the rhumb line, whenever the current gets stronger we'll have to point more directly into it to stay on course. And the closer the current is to being directly on our bow, the slower our speed over ground. So in this case, though the straight line will always be the shortest distance between two points, it isn't always the fastest.

If we avoid pointing into the current we can keep our forward progress at a better pace. The long way can be the quicker way, after all.

USING ELECTRONIC AIDS

Modern marine electronics paired with basic piloting techniques make a great team. Much real-time data can be generated by depth-sounder, GPS, and radar and used to update the DR plot.

DEPTH-SOUNDER

The depth-sounder is a good aid to navigation because it helps you avoid running aground. You can also compare readings from the sounder with chart soundings to help identify your location. If your charted position indicates you should be in 30 feet of water and the sounder reports 10 feet, something is off kilter and you'd better recheck your position.

Information about bottom contours can also be useful. For example, if the depth-sounder shows a rapid change in depth you can look over the chart and find the location of a ridge or shoal that is responsible for the change. In fog, you can follow a contour line on the chart to find the entrance to a harbor or a sea buoy. For example, if you know that the end of the breakwater to a harbor you want to enter or an aid to navigation is in 30 feet of water, you can follow the 30-foot bottom contour line until you find it. Of course you need to know which way to steer to keep on the contour and make sure that the approach to the harbor along the line is clear. And you will need to check the stage of the tide (if there is any) and correct for it if necessary. The charted depth is usually mean lower low water and the actual depth is almost always greater—especially in areas of extreme tidal range. Remember, too, the chart is only as accurate as the last soundings, and some charts rely on old data.

It's also important to keep in mind that a depth-sounder displays the depth as measured from the transducer, which is located under the boat, and not from the surface. You must add this measurement to the displayed depth to get an accurate total to compare with the charted depths.

GPS

The ability to compute your boat's direction and the speed it travels over the bottom as well as its actual location makes the GPS an invaluable navigation tool. This device displays real-time position data and displays a continuously updated fix given in latitude and longitude. Couple this instantaneous readout with its extreme accuracy (often within 30 feet), and you have a navigation tool that's nearly impossible to live without.

Most GPS units can also store waypoints, positions that you choose along the way such as visible objects like a navigation aid or a marina entrance, or simply unmarked spots on the water where you need to make a course change. You can use the GPS to go to a waypoint simply by selecting the *go to* mode and entering the number of the desired waypoint (they are usually saved by number). The unit will quickly display the range (distance) and bearing (direction) you have to travel to get there. You have to be a little careful when you use this feature, as the GPS will calculate and display the rhumb line from where you are to the waypoint you wish to reach. This will always be the shortest straight-line distance, so you must be sure that there is adequate water depth and that there are no rocks (or even land) along the route. But if you check the chart first to make sure the given heading is safe, you'll be OK.

Most GPS sets can also store a number of waypoints (how many depends on the unit) as a route, and take you from waypoint to waypoint without further entry. Some allow you to make the return trip simply by selecting *reverse route* or similar command, while others require you to enter the return trip as a separate and different route. Either way, the ability to pre-enter waypoints and destinations before you even start a trip allows for easier navigation once you're underway, which can be a real boon when cruising.

A GPS will usually show your present position numerically (in latitude and longitude) as its main display. It may show other information such as your SOG (speed over ground) and COG (course over ground) as well. Yet more displays, often optional at any one time,

can include the range (distance) and bearing (direction) to your chosen waypoint. Another useful display is crosstrack error, which shows if you've drifted from your rhumb line course and if so, how far that drift is to the left or right. Some units can even display crosstrack error graphically with arrows or similar graphics to show the amount and direction of the error.

Many newer electronic chartplotters have GPS built in, eliminating the need to interface separate units and enabling the boat's position to be displayed as a moving image—a spot or even a little boat shape—traveling over the chart in pace with the real boat's movement over the ground. Some also display a visible trail of where you've been. Be aware that there will often be a slight offset between the chart display and the GPS position. In a narrow channel, for example, on the screen you may see your boat moving down the shallow water at one side of the channel when it's clear in real life that you are well within the channel. Most sets have a means of correcting this offset, but often the offset changes sporadically, so most corrections are short-lived. The best bet is to never place too much credence in the graphic display.

Instead, compare the lat/long display with the paper chart whenever you need to know your position with extreme accuracy. We've found one drawback with this method, however. Plotting lat and long on the chart can be inconvenient if you use chart kits, where the edges of the chart pages don't always have scales. But here's another trick: GPS plotters allow you to find the bearing and distance of anything visible on the chart by moving the cursor over it. Using a range and bearing from a known object is fast and accurate enough to keep a chart plot up-to-date if you so desire.

But keeping a running paper plot in addition to the electronic plot is an often-unnecessary redundancy. That said, you should keep two things in mind. One, even if you regularly use electronic charts and a GPS plotter, you should practice making paper plots often enough to remain comfortable with the process. That way, when your electronics fail and you have to use the old way, you won't be left scratching your head. And here's a second suggestion that's just as important. Even when you are relying solely on your electronics, you should log your position at regular intervals, say every half hour, so that if your electronics quit, you'll have a fairly recent known position or fix from which to start your DR plot.

You can also use GPS to check your compass by comparing your compass heading against the course displayed by the GPS. Remember, the GPS course is the course made good over ground, the COG, and not necessarily the same as the course through the water. Current will affect the course made good, so the GPS and compass may not agree. In fact, the difference between the compass course and the GPS display of COG is equal to the offset caused by the current pushing your boat off course. If you calculate the strength and direction of the current and record it in your log, you can plot a vector diagram to correct for it the next time you pass this way and the state of the tide is the same. You must also check to see if your GPS displays a magnetic or true course. Most GPS sets can do either, and they will also correct automatically for variation when displaying magnetic. Just make sure that option is active.

RADAR

Radar is a handy navigation tool, and when teamed with input from a GPS and digital compass, it's even more useful. Its main purpose is to avoid collisions, and unless you practice using the set in all conditions, you will find the screen confusing and difficult to understand. Some new sets, those from Ray-Marine for example, have built-in MARPA (Mini Automated Radar Plotting Aid, a small-set version of the ARPA used on all big-ship units) that can analyze targets on the screen and determine if they represent a threat of collision.

If you have an older set, or a newer one without MARPA, it isn't difficult to analyze the relative motion of a target. The technique is simple as long as neither the target nor your boat changes course. You will probably have to remove the sun shield from the set so you can mark the screen. You want to determine the course of the target relative to your boat, which is called the *relative motion line* (RML).

All you need is a grease pencil or white board marker. First, place a mark on the screen over the target you want to track, wait three minutes and mark the target again, then do it once more in another three minutes. That gives you a plot of three relative positions of the target. If these relative positions lie in a straight or nearly straight line, draw a line through the marks, and extend this (RML) beyond the center of the screen. You can now use the radar's *variable range marker* (VRM) to see how close the target will come to your boat.

Unless the RML points directly to the center of the screen (your position) you are not on a collision course. But if you want to know just how close the target will come if neither of you changes course, and you aren't satisfied with estimating the distance from center screen to the RML, expand the variable range marker (VRM) until the ring touches the RML. The reading of the VRM is the *closest point of approach* (CPA). Keep a watch on the target. If it does not continue

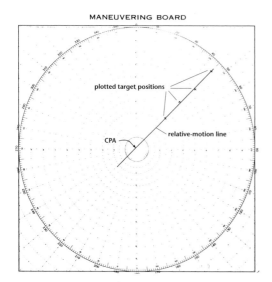

MANEUVERING BOARD

plotted target positions

relative-motion line

CPA

A simple plot, using a grease pencil to mark another vessel's position directly on the radar screen, can show how close it will pass to your boat.

down the RML it has changed course. If the target moves away from the center of the screen then the CPA will get larger; if not, keep a close watch on the target.

Many radar sets can be set to display a track of the target's relative motion. You can use this feature to pick out targets that may pass close by you. If the track clearly shows the target is not heading toward the center of the screen then you don't have to evaluate the CPA. But if your set is on a longer scale, like 6 to 12 miles, you can evaluate a target before it becomes a threat using this technique.

The problem with using the tracking function is that in rough seas a small boat yaws and pitches so much that the target tracks become crooked and landmasses distorted. Some features built into today's radar sets are useful on large ships that don't bounce around in rough weather, but don't work so well on smaller boats when the going gets rough. MARPA, for instance, isn't all that valuable all the time. Even trying to make an accu-

rate on-screen plot can be difficult on a small boat. This is one more reason to use your radar set as often as possible and in different weather conditions—so you can interpret what's happening by screen appearance alone.

Incidentally, though the plotting technique we described above is a part of the procedure ships' officers use while on radar watch, many professional captains on smaller vessels use a simpler one. And when we say simpler, we're not kidding. Here's what to do. Whenever you see a target that you think may present a risk of collision, just swing an *electronic bearing line* (EBL) until it touches the target, then watch. If the target moves off the line, there is no risk of collision. But if it stays on the line and moves closer to center screen, you have the *constant bearing, closing range* situation we discussed in Rules of the Road. There is, indeed, a risk of collision, and you should change course if the target vessel is to your starboard. At the very least, seeing the developing situation should be cause for initiating VHF contact.

NAVIGATING IN FOG

Here are a few tips about navigating in foggy conditions.

- If you're suddenly enveloped by a fog bank, stay put if you don't feel confident operating your boat in fog. Move out of the channel (or to its very edge, at least) before you drop anchor. Drop your anchor, if possible, and wait for the fog to lift. Anchoring in the middle of a channel is never a good idea, and it's especially bad under conditions of poor visibility.
- Know and use proper fog signals. If you're at anchor, ring your bell for at least five seconds every minute. If you're underway, use your horn and give one prolonged blast every two minutes. (See Chapter 17, Rules of the Road.)

- Remember, if you're underway in fog, your radar won't show everything. Post a lookout to call out markers and navigation aids so you can identify your location and progress underway. Fortunately, most navigational buoys these days have radar reflectors that make them quite visible on screen, but radar will not positively identify them. Your lookout can. Of course, your lookout will also have a better chance of spotting other boats that may not show up on your radar either.

- Slow down and give yourself time to make decisions and identify targets on the radar. Also use your ears. Listen for other boats' fog signals, and if you hear one forward of your beam, slow to dead idle until you have a full assessment of the situation and know that no collision is imminent.

- Stay connected to others by monitoring the VHF radio. Scan both channels 16 and 13 and communicate with others in the vicinity. You can also periodically broadcast a *Sécurité* call to announce your location and course to other vessels.

- Use caution when approaching a buoy and be careful not to run into it. Other boats may be setting a course to the buoy or using it as a waypoint so you may not be the only boat approaching it. If it's a sound buoy (bell, gong, or whistle) you may hear it before you see it. But most sound buoys (e. g., bell buoys) depend on wave action, and often in thick fog the seas are so calm that the buoys are silent. If you believe you are near one, or to confirm that a radar target *is* a sound buoy, kick up a wave by putting the engine in forward and giving a short burst of power. If you throttle back immediately and return to neutral, you won't go far. But you should stir up the water enough to rock the buoy and produce some sound.

CHAPTER 22
Cooking on Board

Somehow food just seems to taste better on a boat. Even the most ordinary meal can seem extraordinary in a perfect setting. It's no wonder we so often associate a cruising moment like a magical sunset with the food and wine we were enjoying at the time. It's probably easier to cook in your kitchen than on a boat, but that doesn't mean you can't prepare great meals afloat.

COOKING STYLES

You may look at cruising as an escape from the mundane chore of preparing meals at home, preferring simple meals aboard during the day but eating out at night. Or you may relish the idea of preparing meals aboard to share with others. Whatever your attitude toward cooking, cooking on board is going to temper the way you plan cruising menus and determine how often and what you cook.

Some boaters consider a ham sandwich the perfect lunch; others prefer a Caesar salad with blackened tuna. Barebones cooks spend as little time as possible in the galley and are happy with cereal for breakfast, sandwiches for lunch, and grilling outside for dinner with a prepared veggie or salad. Cruisers who are passionate about food are likely to go to the other extreme with hot breakfasts, fancy salads, and dinners that rival those in fine restaurants.

We enjoy eating more than cooking, so we're likely to cook simple meals aboard, like those we describe in Chapter 30, and then splurge when we eat ashore. The exception is Thanksgiving when we like to roast a turkey, which we buy not by weight, but by its height—our oven will only accept a 6-inch-high bird. If you want to do the same, measure the interior height of your oven from the lowest rack and take a measuring tape when shopping.

GETTING COMFORTABLE IN THE GALLEY

Cooking skills start with knowing how to operate the appliances in a galley. Everyone on board should know how to switch the power source to all the appliances on and off. Propane stoves must have the gas turned on, usually at a remote switch or control. Electric ranges, stoves, and refrigerators are supplied by their own electrical circuits, and require the shore-power switch and circuit breakers to be in the proper positions. The location of these controls varies from boat to boat, so spend some time getting to know the systems.

Read the appliance manuals. If you don't have copies, go to the manufacturer's website and see if they are available. You'll need to know the model and/or serial number of the appliance in order to download one. These sites often show a picture of the appliance, so it's a good idea to have a picture of yours to confirm you're looking at the correct one. The manual might be offered in printed form that you can order for a small fee. If no information is available on the website, leave an e-mail message for the Customer Service department requesting a manual.

MAKING FOOD HOT

Oven thermostats in galley stoves are frequently inaccurate. You may find that your favorite casserole recipe, which calls for 350°F in your kitchen oven at home, requires a higher or lower temperature setting on board. You can use an oven thermometer to confirm the accuracy of the control.

Microwave ovens are 120-volt appliances, which require shore power, a generator, or an inverter to operate. They operate in much the same way on board as they do at home, but they may blow fuses or trip breakers if turned on for long periods of time. By experimenting on board you'll learn how long yours takes to prepare a meal so you can use it to best advantage. If you like to eat but don't like to cook, a microwave is a must-have appliance. You can stock your refrigerator with prepared entrees that you can heat easily and quickly.

Most boats have access to 120-volt power when at the dock, so many cruisers run specialty electrical appliances like a coffeemaker or blender. If you have a generator, you can use these appliances at anchor as well. Often the number of appliances in your galley depends on the amount of storage space

that's available—they can be bulky and cumbersome to store.

KEEPING FOOD AND DRINKS COLD

The galley on our boat is part of the main saloon. It is functional, with a small sink, a three-burner stove with oven, an under-cabinet 3.5 cu. ft. refrigerator/ freezer, a counter, and storage cabinets. Cold food storage can be a balancing act, as the freezer holds two trays of ice cubes and not much else. We use the freezer for frozen chicken, meat, and fish and use a cooler with bags of ice for cold drinks. We try to bring aboard foods that are already frozen to ease the strain on the unit. In the refrigerator we keep perishables and staples, but on an extended cruise we store bulky items like fruits and vegetables in the cooler, along with the beverages.

We have a propane stove so we can make coffee in the morning and cook underway without having to run the generator. We acknowledge that having propane aboard also presents some potential problems, but with proper diligence the system is totally safe, and being free from the generator makes that diligence worthwhile.

The refrigerator probably gets more use than any other appliance in the galley. Most boaters want to keep beverages and perishable foods cold and have ice available, even if they usually eat out or bring prepared foods aboard. Read the manual to see if the unit requires defrosting, and find the suggested temperature to set it at. Some freezer compartments are small but do a good job of freezing their contents; others are more spacious but take a long time to make ice cubes or freeze foods.

With a small refrigerator, it's a good idea to remove food from bulky Styrofoam tray containers and repackage it in plastic bags. It takes up less space. Experiment with different-sized and different-shaped food-storage containers to find the ones that fit best in your refrigerator. Sometimes cold cuts or cheeses stored in one low, rectangular container take up less space than if they're stored individually. Trial-and-error takes time, but once you know what fits best you'll be able to store the maximum amount of food in the minimum space.

If a refrigeration system doesn't operate properly, have the unit checked out by a marine refrigeration service that specializes in your brand. It's money well spent. A unit may need refrigerant, it may need general maintenance service, or it may need a good overhaul, and these operations require skills, knowledge, and tools that most boatowners don't possess.

BASIC COOKING EQUIPMENT

Use your cooking style as a guide when you outfit the galley with utensils. If you like to prepare lavish meals aboard, open your kitchen cabinets and drawers and take note of which items you use most frequently. If galley storage space is at a premium, choose those that can multi-task, like a cheese plane that can double as a spatula.

For those who prefer to eat than to cook, here is a basic outfit.

COOKWARE

Teakettle
Small and large saucepans and fry pans
    with lids
Dutch oven
Small and large roasting pan with rack
Cookie sheet, pizza pan, 8-in. baking pan

ELECTRIC APPLIANCES

Coffeemaker
Toaster
Blender

COOKING UTENSILS

Ladle, turner, spoon, slotted spoon,
    whisk, baster
Knives: paring, utility, vegetable, chef's,
    bread, fish-filleting
Sharpening steel or stone
Can, bottle, and wine openers
Peeler
Scissors
Measuring cups and spoons
Cutting board
Colander
Nesting serving dishes and baking bowls
Hot pads
Food storage containers
Juice pitcher

MEAL PLANNING STRATEGIES

In general, we let the weather be our guide for meal preparation. We try to always have the ingredients available for different types of entree. When it's cool outside we plan dinner entrees that use the oven or we make slow-simmering stews or soups to heat up the cabin. If the weather is hot we're likely to grill out to avoid heating up the interior so that the air conditioning doesn't have to work overtime. And if rain is in the forecast we keep the operation inside.

Whether you're making meal plans for a weekend, a week, or a month, it's a good idea to make a list of the meals you typically serve. Keep it handy and gradually you'll get an idea of how much and how often you eat certain foods. It'll be a big help when you provision. For an extended cruise, we start out with entrees that will give us leftovers for another meal like a roasted chicken (for a salad or sandwiches) and meat loaf (for lunch). On our last night aboard we have an eclectic serving of all the leftovers fit to eat.

A CONTINGENCY PLAN

Even in the best of galleys with every appliance available, it's a good idea to have a supply of provisions to fall back on in case a problem arises. Refrigeration systems break down, ranges and stoves run out of propane—always at an inopportune time—so keep a stash of almost-instant food that requires no refrigeration to store or heat to prepare. Add a supply of bottled water too.

Today's grocery stores are filled with prepared grab-and-go foods. Find food items that you like and will eat, if and when you have a galley breakdown. We've been known to exist on peanut butter and jelly on graham crackers. For a while, that is.

PROVISIONING IDEAS

We like to have a good supply of staples in our galley so that provisioning isn't always a chore. When we're weekending we bring most meals ready to grill or heat so we can spend less time in the galley and more time enjoying the water and being outdoors. We eat more junk food on weekends because we often meet up with friends who are not always a good influence. On an extended cruise we show slightly more restraint, but not always. Meeting new cruising friends or re-meeting old ones is always cause to celebrate and we admit to stocking the boat with many more bags of chips and salsa than with fiber and flax.

Buy canned goods, dry items, and paper products anytime it's convenient and economical before a cruise. Buy meat, chicken, and fish anytime and freeze in serving size packages. Buy dairy foods, baked goods, and produce the day before departure.

We try to take dry goods and staples directly from the store to the boat, to avoid the trek from store to car to house to car to boat. We also keep a shelf in the garage just for boat food so we don't have to bring it inside the house. This works well with heavy, bulky items like bottled water and soft drinks.

The most popular staples used by our boater friends include Parmalat milk, packaged soups, peanut butter, jelly, graham crackers, Boboli pizza crusts, salsa, chips, nuts, microwave popcorn, bread mixes, and canned juices and beverages. For entrees they use marinades, and stir-fry and sweet-and-sour sauces for beef, chicken, and pork.

On an extended cruise we plan meals around non-refrigerated veggies like green peppers, yellow squash, and onions and store them in unsealed freezer bags. For salads we buy a package of three heads of romaine lettuce because it lasts well and stays fresh. When we run low on produce we plan a stop at a town where we can reprovision.

For the freshest bread possible, we look at the color of the twist ties on the wrappers. The ties are color coded for the day the bread is put on the shelf, so we choose accordingly. The colors are easy to remember because they're in alphabetical order: Blue, Monday; Green, Tuesday; Red, Thursday; White, Friday; and Yellow, Saturday.

And we like to get off the boat and dine out occasionally. While we have friends who can tell us which harbors have the best sushi bars and gourmet cafes, we're more likely to head for a casual bar that serves a good burger or steamed shrimp.

GET ORGANIZED

When provisioning for a long cruise, we make a list of the food items we have aboard and where they are stowed. *Where they are stowed* is the key phrase. For example, we write: "Under forward V-berth bunks—cereal boxes, soup cans, pasta, and rice." The list prevents us from finding a forgotten six-pack of canned tuna when decommissioning the boat in the winter—or worse, in the spring after it's been frozen in the bowels of the boat. We keep the list taped to the inside door of a galley cabinet, so we can always remember where it is.

We also designate a small notebook that doubles as a shopping list for galley provisions that need replenishing and another list for boat supplies that we need. In the front we list the food and galley supplies, and at the back we note down what boat gear is needed, and both covers are labeled accordingly. When we've bought the items on the lists we tear out the pages.

PART IV

Keep It Running Well and Looking Good

CHAPTER 23

Routine Maintenance

We are diehard do-it-yourselfers, so we spend a lot of time working on and maintaining our boat. We try to practice maintenance routines to prevent malfunctions, and at the risk of sounding obsessive, we admit that we use checklists. Gene loves Excel spreadsheets and Katie loves to make lists, so we don't apologize—although friends tease us—for using our trusty clipboard to check off jobs to be done and jobs completed. Here's a look at the routines we use for keeping our boat afloat with all its systems functioning.

MAINTAINING THE ENGINE AND SYSTEMS

Regular maintenance is a must if you want to keep ahead of the wear and tear a cruising boat is subjected to. And if you go on extended cruises, remember that one long cruise can put as much time on the engine and systems as a whole season of shorter trips. To keep them in top working order, give them the care and attention they require.

The Engine

Marine engines are run hard, so the quality of the oil and filter you use is vital. After consulting the owner's manual for the engine oil that's specified, choose the best quality brand you can find, and stick with it.

The American Petroleum Institute (API) designates a service rating for oil. Oils with a C prefix, like CH-4, are intended for use in diesel engines and those with S, like SJ, are designed for gas engines. Even if it meets the API standards, an inexpensive brand will not perform as well as top-grade oil.

We use Chevron Delo 400 in our Ford Lehman diesel engine, but many other good brands are available, like Shell RIMULA X. We keep enough aboard so we can top off the oil as needed. For convenience, we purchase gallon containers for oil changes and quart containers to top off—the smaller size is easier to handle.

Once you decide on a particular brand of oil, don't mix it with others since each manufacturer's additives are slightly different. Plus, we believe in having the oil tested at regular intervals, and the testing lab must know the oil brand and type to make an accurate assessment. Do keep in mind, however, that if the engine oil level is low, and for some reason you don't have your regular brand on board, oil of the proper service rating (regardless of its brand) is better than letting the engine run with insufficient oil.

Buy the type of oil filters recommended by the engine manufacturer, not automotive replacements. They may look the same, but they're not the same inside. Oil filters have bypass valves, and as the oil pressure increases, the valves open and allow the oil to bypass the filter. A filter with a bypass valve set to open at the wrong pressure may allow most of the oil to go unfiltered.

The owner's manual for our engine calls for an oil and filter change every 200 hours. We try to do better than that, with a change every 100–125 hours of running time when we're on an extended cruise. Hard running is good for the engine and oil; idling around waiting for bridges and locks to open is not. We consider the manual's recommendations a minimum.

There's a lot more to proper engine maintenance than regular oil changes. Whole books have been written on the subject, and we suggest you read some to familiarize yourself with what's needed. In the meantime, here are a few of the basics that every cruising boater should keep in mind.

Diesel and gasoline engines differ in more ways than just the fuel they burn. When a gas engine is running poorly, for example, or not at all, chances are it's an ignition problem. Fuel problems *can* occur in a gas engine, especially in older, carbureted versions. If fuel sits too long and some of the more volatile components evaporate, the gum that's left behind can cause sticky floats and also block tiny openings inside the carburetor.

But the *first* place to troubleshoot a gas engine is almost always the ignition. Spark plugs foul, and plug wires develop cracks in their insulation that leak current, which makes for a weaker spark. Corrosion can add so much resistance to connections that a wire can essentially stop carrying enough current. And if the engine has breaker points and a condenser, rather than electronic ignition, there's even more risk of failure. Ignition problems, especially in the uncooperative salty atmosphere of a boat, can be many and varied. Fortunately, modern fuel-injected engines with electronic ignition tend to be less trouble-prone. But the ignition system remains the first place to look when a gas engine won't start or isn't running right.

Since diesel engines don't have an ignition system, most of their problems are fuel-related, though diesels also need a good supply of air, and anything that interferes with that can also cause trouble.

The injectors in diesel engines use extremely high pressure to force fuel through microscopic holes as they spray it into the cylinders—a process suitably termed *atomization*. It's important that diesel fuel is very clean, otherwise small particles of suspended dirt can clog these tiny openings. The fuel must also come to the injectors free of water or these holes can rust, which also distorts them and interferes with proper operation. If your boat, or the one you want to buy, doesn't have Racor brand fuel filter/water separators, seriously consider adding them. They are far superior to the standard manufacturers' fuel filters included on most engines.

Racor filters are very good at removing water from fuel and have a clear bowl at the bottom that makes any water easy to see. There is also a small removable plug for draining the water off. The filter element traps finer particles than basic engine fuel filters, and should be changed when you change the other filters on your engines. Often called secondary filters because they are mounted off the engine, these units are really your first line of defense against dirty or water-laden fuel.

Incidentally, if you use a magic marker to write the date and hour-meter readings on oil and fuel filters when you install them, and then also record this information in a maintenance log, you'll never have to wonder if it's time for another change.

Exhaust Tells a Tale

One advantage we have on a boat, but not when driving a car, is that we can most often see the exhaust while underway. This is especially helpful, since the color of the exhaust can tell us a lot about engine performance. White smoke is good. It isn't really smoke, it's condensing water vapor. Burning a hydrocarbon fuel like diesel produces carbon dioxide (CO_2) , carbon monoxide (CO), and water (H_2O). This mixture leaves the engine as a vapor that becomes visible as it condenses in the cooler air. CO and CO_2 are invisible, as are most other normal by-products of an internal combustion engine.

Blue exhaust is not so good. It's a sign that the engine is burning lube oil, which it really shouldn't be doing. If your engine is emitting blue smoke, it's best to get a qualified mechanic to find out why. And expect to pay for the costly internal repairs that will correct the situation.

Black exhaust smoke indicates incomplete combustion——it's black due to unburned carbon. In a gas engine it often means the timing is off and the spark is late (occurring too close to the exhaust stroke) so that the mixture is pushed out of the cylinders before it has had a chance to burn completely. It can also indicate that there's too much fuel in the fuel–air mixture, from either a maladjusted carburetor or faulty fuel injectors. A gas engine producing black smoke usually runs rough and fails to develop its rated power. Again, it's best to call a qualified mechanic.

In a diesel engine, black smoke can mean several things. It's normal to see a little when you first accelerate, because diesels run faster by injecting more fuel. And when more fuel is added, at first the engine is not turning fast enough to draw in sufficient air. While some of the added fuel speeds up the engine, part of it goes unburned until the speed of the engine catches up with the increased volume of fuel. If a diesel engine continues to spew black exhaust smoke after it has revved up, it's usually a sign either that it isn't getting enough air for the volume of fuel or that one or more injectors are spraying too much (or poorly atomized) fuel. An engine that is running too cold will also tend to emit black smoke since the engine may not reach the proper temperature to efficiently burn the fuel.

It's also possible that the fuel you are using has too high a sulfur content. Either way, continuing black exhaust smoke is another clue to the need for professional intervention. If the fuel merely has high sulfur content, additives are available to combat the problem. But it is still wise to have a certified diesel mechanic assess the situation and recommend a solution.

Another problem you may encounter with diesels is air in the fuel lines, which forms bubbles that prevent the fuel from flowing properly to the injectors and thus prevent the engine from starting. Air most often enters the lines when you break their continuity to change filters. *Bleeding* the lines to remove the air is usually fairly simple, but the exact procedure varies with the make and model of the engine, so we'll just explain the basics here and suggest that you find the details for your particular engine(s) from the owner's manual.

In essence, you have to open the connection (fitting) between the fuel line and each injector (using the proper-sized wrench so you won't damage the fittings), one at a time. You only have to open each fitting just enough to let the air out as you build pressure in the lines, either with a manual *priming pump* or as you slowly crank the engine by *bumping* the starter switch. When fuel starts coming out around the loosened fitting, retighten it and that line is free of air. Repeat this procedure for each injector, and you'll get all the air out. Once all the fittings are properly tight again, the engine should start and run normally.

Routine Engine Maintenance

Here are a few more maintenance suggestions that will help keep the engine(s) running smoothly:

- Keep engines properly tuned for efficient fuel consumption, clean exhaust, and economy. With all engines this is a matter of proper timing and valve adjustment. With gas engines, it also means proper adjustment of the ignition system. Engine tuning usually involves hiring a qualified mechanic, but the results will most often be worth the cost.
- Keep your engines clean by wiping them down regularly. This makes it easier to spot and correct small leaks before they become big problems.
- Keep fuel tanks full during winter storage to reduce the buildup of condensation.
- Consider adding a fuel stabilizer to your tanks so that you will not have problems disposing of stale fuel in the spring.
- Routinely add a diesel fuel biocide to your tanks when you refuel to prevent algae growth that can clog filters—and injectors. Some algae absolutely thrive on a diet of diesel fuel and water, and they multiply faster than rabbits if you don't take preventive measures. Biobor is one well-known brand and Racor also has a diesel biocide. You'll find them in marine stores.

Waste Disposal

- Never discharge oil into the water—it is prohibited by law. All boats 25 feet or longer are required to have a sign regarding oil pollution control regulations posted in the engine compartment. These signs are available at most marine supply stores.
- Keep an oil absorption pad in the bilge or below the engine to collect spilled products.
- When performing maintenance tasks, wipe up spills so that they don't get pumped overboard with bilgewater.
- For spill-proof oil changes, use a non-spill pump system that removes crankcase oil through the dipstick tube. Many marinas have these systems available for rent (or even for free use by slipholders); check with the dockmaster. If the marina doesn't have a non-spill pump, they are inexpensive enough to be worth buying. They make the whole oil-change process much easier and cleaner.
- In order to catch the oil traditionally spilled during filter removal, slip a plastic bag over the filter before you remove it.
- Keep the use of engine cleaners to a minimum. Parts cleaning should not be done in the bilge or over open ground. It should be done in a container or parts washer where the dirty fluids can be collected and recycled.
- Never dump waste oils and engine coolants on the ground or into storm drains, dumpsters, and/or open waters.
- Most marinas have specific disposal facilities for waste oils and associated by-products, such as filters and absorptive materials. Ask where they are located and use them. Never dump these items with regular trash.
- When disposing of petroleum-based products, such as fuels and engine oils, keep them separate from each other and from other substances, such as antifreezes, sol-

vents, and water. This lowers the disposal cost charged to your collection facility for contaminated wastes.

Oil Testing

When we bought *High Life,* the previous owner had left reports from earlier engine-oil tests on board. We follow his good example and try to have the oil tested every time we change it. Dirty oil, disgusting as it is, can tell you a lot about an engine. The oil accumulates metal particles and contaminants between changes, creating a snapshot of the engine's condition.

A typical oil test kit you'll find at marine stores is inexpensive and includes containers for the samples, instructions, and a pre-addressed mailer for you to send the samples to the lab for analysis. You can use these kits to test both engine and transmission oil, and some will also test the coolant. The cost includes the report you'll receive back in the mail or by fax.

Some kits contain everything you need to extract the oil sample, including a length of plastic tubing and a bellows container that draws the oil from the engine and stores the sample for shipping. Other kits supply sampling bottles and a mailer; you provide your own vacuum pump and plastic tubing to extract the oil from the engine. This type of kit is best for large diesel engines that provide an oil sampling port. To take an oil sample, simply open the valve on the port when the engine is running and collect the dirty oil in a jar.

Each engine and transmission has different wear rates and so the lab will have baseline data for various types of engines over a range of operating hours. From this baseline they can tell if any of the analyzed contents present in your oil are out of line. With a record of several oil analyses, you can establish a trend for your engine, noting any increase in contaminant levels. A series of good oil analyses is reassuring for you, and when you sell the boat, it's impressive to a potential buyer. It was to us.

THE TRANSMISSION

It's surprising how many boaters don't service their transmission on a regular basis, or even realize they should. Since most people don't change the transmission oil in their cars, they probably think they don't need to on a boat. But even if it remains a nice shade of pink, you should change your transmission oil on a regular basis, according to the guidelines for running time and type of oil recommended by the manufacturer. As with engine oil, use the same brand and keep enough on board so you can top off when needed. Note also that some transmissions actually use engine oil instead of transmission fluid. Always use *exactly* what your owner's manual calls for.

PUMPS

In Chapter 24 we talk about spare parts, and replacement pumps are at the top of the list. Between the engine, generator, water, and air conditioning/heating systems we have ten pumps humming away aboard *High Life.* Some are more critical than others, but if any one of them stops we'll soon know about it.

The bilge and shower-drain pumps are sealed units and don't require maintenance; but others, like the raw-water pumps on the engine and generator, and the freshwater pressure pump, do.

You should replace the rubber impellers in your engine and generator raw-water pumps at regular intervals. Every boat we've owned that had an inboard engine has had this type of pump, so we've changed a lot of impellers. Depending on the pump's location, this can be an easy or difficult project.

Here, in a nutshell, is the process: remove the cover plate (by unscrewing the small machine screws that hold it in place), and the gasket or O-ring. Some impellers may be held in place by a set screw or a snap ring be sure to remove this before you try to pull out the impeller. Use a pair of pliers to remove the old impeller. A couple of screwdrivers with their blades placed on opposite sides of the impeller can also be used to pry out a stubborn impeller. There are tools that are designed to grip the rubber body and extract the impeller. When you replace the impeller, use Never Seize (a silvery paste lubricant available at most auto part and marine stores). Lightly smear a thin film of the lubricant in the bore of the new impeller and over the rubber vanes. Bend the vanes down against the body of the impeller so it will fit into the pump housing. The vanes under the cam inside the housing must be bent almost flat. You can use a large hose clamp tightened around the impeller to compress the vanes. Once it's partway in the housing, remove the clamp. Then push the new impeller onto the shaft (taking note of any flats or other distinctive shapes the shaft may have), giving it a slight twist to engage the splines.

Before you replace the cover, inspect the inside surface for wear. Some scuffing of the surface is normal but if the impeller has worn away enough metal to form a slight depression, order a new end plate and install it at the next impeller change. A tight fit between the end plate and the impeller is essential for the pump to put out maximum capacity. Install a new cover gasket (even if the old one seems OK), and then the cover plate, and you're done.

If the pump easy to reach, the whole process should be a snap. If you have to feel around other engine components and can't see clearly what you're doing, even the seemingly simple chore of removing and replacing the cover plate's mounting screws can test your patience.

We haven't discovered any relation between engine hours and the condition of the impeller. After inspecting many old ones, we've concluded that they suffer more when the engine is not running, as one or more of the vanes stays squished flat against the pump cam. This bends the vane arm at a 90-degree angle and after time it begins to crack. To help prevent this, we install new impellers in the spring before we launch, even if the old ones appear to be in good shape. Though some of the newer materials used to make impellers seem to be longer lived—some manufacturers even advertise that theirs will withstand being run dry—an annual impeller change is good preventive medicine for any raw-water pump.

Freshwater pressure pumps have many internal moving parts, but a three-chamber, direct-drive diaphragm-type pump seems to be a very reliable design. Ours has been in constant service for more than five years and it has never missed a beat. We carry a rebuild kit, but it may turn out that the motor wears out before the pump, in which case we will replace it. We do routinely check for leaks and make certain that all hose clamps and fittings are tight throughout the freshwater system.

REFRIGERATION AND AIR CONDITIONING

Keeping food, the skipper, and the mate cool on a boat is a demanding job. However, refrigerators and air conditioning systems require little maintenance except for keeping them clean and servicing the raw-water circulating pumps and their associated strainers.

You should clean the air vents around an air-cooled refrigerator on a regular basis, at least monthly. An amazing amount of dust can be drawn into the system, especially if the air enters at floor level. Also clean the evaporator plates located on the refrigerator motor assembly.

Air conditioner evaporator units also have a set of fin coils that should be cleaned monthly. Turn the unit off to allow the coil to warm up and dry out before you attempt to remove any dust and dirt. If the unit doesn't have a filter, you can make one by cutting a piece of air-conditioner filter replacement foam to the size of the coil. Then fasten it in place in front of the coil.

Check that the condensation collection pan (under the coils) and its drain lines are operational and clean. One particular problem facing almost every AC system is that cruising boats so often moor or anchor in relatively shallow water over bottoms alive with eelgrass. This grass can soon overwhelm the system's raw-water strainer, which can become so clogged that water flow drops to barely a trickle—if it flows at all.

It's a wise move to clean out the raw-water strainer daily—more frequently if the system doesn't seem to be working right. Also check that the circulation pump is working; the impeller here can need frequent attention. In a worst-case scenario, in which some eelgrass gets through the strainer and starts to clog the tubing in the AC compressor's heat-exchanger coils, you may have to resort to back-flushing the system to get the seaweed out the way it came in. Hook up a dock water hose to the system's overboard discharge hose using adapters, hose clamps, or whatever you need to make a watertight connection. Then let the water flow, at moderate pressure, back through the system and out the intake through-hull. After a few minutes, you should find that any clogs have disappeared. This can be a wet and messy job.

CONNECTORS FOR THE ELECTRONICS

At least once a season, clean the connections between the antennas or senders of radios, depth-sounders, GPS units, and radar sets. Remove all the connectors and clean the contacts. This is especially important for a radio antenna or any electronic device that's exposed to the elements. We always notice that the electronics on our bridge—GPS, VHF radio, and depth-sounder—perform better after we've cleaned the antenna connectors.

Use fine emery cloth to remove any corrosion from the contacts. If there is any buildup of salt deposits, a good washing with a mixture of water and TSP (trisodium phosphate, an industrial cleaner available at hardware and home stores) will remove them. Be careful not to get water inside the electronic gear. Dry the fittings completely before reassembly. A little silicone grease applied to the outside of the connectors after they are reassembled will help prevent further corrosion.

FRESHWATER SYSTEMS

While underway, we need to replenish the water supply at least once a week, so keeping it fresh is not a problem. We cruise in areas where there is a good supply of potable water. To keep our water drinkable, we periodically add bleach to each of the tanks (a capful for each 100 gallons) when we refill them.

When the boat is out of service for the winter, we drain the tanks and pour in a few ounces of bleach. We add nontoxic antifreeze to the freshwater system because Murphy's Law tells us that no matter how well we drain the system, there will always be at least one place, and maybe more, where we are unable to drain the water out completely. And when that lingering water freezes, it will expand to break the hose or fitting. These breaks are

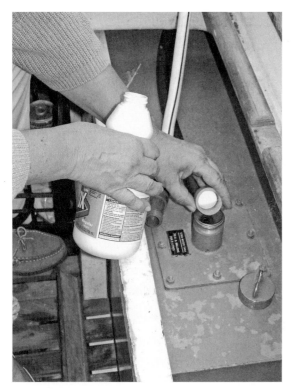

We add a capful of household bleach to each water tank each time we refill.

because the paint on the propeller loses its anti-fouling properties long before the paint on the bottom. Even a few barnacles on the propeller will hurt its efficiency. Protective sacrificial zincs will also be eaten away.

Every time we go swimming we check the condition of the prop and the zincs. In salt water it takes a while for barnacles to grow on the prop, so if you clean it at every opportunity, they won't have a chance to get started. We usually have to replace the zincs at least once a year and sometimes more often. In cold waters we have a diver check them at least twice a year or replace them when the boat is hauled out of the water.

Carry extra zincs aboard, especially those that are hard to find, like this one on the prop nut of our propeller.

never easy to find and fix. Nontoxic antifreeze is available at most marine stores in cooler climates.

When we recommission the boat, we pour about ten gallons of water in each tank to dilute the bleach we added at the beginning of the layup and run this mixture through the hot and cold water system. The strong bleach mixture sanitizes the plumbing, and when the tanks run dry we refill them with water. This technique also flushes out the nontoxic antifreeze from the system.

UNDERWATER

Propellers and running gear must be protected from corrosion and marine growth,

ONGOING INSPECTIONS

We perform a number of ongoing chores and checkups throughout the cruising season, especially when we're underway and using the boat continuously for a month or longer. We've grouped these "messing about" chores by their function and/or where they're located on the boat so they're easy to complete in an hour or less. We use this list to work from if we're weathered-in and have time to kill. When they're accomplished, we get great satisfaction from checking the items off the list.

ENGINE ROOM

Besides the day-to-day engine checkup, you should inspect the engine room thoroughly once a month with a flashlight. Use paper towels to clean up any dirt, leaks, or grease you find. Even if the engine room lighting is good, a flashlight lets you see into corners, as well as behind and under components.

Engine Pan

Liquid leaking from the engine collects in the drip pan, so place an oil-absorbent sheet below the engine to help locate leaks and avoid potential trouble. Check the sheet for signs of leaking oil, fuel, water, or coolant. Each will leave spots of a different telltale color.

Oil and Filters

Most conscientious skippers make it a habit to check the oil level in the engine before they start it each day and top it off if needed. But it's also important to look carefully at its condition. The presence of more oil than expected can signal a leaking fuel pump, especially if the oil seems thinned out. Milky-looking oil indicates a water leak somewhere within the engine, such as at a head gasket.

Either of these conditions tells you that you need to call a qualified mechanic to find and fix the problem. If the oil filter shows signs of leaking, tighten it, but be careful not to over-tighten.

Fuel Pump

Check the fuel pump for signs of oil or fuel leaks, and tighten anything that's loose.

Primary Fuel Filter on Engine

Inspect the fuel filter on the engine for signs of leaks. Tighten the bleed screws or filter if needed.

Injector Pump (Diesel Engine)

Check the injector pump for signs of fuel leaks. Check the throttle linkage and lubricate if necessary. Check the pipes that lead from the pump to the injectors for signs of leaks.

Carburetor (Gas Engine)

Remove the flame arrestor and check the carburetor for signs of leaks. Inspect and clean the flame arrestor.

Secondary Fuel Filter

Inspect the fuel-filter bowls and drain any water or other contaminants if necessary. Check the filter for signs of leaks.

Belts

Check all belts for tension and tighten if necessary. Belts that are too loose are inefficient and will also wear prematurely. But if they are too tight, they can cause premature wear of the pulley shaft bearings by creating too much side pressure. Read your owner's manual to learn just how much tension is right. Change belts if they are glazed from excessive slipping or if they show signs of age, like fine cracks on the surface. Belts that are becoming stiff need changing, too; they're getting close to the breaking point. Dual belts on high-output alternators should be purchased as a set and changed together.

Also check the alignment of the engine and alternator pulleys. If you see a fine black powder that looks like oil on the front of the alternator or engine, it's coming from belt wear. It's a sure sign that the belt is either too loose, or more probably that the pulleys are out of alignment.

Batteries

Top off the water level in flooded lead-acid (wet-cell) batteries with distilled water. The water should cover the plates, but don't over-fill since the electrolyte expands when it heats up during use. Check the charge level with a hydrometer, which measures the specific gravity of the electrolyte—but not just after you've added water. A fully charged battery will read 1.262 and a half-discharged battery will read 1.190. The cells should all read about the same. One low-reading cell is an indication of a failing battery. Clean up any signs of dirt or corrosion on the top of the battery and around the battery posts.

Sealed lead acid, gel, and AGM batteries don't require water, but do keep them clean.

Coolant

Check the level of the coolant in the engine and top off if necessary. It should appear semi-transparent; a milky-looking coolant is a sign of a possible head-gasket leak. Find the source of contamination and replace the old coolant with new. Also check the condition and contents of the overflow bottle and radiator cap.

Hoses

Inspect all hoses on the engine. Tighten hose clamps if they're loose, and replace rusty or damaged clamps. Use all-stainless clamps; those with regular steel tightening screws will eventually rust and fail. One way to test whether the screw is stainless or not is with a magnet. Stainless steel, because of its higher chromium content, is much less attracted to magnets.

Transmission

Check the transmission for leaks at hose fittings and the shaft coupling. Check transmission fluid level and top off if necessary. The transmission fluid should be a clear red if it's Dexron. A milky look is a sure sign of a water leak in the transmission oil cooler and should be addressed immediately. To get a correct reading, some transmissions must be running at idle and in neutral when you check the fluid level. Read your owner's manual to be sure.

Through-Hull Fittings

Each of your through-hulls—the fittings where seawater comes into the boat for engine cooling, AC heat exchange, and so on—should be examined to see that the fitting is sound. They can corrode or be eaten away by electrolysis. Also check that the hose clamps (there should be two on each connection) are solid and securely tightened. If any are leaking, find out why and correct the problem.

Most through-hulls use ball valves or seacocks to shut off the water flow, though on some older boats you will find the less desirable gate valves. (Gate valves are designed for home plumbing applications and are subject to failure through corrosion in marine applications.) To keep the valves operating freely, you should open and close valves routinely, at least once a month—weekly is better. Some ball valves have zerk grease fittings so they can be lubricated with a grease gun. If yours do, add waterproof grease once a month.

Clean all raw-water strainers, those glass or glasslike cylinders connected to the through-hulls by hoses. To do this, close the valve and remove the unit's cover. Some covers are threaded and screw off by inserting a special wrench into a series of small, round indentations and turning counterclockwise; others are held in place by a wing nut on a threaded rod. Be careful not to lose the O-ring between the cover and the base. Once the cover is off, remove the strainer from inside and empty any contents into the trash. If necessary, rinse and scrub the metal strainer before you reinsert it into the glass, and reseal the unit by following the removal procedure in reverse. Make sure the top is on tight, but not too tight—you'll need to remove it again. Tighten any hose clamps if necessary and replace any that have rusted.

Fuel Tanks
Check fuel tanks and fittings for leaks. Inspect tanks for signs of rust or corrosion.

Bilge Pump
Operate the bilge pump and test the float switch. Test the high-water alarm. Clean the bilge and mop up any oily water before discharging anything overboard.

Generator
Check generator fluids, belts, and pumps. Use the same routines as for the main engine.

Circulating Pumps
Check for leaks in the circulation pumps for refrigeration and/or air conditioning systems. Inspect the raw-water strainers and clean out if necessary.

Stuffing Box
Check the stuffing box, the gland that surrounds the propeller shaft where it penetrates the hull, for leaks. This device is meant to keep water out of the boat, but a tiny drip is usually necessary when the prop is turning. The packing inside the stuffing box must be lubricated to prevent the shaft from overheating and wearing, and a very small amount of water flow accomplishes this quite well. Older stuffing boxes have flanges that you tighten with a wrench to pack the stuffing (usually waxed flax) tighter. Resist the urge to tighten a flange until absolutely no water flows. This can cause premature shaft wear and actually grind a groove in the shaft that will make future sealing almost impossible.

Always allow a very slight drip from a turning shaft and all should be well. The packing should be tight enough to prevent dripping when the shaft is still. Of course, too much dripping is not good; it can overwork your bilge pump. If the stuffing box is connected to the prop shaft tube by a hose and clamps, inspect them for leaks and tighten any loose clamps.

Steering
Inspect steering cables for wear, and lubricate pulleys if necessary. If you have hydraulic steering, check for leaks at the ram that's attached to the rudder. Top off the fluid if necessary.

INTERIOR AND SYSTEMS
Inside the boat there are many pumps, hoses, drains, and other systems that require regular maintenance. A quick inspection on a routine basis will usually discover potential problems before they arise.

Windows
Check windows for proper drainage. If the tracks have drain holes at the ends, probe

them with a pipe cleaner to keep them clear. These holes are small to begin with and are usually somewhat hidden for cosmetic purposes, so be sure to seek them out and keep them clean. Standing water always means trouble, and even the small amounts that can accumulate in a window track can eventually cause problems.

Surfaces

Inspect interior surfaces for mildew, especially the inside face of teak drawer fronts where it tends to accumulate.

Lighting

Check all light fixtures and replace any faulty bulbs.

The Galley

Heavy layers of frost reduce refrigerator/freezer efficiency, so defrost and wash interior surfaces. Clean the galley exhaust fan and filter. Check all stove burners by turning them on and lighting them to see if they are working efficiently.

If you have a propane system, test it for leaks. After you've lit and checked the burners as suggested above, close all the burner valves, but leave the solenoid switch on. Read the pressure gauge, and then turn off the manual valve on the tank. After 3 minutes, read the pressure again. If it is unchanged, wait 15 minutes and read it again. Any drop in pressure indicates a leak that must be located (with soapy water) and stopped. If the system is leak-free, reopen the valve on the tank, light a burner, then shut off the solenoid as normal. This leaves the tubing inside the boat empty until you turn the solenoid on again. Finally, don't forget to turn off the burner.

The Head

Clean the shower pan and remove soap scum and dirt from the drain pump sump.

Check that the sump pump works. Clean and inspect the toilet for leaks, and add deodorant to holding tanks.

ON DECK

A quick walk around the deck usually turns up several should-do chores, because anything exposed to the elements requires regular maintenance to keep it functioning.

Deck Lights

Inspect the running lights, spreader lights, and anchor light and replace any burned-out bulbs.

Lines and Fenders

Check docklines for chafe. Swap lines if necessary to spread the wear more evenly among them. Inspect anchor lines for signs of wear. Check that shackles are tight and the chain/rope splice is in good shape. Inspect fenders for proper inflation and to ensure that their lines are in good shape.

Deck Pumps

Check the washdown pump and clean the intake strainer if necessary. Check the freshwater deck shower for proper function.

Canvas

Inspect canvas for signs of wear, especially around fasteners. Lubricate zippers with a dry lubricant like a silicone spray and clean both the exterior and interior, where mildew can grow.

Dinghy and Outboard

Clean the inflatable boat or hard dinghy and check for signs of wear. Inspect the outboard and its spark plugs, starter cord, and gas tank.

Safety Gear

Check safety gear like flares, VHF radio, and EPIRB to see that they are in working order, and make sure that the first-aid kit is well stocked. Make sure flares are not outdated and that there are fresh batteries in all units that require them.

Give fire extinguishers a shake to reactivate the contents. Also make sure their inspection tags are up to date—they should be inspected annually by a professional and replaced, refilled, or retagged as appropriate.

CHAPTER 24

Tools and Spare Parts

When we asked a lot of boaters what tools and spare parts they keep on board, we were not surprised to learn that choices range from bare essentials to a list as long as your arm. It seems that the more mechanically inclined a cruiser you are, the more tools and spares you will carry.

Vic Hansen from Southwest Florida Yachts, where *High Life* is chartered during the winter months, has some sage advice. He says if it pumps, sucks, or spins, a spare should be on board. Anyone who owns a boat knows the wisdom of those words.

Even if you neither intend nor have the inclination to use any tools, a basic set should be on board for emergency repairs. Exactly what spare parts you need to carry is a more subjective question.

WHAT SHOULD YOU KEEP ON HAND?

For the boater who doesn't plan to cruise to remote places, carrying a large store of spare parts and all the tools to install them probably doesn't make much sense. We carry a reasonable store of both to prevent any delays in our cruising. If we have the part we can fix the problem; and even if we don't make the repair ourselves, there's a good chance we can hire

someone who can. But we don't carry major parts like fuel injectors that require real expertise to install. And depending on where we cruise, fast delivery by FedEx, UPS, or other shippers makes most replacement parts available in a matter of days.

When we purchased *High Life*, she had 5,000 hours on the engine. Since then we've begun a systematic overhaul of the engine and generator and replaced everything outside the engine that moves, pumps, or comes in contact with seawater. Our stash of spare parts contains both new and used items. Many of the parts we replaced, like the main heat exchanger, transmission, and oil coolers, were still serviceable, so we cleaned them up and saved them as spares. The same is true for the fuel, raw water, and circulating pumps. All are in working order and could easily replace a failed part.

If you have a newer engine, you probably don't need to carry so many parts, unless you plan to cruise to areas where you can't rely on a next-day shipment. There are, however, parts that begin to wear the moment you commission the boat—belts, pump impellers, and hoses all age. These are the parts for which every boat should have spares, along with the necessary tools to install them.

The parts dilemma extends beyond the engine room. Every time you turn on the water, that faithful pressure pump is a bit closer to failure. And bilge pumps, shower drain pumps, washdown pumps, air conditioner pumps, and refrigeration circulation pumps are all going to fail sooner or later.

One of the best ways we've found to answer the question "What's going to break next?" is to talk to boaters who own similar boats. Look for your boat manufacturer's website. Many of these sites feature an owner's discussion forum either on the site or on a user group's website. Find one on Google and join in. Both Yahoo and MSN host many active forums. Each boat has its strong points and its unique weaknesses, and by reading what other owners say, you can ferret out potential problems that you should anticipate.

Sometimes manufacturers publish a newsletter. It's another resource to read and ponder.

TOOLS TO HAVE ABOARD

We draw a distinction between tools to maintain the boat and those required for making repairs. Tools like an electric buffer we keep at home and bring aboard only when we plan to wax and polish the topsides. Any tool that we think we might need for an unplanned repair we keep on the boat.

We think it's better to have a collection of small specialty toolboxes, containers, or canvas sacks than one large one that's difficult to stow and too heavy to lift. We also think that quality is better than quantity when it comes to tools. Better to have a few good screwdrivers with hardened tips that won't strip a screw head than a full set of cheap ones. The same goes for wrenches: cheap ones distort under pressure and will slip and round the corners off bolts or fittings. And don't rely on adjustable wrenches to loosen really tight bolts. Have combination (box end on one side, open end on the other) wrenches of the proper size for every application. Buy the best quality tools you can afford and keep them on board.

General Tools

- Measuring tape
- Hacksaw
- Cordless ⅜-in. drill
- Wrench sets: complete sets of open-end and box-end; US standard ¼ in. to ⅞ in., and metric 9 mm to 19 mm
- Sockets: standard ¼ in. to ⅞ in., and metric 9 mm to 19 mm
- Ratchet handle and extensions
- Pliers: regular fixed joint; needle-nose; slip joint; locking; hose pinch-off clamp
- Screwdrivers: Straight or slot drive of assorted lengths and tip sizes; Phillips head #0–#4 in assorted lengths; stubbies in both straight and Phillips head; precision micro set
- 6 in., 8 in., and 10 in. adjustable wrenches
- Oil filter wrench
- Regular and long-reach side cutters
- 12 oz. ball peen and soft-tip hammers
- Set of cold chisels, punches, and drift pin alignment tools
- Feeler gauge set (to measure thickness)
- Scratch awl
- Metal files
- Heavy-duty scissors
- Small and large prybars
- Standard and metric Allen/hex wrench sets
- Impeller removal tool
- Gasket scraper
- Magnetic pickup tool
- Portable work light
- Ear muffs

We store our electrical tools in a fishing-tackle box. It holds everything we need for minor electrical repairs and installations.

We use this small drawer under a step into the main cabin to keep openers, gizmos, and the tools we need most often for a quick fix.

Electrical Tools

We use a small plastic tackle box for electrical tools that contains:

- Digital multimeter
- AC outlet tester
- Battery-terminal cleaner
- Wire cutter/stripper
- Ratcheting crimper
- Seizing wire
- Assorted connectors, wires, wire ties
- Electrical tape
- Emery paper

THE TOOL DRAWER

We store small tools that we need for quick repairs under a step in the main saloon. We keep the basics: a measuring tape, utility knife, small and large adjustable crescent wrenches, Phillips and slotted-head screwdrivers, adjustable Robogrip, needle-nose pliers, hammer, cordless Wizard power tool, cordless power screwdriver, and a ditty bag with assorted small lines.

OTHER USEFUL NON-TOOL ITEMS

Over the years we've acquired useful bits and pieces that help us keep the boat working. Here's a list:

- Flashlights: pocket light in nav station, 8-inch flashlight in engine room, 6-inch flashlight in main salon, spare flashlight on bridge
- Handheld power vacuum (with a crevice tool)
- Washdown hose and spray nozzle, buckets
- Silicone sealant, bedding compound
- Spare nuts and bolts, stainless steel screws, fasteners
- Miscellaneous: duct tape, funnel, pipe cleaners, mirror, magnet, bungee cord, spray bottle, adhesives, sealants, lubricants, WD-40

A–Z TOOL BAGS

One long-time cruising friend of ours likes small, separate Ziploc tool bags that are easy to pick up and carry where they're needed. He labels the bags on the top and sides in large letters for quick identification. Here's his system:

- Bag A—the most often-used tools such as a selection of screwdrivers, adjustable wrenches, pliers

- Bag B—spare and less-used tools
- Bag C—small spare parts
- Bag D—sealants, lubricants, snaps
- Bag E—electrical supplies
- Bag F—socket wrenches, electric screwdriver
- Bag G—assorted screws, nuts, bolts, etc.

SPARE PARTS

We were enjoying ourselves in West End on Grand Bahama Island, waiting for the Gulf Stream to lie down before returning to Florida, when a sportfishing boat limped in and docked next to us. One of its engines had a blown coolant pump. The owners made a few calls, found a replacement pump in Miami, and had it overnighted to them. When they went to pick it up they discovered that the import duty was almost as much as the pump itself. We remember that incident when we question the money we've invested in our spare parts.

We think that spare parts can be split into those you must have on board, and those that are nice to have.

MUST-HAVE PARTS

These consumable spare parts are part of our inventory:

- Fuel filters, both for the filters mounted on the engine and for remotely mounted filters
- Oil filters

- Engine oil, transmission fluid, hydraulic steering fluid, engine coolant
- Zincs for engine, heat exchangers and coolers, shaft(s), and rudder(s)
- Belts for alternator, freshwater pump, seawater pump, refrigeration system, engine, and generator
- Several seawater impeller replacements and gaskets
- One tested thermostat with gasket
- Radiator cap
- Spark plugs
- Air cleaner elements
- Inflatable repair kit

BASIC BOAT SYSTEM SPARES

Each boat is unique but here are the basic parts and rebuild kits for the systems of a cruising boat that should be aboard.

Water System
- Pressure pump rebuild kit
- Shower-drain pump rebuild kit or spare pump
- Bilge pump rebuild kit
- Manual bilge pump rebuild kit

- Extra water filters
- Assorted ABA-type hose clamps

Head
- Head rebuild kit and gaskets
- Assorted ABA-type hose clamps

Electrical
- Assorted bulbs for interior light fixtures, running lights, masthead light, instrument panels, compass, and electronics
- 4 Spare fuses for all navigation electronics, radios, entertainment units, and so on
- Spare batteries for radios and cameras

Outboard Spares
- Spark plugs
- Propeller
- Shear pins

NICE-TO-HAVE PARTS

Many of the parts listed below are made of rubber and will eventually deteriorate, or they have moving parts that will wear out. All have a long service life, but remember that, as any engine reaches more than a couple of thousand hours the bolt-on items need attention. It's a simple case of buy them now or buy them later.

Engine
- Factory hose kit
- Oil coolers for engine and transmission
- Starter solenoid
- Alternator and mounting bracket
- Set of oil cooler hoses
- Transmission cooler hoses
- Start and stop control solenoids
- Spare raw-water pump with gaskets, pulleys, and pipe and hose fittings

- Raw-water pump cover plate with gasket and screws
- Raw-water pump cam and screw
- Engine coolant freshwater pump with gasket, gears, and pulleys
- Spare fuel pump with hose fittings
- Engine valve cover gasket
- Heat exchanger
- End cap gaskets

Air Conditioning System
- Seawater cooling pump with fittings
- Spare electric pump with switch

Finally, here's a piece of advice about buying parts for your boat. Whatever you need for your boat, always look first to the marine store that's closest. The price may be higher than elsewhere, but buying locally has many advantages. There's the convenience, and the fact that local sales associates can often answer questions to lead you toward exactly what you need. And when you take into account the ease of return if you select the wrong part, and the lack of shipping charges, the price may not be so different from that of a large discount store or online supplier.

But when you need a rare item that doesn't sell well enough for the local store to stock it, going online or calling an 800 number can often be the answer. Just remember that, though "long distance" prices are often much lower (thanks to volume sales and the economies of scale), by the time you add shipping and handling charges you may not have saved that much. The value of these sources lies in being able to get whatever you want—when you want, if you opt for overnight delivery.

CHAPTER 25
Keeping It Clean

Some people who live to cruise are oblivious to dirt, bird droppings on deck, and the scent of mildew down below. And there are others who live to clean and polish their boat and rarely leave the dock. Most of us fall somewhere in between—at least we do. We're not clean freaks by any stretch, but we do find cleaning our boat much more rewarding than cleaning our house or car.

Any boat—tied to a dock, swinging at a mooring, or sitting high and dry—is susceptible to dirt from its surrounding area, from air pollution, and from salt spray. In this chapter we'll tell you our solutions to keeping a boat clean and share some ideas we've learned from boating friends. These techniques work for us, whether we're uncovering a boat that's been laid up all winter or doing regular cleaning routines during the season.

We schedule interior cleaning before or after—never during—the time Gene is at work in the engine room. When he's down there we have to remove the floorboards in the main cabin. That simple action leaves nowhere to go. The main cabin's out of action. Working up forward isn't possible because there's no access, and we move the dinette table from the main cabin to the aft

cabin while Gene's working, so that's off limits as well. We learned the value of scheduling the work this way during our first season. Katie was in the forward cabin cleaning away as Gene got to work in the engine room. She only escaped by wiggling out of the forward hatch with some clever maneuvers and with great difficulty.

On some boats, the teak trim, or *brightwork*, requires nothing more than a hose-down. This is generally the case when the wood is either well-oiled or properly varnished. (Some boatowners go as far as to have a coat of clear Awlgrip professionally applied over the varnish for further protection.) Oiled or varnished brightwork will last a long time if you rinse it daily to remove the salt and then use a chamois to remove the water drops, which (because of their lens-like shape) can magnify the sun's intensity and increase its potential damage. On other boats the owners neglect the brightwork until it gets so bad that it's beyond routine maintenance. Then it always becomes a major refinishing project.

Call us crazy, but we enjoy making the wood trim shine and sparkle. After we give you our take on boat cleaning we'll describe the Hamilton approach to the fine art of finishing teak.

CLEANING TOPSIDES AND DECKS

Scrubbing the decks of a boat provides a sense of satisfaction like no other, and for many it's a Saturday morning ritual. When we arrive at the boat, we unload our stockpile of food and gear, and before opening all the hatches and windows, we haul out the hose and dutifully remove the layer of dirt on the topsides and deck that has built up while we were away. It's a good workout and a routine that kick-starts our weekend cruises. Before we put the hose away, we top off the water tanks and we're ready to cast off in a clean boat. It goes without saying that our smaller boats were a cinch to clean and we were off the dock in no time; larger ones take more time and attention.

Once a boat's been scrubbed and polished, a weekly routine of cleaning chores is all you'll need. Some people even find these chores to be therapeutic. Many boaters tell us that after working all week at a desk job, the physical exertion of cleaning comes as a welcome change, not to mention the sense of satisfaction that comes from having a squeaky clean boat.

At the beginning of the boating season, it's prudent to give the boat an overall cleaning: hull, topsides, decks, and all the interior surfaces, spaces, and windows. But regular cleaning throughout the season is important too. Debbie Roark, who cruises aboard *Still Water* with her husband Roger, is a boat-cleaning phenomenon at our club. Here's how she tackles it.

When they come in from a day on the water, Debbie hoses down the boat with water, then she applies a water and boat soap solution (using a soap dispenser attached to the hose). Once a week she scrubs the boat thoroughly with boat soap and water and uses Absorber rags—the brand of artificial

Many boaters get into the habit of cleaning their boat soon after tying up.

chamois that claims to absorb three times faster than the natural type—to dry the glass and chrome. To clean the heavy vinyl enclosure panels on the bridge, she likes Aqua-View 210, a cleaning and polishing product used with a squeegee. To keep teak trim bright, she likes Semco sealer because it's easy to apply and gives the wood a nice finish.

To clean dirty power cords and fenders, she prefers GoJo, an orange pumice hand cleaner. If they're particularly dirty she applies it with a scrubbing pad. This works on dirty water hoses too.

WASHING A BOAT 101

Beginning on the flying bridge or top of the boat, work your way down to the decks concentrating in one area—about 3–4 square feet—at a time.

1. Close all openings like hatches, windows, and doors and clear the decks of chairs, coolers, etc.
2. Haul out a hose (long enough to reach all areas of your boat) with an adjustable spray nozzle and attach it to a dock water spigot.

3. Gather together cleaning supplies that include a bucket, brush, sponge or pad with a pole handle, rags, a hand scrub brush, boat soap, and absorbing chamois.

4. Don't scrub a dry surface. It's best to wash it down with a spray of water before cleaning. The water can loosen and wash away the dirt.

5. Mix a boat soap and water solution (according to the manufacturer's directions) and scrub the surface with a pole handled brush or non-abrasive scrubbing pad.

6. Use a hand scrub brush to remove bird droppings, bug nests, or other tough to remove spots.

7. Rinse the soapy area with a spray of water.

8. Use rags to dry surface areas and an absorbing chamois on teak trim and rails, chrome, display panels, and electronics to prevent spotting.

9. As you complete one section of the boat, continue working your way down and around the boat to wet, wash, and dry the rest of it.

CLEANING TEAK DECKS

The teak decks on our 1984 trawler are original and have withstood many years of dirt, wear, and weather. To keep them clean, we use a deck brush or non-abrasive scrubbing pad on a pole.

We fill half a bucket with water and liquid TSP, mixed according to the directions. The job is divided into four parts beginning on the bridge, then along the port and starboard sides, and finishing in the cockpit. On hot days we try to follow the sun, working on the shady side first so the heat doesn't dry the decks before we've scrubbed them. We change the solution for each area of our cleaning process. Here's a short rundown:

Close hatches, windows, and door openings. Hook up the hose to a water spigot on shore and gather cleaning supplies so you have everything you need. If your skin is sensitive, wear rubber gloves. Remove everything from the decks so all the surfaces can be scrubbed. Don't forget to lift the tail ends of docklines and hang them over the railing, and make sure the scuppers are free so the washdown water will flow freely.

FIXING SCRATCHES

To remove scratches from Plexiglas windshields or windows or covers made of plastic, you have two choices, depending on the severity of the scratch. Minor scratches can be filled with a gelcoat polish with one application. Let it dry to a haze and follow up with a good buffing.

For a scratch on a plastic surface, use a rubbing compound that has a cutting agent, designed to remove oxidation from the boat's gelcoat. Apply the rubbing compound to the area of the scratch, gradually removing some of the surrounding surface to make the scratch and area around it smooth and shiny. Make several gradual applications and work slowly until you can run your hand over the scratch and barely feel it. Then apply a good buffing polish to remove any marks left by the rubbing compound. To protect the surface apply a good quality boat wax or polish.

Before applying soap to dirty decks, hose them down to give the cleaning solution a wet surface to work itself into.

- Hose down one section of the deck and then dip the brush or scrubber into the bucket of liquid TSP and water solution and slop it onto the surface.
- Let the solution set on the teak for a few minutes and then work the brush or scrubber into the wood fibers. Gently scrub the deck across the grain of the wood and in a circular motion. As you scrub you'll see the color of the wood lighten and dark spots disappear.
- Rinse off the solution with clear water and make a second application to any areas that are particularly dirty or darkened.
- For narrow pieces of teak trim use a variety of different-sized brushes that fit the situation. We use a small toilet bowl brush and kitchen brushes.
- As you complete one section, give it a final rinsedown and let it dry.

Instead of TSP, teak decks can also be cleaned with any of the commercially available teak cleaners that are used to prep teak brightwork before refinishing. Since most of them have been on the market for a while; each has its devoted proponents who swear "nothing is better." Some are best suited to refinishing work, others are OK for cleaning.

A hose and scrubbing pad work together to remove mildew and dirt from old teak decks.

If you decide to try one for yourself, be sure to read and follow the directions on the package. We can't help but notice that when people aren't satisfied with the results obtained from using a product that others say works

Use small brushes to scrub difficult-to-reach areas.

well, it's most often because they failed to properly follow the manufacturer's instructions.

WAXING AND PROTECTING THE GELCOAT

A layer of wax gives a fiberglass boat a protective finish against damaging ozone and ultraviolet light, dirt, and soot. With a big boat, this is not a job for the faint of heart. Waxing can be a time-consuming project, depending on the size of the boat and condition of the gelcoat—the usual outer layer of a fiberglass structure.

First, clean the boat, then apply wax using a clean rag or foam pad, following the manufacturer's directions. Apply the wax in a circular motion and work it into the gelcoat. Change the applicator often to avoid scratching the surface with any dirt or particles you may pick up during the wax application.

When the wax dries to a light haze, power up an electric buffer to polish the surface and remove the wax. Change the pad, also called a *bonnet*, frequently to create a clean surface. We've also heard rave reviews for both terry rags and microfiber towels for hand buffing and polishing.

Avoid getting wax on any unfinished wood, including brightwork or nonskid areas of the deck. It can leave residue and change a nonslippery surface to a slippery one.

Consider polishing old or dull gelcoat with a rubbing/polishing compound to restore its finish. The compound first works as an abrasive paste to remove dirt and chalking (a light dusty residue), then as the compound dries it can be used to polish the surface. Apply the compound, working on a small area at a time, and then use an electric buffer to remove the compound and restore the gelcoat.

CLEANING A BOOTSTRIPE

A bootstripe, the thin strip of contrasting color often applied at the waterline just above the bottom paint, is an eyesore if it accumulates oil and grime, but it doesn't have to be. If your boat is out of the water, it's easy to scrub. You can usually reach it from a comfortable standing position or from a stepladder. If the boat's in the water, you can clean it from an inflatable boat or work float without too much effort.

We use green 3-M (or Scotch) scouring pads soaked in a biodegradable cleaner. We scrub our way around the boat, and then rinse it off with a sponge and clean water. If the boat is out of the water, we give it a quick coat of wax to keep the stripe cleaner longer.

If you're a strong swimmer, you can get in the water and swim or paddle around the hull. Be sure to wear a life vest or use a swim tube for support. To help tread water, wear swim fins. To hold yourself close to the boat, you can use a suction-cup handle that sticks to the hull. These handles are sold at many large boat supply outlets and hardware stores.

Before we go below to start cleaning up the boat's interior, here are three other tips we'd like to pass on. First, to clean docklines, wash them in Woolite in the gentle cycle of a washing machine and drape and snake them over a fence to dry.

Second, to avoid a diesel stain when refueling, spray the decks with water before taking on fuel. If there is a spill the fuel will float on top of the wet deck and be easy to clean up with an oil-absorbing pad, rag, or paper towel. It will not stain the teak.

Third, if your hull material is steel, there is a product called Ospho (www.ospho.com) that, if added to wash water, will penetrate the inevitable pinholes in the finish and chemically restore any new rust (iron oxide) to pure steel as you wash the boat. It will help in maintaining a steel boat above the waterline both cosmetically and structurally.

A SQUEAKY CLEAN INTERIOR

The nooks, crannies, and confined spaces inside a boat create perfect conditions for mildew to grow and spread. And all the gear you bring aboard and store makes cleaning those spaces more difficult. The first step in cleaning the interior of a boat has nothing to do with actually scrubbing and polishing: it involves removing cushions, dishware, and curtains and relocating toolboxes, storage containers, and other items from their designated spaces to give yourself access to all the compartments and hidden corners. It's the only way to clean the surfaces below bunks or tucked behind bulkheads.

We try to tackle a major cleanup of the interior on a sunny, windy day. To give cushions a dose of freshness and prevent mildew we spread them on deck bottom-side-up and let the sun do its work. We open all the hatches, windows, and doors to ventilate the interior.

If you store the boat out of the water during the winter months, remove linens, dishes, and so on and store them at home. In the spring, bring them back washed and ready to use. If you keep the boat in the water all year, schedule a boat "strip" twice a year and do the same thing—empty the boat and clean it from stem to stern.

With its appliances, compartments, dishes, glassware, and pots and pans, a galley requires a lot more cleaning attention than you'd expect from its relatively small space. We take all the dishes, cookware, and utensils home to run them through a dishwasher and schedule galley cleaning while it's empty.

Product-wise, we stick to store-bought cleaning solutions that can be used for more than one task. Storage is always at a premium,

CLEANING SECRETS FROM SEASONED CRUISERS

Here are some cleaning tips we've gleaned from boaters far and wide:

- Use a hand vacuum to clean carpeting on interior hull sides to remove dust. For the best results, remove the carpeting from the boat and bring it to a professional cleaner. If the carpeting is held down with snaps, be careful when lifting it. Pry the snaps apart slowly with a putty knife rather than yanking on them.
- Keep a terrycloth face towel handy in the head to wipe up excess water and moisture every time you use the sink and (especially) the shower.

- Use an old toothbrush to scrub around sinks, and cotton swabs to get fine dirt out of hard-to-reach spots.
- Make cleaning the head after use an easy routine for everyone by leaving a pull-top container of wet disinfecting wipes handy.
- After every shower, open a window to air out the space and help dry the damp towels and shower curtain.
- After pumping out a holding tank, flush it with water and then pump it out again. Use a holding tank deodorant applied directly into the tank or the toilet.

HEATING AND COOLING SYSTEMS

Check the drainage pan that collects condensation under the air conditioning evaporator coils: it's a natural breeding ground for mildew and odors. Make sure the drain is not clogged. The air conditioner can remove a lot of moisture (several gallons at least) from the air every day, and this water should go overboard or at least into the bilge, not onto the cabin sole. Clean the air duct filters too. Even though the boat is a rather clean environment, a lot of dirt accumulated in the filter will lower the efficiency of the air conditioner. Clean the filter with soap and water, and let it air dry before reinstalling it.

so we buy these items in normal-sized, not jumbo, containers and keep an extra one tucked away. We like Pinesol for cleaning interior surfaces, especially in the galley and heads, and Murphy's Oil Soap for the teak bulkheads, cabinets, table, and floors. For brass and metal we like King Midas Metal Polish and Bar Keepers Friend; both are small in size and can be used on deck as well as down below.

When the interior surfaces are clean, we wash the windows inside and out.

To keep the head clean, we remove everything that's not bolted down and pay particular attention to the storage compartments, where mildew can take hold. We wash all the surfaces, and use a narrow brush to clean small, hard-to-reach areas. After we've cleaned the toilet we flush it with a solution of household vinegar and water and then add a few drops of cooking oil to lubricate the seals.

Although the head is the smallest cabin on most boats, it requires regular cleaning and upkeep. With a tub or shower, the close, damp conditions contribute to the growth of mildew. If there's a floor grate in a shower pan, don't forget to clean the water reservoir below it where the float switch for the shower sump pump sits. Hair, soap scum, and dirt tend to accumulate there.

BRIGHTWORK

There are two types of brightwork: 1) the teak trim we discussed earlier, and 2) the many stainless steel and chrome fittings that you'll find on a boat.

We're suckers for teak brightwork, so over the years we've tested various finishes aboard the different boats we've owned. We've used teak oil, Cetol, and different brands of varnish. Our current finish of choice is Epifanes varnish. We admit that a high-gloss varnish is the most time-consuming, but we think it's worth it. Yes, it's labor-intensive and demanding work, but we love the shine that only a good marine varnish produces.

OUR TRIED-AND-TRUE VARNISHING ROUTINE

Anyone who refinishes brightwork knows that the real work lies in preparing the teak; applying the finish is the finale. First we remove deck hardware, like the port and starboard stainless steel rub rails, gate hardware, and other fittings, and then we apply low-tack (light adhesive), waterproof, blue masking tape to protect the gelcoat from splatters of varnish and to catch drips. We cut old drop cloths into strips slightly wider than the decks to protect them. The skinny drop cloths are easy to move around the boat and to shake out.

We create a workspace on the aft cabin with a layer of newspapers to protect the sole, and assemble the supplies. Key to the operation is a varnish box and a few large coffee cans to clean the brushes and mix the varnish and thinner. The cardboard box should be about 10 × 14 inches or smaller—just the right size to hold a can of varnish and a rag, and to provide a convenient resting place for the brush.

Here's how to do it:

1. First, tape around the teak with water-proof blue masking tape to protect the gelcoat. We've found that non-waterproof blue tape leaves adhesive residue *everywhere*. Our experience gave us a keen respect for 3M adhesive remover (after we'd tried every other adhesive remover we could find). We never leave the tape on if rain threatens, and as soon as the finish tacks up we remove the tape. A well-waxed boat will prevent most of the tape problems.

2. Use a piece of folded 220-grit sandpaper and a foam sanding block to remove the top layer of finish until there's a dull shine. Sand with the grain of the wood to remove any dark spots or blemishes in the varnish and create a uniform surface.

3. When sanding is completed, use an old paintbrush as a duster to remove sanding residue from the surface, and then use the crevice tool of a portable vacuum to thoroughly clean the area surrounding the teak. Then wipe down the teak with a rag dampened in mineral spirits. After this, you should wipe down the surface again (thoroughly) with a tack cloth to lift all sanding dust. Keep refolding the cloth to constantly present a clean part. It's best to use a tack cloth bought from a marine store: home-supply cloths often contain a waxy substance that will spoil a good varnish job.

4. Always read the manufacturer's directions about stirring and mixing the varnish with thinners. Most often, you'll have to thoroughly stir the contents of

Our varnishing kit. A simple box keeps everything together: varnish, thinner, brush, blue masking tape, and rags.

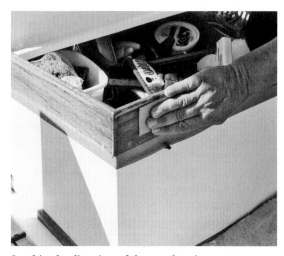

Sand in the direction of the wood grain to remove any blemishes or imperfections.

the can before you do anything else. But do any thinning and remixing in your *working* container, NOT in the varnish can. In fact, once you pour the amount of varnish you need into the working container, you should put the lid back on the can as tightly as possible. Don't hammer the lid, unless you use a rubber mallet. Hammering can distort the top of the can and prevent an airtight seal.

5. Mix the varnish thoroughly with the correct amount of thinner (stirring as gently as possible to avoid creating bubbles that can spoil a good varnish job). Now you're ready to grab your brush.

6. Some people swear by foam brushes because there are no bristles to leave streaks. We disagree. In our opinion, there's only one type of brush to use of you want a spectacular finish: badger hair. And don't skimp; buy the best quality you can find (a 2-inch width is adequate for most projects) and treasure it like the family jewels. Use it *only* for varnish, clean it thoroughly after each use, and store it so it will maintain the proper shape. When you buy a good brush, it comes with a light cardboard wrapper held shut with string wrapped around a couple of small paper disks. It's tempting to toss the wrapper as soon as the brush is removed. Don't! Keep it to use as a bristle protector, and your brush should have a long and useful life.

7. Dip just the tip of the brush into the varnish and tip it off on the edge of the can to remove any excess. Apply the finish in a sweeping motion in one direction and return over the wetted area in the other direction to fill in any voids. Blend each brush stroke back into the previously covered wet area, and you should get a clean, line-free finish.

[fc 24.6] Keep varnish flowing onto the sanded wood by applying even strokes, following the grain of the wood.

8. After applying the finish carefully, dispose of any leftover varnish in your working container. Never return it to the can. Don't even keep it for another coat unless you are absolutely sure it won't start to set up while you are waiting. You will get a better result by using a fresh batch for the next coat. It's worth a small amount of waste.

9. Clean out the brush thoroughly in mineral spirits and dry it with a brush spinner, a tool that works like a kid's toy top. Spin the brush inside a bucket lined with newspaper to avoid spraying the surrounding area with mineral spirits. When the brush is thoroughly dry, wrap it in its protective cover and hang it by the handle so that the bristles will maintain their shape and flexibility.

10. For a long-lasting and durable finish, and one that looks great, too, you should apply a minimum of four to six coats if you are starting from bare wood. For routine touch-up of cared-for wood, a single fresh coat, if applied frequently enough, should maintain the finish

well. Follow the manufacturer's instructions, of course, but when you are applying multiple coats, usually you must wait until each coat is dry enough to withstand a light sanding with 220-grit wet-or-dry paper. This breaks down the gloss to provide a roughened surface for the next coat to adhere to. After each sanding, follow the suggestions outlined above (dusting with dry brush, vacuuming, wiping with mineral spirits and tack cloth) to thoroughly remove all sanding dust before applying another coat.

If you follow this refinishing procedure whenever your brightwork starts to lose its gleam, and keep up with it by proper cleaning and drying on a daily basis, it will always look good. Ultraviolet light is the prime enemy of varnished surfaces. The closer your cruising takes you to the equator, the more often you'll have to renew the finish, even if you follow your daily maintenance routine religiously.

If you don't keep up with it, either by neglecting proper daily maintenance or by not renewing the varnish surface coat often enough, you'll have to remove the whole lot and start from scratch. And even if you do everything right, eventually those multiple layers of varnish will cease looking like a shining gem and become a thick opaque mess that must be removed. That's exactly the situation we faced when we bought *High Life*. Most of her varnish had to be removed, a process called *being wooded*. Here's how it goes:

STRIPPING OLD VARNISH

When the brightwork finally loses its luster, and needs stripping back to bare wood, we use a pair of heat guns, each with a long, heavy-duty extension cord to give us access to all areas of the boat. We also use two Red

You'll need to bring out the heavy artillery—a heat gun—to remove peeling and cracked varnish.

Devil hand scrapers, small and inexpensive, but mighty powerful for scraping off heavy layers of varnish. We bring a small tool sharpener aboard so we can sharpen the scraper blades frequently. They should be razor sharp. We lay down the drop cloths and use kneepads to ease strain on the knee joints.

It takes some experimentation to handle the tools comfortably—to learn how far to hold the gun from the varnish, and to find out which setting (high or low) works best. Be careful with the heat gun; it gets very hot, and will burn any surface it gets too close to. Practice using it so you won't damage the boat or hurt yourself. And be sure to wear safety glasses to protect your eyes. The job is painstakingly slow, so be patient.

Once removed, the curls of old varnish dry quickly and you can gather them up in the drop cloths when each section of the job is completed. Use a shop vacuum to pick up all the other pieces that blow around the boat, before they get lodged in the scuppers or tracked below decks.

A small hand scraper with a sharp blade removes layers of dried varnish.

If you take your time and use a very sharp scraper the teak will be smooth and almost ready to varnish. Give all bare surfaces a light sanding with 220 paper, then dust the areas to remove the sawdust. Next, check out our varnishing tips in the section above.

OTHER FINISHES

Before we leave the subject of teak care, we should acknowledge that not everyone shares our love of a patent-leather shine. Some prefer the warm, soft-matte finish of well-oiled wood, while others delight in the silvery, natural look of unfinished teak. Whatever floats your boat. But whatever finish you choose, while the type of work involved may differ, good-looking teak always requires work of some kind.

Take the natural look, for example. To keep a nice, even finish, the wood must be kept clean. It's ultraviolet light—our enemy in so many ways—that helps this look to develop. This is probably why the natural look seems to develop so much better in sunnier climates; up north, it often becomes more black than silvery. If you don't keep the wood clean and follow the same rinse and wipe routine we recommend for finished wood, you'll end up with dirty, blotchy teak that screams its lack of care.

Similarly, oiled teak must be washed, rinsed, and wiped dry every day, or it too will start to look less than perfect. And though an oiled finish is in some ways easier to maintain than a gloss, it occasionally requires a thorough cleaning with teak cleaner (usually a one- or two-part product that combines a detergent with a wood bleach), followed by one or two coats of fresh oil. This removes sub-surface dirt and evens out color differences in the wood that result from differing responses to ultraviolet light, for a smooth, even finish.

As always, the particular cleaner or finish you use will often be less significant than whether or not you follow the manufacturer's instructions. If you do, all products work well. If you don't, you've wasted your time and money. We recommend that you first try several brands to find which one you prefer to work with, then stick with that one. As with so many aspects of boating life, the more familiar you are with a process, the easier it becomes and the better the results.

CHROME AND STAINLESS STEEL

Besides finished wood, boats have plenty of chrome and stainless steel that need care as well. As with wood, one of the keys to maintaining metal fittings is to keep them as salt-free as possible. The same "wash it, rinse it, wipe it" technique works here, too. The big difference is what you do afterwards to make the process easier in the future.

Some boaters use a slightly abrasive metal polish like Flitz (www.flitz.com) to get the brightest shine, then wax the metal so that it will repel dirt and salt. This works, but others take a different approach. There is a liquid polish called Sheila Shine (http://www.sheilashineinc.com), which does an excellent job on chrome or stainless steel (or any other hard surface). It both polishes and protects in a single application. Sheila Shine works best when applied in a very thin film. Wipe it on any clean, dry surface, wipe again with a clean cloth to remove any remaining dirt and/or oxidation, then wipe once more with a very thin film. This film will shun water, salt, and just about anything else, making the surface easy to clean in the future with just a rinse. Used on a weekly basis, Sheila Shine will keep metal brightwork and other hard surfaces like consoles, bars, and galley countertops looking like new. Just remember to apply it sparingly. A little goes a long way.

PART V

Live the Cruising Life

CHAPTER 26
How to Live the Cruising Lifestyle

Cruising has always been a part of our lives. As first-time boaters in the late 1960s, we counted the long winter days in Chicago until spring when we could get our boat ready for a season on Lake Michigan. Come summer, we spent our weekends and vacations on the lake, first crossing to southern Michigan harbor towns, and later venturing further north up the coast. We discovered Door County, Wisconsin, in the same way, poking into lakeside towns along the shoreline. We used vacations to help friends move their boats from the Great Lakes to the Erie Canal and to deliver boats from Maine to Cape Cod. We jumped at every opportunity to cruise. We even took a year off from work and cruised from Chicago to the Bahamas and back.

Today we live on the eastern shore of Maryland on Chesapeake Bay, and nowhere will you find more idyllic cruising grounds. In the fall we enjoy an annual cruise on the Intracoastal Waterway (ICW) as we take our boat to Florida, where it's chartered during the winter months.

Your own style of cruising will depend on how much time you are able to devote to it. In this chapter we'll describe three cruising scenarios based on the amount of time you have available: at weekends and on vacations; for an extended, flexible cruise; and for an unlimited period.

WEEKEND AND VACATION TIME

Weekend cruising is a wonderful way to leave behind the day-to-day concerns of land life and climb aboard a moving escape pod with all the comforts of home. We moored three of our previous boats on Chicago's lakefront, an hour's drive from where we lived. Another we kept in a Wisconsin marina, four hours away. But wherever the boat was located, we felt the commute was well worth the time.

Every Friday night and Saturday morning boatowners take to the nation's highways en route to their waiting vessels. Their cars and vehicles are packed with duffel bags, canvas sacks, and coolers filled with food and drink for their getaway. Many trailer their boats to a ramp where they'll launch.

There's no better way to gain experience on the water and to get acclimated to the boating life than by cruising on weekends and during vacations. You're likely to encounter different wind and weather conditions. For a first-time boater, the weekends become adventures to new places, and cruising becomes an enriching element of life. The boat becomes a summer cottage, and the marina, where you meet other boaters who share the same interests, becomes the center of your summer social life. You may have a slip at a luxury marina that offers

Like many boaters, we enjoy the camaraderie of cruising—making friends and sharing experiences.

resort living accommodations, or at a more basic boatyard. But no matter where you keep your boat, you're likely to feel the sense of community of like-minded cruisers who enjoy being on their boats as much as you do.

One of the easiest ways to go on a weekend cruise is to make a reservation at a nearby marina. Or join a local cruising group, travel with a fleet, and enjoy the companionship and security it offers. The group fleet captain creates the itinerary and you just follow along. We looked at these groups in Chapter 16, Learning Skills.

If you want to plan your own cruise, decide how much time you want to spend aboard and find a destination you can reach within that time. For example, if your boat cruises at 10 knots, a 50-mile run will have you underway for five hours. That's five hours *running time*. It doesn't include time spent getting ready to leave the dock, waiting for a bridge to open, or circling around at your destination waiting to get into a slip. When you're planning a cruise, always figure on additional time before and after you slip your lines to reach an overall estimate. Add an hour or two to allow for unpredictable

events that might lengthen your cruise. Sometimes Mother Nature hasn't read the day's forecast and decides to deliver some weather that's nastier than expected.

If you're early risers, a five- to six-hour run will get you to your destination in the early afternoon with time to enjoy the new harbor. If you leave at noon you'll still arrive with time to dock and unwind before dinner.

Most families who cruise with kids make shorter runs to keep everyone happy, and try to include a stop midway to anchor off a sandy beach for swimming. Some like to arrive early in a harbor town with time to explore the shops and sights. People who cruise with dogs must allow time when they arrive for a walk in the park or on the beach. We'll talk more about cruising with kids and pets in Chapter 28, Planning a Cruise. Kids or not, it's not a good idea to schedule long runs for your first cruise. It's better to ease into a routine and determine just how long everyone is comfortable being underway.

Of course, weather plays a key factor in planning a cruise, so have a bailout plan or alternate destination within a shorter distance in case it kicks up. A few days before a weekend aboard, we check a local marine

Rafting up is a popular way for boaters to get together at anchor. Often it feels like you're at a slumber party, but with your own bedroom.

THE BOAT AND BED ASHORE OPTION

Not all cruising boats have the creature comforts that make for a good night's rest, so many owners choose a destination where they can stay at a nearby motel or bed and breakfast. A marina affiliated with a motel is a good choice. You can spend the day on the boat, tie up to a slip and meet other boaters, and then take a short walk to more comfortable accommodations.

weather website where we can see what conditions are predicted. We'd rather know what's coming our way than be surprised when we're out there.

EXTENDED FLEXTIME CRUISING

When you can control your time off or have a flexible work schedule, you have more opportunities to go farther and stay longer. You can cruise your boat to distant shores and leave it in a safe place, then return to it when you have more time to spend aboard and continue the cruise. Although you won't have the use of your boat at home, you will have a new cruising area to explore.

We know many cruisers who take their boats to a favored cruising ground like Maine for winter storage so they can spend the next cruising season in the area. Others leave their boats in dry storage all summer on the east coast of Florida on the Okeechobee Waterway near Stuart—an easy jumping-off point for the Bahamas. The owners return in the winter to spend three or four months in the Bahamas. If you're inclined to cruise on an interim basis and can schedule your time aboard, roaming from cruising grounds to cruising grounds offers a lot of possibilities.

This cruising style isn't available to nine-to-fivers, but it's popular with teachers who have two months off in the summer, professionals in the medical field or in high-tech industries with interim jobs, and those who do contract work. Although they don't live aboard permanently, they make the most of cruising time by leaving their boat in a destination they want to explore. It takes legwork to find a good marina or boatyard where you'll feel confident about leaving your boat, but the time and effort will pay off when you consider the cruising opportunities that open up when you use your boat as a movable home.

Another benefit of this type of cruising is that it provides an opportunity for people looking for a place to retire. Cruisers can visit coastal communities and live aboard in a marina for a few weeks while getting a complete view of the area.

It's also possible for cruisers to break up a long passage into segments, leaving their boat at some point during a trip and returning to it later. Many cruisers making the 6,000-plus mile Great Circle or Loop Cruise, for example, like to leave their boat after a few months and return home. On this cruise, if you start with the Intracoastal Waterway on the East Coast, you then go north to the Hudson River and into the Erie Canal. From there you go across Lake Ontario to Canada's Trent-Severn Canal, to Georgian Bay, and south down Lake Michigan to Chicago. Then you take the Illinois River to the Mississippi, and on to the Ohio, Tennessee, and Tombigbee Rivers to the Gulf of Mexico. From there you go to the Panhandle and West Coast of Florida and the Keys, and back to the ICW on the East Coast. Often boaters beginning the trip in the spring leave their boat in inland waters for the winter and return the following spring to resume their cruise.

Transportation to and from the boat in more remote locations can be a challenge. How do you get home from your boat without a car? There are many options. You can arrange with a friend or family member to pick you up where you're leaving the boat. If the cruising area is within driving distance of your home, you can drive your own car back and forth to the marina that you use as your cruising base, leaving it in the marina's parking lot while you're cruising. You can take a bus, train, or jet to the destination, or use a one-way rental car.

If you rent one-way, the proximity of the marina to an airport is a key consideration. An airport is often the best and sometimes the only place to rent one-way without paying a high drop-off fee. While the cost of this kind of rental is higher than daily or weekly rates, the convenience factor is worth it. Just allow enough time to pick up the car and load or unload the boat.

We find one-way car rental more convenient than flying. (No matter how hard we try, we always travel with a pile of canvas sacks and duffel bags. They take up less room in the boat than rigid suitcases.) And we're not alone. Most cruisers that we know use one-way rental cars to get to and from their boat. And they use the car to provision the boat before returning it to the rental agency.

WHEN ONLY ONE OF YOU WANTS TO CRUISE

What do you do if one partner in a relationship doesn't want, or can't take off time, to go cruising? One Canadian solo sailor we met took his boat to the Bahamas for the winter and then his wife joined him when she had vacation time. He sailed his boat alone, but teamed up with other boats going the same way so he wasn't always on his own.

We met a "rotating" crew aboard a boat on the Erie Canal, taking a boat south for the winter. The owner had enlisted several friends to join the boat and help deliver it because his wife couldn't take unlimited time off. Each crew member was on a one-week stint. At the end of the stint, someone else replaced him. Each departing member of the crew returned home in the car driven by a newly arriving one. Where there's a will, there's a way.

UNLIMITED TIME ABOARD FOR LONG-TERM ADVENTURE CRUISING

We continue to meet people who reinvent the cruising lifestyle and combine cruising with their careers. Some are retired; most work part or full time; some live and work aboard and raise families. Sometimes they stay in one place and make permanent ties to a community while others follow the sun and move to new cruising areas. Their diverse cruising lifestyles show us clever and creative ways to have it all.

LIVING ABOARD

There's a growing number of liveaboards, who have sold their houses and replaced them with boats that they call home. They range from twentysomethings to 80-year-olds, and include couples, families, and solo sailors. Some work, others are retired, and most of them are living in marinas in locations where the weather suits them. Anyone interested in the liveaboard lifestyle should get the magazine *Living Aboard*, which has a wealth of useful tips, resources, and advice about the lifestyle from people doing it. For details, see Appendix 1.

We lived aboard at two different periods, for a year or so each time. They were wonderful adventures, but neither of us wanted to totally give up our land life. We had strong ties with family, friends, and community and looked at each of our years aboard as a life experience and experiment—not an escape. At the end of each of the cruises we were ready to return to our home, which we had rented out, and resume our life ashore. We were also aware of the financial advantages of owning a house, not a boat, and watched as our real estate appreciated in value.

WORKING FROM YOUR BOAT

Many people who live aboard work ashore in full- or part-time jobs. They use their boat *as* a boat mainly on weekends and vacations—the rest of the time, it's essentially their house. Their boats range from small to large. They are found mainly in warm climates, where living aboard is more comfortable. Their jobs are as varied as their ages and boats, and they usually have some but not all of the trappings of a land life—like a car to get to work, bikes to get around, and a cat or dog as part of the crew.

Some marinas don't want slipholders who are continually on site using their facilities. Others welcome liveaboards and see the benefit of having a lively, engaged community of boaters on the dock. Work-aboards are cruisers who work and cruise to different locations. Some move from one job to another, like those in the hospitality field (waitstaff, bartenders) and seasonal workers (scuba instructors, tour guides) who can live, work, and cruise in the Great Lakes in the summer

and move to similar jobs in warmer climates come the end of the season.

With staffing shortages in the medical field there's a growing number of traveling healthcare professionals who work for a 13-week period as a nurse, doctor, imaging professional, or therapist. These work-aboard professionals cruise their boats to a marina near one job, and then move to a new job or destination when they want.

One group of work-aboards consists of cruisers who are self-employed professionals, contractors, or consultants who are not tied to a specific location. They can take their job with them, and perform their service while underway. Another group consists of seasoned professionals who choose to forgo full retirement and want to work on a part-time or flextime basis. Some pick up a new client or boss, others work for their former employer. Lawyers who want to stay engaged, but not practice law, do research for their firm; engineers take on project work; accountants take the overload at tax time. With a cell phone, Internet connection, and laptop, many professionals can manage and maintain their career or business while cruising.

DEVELOPING YOUR OWN CRUISING STYLE

We've met some of the most interesting and independent people aboard boats, pursuing cruising in a wide variety of ways, and the three cruising styles we've talked about in this chapter are merely our attempt to define and organize them. Only you can decide for how long and on what type of boat you'd like to cruise. And your best laid plans can fall apart when an injury or illness, a business complication, a sick parent or child, or any number of life's challenges get in the way and force you to reassess your commitment to cruising. But don't let that stop the dream—those factors can just as easily interrupt any lifestyle.

If we achieve nothing else, we hope to encourage you to find a way to cruise for however long and however far you want. Take advantage of the thousands of miles of coast, rivers, lakes, and other waterways there are to discover, for an afternoon or forever after.

CHAPTER 27

Supporting the Cruising Lifestyle

Financing a house mortgage, car loan, or college tuition takes a big bite out of most paychecks. So does financing a boat. In this chapter we'll take a look at the costs associated with owning and operating a boat for short- and long-term cruising. Then we'll suggest some ways to finance a cruising adventure.

WHERE TO FIND A BOAT LENDER

All lenders are basically interested in two things: your ability to repay the loan, and the value of the boat used to secure the loan. If both halves of the equation balance, the loan is approved.

CLOSE TO HOME

You most likely have a relationship and good track record with your local bank already, so that's a good place to start. Check with your local banker and inquire if he or she makes boat loans. A good reputation with the bank may win you more favorable terms than those offered by lenders who don't know you. If you belong to a credit union, ask if boat loans are available for members.

DEALERS AND COMMERCIAL BANKS

Boat dealers and brokers have a vested interest in helping you secure a boat loan since the sale of a boat hinges on the buyer being able to pay for it. They often have a finance department or can suggest available financing options and programs.

You'll find a host of marine loan providers advertising their services in boating magazines. Choose the magazine for the type of boat you're buying. Lenders who regularly write loans for new and used power cruisers, for example, advertise in magazines like *Yachting* or *Motor Boating*.

Boat shows are a good place to look for a boat loan. In fact, they're great places, since you can talk to the lenders in person, learn their current rates and requirements, and do some on-the-spot horse-trading. If you go to a boat show (or boat dealer) with your personal financial statement, or are already prequalified for a specific amount, you have leverage because you're as good as a cash buyer.

Use the Internet to find sources for marine loans on the commercial websites where boats are sold. Use a search engine like Google, type in "Boat Loan" in the search box, and you'll find a long list of marine lenders. Yachtworld.com and firstboat.com are good examples of new and used boat-selling sites that link to marine loan companies. They feature interactive calculators that let you plug in numbers to find the best deal,

COMMON LOAN TERMS	
Loan Amount	Term in Years
$5,000–$9,999	7
$10,000–$14,999	10
$15,000–$24,999	12
$25,000–$74,999	15
$75,000+	20

and online application forms. Another good source is a boatowners' organization like BoatU.S., where members can get a quote on-line or by telephone.

National Marine Bankers is a trade organization of marine lenders. You can find a listing of members in your area on its website (www.marinebankers.org). It has a loan calculator to help you determine a monthly payment on a given loan amount, or find out how much you could borrow based upon a desired monthly repayment.

Most lenders will require 15 percent down, but this may vary from lender to lender and upon your credit rating. Lenders offer different programs with fixed rates or adjustable rates that vary with the current financial climate. A fixed rate loan with simple interest is the most basic arrangement. You agree to pay back the borrowed money plus interest at a specific rate over a certain number of years. The average length of a boat loan depends on the cost of the boat.

THE LOAN APPLICATION PROCESS

Years ago, getting approved for a boat loan used to take a lot of time and paperwork. Today you can get two- or sometimes one-day approval. Most lenders require a personal financial statement and copies of your tax returns for the past two years, and they review your credit history. To find the most favorable financing, take the time to organize your financial history, including current debt obligations. Have this information readily available before you apply.

Your personal financial statement should include an estimate of your personal assets such as house, car, and other personal property, and also your outstanding debt (car loans, credit card debt, and so on). In addition you should collect the name of your bank(s) and account numbers, details of the lender who holds the mortgage to your house, the name of your employer, and the length of your employment.

Before talking to a lender, get your credit report and your credit rating. Correct any errors if they exist and add up the total of your loans and revolving credit lines. Having a large line of credit isn't advisable because lenders view a large unused balance as a risk. Consider canceling any cards you don't use, and make sure the credit report notes that the cancellation was at your request, not because of a problem. If you're taking out a loan with a co-applicant the lender will require the same information from him or her.

You'll also need detailed information about the boat that you plan to purchase. This includes whether it is new or used, the manufacturer, model, year, length, and hull construction. In addition, you'll need the engine details, such as type, size, and the manufacturer. The total cost of the boat includes the purchase price, any equipment upgrades or accessories you're considering, and any sales taxes and registration, title, or documentation expenses that must be paid out at the time of purchase.

The lender sends your personal information to a credit bureau. If it is verified, and the boat's valuation is in line with the loan, the loan is approved.

THE SPECIAL TAX ADVANTAGE

It may be frosting on the cake, but there is a nice tax advantage to consider when you're planning your purchase. Most cruising boats will qualify as second homes, which the Internal Revenue Service defines as having "basic living accommodations, such as sleeping space, toilet, and cooking facilities." If your boat qualifies, the interest paid on the loan is fully deductible. However, to qualify, the boat loan must be a secured loan, or one where the lending institution holds the boat as collateral. Because most banks or credit firms that finance boats will want to hold a *Preferred Ship's Mortgage* (a lien that takes precedence over all other in case of default), meeting this qualification is rarely a problem.

Will the lender care if you take your boat off on a long cruise? The answer again lies in the Preferred Ship's Mortgage. As long as you make your payments, most lenders don't care a bit where you happen to be at the time. And if you don't make your payments? Well, that Preferred Ship's Mortgage is filed with the Coast Guard, so it has considerably greater reach than most other liens. It allows the lending institution to feel quite secure about getting either its money or its collateral.

COSTS OF OWNING AND CRUISING A BOAT

Sometimes we don't like to admit just how expensive owning and operating our boat is, but for all the enjoyment we get out of it, it's money well spent. Some owners describe a boat as a black hole that sucks up every available dollar. There's truth to that; owning a boat is not cheap. The urge to spend money on her can be irresistible, but the addiction can be managed.

Spreadsheet and accounting software make it relatively easy to keep track of boat expenses. We use Quicken to set up different categories. Other boaters use a basic spreadsheet program to keep track.

Online you can download your bank and credit card balances into most major financial programs, like Microsoft Money and Quicken. That makes managing your finances easier than ever before. When we're on an extended cruise, we connect to the Internet with our cell phone and conduct most of our financial transactions online. If you need more bandwidth (for a faster connection), most marinas provide a shoreside modem connection, and many now offer high-speed wireless Internet connections.

Here's a list of our typical expenses for a 36-foot trawler based in the Chesapeake Bay. The costs for your own boat will vary considerably depending on its size and where it's located, and whether or not you do your own maintenance. We do most of the maintenance like oil changes, engine work, painting, and varnishing ourselves. Our trawler has a lot of varnished teak trim and that would cost $2,500 a year (at 2005 prices) if we had to pay a boatyard. And keep in mind that the cost of owning a 46-foot trawler will be more than double the cost of owning a 36-foot trawler. For example, our boat takes just under two gallons of bottom paint; a 46-footer would need at least five gallons. That makes quite a jump in the cost of bottom paint for an additional 10 feet of boat.

We divide the costs of ownership into two categories: fixed and variable. Fixed costs are recurring as long as you own the boat, even if you don't use it. Variable costs are related to how much you use it. Maintenance costs are in the fixed-cost category since a boat always requires upkeep. But the more you use a boat, the higher the repair factor, so we place repairs in the variable category.

FIXED ANNUAL COSTS	
Boat loan payment (if applicable)	None
Insurance	$2,200 (extra if going to Florida or Bahamas)
Haulout and launch charges, bottom paint	$1,275
Slip rental	$1,800
Winter storage	$ 800
Maintenance	$ 600
Total	$6,675
VARIABLE ANNUAL COSTS	
Repairs	$ 900
Fuel	$ 600 (150 hrs of use)
Slip rentals when cruising	$ 350
Total	$1,850

CRUISING COSTS

In addition to the annual cost of owning a boat there's the actual cost of going on a cruise, which is tied directly to your lifestyle. The figures below reflect our style of cruising and may be more or less than the cost of operating your boat in your cruising area.

ONE-MONTH CRUISE	
10 nights at marina	$ 810
Fuel	$ 680
Food (groceries, restaurants)	$ 650
Cruise total	$2,140
Monthly portion of fixed annual costs ($7,575/12 months)	$ 630
Total Cost	$2,770

These one-month cruise figures are from the 2004 records of our 1300-mile, 21-day trip from St. Michaels, Maryland to Fort Myers, Florida via Chesapeake Bay, and the Intracoastal and Okeechobee Waterways. The total cost of the cruise was $2,140 for fuel, dockage, and eating aboard and ashore.

FUNDING AN EXTENDED CRUISE

For some cruisers, money is not an issue. But for the majority of us, finding the money to pay for cruising is a concern. Working at a job buys you the time to go cruising, but there are other ways to raise the funds.

USING YOUR HOUSE

Over the past few decades, the U.S. real-estate market has done very well. Equity in our property has fueled more than one cruise.

And along the way we've met many other cruisers who have devised ways to generate a cruising kitty using their property. Some rent their house while cruising for several months or more. This strategy not only helps defray the cost of the cruise, it also avoids leaving the house empty for a long period of time. Most realtors will manage the property, collect the rent, and make the necessary tax payments.

Some cruisers sell their house, downsize to a smaller one, and use the proceeds to fund a cruise. Then they store their furniture and rent the place while they're cruising.

CHARTERING YOUR BOAT

We've chartered our boat out of Choptank Charters in Oxford, Maryland for three summer seasons and from Southwest Florida Yacht Charters in Fort Myers, Florida for two winters. The arrangement works for us because we enjoy the Intracoastal Waterway trip in the spring when we return to the bay, and again in the fall when we head to warmer cruising grounds. The charter fees help defray the costs of owning and operating the boat.

If you think of your boat as a second home, a charter company is like a property management firm that handles the business of securing tenants or customers. Their responsibilities include advertising and marketing the boat, booking it with screened and qualified customers, checking them out before they leave the dock (so they know how to operate the boat), and administering the day-to-day details of having the boat ready and able to cruise.

The boatowner is responsible for the cost of insuring the boat (usually as part of a charter fleet under a plan offered by the chartering company), keeping the boat in sound working order, and maintaining it in Bristol condition. So you don't get to keep all of the

money your boat earns in charter. And of course, you don't get all the receipts to begin with. Some companies and boatowners operate on a 50:50 split; in other arrangements 60 percent goes to the boatowner and 40 percent to the charter agency. Some agencies charge a monthly fee for the time spent aboard cleaning, maintaining, and checking on the security and seaworthiness of the boat. Others charge on an hourly fee basis.

Naturally, there are pros and cons to chartering your boat. For some, it is completely out of the question because they don't want strangers using their boat. Ever! But for people who feel a tad less personally involved with what is, after all, just property—albeit beloved property—chartering solves several problems. For one, it helps defray the cost of owning the boat and having it available year round. We don't believe anyone ever got rich from chartering their boat, but the income is a definite plus.

Perhaps even more important, a boat in charter service is used often enough to keep things moving. It's a sad truth that if a boat doesn't get used often enough, problems soon develop. Salt air gets into everything, and parts that normally move eventually become so corroded they refuse to budge. People do keep boats in the water hundreds of miles from home in the hope of using them occasionally, but they usually discover that when they finally get to go boating, they actually go fixing instead. Boats in charter service get the attention and use they need to prevent this.

The key is to select a reliable charter service that will really care for your boat as well as handle the paperwork and the legalities involved in chartering. You also want to pick a service that actively markets its fleet, otherwise you'll get little of either maintenance or income. Word of mouth is the best recommendation. Ask around town or inquire in boater chatrooms. Either way, you should get a good indication of companies that work and those to stay away from.

BOAT INSURANCE

The purpose of boat insurance is to cover the cost of loss or damage to a boat and its equipment and to protect the owner from liability for injury or property damage. You need coverage for your boat when you are using it on the water, launching, hauling, and storing it. A good policy will protect you against theft, vandalism, windstorm, hail, lightning, fire, explosion, collision, and grounding. You also need insurance if you're buying with a boat loan. Most lenders require it as a way to protect the value of the loan.

We've always had good luck using a local agency that specializes in selling marine insurance, but many others swear by boatowners' associations like BoatU.S. The important point is to choose an insurer who knows the type of boat you own and the area where you do your cruising. This is particularly important in areas where weather-related issues apply, like hurricane clauses in southern waters. Travel restrictions can apply in any waters.

A good boat insurance agency will explain the difference between a policy based on the *actual cash value* and the *agreed amount* or *stated value* of your boat. An agreement based on the actual cash value pays for replacement costs minus depreciation at the time of the loss, so it's usually the less expensive policy. A policy based on the agreed amount value provides more complete coverage since you and the insurer have agreed on the value beforehand, and if the boat is totally lost you will be paid the agreed-upon amount.

Many boaters insure their boat under their homeowner's insurance policy. This type of insurance may be less expensive, but unless it is a true yacht-type policy it may not cover liability for environmental damage from oil or fuel spills that your boat causes, and other contingencies that *are* covered in a yacht policy.

Read the policy carefully, and make a list of questions to ask the agent so you understand what is covered and what is not. For example, many policies cover unattached equipment, like an inflatable or outboard motor, for an additional charge. And understand clearly the limits of liability coverage a policy offers for any accidents or injuries that occur on your boat.

THE APPLICATION PROCESS

In Appendix 1, you'll find information about marine insurance providers. Many include application forms on their websites so you can fill it out and submit it at any time.

Be prepared to answer questions about the following:

- Boat's name, type, year, model, hull type, hull number; engine type, horsepower
- Boat's insured value and liability limits
- Navigation area for coverage
- Boat's location

You'll need to provide personal information, including your occupation, driving record (and any moving violations you've had within the last three years), years of boating experience, years as a boatowner, the size of boats you've owned and operated, if you are a member of a boating organization, and if you have completed any boating education courses. Some insurance programs offer discounts to boaters who have completed a safe boating course that is approved by the National Association of State Boating Law Administrators (NASBLA). These include courses by the U.S. Coast Guard Auxiliary, the U.S. Power Squadrons, the Red Cross, and others.

If you're buying a new boat, have the spec sheet detailing its model number, Hull Identification Number (HIN), and other identifying information, along with a list of the equipment and gear it comes with. If you're buying a used boat you'll need at least a recent survey, and many insurers will require a new and current survey of any boat. You'll find more about boat surveys in Chapter 7, Buying the Boat.

TOWING INSURANCE

Many boat insurance policies provide for limited towing expenses. Specific towing insurance, on the other hand, provides coverage for you if you get in trouble. Maybe you've run aground, the engine's broken down, or you've run out of fuel. For whatever reason, the coverage provides on-the-water assistance when you need it. It is sold in the form of a membership for about $100 a year based on the level of towing service you select.

We're members of BoatU.S. and are big fans of its Towboat U.S. towing service, which we had occasion to use when our boat broke down in Georgetown, South Carolina. Our $100 policy covered the $750 charge to deliver our boat to Myrtle Beach, where it was serviced.

All it takes is one light grounding or breakdown and towing insurance pays for itself. You'll find a list of nationwide towing insurance networks in Appendix 1. These networks of on-the-water and ready-anytime commercial towboats are available 24-7 to help boats in distress. They also act as harbor ambassadors, providing visiting cruisers with radio checks, navigational assistance, and local sea condition information.

SALVAGE

Towing insurance only covers being towed as a result of minor situations that are easily dealt with by one small tow vessel. Anything more serious usually becomes salvage, and is not covered by your towing insurance.

According to BoatU.S., salvage is "any voluntary and successful rescue of a boat, its cargo and/or its passengers from a peril at sea." Salvors can demand a percentage of the boat's value, so salvage can cost a great deal more than a tow, which is typically billed at a rate of about $140 per hour.

Salvage should be covered by your basic insurance. So when you insure your boat, make sure your policy:

1. Specifically covers salvage charges (or the costs of rescuing the boat from a peril at sea).
2. Provides salvage coverage equal to the value of the boat.
3. Provides the salvage coverage in addition to the repair of any damage to the boat.
4. Does not apply a deductible or other adjustment to the payment.

Most good marine policies provide this coverage, but you need to be sure yours does too. That's another good reason for not relying on your homeowner's or other insurance to cover your boat as well. Marine insurance has many specific needs that other policies will not address.

Never assume that a tow will be billed as a tow. Any ambiguity can result in you receiving a demand for payment as salvage. Before accepting a tow, clarify with the towing captain that the service is a tow and not salvage. If at all possible, get a written estimate for the price of the tow. If the situation calls for immediate action and a written document is impractical, have someone witness the oral agreement.

Since in many cases getting a tow as quickly as possible is of more immediate concern than anything else, including the cost, having a good insurance policy (and agent) is of the utmost importance.

CHAPTER 28
Planning a Cruise

A weekend cruise to a familiar area doesn't require an extensive cruise plan, but when you want to explore new waters and invite others to join you, a thorough plan is a good idea. Make one that's flexible, and be prepared to change it according to the wrath or pleasure of Mother Nature. It might be an easy run to a marina near a favorite restaurant, or a longer cruise that involves exploring several harbor towns and anchorages. The longer the cruise, the more options you will need to consider, and the more detailed your plan will need to be. Also, the longer the cruise, the more uncertain the itinerary, and that's why it should be flexible.

Family, friends, and pets all add new dimensions and perspectives to cruising. Kids and crew often make you look at a familiar area in a new light, and meeting new friends along the way generates a lasting bond from a shared experience. Add a cat or dog or both to the mix and you'll enliven and enrich all your boating adventures. Few people would disagree that a furry friend is their best crew member, a devout companion and soul mate. In this chapter we discuss how to make a cruising plan and create a happy environment aboard.

RESEARCH DESTINATIONS

First of all, gather charts of the area and plot your course so you can estimate the time and distance you'll be underway. You can do this at home (or at the office) if you have the paper or electronic charts available. We keep new charts aboard and old ones at home for planning purposes. If we're returning to a harbor we've visited in the past, we will already have the routing stored in the GPS. Look over the chart, make your navigation plan, and become familiar with the route, especially any low bridges with restricted operating hours, which you want to avoid.

We plan ahead and leave early to explore a new area. If we intend staying in a marina we like to have the security of a reservation. When we're going to a popular area during the busy summer season we always phone ahead, sometimes weeks in advance, to get a reservation. When we're underway it's easy to call the marina by cell phone. Marinas and boatyards almost always answer the phone, but they may not monitor the radio except in the afternoon, when boats are expected to arrive.

If we're anchoring out we like to arrive early in the afternoon so we can pick and choose where we drop the hook.

CRUISING GUIDES AND OTHER RESOURCES

Check out a cruising guide for the area to learn about the marinas and approaches. Most guides are not designed for navigation, but they give you an overall idea of what to expect and look for on the chart. They list marinas, boat clubs, and launch ramps, and many include links to websites. The guides also include the location of anchorages, with information about the bottom, depth, and protection from the wind. Some have drawings illustrating the approaches; others are less precise. They usually also provide information about the history of the area, shopping, dining, and the overall personality of the place.

A local tourism office is another good source of information. The staff can tell you about upcoming events, like a music festival or a fireworks display. To find the office use the Internet and a search engine like Google. Type the name of the town and *tourism* in the search box. Or pick up the telephone and call the local tourism office. They'll mail you information or direct you to a site where you can find out what's going on.

Many cruisers choose a marina for its amenities. A swimming pool is a popular draw for cruising families during warm weather, as are nearby walking trails and tennis courts. The dockmaster or local boaters at the marina can give you directions to specialty shops and tell you if there's a trolley or shuttle bus to take you there. Advertisements for marinas in magazines and cruising guides include details of their websites, which you can check out to get full descriptions of their facilities, rates, and drawings or charts showing how to approach them.

Of course, many boaters simply want to arrive at the marina safely and then do noth-ing, except perhaps appreciate having the time to read a book, do a crossword puzzle, or some needlepoint, or just take a nap.

FLOAT PLAN AND PRE-DEPARTURE CHECKLIST

The U.S. Coast Guard suggests that you fill out a float plan and give it to a land-based friend or relative if you're going on a cruise. Why have a float plan? It's a safety precaution so someone can alert authorities if you don't reach your destination or return home. Don't forget to notify whoever's looking after the float plan when you return.

This is the form that you'll find in the Coast Guard pamphlet *Federal Requirements*

Float Plan

Complete this form before going boating and leave it with a reliable person who can be depended upon to notify the Coast Guard or other rescue organization, should you not return as scheduled.

Do not file this plan with the Coast Guard. Remember to contact your friend in case of delay and when you return.

1. Person Reporting Overdue
Name_____Phone_____
Address_____

2. Description of Boat
Name_____
Registration/Documentation No. _____ Length_____
Make_____ Type _____
Hull Color_____ Trim Color_____
Fuel Capacity_____ Engine Type____No. of Engines__
Distinguishing Features_____
_____

3. Operator of Boat
Name_____
Age _____
Health _____ Phone _____
Address_____
Operator's Experience _____
_____

4. Survival Equipment (Check as Appropriate)
❏ #___PFDs ❏ Flares ❏ Mirror
❏ Smoke Signals ❏ Flashlight ❏ Food
❏ Paddles ❏ Water ❏ Anchor
❏ Raft or Dinghy ❏ EPIRB
❏ Others

5. Marine Radio: ❏ Yes ❏ No
Type _____ Freqs. _____
Digital Selective Calling (DSC) ❏ Yes ❏ No

6. Trip Expectations
Depart from _____
Departure Date _____ Time _____
Going to_____
Arrival Date _____ Time _____
If operator has not arrived/returned by:
Date_____ Time _____
call the Coast Guard or Local authority at the following number:
_____
_____

7. Vehicle Description
License No. _____ Make _____
Model_____ Color _____
Where is vehicle parked? _____

8. Persons on Board
Name   Age   Phone   Medical Conditions
_____
_____
_____
_____
_____

9. Additional Information
_____
_____
_____
_____

You can download this float plan from the USCG Auxiliary's website at http://www.uscgaux.org/~floatplan.

and Safety Tips for Recreational Boats. It's also available as a PDF file online (www.uscgboating.org).

Before you slip the docklines, go through the following checklist to make sure all the boat systems are working OK. This routine will become a common practice that might spare you from an engine failure or system breakdown. Run through it the night before departure or first thing in the morning, whatever works for you.

- Write a float plan
- Check the oil, water, and transmission fluid levels
- Check that the batteries are fully charged and that the water level is topped up
- Check the engine to see that all its parts and pumps are working
- See that the running lights are working
- Inspect the head to see it works properly
- Make sure the holding tank is empty
- Check the supply of cooking fuel to make sure it's full
- Fill the water tanks
- See that the refrigeration system is working
- Inspect all safety gear
- Make sure the VHF radio works; if it's handheld, check that you have extra batteries
- Check to see the anchor is free to drop in case of an emergency
- Make sure docklines are set up for departure and fenders are on board
- Wash the topsides so you'll leave in a clean boat
- Make sure the ensign and any other flags are flying properly
- Unplug the power cord
- Unplug the water hose
- Check to see you have the charts you'll need and binoculars

- Turn on DC switches for the wiper, running lights, and horn
- Turn on the VHF, GPS, depth-sounder, and other electronics

WHEN KIDS ARE CREW

Any boating family will tell you that some of its fondest memories involve being together on the boat. Cruising provides a wealth of family lore to chronicle—favorite places or stormy seas—and countless boating pictures fill the pages of family photo albums.

Here's some advice from cruising parents who tell us that the best way to make kids feel part of the cruising routine is to create goals they can achieve and to allow for downtime so everyone can rest and regenerate.

- Take every opportunity to teach kids how to be useful crew members. Teach them how to use the VHF radio, take a compass bearing, read a chart, and take part in the docking procedure. Kids love to cast off the lines or jump ashore with a spring line. They can take on responsibilities like being captain of the dinghy and outboard. If you teach kids safe and useful boating skills, they will feel they have something to contribute and grow up to be enthusiastic crew members or skippers for life.
- Kids have a love of nature and animals that drives their curiosity and can keep them busy. Keep a bag of food scraps to feed to gulls and ducks.
- Give a kid a fishing pole, and get him or her hooked for life.
- Limit the stuff kids bring aboard so their choices are not overwhelming. The amount depends on the age of the kids, and of course, the storage space available. But clearly less is better because it narrows the choices.

- Many marinas have free charts of their location. They make ideal pretend charts so that kids can refer to where they are and where they're going. When you're underway and passing green and red markers, have the kids find them on their own charts and show where they're displayed on the GPS. Little kids love to color these maps, too.
- Speaking of coloring, find a boating coloring or activity book where they can learn to identify nautical items, birds, or fish. Kids like to see and learn what's around them so take advantage of their eagerness to spot a heron or dolphin or identify different types of boats.
- Designate a quiet time every day so kids (and parents) can enjoy reading.
- Keep a stash of movies and electronic games on board and encourage kids to bring their favorites. When the weather keeps everyone down below, a good movie can have a calming effect on kids of all ages.
- Cruising gives kids an opportunity to meet new friends: other cruising kids. Many cruising families have discovered that these chance meetings can sometimes evolve into lifelong friendships, based on the common bond of boating.

With kids, a warm sandy beach is always a hit. They can get off the boat and swim before you stop for the day.

Cruising with Guests Aboard

Sharing your boat with friends can expand your enjoyment. The perfect guest brings a small duffel bag of clothes, a large bag of food and drinks, and treats your boat with as much love and kindness as you do. Talk about your cruise plan in advance, so guests know what to expect and how to participate.

Let them help with provisions, and be specific. Tell them what to bring, and how to prepare it. Some boat refrigerators and ovens are small, so large dishes will not fit inside them. If you have a no-glass rule on board, tell guests you prefer canned, not bottled, beer. If your galley sink is small and you avoid doing dishes, suggest a casserole in a throwaway aluminum pan, not one that needs washing.

If you have limited water tanks, explain that you use the showers at marinas, so they can bring a small tote to carry their things in. If you have bed linens and towels aboard, let them know so they don't bring them.

Establish a firm departure and return time so they'll know when to arrive to cast off and when they can expect to be back. That said, impress on them that cruising is not the same as driving down the highway from motel to motel. The longer their time on the cruise, the more flexible their schedule must be.

Unfortunately, not all shoreside friends and family members make good boating companions, so consider their personalities and your creature comforts and cruising style before extending an invitation. Type A personalities who are used to following a tight schedule are not a good mix if you're a laid-back cruiser bent on relaxation. If your boat is small and lacks privacy, it's probably not a good fit for people who like their own space. Most of the friends who come along with us are boaters, or have been, and they know the agonies and ecstasies of cruising, so they make welcome guests.

Consider this advice about inviting friends to join you on your boat:

- Before going on a cruise of a week or more, take your guests on a shakedown cruise for a long weekend. This lets everyone get to know one another and allows your guests to experience all the boat's idiosyncrasies. Better to find out they are high-maintenance on a short cruise than on a long one. Ideally, one of those days you'll be weathered in to see how they react to the dark side of cruising.

- Resolve money issues before you go. Are you sharing expenses like fuel, dockage, and food? If so, many people have a cash kitty where they put in the same amount and use the money for provisioning, eating out, or refueling. Others use credit cards and divvy it up at the end of the cruise. If you want to foot the bill entirely, make it known beforehand to avoid that annoying "no, let me pay for it" dialogue every time the boat needs a block of ice or a new chart.

- Guests usually bring too many clothes and too much stuff so give them clear direction about using duffel bags or a soft suitcase, which can be stowed more easily than a hard one. Be specific about the number of bags so you'll have space to store them. Decide beforehand where you want to stow snorkeling, camera, or any other gear that guests want to bring along.

- Most guests want to bring gifts. Instead of letting them surprise you with something you can't use or don't want, tell them what you'd like. Anything consumable—food, liquor, soda pop, water bottles—that you will use and enjoy is easy for guests to bring. Don't forget you'll need a place to store the gifts.

- If you have a large water tank or go to marinas every night and tap into a shoreside water supply, water is not a concern. But hearing a galley faucet or shower run incessantly by your guests can frustrate even the most laid-back skipper. Sensitivity to using too much water is not something non-boaters easily understand because we use it so frivolously in our homes. But on a boat with limited water tank capacity, conserving it is key. This is another reason to have a shakedown cruise, so guests get an idea of just how much water they can use without becoming *persona non grata*.

- Don't forget, newcomers to your boat, or even old friends who haven't been aboard in a while, need to be told where they will find PFDs and fire extinguishers, where to meet in case of an emergency at night, and any other basic safety guidelines you may wish to lay down. Some skippers we know go so far as to conduct a drill at some point during their guests' first day aboard, like they do on cruise ships. This may be a bit extreme, but conducting a drill, and pointing out safety requirements ahead of time while all is calm, is far better than having to try to explain it all during the heat and stress that a real emergency might generate.

A sunny day on the water with good friends. That's what good times and fond memories are made of.

MAKING FRIENDS WITH LIKE-MINDED CRUISERS

The people we meet along the way come in all sizes and shapes, just like their boats—young families, single folks, and couples. And we're all out there enjoying the water and sharing experiences together. Admittedly, some of the sea stories can be harrowing, but more often cruisers share news of a favorite anchorage, an ice cream shop, or a good restaurant.

Meeting other boaters may come naturally to some people because of the common bond they share, but talking to strangers isn't easy for everyone. If you're the shy type but would like to strike up a conversation with other boaters and don't know how, here are a few ideas.

BE USEFUL

Anyone who catches our lines when we're docking is our new best friend. After we're squared away, we always make a point of finding the person who helped us, so we can

When we arrive at a new destination, it's always a treat to have someone waiting on the dock to catch our lines and welcome us.

extend our gratitude. The flip side is true, too. When we're on a dock and see a boat approaching with no dockhand in sight, we make ourselves useful and catch their lines.

AT THE DOCK

We take the direct and obvious approach of walking the docks, usually with a cold drink in hand, around 5:00 P.M., looking at boats and chatting with anyone who wants to. It's the most natural thing in the world to ask, "Where'd you come from today? Where're you headed?" Probably not the approach Miss Manners would approve, but it's a good way of meeting other interesting and entertaining cruisers.

AT ANCHOR

When we've set the anchor and tidied up the boat we like to go for a dinghy ride around the creek or harbor where we're anchored. We cruise along the shoreline and go by other boats on the hook. If someone's on deck we stop by to see if they want a visit—it's pretty clear whether they do or don't. A boat's hailing port is usually the icebreaker, and a conversation begins from there. If it's an obvious fit, we usually invite them over for a drink. If not, we go on our way.

BE OBSERVANT ASHORE

Keen observation ashore begins at a marina, but it extends to the surrounding area as well. We've met countless boaters walking through a harbor town simply by noticing that they *are* boaters. Here are some common indicators that will help you identify other boaters ashore:

• Anyone standing in line at a grocery or liquor store checkout line with canvas sacks

- Anyone wearing a foul weather jacket in a restaurant, marine store, hardware store, ice cream parlor, or library near a marina
- Anyone in the laundromat at or near a marina
- Anyone riding a foldaway bicycle or walking with a canvas sack near a marina

CRUISING WITH OTHER BOATS

In any popular anchorage on the weekend you'll find a flotilla of boats rafted together. Marina docks, too, are often filled with members of a cruising group. We belong to several boating groups and enjoy participating in their cruises, especially to destinations that are new to us. The fleet or cruise director of the group does all the planning, makes marina arrangements, schedules activities and events, and makes dinner reservations, so it's an easy way to go on a cruise and meet other boaters while you're at it.

But you don't have to be a member of a group. You can plan a cruise in convoy with friends' boats, making the same sorts of decisions about where to go and stay. We always joke that we have such "fast friends" we have to leave at dawn while they leave at 10:00 A.M., so we can arrive at the destination at the same time. Sometimes we plan ahead and bring a dish to share; at others we agree to eat out. Sharing a night or weekend with other like-minded cruisers makes it quality time for everyone.

SOLITUDE SEEKERS

Sometimes cruisers want to be left alone to enjoy the peace and quiet of being on their boat. And who can think of a better escape from a busy land life than getting aboard and leaving it all behind? Whether they are snug in a marina slip or tethered to an anchor in a remote cove, we always respect the privacy of boaters enjoying their solitude.

HAVING PETS ON BOARD

The dogs and cats we've met on boats are clearly a part of their cruising families, and they often create opportunities to meet other boaters. Passers-by stop when they see our cats, Pete and Repete, curled up on a forward hatch or peering down from a perch on the flying bridge. And anyone who walks his or her dog down a dock knows that a wagging tail is an open invitation to engage in conversation. Animals bring out the best in people and their presence on a boat seems to make everyone happier.

We've always cruised with cats and found they've gotten us invited to some very nice places. We were tied to a dock at Bucksport, South Carolina one time when a 64-foot Burger pulled in behind us and tied up. Once the boat was secured, the gangplank was lowered and out stepped the captain, who walked directly to our boat and invited us for cocktails. Never ones to pass up a drink (and curious to know why we were invited), we accepted.

"We wanted to meet you," said the owners, "because we know your two black kittens." We were stunned to find out that, months before, when we were in a Fort Laud-

Cats, like Pete and his brother Repete (not pictured), are cruising companions who demand little and give back so much more.

erdale marina, our cats at the time, Puss and Boots, had visited their boat every morning, and were treated to a can of tuna fish. Their captain had followed the cats back to our boat to find out where they lived.

Another time we were heading north on the ICW, hailing a marina in Morehead City, North Carolina, to ask for a slip for the night. We were concerned about the water depth. When we signed off with the marina we were hailed by *Inverness*, a boat name we didn't recognize. They assured us that they too had a deep draft but always stopped at the marina, where there was plenty of water. The caller invited us for a drink when we got in and we quickly accepted.

About an hour later an enormous blue-hulled trawler with a car on its aft deck overtook us. We were amazed to read *Inverness* on the stern. Later that day when we joined the owners, they said they recognized us by our cats. At the time we had Puss and Boots and their three little black kittens. Apparently the owners had been visiting friends on a boat tied next to us one afternoon in Nassau when we were ashore. One of the kittens had fallen overboard and they had rescued it. We were eternally grateful and happy to meet them.

First-Time Furry Cruisers

It may seem like common sense, but it's important to remember that animals may not adapt to the unfamiliar surroundings of a boat easily or immediately. To introduce your pet to cruising, make their first boat trip a short one, and bring water and food from home that they're familiar with. They're usually smart enough to find a shady place and avoid strong sunshine, and they often find a cozy spot down below. Bring along a favorite blanket and toy from home to make the new surrounding more familiar (though pets will quickly discover a new set of boat toys to play with). And get advice from your veterinarian about seasickness, just in case.

Pet-Friendly Boating Ideas

Some of the best advice about keeping four-legged crew members safe and comfortable comes from boaters who regularly take along their dogs and cats.

- Give your pet an ID tag for the boat, imprinted with your name, boat name, marina or yacht club, and most importantly, your cell phone number. If the pet is lost, that information—not your home address and phone number—will make it easy to find you. It helps to have a handy photo of your pet if he goes missing so you can show people what he looks like.
- Fishing gear like hooks and poles can be dangerous for a pet, so keep them stored out of reach and out of the way.
- Outfit your pet with an animal-style PFD—a *pet* flotation device—that fits him. And use it. Most pet flotation devices have handles on top to let you quickly grab the vest and lift him out of the water. Do a pet overboard drill by giving him a gentle dunking in shallow waters to see how he reacts and to find out what you have to do to get him out of the water.
- A pet wearing a harness can be retrieved from the water more easily than one wearing a collar.
- If you're leaving home port, make a copy of your pet's vaccination records and keep them with your boating documents, just in case a marina wants to see them.
- Schedule your day's cruising with time to exercise a dog, especially a large one. Give him a run in the morning before you leave, and again when you reach port at the end of the day.

- A retractable leash with a built-in flashlight is very convenient for nighttime dog walks.
- If you're anchoring out, make sure there's public shore access nearby so you can take the dinghy ashore to walk a dog.
- If you're anchored out with a cat, throw a heavy line long enough to reach the water over the stern at the swim platform so he can grab the line and climb up if he falls overboard.
- Always have a bowl of water available for your pet, especially during hot weather.
- Keep a wide fishing net on a pole handy to quickly retrieve a small animal that might go overboard.
- Carry a litter box in a place where it's easy to clean and refill.
- If your cat is an outside creature at home and wants to roam the docks, keep him locked inside when you're docking the boat.
- If your pet stays down below while you're underway, make sure to open the windows and create a flow of air so it's not too hot.
- Most puppies adapt to cruising faster than older dogs. If there's a dog in your future, bring him aboard sooner rather than later.

CHAPTER 29

Diversions

Boaters spend their time aboard in different ways. Some use it to putter around their boat, fixing, tweaking, and studying all its components and systems. Others use it as an escape from their day job—they run fast and far and enjoy where the boat can take them. Still others use their boat as a private refuge, a holy place where they can do whatever they choose. The diversions boaters enjoy while they're aboard are as varied and as different as the boaters themselves. Here are the ways we see cruisers spending their time.

FUN ON THE WATER

Spending quality time on the water tops the list of cruisers' favorite activities. One of the most popular on-board activities by far is fishing. Many a cruising boat is loaded with rods, reels, nets, bait buckets, and tackle boxes. On a cruising boat fishing takes on a status all its own, especially when the end result is a nice fillet dinner.

Many cruising boats carry a personal watercraft (PWC) and enjoy using it for an afternoon on the water. It makes short work of exploring creeks and rivers and is often used instead of a dinghy for getting ashore.

Once you've paddled a kayak around a harbor or anchorage, you'll understand why it's becoming a popular cruising take-along.

Kayaks come in sit-on-top or sit-inside designs for solo or two-person paddlers, and they're lightweight for easy transport. They're made of fiberglass, rigid plastic, or inflatable materials. Inflatables are a good solution for small cruising boats where there's no deck space to store them.

Other popular activities include dinghy rides to nearby beaches, swimming and snorkeling with swim fins around the boat or off a beach, and water toys like towable tubes and floats that you inflate with a simple 12-volt or foot pump. If your boat or dinghy is fast enough, you can use water skis, kneeboards, or wakeboards.

These boaters are ready to launch the personal watercraft and go for a quick spin around the harbor.

Today many cruisers carry a kayak as a means of transportation and for enjoyment when at anchor in a quiet cove.

FUN ABOARD

Some cruisers outfit their boat with a television and DVD or VCR. These devices require a power connection to a dock or a generator, and as a result, many of today's cruisers are equipped like small cruise liners to keep the electronics up and running.

Listening to music is a popular on-board activity, and a stereo system is almost a standard feature on most cruising boats. Some have high-end surround-sound speakers from bridge to bilge; others have more traditional built-in systems in the main cabin. Those that combine a radio and CD player take up a small amount of space but provide a large amount of listening pleasure. Some boats carry a laptop to play electronic versions of bridge, or a PDA with a favorite game. Many boaters we know are card-playing fanatics, and their addiction doesn't stop when they're on board. And there are others, like us, who prefer the quiet pleasure of reading a good book or having the time to pursue a needlework project.

These indoor diversions are enjoyable anytime aboard but they take on new significance when there's foul weather. Many cruising-family legends have emerged from a hotly contested Monopoly or Scrabble tournament.

BIKES AND SCOOTERS

Many cruisers wouldn't leave the dock without a bike or scooter to provide transport when they go ashore. A standard bike is an easy choice if you have plenty of open deck space, and it can be protected with a cover.

A folding bike is another option if space is at a minimum. They usually weigh around 40 pounds, and come in 18- and 20-inch frames with any number of gears. Typically an 18-inch frame is suitable for riders under 5′10″; the larger 20-inch frame is better for larger riders.

Human-powered and electric scooters are becoming a popular, economical mode of transportation. They're small and easy to stow aboard, taking up less space than bicycles, folding or otherwise. We see more and more adults toting lightweight scooters off their boats and heading out to explore. Man-powered scooters take more stamina to operate; electric ones need to have their batteries recharged.

CHAPTER 30
Favorite Cruising Recipes

Here are some favorite recipes we've gathered over the years. Some are make-aheads for weekend cruising, others require a minimum of ingredients and little preparation time. All are easy to make, easy to serve, and delicious.

APPETIZERS

Hot Cheese Dip

1 8-oz. package cream cheese
1 cup cheddar cheese, shredded
¾ cup sour cream
¼ cup salsa

Let cream cheese come to room temperature, then mix with salsa, cheddar cheese, and sour cheese. Heat in microwave for about 4–5 minutes and serve with crackers.

Make-Ahead Pepperoni Dip

Kay Wurst aboard *Katie Lynne* makes this dip before heading out on a cruise so she's always ready to entertain.

1 8-oz. package pepperoni slices, minced or diced
1 pt. sour cream
1 bunch scallions, finely diced

Blend ingredients together and refrigerate for at least a day before serving. Serve with crackers and/or celery sticks cut into bite-sized pieces.

Onion Appetizer

Aboard *Sandalwood* this is a signature dip from Brenda Appel. It couldn't be easier to make or more delicious.

1 cup Vidalia onions, chopped
1 cup sharp cheddar cheese
1 cup real mayonnaise

Stir ingredients well and bake in a warm oven until the cheese is melted and the onions are soft. Serve with crackers.

A Soup and Some Salads

Gazpacho ala Otter

Martha Austin, with her husband, captain Jack, serves this delicious cold soup aboard *Otter*, to the delight of everyone.

```
   2  1 lb. 12 oz. cans diced tomatoes
   1  14 oz. can beef broth
   4  stalks celery, chopped finely
   1  green pepper, chopped finely
 ½  red onion, chopped finely
   1  cucumber, seeded and chopped
      finely
   1  bunch scallions, chopped finely
   1  tbsp. balsamic vinegar
   2  tbsp. olive oil
   2  tbsp. Worcestershire sauce
5–10  second shake of Tabasco sauce
      Minced garlic to taste
      Feta cheese
```

Combine all ingredients except the cheese and refrigerate overnight. Then test seasoning and add more Worcestershire or Tabasco sauce as needed. Serve cold, topped with crumbled feta cheese.

Minestrone Salad

Gail Greco, who cruises aboard *Greco Roamin'*, a 28-foot cruiser, with husband Tom Bagley, makes this colorful, flavorful, and oh-so-portable salad that will accompany almost any meat, poultry, or fish. If fresh basil is not available, substitute a generous tablespoon of dried basil.

Dressing
```
   2  cloves garlic, peeled and coarsely
      chopped
   2  shallots, peeled and coarsely
      chopped
 ¼  cup balsamic vinegar
 ¼  cup Dijon-style mustard
   2  tbsp. honey
 ¾  cup olive oil
   1  cup fresh basil leaves
      Salt and pepper
```

Salad
```
   2  cups fresh green beans, trimmed and
      halved lengthwise
   2  cups carrots, peeled and quartered
      lengthwise, then thinly sliced
   2  cups canned chickpeas, drained
1½  cups fresh ripe tomatoes, diced
```

Prepare dressing in a small food processor. Mince the chopped garlic and shallots and add vinegar, mustard, and honey. Slowly drizzle in olive oil, then add basil leaves. Whirl until smooth. Season with salt and pepper to taste.

To prepare vegetables, boil a large pot of water and blanch green beans for 1 minute. Add carrots and cook for another minute. Drain and rinse vegetables under cold water, and again drain well. Place in a large portable salad container and toss gently with some of the dressing. Add tomatoes and chickpeas and toss again with more dressing. Use only enough dressing to coat the salad. Place remaining dressing into a small portable container to use later when serving on board.

Serves 6 to 8 as a side dish.

Suellen's Spinach Salad for 6

This salad is ideal for boating. It's easy to bring aboard in plastic bags and quickly assemble when dinner's ready. We first tried it with John and Suellen Gargalli aboard *Nana Suey* and have been serving it ourselves ever since.

- 1 package baby spinach
- 1 cup mushrooms, sliced
- ½ cup red or white onions, sliced
  Ken's Raspberry Vinaigrette Dressing
  Blue cheese, crumbled (to taste)
- ¼ cup walnuts

Empty the package of baby spinach into a salad bowl along with the sliced mushrooms and onions. Lightly coat with 2–3 tbsp. of dressing then toss. Serve topped with crumbled blue cheese and walnuts.

Make-Ahead Layered Salad

We like this recipe when we're weekending and having a potluck with other boaters. Make it on Friday and it's ready to serve 6–8 for a raft-up on Saturday night.

- 1 head lettuce, cut into bite-sized pieces
- 1 cup frozen peas
- ½ red onion, thinly chopped
- 3–4 stalks celery, thinly chopped
- 4–5 hard-boiled eggs, diced
- ¼ lb. grated cheese (cheddar or Swiss)
- ½ cup fried, drained bite-sized pieces crisp bacon or finely chopped ham
- ¾ cup mayonnaise or ranch dressing
- ¼ tsp. paprika
- ¼ tsp. salt
- ⅛ tsp. pepper
- 1 tsp. dried parsley
- 2 tbsp. grated Parmesan cheese

Layer ingredients in a large bowl in the order listed. The bowl should be full to the top. Spread mayonnaise or dressing evenly over top of salad, covering ingredients to edge of bowl. Sprinkle herbs on top and cover tightly with plastic wrap. Chill overnight and toss gently in a wider salad bowl to mix just before serving. Serves 6–8.

ENTREES

Chili

There's nothing better than chili and corn bread (made from a box mix) on a chilly night. This easy-to-make recipe is a meal in itself. If you're weathered-in for a few days this really hits the spot.

- 1½–2 lb. ground turkey or beef or combination
- 1 onion, chopped
- 1 green pepper, chopped
- 2 tbsp. olive oil
  Garlic to taste
- 1 28 oz. can diced tomatoes
- 1 8 oz. can tomato sauce
- 1 cube beef bouillon
- 1 19 oz. can red kidney beans
- ¼ cup ketchup
- ¼ cup chili powder
- ½ tsp. cayenne
- ½ tsp. salt
  Shredded cheese to garnish

Brown ground turkey, beef, or a combination of both in 2 tbsp. olive oil in frying pan. Add garlic to taste. Remove to larger pan and sauté chopped onion and green pepper in oil until soft. Add onions, green pepper, diced tomatoes, tomato sauce, beef broth, kidney beans, and ketchup to large pan and mix thoroughly. Add chili powder, cayenne, and salt and bring to a boil. Then lower the heat and cook for 30–45 minutes. Top with shredded Swiss or cheddar cheese to serve.

Serves 6.

Jayne's Teriyaki Beef and Green Peppers One-Dish Dinner

Irv and Jayne Hetherington serve this dinner aboard *Karaya*. It's delicious and easy to prepare. The recipe serves four, so it's great for company. Or divide it and save half to reheat for another dinner.

¾–1 lb. sirloin steak (or ground beef)
2 green peppers, cut into 1-inch chunks
2 onions, cut into 1-inch chunks
2 tbsp. olive oil
1 14.5 oz. can diced tomatoes
1 4 oz. can mushrooms, drained (optional)
1 8 oz. can sliced water chestnuts, drained (optional)
1 10.5 oz. can beef gravy
¼ cup (approx.) teriyaki sauce
½ cup Minute Rice

Fry the meat in half the olive oil until brown and tender. Remove steak and slice into 2-inch strips. Sauté green pepper and onion chunks in remaining olive oil until slightly soft (peppers should still be a bright green color). Add steak slices, tomatoes, mushrooms, water chestnuts, gravy, and teriyaki sauce. Heat thoroughly (about 5 minutes). Stir in rice and cover. Serve promptly after rice is ready, adding more teriyaki sauce if desired.

Serves 4.

Raisin-Laced Beef on the Range

1 tbsp. olive oil
1 onion, finely chopped
2 tsp. garlic
1½ tsp. cinnamon
1 tsp. oregano
1 tsp. ground cumin
1 lb. ground beef or turkey or combination
14.5 oz. can diced tomatoes in juice
¼–½ cup raisins
⅓ cup stuffed green olives, sliced
¼ tsp. salt
Cooked rice or pasta

Brown onions in olive oil in skillet until soft and add garlic, cinnamon, oregano, and cumin. Add beef and cook until lightly browned, breaking it into small pieces as it cooks. Add tomatoes, raisins, olives, and salt and heat to a boil. Stir, lower heat and simmer with cover for 30 minutes or until ingredients blend. Serve over hot cooked rice or pasta.

Serves 6.

Easy Oven Chicken Entrée

 2   boneless chicken breasts
 6   oz. jar quartered and marinated arti-
     choke hearts
14.5 oz. sliced potatoes, drained
 ¼   cup Parmesan cheese

Brown chicken breasts in small, oiled roasting pan in oven at 350°F until browned on both sides. In small bowl mix together jar of artichoke hearts, drained potato slices, and Parmesan cheese. When chicken is browned, spoon mixture into roasting pan around chicken breasts and bake for about 45 minutes. Stir occasionally to distribute potato slices and artichoke hearts so they blend with cheese, creating a thickened sauce.

Serves 2.

St. Simon's Pizza (entrée or appetizer)

This is a rendition of a pizza we had on St. Simon's Island, Georgia. We like it because it only requires a few basic ingredients, and it uses up leftover vegetables.

 1   ball of pre-made pizza dough
 ¼–½   cup Alfredo sauce
 1   cup sliced veggies (any combination
       of mushrooms, onions, peppers,
       broccoli, and asparagus)
 1   cup leftover chicken, scallops, shrimp
 1   cup shredded mozzarella cheese
       Herbs and seasonings to taste

Preheat oven to 425°F and roll pizza dough onto a cookie sheet. Bake dough for about 8 minutes and then remove to add toppings. Spread Alfredo sauce to cover dough, but not heavily. Add other toppings, herbs, and seasonings and cover with mozzarella cheese. Return to oven to bake until dough is brown around the edges and toppings are heated thoroughly. Remove from oven and let sit about 5 minutes before slicing. Cut into bite-sized pieces for appetizers, or individual servings for an entrée.

Low-carb version: when we're watching our diet and counting carbs we substitute low-carb soft tacos for the pizza dough and Marzetti's Buttermilk ranch dressing for the Alfredo sauce. Add toppings and low-carb shredded mozzarella cheese. The thin tacos take less time in the oven than pizza dough so watch them carefully. They're ready when the cheese bubbles and the edges of the taco are brown and crisp.

Meatloaf Made Easy

This is our favorite menu if we're making an overnight passage. The smell of simmering meatloaf wafting through the air is intoxicating, and the leftover meatloaf is great for snacking later. We serve this entrée with baked potatoes started half an hour before the meatloaf goes in the oven so they're soft to the touch about the same time the meatloaf is ready to serve.

 1½   lb. ground turkey or beef or a combi-
      nation of both
 1   onion, finely chopped
 ½   cup ketchup, salsa, or chili sauce
 ¾   cup dry oatmeal, old fashioned or
      quick
 1   egg, slightly beaten
 1   tbsp. Worcestershire or soy sauce
      Salt, pepper, and garlic to taste

Preheat oven to 350°F and mix ingredients in a large bowl. Shape into a meatloaf pan or on a cookie sheet. Bake for about 1 hour and let stand for 5–10 minutes before slicing to serve.

Serves 6–8.

One-Pan Wonder

Jim, a retired doctor and solo sailor, taught us this ever-so-easy way to make a quick dinner.

Prepare a 1 lb. package of spaghetti in boiling water according to directions. Let the pasta drain in a colander while pouring a 20–30 oz. jar of marinara or spaghetti sauce into the pan. Return the drained pasta to the pan and mix it with the sauce. Serve immediately so both pasta and sauce are heated. Serve with a salad, bread, and Parmesan cheese.

If you prefer a white sauce, try this with Alfredo sauce.

Serves 4.

Roasted Veggies and Sausage on Pasta

- 1 lb. Italian-style turkey sausage links
- 4 sweet peppers (green, red, or yellow) cored, seeded, and cut into thick slices
- 2 large onions, quartered
- 2–3 tbsp. olive oil
- 4–5 cloves garlic, chopped
- 2–3 tsp. dried oregano
  Salt and pepper to taste
  Cooked spaghetti

Heat a frying pan, prick the sausages, and cook until browned on all sides (or prepare in microwave or grill). Heat olive oil in a roasting pan in a hot oven (about 425°F). When oil is hot, lower heat to 375°F and add peppers and onion seasoned with garlic, dried oregano, salt, and pepper. Bake for about 15 minutes.

Cut sausage into serving-size pieces and add to vegetables. Heat entrée another 30 minutes or until vegetables are tender and sausages are cooked. Stir frequently to prevent vegetables and sausage from sticking to the bottom. Serve over hot spaghetti.

Serves 4.

Baked Shrimp with Salsa

- 1 lb. cooked frozen shrimp, thawed, with tails removed
- 1 15 oz. can corn, drained
- 1 cup salsa
- 4 tsp. lime juice
- 1 tsp. olive oil

Layer the corn, shrimp, and salsa in a 2 qt. baking dish. Cover with lime juice and olive oil and bake in a hot oven for 10–15 minutes, or until ingredients are cooked throughout. Serve over rice or flavored rice mix.

Serves 3.

Shrimp Stir-Fry

- 2 tbsp. olive oil
- 1 lb. cleaned shrimp
- 1 lb. bag frozen oriental vegetables
- ¾ cup chicken broth
- 2 tbsp. cornstarch
- 3 tbsp. soy or teriyaki sauce
  Cooked rice

Pour olive oil in high-sided frying pan and heat until sizzling. Add shrimp and stir fry until it turns pink. Remove shrimp and add enough oil to coat pan. Stir fry frozen vegetables until slightly tender. Mix cold broth, cornstarch, and sauce in measuring cup. Add shrimp to vegetables and sauce. Heat and stir until sauce thickens. Serve over hot rice.

Serves 3–4.

Grecian Feta-Shrimp

Nancy and Bob Bartell aboard *Winsome* serve this winning entrée hot over rice or pasta or cold over romaine lettuce. It's delicious both ways. The two recipes that follow are from them, too.

    ½ cup olive oil
    2 tbsp. butter
    1 onion, thinly sliced
    1 lemon, juice of
    1 tsp. oregano
    4 oz. feta cheese
    1 lb. large raw shrimp, peeled and "butterflied"

Saute onion, butter, lemon juice, and oregano in oil. Add shrimp and simmer until shrimp turns pink. Just before serving add feta cheese in large chunks.

Serves 3–4.

Easy Mayonnaise-Dill Sauce for Grilled Salmon

    ½ cup mayonnaise
    ½ lemon, juiced
    ½ tsp. dill

Mix ingredients together. Serve with grilled salmon.

Grilled Eggplant

    1 large eggplant
    ½ cup olive oil
    2 tbsp. lemon juice
    1 garlic clove, minced
    ½ tsp. sage
       Parmesan or fortina cheese

Cut eggplant into ½-in. slices and sprinkle both sides with salt. Set on a paper towel for an hour, rinse, and pat dry. Prepare a marinade in a Ziploc bag by combining olive oil, lemon juice, garlic, and sage. Add eggplant slices, close bag and shake to cover slices. (This marinade is great on other grilled veggies, too.)

Grill the eggplant slices, turning once or twice, brushing with the oil mixture until done—about 8 minutes. Sprinkle with shredded or grated Parmesan or fortina cheese, and when melted serve immediately.

Serves 3–4.

Three Easy Ways with Chicken Breasts

Chicken breasts are easy to store, especially in small freezers, so we buy large packs and repackage them in freezer bags, each containing two servings. Here are three ways we prepare them, depending on what we have available. Served with a vegetable and salad they make a nice meal.

Marinade for Grilling
    ½ cup soy sauce
    ¼ cup white wine
    2 tbsp. honey
    2 tsp. minced garlic
    ¼ tsp. ginger

Combine marinade ingredients in a Ziploc freezer bag and marinate chicken breasts for a few hours. Remove from marinade and grill until tender. Heat marinade and brush on chicken during grilling.

Fried in the Oven
    1 egg white
    ¼ cup Parmesan cheese, grated
    2 tsp. dried thyme
    2 cup crushed cereal (corn flakes, Wheaties, or Rice Krispies)
    ¼ tsp. salt and pepper

Mix dry ingredients—cheese, cereal, thyme, salt, and pepper—in a shallow pan. Beat egg white until frothy and pour into bowl large enough for chicken. Dip chicken first into egg white, then transfer to dry mixture and coat well. Bake chicken on a cookie sheet sprayed with vegetable oil until tender, about 20–30 minutes.

Skillet Cacciatore
- 1 tbsp. olive oil
- 1 onion, cut into chunks
- 1 green pepper, cut into chunks
- 1 14.5 oz. can diced tomatoes with basil, garlic, and oregano

Heat oil in skillet and brown chicken on both sides (about 2–3 minutes each side). Add remaining ingredients and heat to a boil. Reduce heat to medium-low and cook for 20 minutes. Serve over rice or pasta.

DESSERTS

Pudding Cups with Dippers

Serve Vanilla Wafers or any small thin cookie with chilled individual-serving pudding cups. Use the cookies to dip into the pudding.

S'Mores for Four

We like this treat for dessert when we use the grill for the entrée. Just before serving dinner, we give guests a piece of aluminum foil and the ingredients to assemble their own dessert: a graham cracker sandwich with a chocolate bar and two marshmallows as filling.

- 8 graham crackers
- 4 chocolate candy bars
- 8 marshmallows

After serving the entrée, turn off the grill, place the wrapped treats around the outside of the grill to slowly heat and turn them once. Allow about 15–20 minutes to melt the chocolate and soften the marshmallows.

Serves 4.

Easy Chocolate Pie

- 9-in. graham cracker pie shell
- 1¼ cups milk
- 8 oz. Cool Whip
- 2 4-serving packages of chocolate pudding
  Chopped nuts or candy bar

In a medium size bowl combine pudding, milk, and half the Cool Whip. Stir until blended into a thick mixture. Pour into pie shell, spread remaining Cool Whip on top, and decorate with chopped nuts or a candy bar.

Serves 6.

No-Bake Cheesecake

We've been serving this favorite on board for years because it's simple to make with prepared foods we can find anywhere.

- 1 9-inch graham cracker pie shell
- 2 8-oz. packages cream cheese, softened
- 1 14-oz. can Eagle Brand sweetened condensed milk
- 2 tbsp. lemon juice
- 1 14 oz. Cool Whip

Gradually add condensed milk to cheese while beating, until smooth. Stir in lemon juice and Cool Whip. Pour into pie shell and refrigerate for 3 hours.

Serves 3.

PART VI

Cruise These Great Destinations

CHAPTER 31
Erie Canal

The Erie Canal is a 338-mile waterway in upstate New York that connects Albany, on the Hudson River, with Buffalo, on Lake Erie in the western part of the state. It is part of a network that connects a state canal system to hundreds more waterways that make intriguing side trips. One is the Oswego Canal that leads northwest from the Erie Canal to Oswego on the shores of Lake Ontario. Another is the Cayuga-Seneca Canal that runs south into the pristine Finger Lakes region. And from the junction of the Erie Canal and Hudson River you can turn north and follow the Champlain Canal. It leads into Lake Champlain and eventually, all the way to the St. Lawrence River.

The Erie Canal is busy with traffic during its May–November season. Recreational boaters are joined by a fleet of passenger boats—narrow canal boats, tour boats, and overnight cruise liners—along with local fishermen and a few commercial boats.

In the spring and summer, boats from all over the world use the Erie as they head to Canada's fine cruising grounds. Long-distance cruisers on the Great Circle Route take the canal to reach the Mississippi and Tennessee–Timbigbee Waterway via Lakes Erie, Huron, and Michigan. And in the fall the canal transports inland cruisers and snowbirds heading to the Atlantic seacoast and

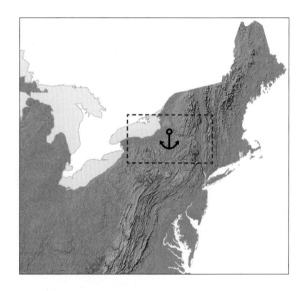

the Intracoastal Waterway. This scenic waterway along New York's Mohawk River Valley just keeps getting better and provides a unique boating experience for cruisers of every size.

Along the canal you'll see ever-changing scenery of pastoral farmlands, quiet tree-filled wilderness, steep cliffs and hills, and cityscapes of warehouses and factories. Waterfront homes are often clustered together, with people fishing off their docks and kids splashing into the water from a rope-and-tire swing hung on a shoreline tree.

The canal passes through scenic historic

towns that welcome boaters, so you can stay at marinas or use free docking facilities (most without electricity) at canal parks and town terminals. Since many of the locks have towns nearby you can find shopping, specialty stores, and restaurants within easy walking distance. Make a long day's passage, or cruise for a few hours and have time to enjoy shopping, hiking, or biking on the towpath trail system along the shores of the canal.

Heading west on the canal from its eastern end, you'll find the town of Amsterdam, with its waterfront facility and public dock. At Rome there is the restored Fort Stanwix, a reproduction of a Revolutionary War wooden fort. A short cab ride away is the Erie Canal Village, which features a restored section of the original canal and a replica of an old canal boat. Further west in Fairport you'll find another nice stopover.

You'll traverse a 20-mile stretch of Oneida Lake, which the Erie Canal crosses, and find Brewerton, a lively little town with plenty of marinas, boatyards, services, and restaurants.

At the western end of Oneida Lake many boaters take a side trip to Oswego on the 24-mile long Oswego Canal, a section of the Oswego River that has been turned into a canal and flows through seven locks. Plan a stop at Phoenix, famous for its Bridge House Brats: local kids who help out at the town dock and welcome visitors. Oswego, on the shores of Lake Ontario, is a hip town with all the stores and services a cruising boater might need. It's also the gateway to cruising the Thousand Islands, the Trent-Severn Waterway, and other Canadian cruising grounds.

The Cayuga-Seneca Canal is another interesting side trip to the Finger Lakes region. Cayuga and Seneca Lakes are popular cruising grounds with parks, marinas, lakeside wineries, and restaurants.

Lyons is a popular canal stopover before the canal passes by Rochester, and so is Lockport, near the western end, where you'll find an Erie Canal museum, shopping, and marinas an easy walk from the lock.

The town of Tonawanda is at the western end of the canal and leads to the eastern portion of Lake Erie. There you'll find city docks, marinas, plentiful shopping, a museum, and public transportation.

The original canal, completed in 1825, was built in seven years and was considered an engineering marvel of its day. Cutting through miles of wilderness it featured 18 aqueducts and 83 locks, with a rise of 568 feet from the Hudson River to Lake Erie. It spurred the westward migration of settlers and opened the only trade route west of the Appalachians. The canal was enlarged over the years to meet growing traffic and larger barges.

You'll notice that sailboats on the canal look a bit strange because they've had to lower their masts and secure them to the deck on sawhorses so they can get under the low bridges.

Most powerboats can fit under the controlled heights on the canal. At the western end there's 15-foot bridge clearance to the Oswego Canal. Beyond that, to Troy, the controlled height is 20 feet. But this clearance can vary depending on rainfall. There are also several lift bridges, many of them just a few miles apart, which are opened by a single bridge tender, called a roaming operator.

The water depth is usually 12 feet, but it fluctuates with the rainfall.

There are 34 locks on the Erie Canal and one federal lock at Troy, so running the entire canal you'll pass through a total of 35 locks. Before we entered the Erie Canal we'd heard horror stories about the difficulty of negotiating the locks. While the procedure was at first unfamiliar, we quickly became adept because we had so many times to practice and could then anticipate what would happen.

Use VHF channel 13 to communicate with lock tenders, who are usually very helpful. Be prepared and bring a pair of waterproof gloves to wear when you're handling lock lines, which can be slimy and grungy because of the lock walls. See Chapter 16, Boat Handling, for suggestions about how to maneuver and secure your boat in a lock.

Just like in the old days of the canal there are tolls, but they are a small price to pay for the charm and enjoyment of cruising on the canal. In 2005, a 10-day pass for a cruising boat cost between $12.50 and $50.00, depending on the length of the boat. For example, a 10-day pass for a boat 26–39 feet costs $37.50. It's $75.00 for a season pass.

Trailer boats have access to the canal at many locations so it's suitable for a short or a long cruise. Use the New York Canal System 800 phone number and website listed in Appendix 3 to obtain marina and launch site information. You'll also find the calendar of events in towns along the canal so you can plan your cruise to include them on the website.

CHAPTER 32

Chesapeake Bay

Along the shores of the Chesapeake Bay you'll find coastal cruising at its finest. From the Elk River at its northernmost reaches to its outlet at the Atlantic Ocean, the Bay offers cruising for every style and mood. You'll find thousands of miles of shoreline, with countless anchorages tucked away in creeks and coves. The finest accommodations are only a short walk away from charming old harbor town and big city marinas.

Since we live on the eastern shore of the Bay and cruise the area extensively, we're more than a little partial. The tremendous diversity and scope of destinations make the Chesapeake Bay a special place for us and countless other cruisers. If you're a history buff, pick up a copy of *Chesapeake* by James Michener to enjoy while you're underway.

The Bay's variety makes it popular with boaters from all the states bordering its shores. At the northern end of the Bay as many boats hail from Pennsylvania and New Jersey ports as hail from Maryland and Delaware. The same is true on the western shore, where Virginia and Washington, D.C. boaters keep their boats. Of course, the Bay is also home to a thriving commercial fishing industry.

Summer months bring out most regional cruising boaters as well as fishermen. Independence Day is one of its busiest times, with

many harbor towns on both sides of the Bay celebrating the holiday with fireworks.

In the spring, the Bay sees a lot of snowbird traffic, as cruisers head back from southern waters to their home ports in Canada, New England, and the Great Lakes. In the fall, the traffic heads south, especially after the Annapolis U.S. Powerboat and Sailboat Shows.

Commercial freighters, tugs with barges, cruise ships, and naval vessels plow the center of the Bay in the shipping channels. Outside the channels, in shallower waters, you'll see clusters of fishermen in traditional dead-rise fishing boats tending their catch of blue crab, oysters, and clams, depending on the season. The brackish waters—a mix of salt and fresh water—provide fertile breeding grounds for fish in this expansive bay.

Crab pots pepper some of the waters outside the shipping lines of the Bay so be mindful of snagging one. They're easy to spot because there's rarely just one—there's a minefield of them! Be cautious also of sea nettles—jellyfish that sting swimmers. The nettles prefer salt water, so they're mostly found south of the Bay Bridge. The brackish waters of the northern sections of the Bay can be relatively nettle free, especially in times of heavy rainfall.

Many cruisers know the Bay for its uncrowded anchorages, which are tucked up rivers and coves and provide plenty of protection and room to swing. But they're not visible to the naked eye until you meander along a shoreline and get closer. Then you'll spot a navigation aid marking an opening, or notice a break in the treeline. Some of our best cruises on the Bay have been spent sitting at anchor and listening to the music of Chesapeake troubadours like Janie Meneely or Them Eastport Oyster Boys.

But Chesapeake Bay offers much more than isolated gunkholes; some of the liveliest cities line its shores. At the north of the Bay on the western shore there is Baltimore on the Patapsco River, a boater-friendly city if there ever was one. Known as the Inner Harbor, this area is rich in history, not to mention shopping, world-class museums, and fine dining in nearby Little Italy. Neighboring Fells Point is a small city with its own distinct atmosphere, specialty and antique shops, and seafood restaurants. You can dock your boat at one of the many marinas on the Inner Harbor and use the ferries that crisscross it to see and do everything this historic city has to offer.

Annapolis, about 30 miles south of Baltimore, is a must for anyone cruising the Bay. While our friends in Newport, Rhode Island would disagree, many seasoned boaters say Annapolis is the center of the yachting world. When it comes to marine services and products, if you can't find it in Annapolis, you probably won't find it anywhere. The city lies on the Severn River, just south of the Chesapeake Bay Bridge. There are in-town marinas and moorings. The U.S. Naval Academy occupies a large part of the shoreline, with the town of Eastport and marinas across the harbor.

For live entertainment that's hard to beat, sit at a waterside restaurant and watch the harbor activity. Dinghies from cruising boats use the city dock to land their crews in the center of town in front of the Market House. Show-off boaters strut their stuff along "Ego Alley," a stretch of the harbor in clear view for all to see. Harbor taxis and tour boats scoot in and out, racing sailboats tack and jibe between the moored boats—and that's all on a dull day.

One of the most popular destinations on the western shore is Solomons on the Patuxent River, some 40 miles south of Annapolis. This somewhat sleepy area has become a haven for boaters due to its wealth of fine marinas and services and nearby gunkholes and anchorages. Solomons is home to the Calvert Marine Museum, well worth a visit, with nearby waterside restaurants and specialty shops.

The eastern shore of the Bay offers cruising grounds similar to the middle and lower western shore—remote anchorages, charming waterfront towns, and marinas that range from good-ole-boy boatyards to the luxury resort variety. On the northern part of the eastern shore the Sassafras River has one of the prettiest and most pastoral shorelines, with rolling farmlands punctuated by protected coves. Up the river, Georgetown is a popular destination, with full service marinas and yachting centers that offer all the amenities as well as fine restaurants and inns.

Rock Hall, a fishing village that sits right off the Bay on the eastern shore across from Baltimore is another yachting center in an otherwise laid-back country town. There are actually two harbors here, brimming with boats: one at Rock Hall Harbor, the other at Swan Creek just to the north. You'll find a charming old town a short walk from the harbors and a trolley service that picks up passengers from marinas outside town.

Just south of Rock Hall is the entrance to the Chester River, another river that meanders through rolling countryside as it heads to Chestertown. You can anchor off the town or go to a marina within walking distance of this charming riverfront town with its historic homes and a treasure of specialty shops and restaurants.

The Eastern Bay on the eastern shore is the entrance to two favorite destinations on the Chesapeake, Wye River and St. Michaels. Wye River is known for its abundance of protected anchorages, and St. Michaels is the historic harbor town where we live. The town is the home of the Chesapeake Bay Maritime Museum, where you'll find extensive collections and exhibits recognizing the culture and maritime heritage of the Bay. On weekends you'll see log canoe races on the river. On Thursday nights in the summer you can enjoy a concert in the town park on the water. Stay at a marina or anchor in the harbor and dinghy ashore, and within a few blocks you'll find groceries, restaurants, and boutiques where you can shop 'til you drop.

Further south is the historic town of Oxford on the Tred Avon River, a popular anchorage and stopover, revered for its quiet, tree-lined streets and tranquil setting. As you approach Oxford you'll probably notice a car ferry on its regular run to the harbor from nearby Bellevue. Oxford is the kind of town that cruisers choose if they want to get away from the crowds. An afternoon is busy here if it's spent eating an ice-cream cone in the waterfront park. It may be quiet, but Oxford is a well-known yachting center and home to brokers, classic yacht restorers, several full-service boatyards, and a collection of shops and restaurants.

Nearby Cambridge, on the lower Choptank River, is another popular harbor town with riverfront marinas, museums, restaurants, and shopping. Upriver there's a resort marina and plenty of shoreline to explore. You can head your boat up the Choptank, or board the *Cambridge Lady* for a 40-mile trip upriver and learn the fascinating history of this broad and bountiful river.

CHAPTER 33
Intracoastal Waterway

The Atlantic Intracoastal Waterway (ICW) is a 1,000-plus mile waterway of connected rivers, sounds, creeks, bays, and land-cuts along the southeastern coast of the United States. As a cruising area it offers boaters a host of opportunities to visit historic harbor towns and cities, remote islands, lush forests, and saltwater marshes. The ICW begins at Norfolk, Virginia at Mile 0 and ends at Miami, Florida at Mile 1,095, all the while providing a sheltered route for pleasure boats, passenger cruise ships, and barge traffic carrying agricultural products, sand, gravel, and petroleum products. The waterway continues from Miami to Key West following Florida Bay on the northern and northwestern sides of the Keys for shoal-draft boats. For boats drawing 5 feet or more there is the Hawk Channel, known as the outside route, which runs along the southeastern or ocean side.

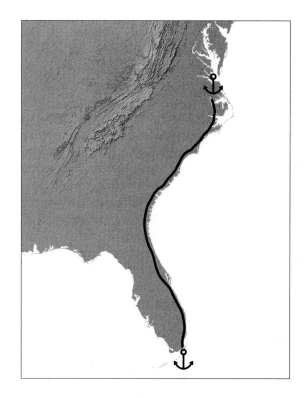

As a cruising boater you can make your way along the entire path of the ICW or choose one section to explore. If you can trailer your boat, you'll find any number or launch ramps or marina facilities along the way.

We've made 12 trips on the ICW since our first one in 1975 and we've always felt like we were part of a moving community of cruis-ers. You're all on this long string of water headed in the same direction, so you quickly recognize a familiar voice on the VHF calling a marina or spend time idling with others waiting for a bridge to open. Boats traveling at the same speed and with the same cruising style seem to travel in packs, so it's common to meet at the end of the day. We've seen dramatic changes in the landscape along the waterway due to continued expansion and development, but the ICW remains one of our favorite trips.

Our favorite stops begin at Coinjock, at Mile 49, where there's a marina on either side of the waterway, both with restaurants. Once we've crossed Albermarle Sound we like the anchorage at Little Alligator River, near Mile 82, and further on in the creeks off the Pungo River that runs from Mile 129 to Mile 145 near Belhaven. For some interesting side trips in North Carolina see Chapter 34.

As we approach Mile 200, we have to decide between having a fresh fish dinner in Moorehead City or at nearby Beaufort—either one is a good choice. At Mile 244, near New River Inlet, we often anchor at Mile Hammock Bay. It's a popular spot so we try to get there early. As we make our way south and across ocean inlets we enjoy seeing dolphins swimming and diving to their hearts' content.

We occasionally stop at Wrightsville Beach, around Mile 283, if we want a night out or need parts or service. One of our favorite layovers is Southport, a historic seaport town, at Mile 308, and nearby Bald Head Island at the mouth of the Cape Fear River. About 10 miles after entering South Carolina in the Myrtle Beach area we stop at the free dock at Barefoot Landing, at Mile 354. We also like the quieter side south of the Strand on the Waccamaw River between Mile 375 and Mile 402, where there's a growing number of marinas and wonderful wilderness anchorages in oxbows and creeks we can duck into.

Georgetown, at Mile 403, is another old, gentrified harbor town that's a solid day's run from Charleston, at Mile 470, where we like to stop to visit when we have a few days.

Often we anchor at Rock Creek, at Mile 516, a narrow cut that's well protected. And then there's Beaufort, at Mile 535, which tops the hit parade of places to lay over or anchor before crossing Port Royal Sound. We like Hilton Head, from Mile 555 to Mile 565, where we stop at a marina or anchor nearby before crossing the Savannah River and heading into Georgia.

Thunderbolt at Mile 583, and Isle of Hope at Mile 590, are charming villages to visit, but we also like anchoring at Kilkenny Creek, at Mile 614. Further south we often return to New Teakettle Creek, at Mile 646, where we find good holding and protection, before crossing the Georgia sounds.

Fort Frederica, just off the ICW at Mile 665 on St. Simons Island, is a national monument with a snug anchorage where we like to go ashore to walk the nature trails and visit the historic park. Jekyll Island, at Mile 684, is another nice place to stop and visit. Further south, between Mile 705 and Mile 715, we like the anchorages at Cumberland Island and St. Mary's River, both just off Cumberland Sound.

And then there's Fernandina Beach, at Mile 716, which welcomes boaters to Florida. Depending on the weather, we anchor off or tie up at the city dock to be in the center of this lively, restored town; there's a nice marina a few miles south. We haven't found a marina we didn't like in St. Augustine, at Mile 778, and when we anchor there we prefer being just off the fort, north of the Bridge of Lions. If we need a marine store we stop at Daytona, at Mile 831, where there's one within walking distance of the marinas.

From there we make stops in Titusville, at Mile 878, or Cocoa, at Mile 897, both with marinas and anchorages in the heart of town. Melbourne, at Mile 918, has two nice marinas, and Vero Beach, at Mile 951, has a marina and moorings. Fort Pierce, at Mile 965, is a good stopover and a major inlet for going offshore. Some 20 miles south, at Mile 988, is St. Lucie Inlet, which leads into Stuart on the St. Lucie River, and the Okeechobee Waterway that leads to the west coast of Florida.

The bridges get closer together as you enter the busy waterways approaching Jupiter Inlet, near Mile 1005, and Lake Worth Inlet, at Mile 1018, where there's a string of marinas to choose from. We often anchor in the northern end of Lake Worth. We like to go offshore from these inlets for the remaining stretch of the waterway to avoid the congested traffic and bridges in southern Florida. We come in again at Fort Lauderdale at Port Everglades, at Mile 1066, or continue south to Miami, staying at any of the marinas close to these bustling boating centers.

If you're planning an ICW cruise there are a few things to keep in mind. While you're cruising through busy boating centers there are plenty of marinas with slips and fuel, but in remote backwaters and tidal sounds the facilities are few and far between, so you have to plan ahead. The same is true about good anchorages. The broad reaches of the some of the wide rivers have an abundance of anchorages, but where the waterway is primarily a series of landcuts, a protected cove or creek is hard to find.

The controlling depth of the ICW is supposed to be 12 feet to central Florida and then 10 feet further south. But water depth and shoaling are a concern, especially where the waterway crosses an inlet or sound and is affected by tides and currents. Years of neglect and lack of federal funding have made matters worse. You'll find updated information at the website of the Atlantic Intracoastal Waterway Association listed in Appendix 3.

The waterway is clearly marked with nav-igational aids—red ICW markers on the starboard side and green markers to port going south. But you may get confused when the waterway joins or crosses another body of water and the markers are shared. The inland rules apply (we discussed this in more detail in Chapter 17, Rules of the Road). To minimize confusion we navigate the ICW with an electronic chart for our GPS, and we refer often to the *Intracoastal Waterway Chartbook* (listed in Appendix 3). It's an invaluable reference of every mile of the waterway in detailed, mile-by-mile strip charts. We also have a collection of cruising guides so we can plan our marina stops and visits ashore.

More than 100 bridges cross over the ICW. Several have restricted hours of opening; others open on demand. As you make your daily plan, use bridge schedules and VHF channels noted in the cruising guides to decide when to arrive at a bridge. Find out the height restriction of your boat so you'll know if you can safely clear below it. If not, request an opening. The bridge operators on the waterway are courteous and helpful, and by the end of the cruise you'll be able to distinguish the accent of a North Carolinian from that of a Georgian.

Going down the ICW you'll negotiate one lock and learn how to read ranges, both useful skills to master. The lock is small and it's located at Great Bridge, Virginia, just south of Norfolk, at Mile 11. In the areas of strong currents in the Carolinas and Georgia you'll get practice using ranges to keep your boat in the channel. You'll find more information about locking through and reading ranges in Chapter 16, Boat Handling.

Some fast boats blitz the ICW in two weeks; for others it's a month-long trip. To estimate your travel time, figure your average speed and multiply it by the number of hours you like to cruise each day. On long days we run at 7.5 knots for about 10 hours, so we average about 75 miles a day. We leave at sun up and go to bed earlier than we care to admit. On short days we stop at noon and spend the day ashore.

Nasty weather can affect any passage along the ICW. Wise boaters stay put until it passes. Strong winds and tides are of special concern when you cross open waters or inlets. It's impossible to forecast the weather or know when bridge will be broken (and not open), so plan an ICW cruise that's loose and flexible, with time to enjoy the riches and wonders you'll find there.

CHAPTER 34

North Carolina

The river towns of northeastern North Carolina offer some of the prettiest cruising destinations we know. You can plan a cruise to begin at any one of them—Elizabeth City, Edenton, Belhaven, Oriental, or New Bern—and spend as much time as you like exploring the nearby waters. The distance between towns is a comfortable run, no matter what speed you cruise at. And along the way you'll find marinas and tree-lined, protected anchorages hidden up creeks and tucked in coves.

The towns are poised along rivers that flow into Albermarle and Pamlico Sounds, which lie inside the Outer Banks along the Atlantic coast from the Virginia border to Cape Lookout. A stretch of the Intracoastal Waterway meanders through the sounds and rivers, providing an inland passage between them. In a long weekend you can launch a trailered boat and cruise nearby or spend a week in the area going from town to town. Snug anchorages, friendly people, and fine marinas and restaurants all combine to make good cruising grounds.

In our country's early history, the location of these towns made them major shipping and commerce sites, the river banks lined with prominent homes. Today many of the neighborhoods have been reclaimed as historic landmarks with restored homes and commercial buildings dating back to the Revolution-

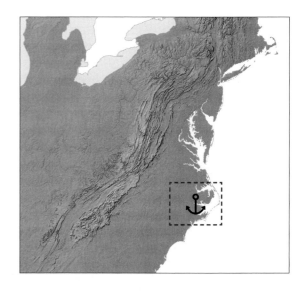

ary and Civil wars. All of them welcome cruising boaters to visit and stay awhile.

The northernmost town is Elizabeth City on the Pasquotank River off Albermarle Sound. The town has gained a reputation as a harbor of hospitality. For years its "Rose Buddies" or local folks have welcomed visiting boaters with wine, cheese, and roses. The town's Mariners' Wharf offers free docks on a first-come, first-serve basis—another way the charming old town provides a warm reception to boaters. The Pelican Marina also has slips, and there's an anchorage just off the channel.

The town is the gateway to the historic Dismal Swamp Canal, a 22-mile long waterway listed in the National Register of Historic Places, and designated a National Civil Engineering Landmark. The Canal is an interesting side trip that includes two locks, a landcut and winding river, and miles of beautiful scenery along its shores. In some areas your boat is draped in the grapevines that overhang the canal; in others it feels like you've stepped back to a forgotten time. Conditions in the canal depend on rainfall and other weather events, so contact the Dismal Swamp Visitors Center, listed in Appendix 3, for current water depths.

Edenton is 30 miles off the ICW, near the headwaters of Albermarle Sound. The cypress groves shade the broad river and create habitat for bald eagles, ospreys, and thousands of migratory birds. You can stay at the Edenton Marina or anchor in Pembroke Creek and row ashore. Visit the town's waterfront National Historic District, where you'll find boutiques, antiques, and restaurants on tree-lined streets. And take a guided walking or trolley tour to see the "South's prettiest town."

The inside passage between Albermarle and Pamlico Sounds is the Alligator River and the Alligator River-Pungo River landcut. The cut feeds into the tree-lined Pungo River and leads to Belhaven, where there are several snug anchorages and marinas to choose from. A few miles north of town you can anchor in Scranton Creek or tie up at Dowry Creek Marina in a peaceful setting on Upper Dowry Creek. Two-story, wide-open porches wrap around the marina building and a footbridge over wild marshland connects to a boater's lounge that's just like home, maybe nicer.

In the harbor of Belhaven you can stay at Waterway Marina or other marinas, or anchor inside the breakwater. You'll be right downtown within walking distance of everything the small town offers, including restaurants serving local seafood and southern home cooking. Nearby you can anchor at Pungo Creek or a few miles beyond in Slade Creek.

The shoreline of the Neuse River that flows into Pamlico Sound offers both quiet coves for anchoring and upscale marinas with full-service facilities. Depending on the wind and current the wide waters can be calm or cantankerous, so follow your course with caution, especially if you're new to the area. The village of Oriental on the river's northern shore may look like a quiet hideaway, but on weekends it's hopping. It's known as the "Sailing Capital of North Carolina," and you'll see all kinds of boats there at almost any time of year.

Oriental Harbor is the newest of the marinas in town. In this coastal village you'll find restaurants, a historic hardware store, and a train station that's been restored to house several retailers and a wide selection of marine-related services. There's also the Oriental Marina and Inn and Whittaker's. You'll find spots to anchor beyond the 45-foot fixed bridge in both Smith and Green Creeks in the harbor.

Cruising further up the Neuse to its headwaters you'll find New Bern, a picture-postcard town that looks like it belongs in New England rather than in the South. It's known for its Swiss heritage, as the birthplace of Pepsi, and as the home of Hatteras Yachts. As you approach the harbor you'll pass under a high-rise bridge and then a swing and railroad bridge into the Trent River. You'll find a renovated cityscape with a city wharf and marinas within walking distance of restaurants and shopping. New Bern was the state capital until the late 1700s, so it's steeped in history. Take a stroll down its tree-lined streets and visit the Fireman's Museum with its extensive collection of early fire-fighting equipment, or go on a trolley tour to see some of the 400-plus sites on the National Register of Historic Places.

CHAPTER 35
Abacos, Bahamas

The Sea of Abaco is a protected passage that provides miles of emerald green water, dotted with lovely anchorages, small towns, and settlements for the cruising boater to explore. On the western side of the passage lie two large islands, Great and Little Abaco. A string of smaller barrier islands on the eastern side shelters the passage from the Atlantic. This island chain, called the Abacos, runs some 130 miles from Walkers Cay (pronounced key) at the northern end to Hole in the Wall at the southern end. Some of the islands are uninhabited, and others have small settlements with shops and homes. Yet others have mega-villas and resorts lining their shores.

The waters splash ashore on dazzling white beaches lined with coconut palms. It is generally shallow here and the water color depends on the nature of the bottom—grassy patches, shallow coral heads, or sand. Depth is always a concern for the thousands of boaters who cruise in the Bahamas, but with a good chart and sound judgment you'll be all right. Snowbirds spend the winter in the Bahamas and Florida; southern boaters make the crossing in the spring when the weather and wind are more settled.

For years fishermen and snorkelers have flocked to the Abacos for their bountiful sea life. Today cruising boaters join them and find pristine beaches and anchorages all within an easy day's run. You can anchor off a quiet beach and swim from the boat, then take a dinghy ride ashore to comb the beach. You can choose a small settlement with charming out-island appeal or pamper yourself at a luxurious resort and marina. There's a tremendous variety of marina facilities and anchorages to choose from, and restaurant fare ranges from good local seafood gumbos to the best of fine dining.

Making a cruise to the Abacos or anywhere in the Bahamas involves more preplanning than the other cruising areas we cover in this section because you're visiting a foreign country. Before leaving call U.S. Customs (listed in Appendix 3) to find out what you are required to do on returning stateside. It usually involves calling them to declare that you have returned when you arrive in U.S. waters.

Seasoned Florida cruisers tell us the best route to take crossing the Gulf Stream between southern Florida and the Bahamas is Key Largo to Bimini. They prefer anchoring in Angel Fish Key at the north end of Key Largo before heading across. Biscayne Bay's No Name Harbor is another good departure point. We've also crossed from Port Everglades in Fort Lauderdale to Nassau. On our most recent cruise to the Abacos we crossed from West Palm Beach to West End on Grand Bahama Island, where we cleared Customs and Immigration. From there we headed to Great Sale Cay, and then headed down the chain of islands.

If you're intimidated about crossing the Gulf Stream, consider participating in one of the Bahamas Summer Boating Flings. These guided flotillas run from June through August and depart from various eastern Florida inlets like Fort Lauderdale, Palm Beach Shores, and Stuart. The Bahamas Ministry of Tourism and the Marine Industries Association have sponsored the Flings for the past 21 years, in an effort to encourage boaters to discover the beauty of Bahamas cruising while providing the security of a supervised group. There's a schedule of upcoming Flings, information about joining the group, and registration on the Boating and Sailing page of the Bahamian Government website (listed in Appendix 3).

Several websites (also in the Appendix) explain the requirements for cruising boaters entering the Bahamas. In general you must clear Customs and Immigration at a port of entry (usually located at a government dock

or marina). As you enter the port, fly the yellow quarantine flag and notify Customs and Immigration of your arrival. No one other than the captain is permitted to leave the boat until your vessel has been cleared. In some cases Customs and Immigration will come to your vessel; in others, everyone on board goes to the office with proof of citizenship to fill out an immigration card. As a courtesy, visiting boaters should fly the Bahamian flag.

In 2005, the entry fee was $150.00 for boats up to 35 feet in length and $300.00 for boats over 35 feet for two entries during a 90-day period. The Bahamian Government has been appraising its fee structure and is considering an annual fee. Again, its boating website is the best source of current updates on this information.

If you're cruising with a pet aboard you must apply for an import permit ($10), required by the Bahamas Ministry of Agriculture, and have a valid certificate of rabies vaccination and a Veterinary Health Certificate. Details are also on the government website.

Food and drink in the Abacos are more expensive than in the States, so it's a good idea to stock up with provisions before leaving. In larger towns like Marsh Harbour, grocery and liquor stores are within an easy walk of the marinas. Also, before you go to the Bahamas, be sure to stock up on a good supply of spare parts and any consumable materials you need to maintain your boat. You never know when you'll need to make a repair, and if something is going to break down it will likely be in a remote spot where spare parts aren't available.

Restaurants in the Bahamas are laid-back, so you won't need to make reservations to savor the local cuisine. Plan to eat out in some of the charming native eateries where you'll find seafood served in some delicious ways. A basket of conch fritters and a cold

Kalik—the native beer of the Bahamas—is island living at its finest. And if you want to get into the island swing, pick up an Island Boys CD with calypso and junkanoo music. You'll soon be in the groove.

We think a dinghy and outboard are essential when cruising the Bahamas. The water is so inviting, and it's the only way to get to remote anchorages and visit other cruisers. On our first visit to the Bahamas we had a hard dinghy and, although it was a salty, seaworthy vessel, it was only good for transportation. It just wasn't fun. We tagged along with friends who had an inflatable and used their boat for swimming and snorkeling almost every day. We got our own soon after.

Spanish Cay has a nice marina and restaurant, with beautiful beaches on its ocean side, all an easy walk from the marina. Green Turtle Cay offers anchorages and marinas and a charming little settlement in New Plymouth, where you'll find restaurants and small resorts, and feel the pull of the laid-back life.

Going south, Powell Cay and Delia's Cay on Great Guana Cay are two nice anchorages. Ashore at Great Guana Cay don't miss a stop at Nipper's Beach Bar, and stroll the miles of beautiful beaches. Across from Great Guana Cay, on Great Abaco Island, there's a full service marina and more extraordinary beaches at Treasure Cay, a fisherman's paradise.

The red and white candystripe lighthouse of Hope Town rises high above lush green palms against a backdrop of turquoise water. Boats bob on their anchor lines in this picture-postcard harbor, its shores lined with colorful cottages, inns, and resorts. If you don't go to Hope Town on your boat, take the ferry from Marsh Harbour.

You can anchor at Marsh Harbour, the largest town in the Abacos, or stay at a marina. You'll find boating facilities and services as well as restaurants and shopping. There's even an airport and a "cruisers' net" on the VHF, if you want to hear the latest marine conditions and boaters' gossip. The airport has daily flights to Florida, so it's a good spot to plan a layover, or to pick up and drop off visiting crew members.

When you're in the Bahamas it doesn't take long to adjust to a slower-paced island life. We agree with the Bahamians: it really is better in the Bahamas.

CHAPTER 36

Florida Keys

Anyone who cruises south of Miami can't help but appreciate the pristine waters of the Keys, the sweeping string of islands that extend 130 miles southwest from the Florida mainland. The Keys, which are connected by a series of highway bridges, begin south of Miami and end at Key West.

There are two routes south through the Keys. Your choice depends on the draft of your boat. On the northern and northwestern sides of the Keys, the shoal-draft Intracoastal Waterway follows Florida Bay. The deeper Hawk Channel, known as the outside route, runs along the southeastern or ocean side and is a better choice for boats drawing 5 feet or more. Many cruisers combine both routes, using crossover channels if weather conditions and their boat's draft allow for it. There are many places to crossover and local boaters run them regularly, but visiting boaters should avoid most of them. They are often uncharted, with swift currents and shifting depths. The three passages that are known for being deep and well marked are the northernmost cross over at ICW Mile 1096, at Cape Florida and Biscayne Channels; Channel Five, which is further south at ICW Mile 1170; and Moser Channel, at ICW Mile 1197.

As you cruise the Keys and travel ashore, you'll find two different mileage systems.

The Intracoastal Waterway, which begins at Mile 0 in Norfolk and ends at Mile 1095 in Miami, is extended to Key West as the Florida Bay Intracoastal Waterway. Another set of mileage markers begins in Key West at Mile Marker 0, making it the "Southernmost City" in the continental United States. These markers are part of the Overseas Highway system, which ends at Mile 128 in Florida City on the South Florida mainland. They follow the Hawk Channel, or ocean-side route. We mention this because you'll find that some marinas advertise their location by their Mile Marker. Here's an example.

There are two very nice Faro Blanco marinas in Marathon, considered the center of the Keys. One is the Faro Blanco Marine Resort Bayside on Florida Bay at ICW marker 1193. The other, Faro Blanco Marine Resort Oceanside, is at Mile Marker 47.5, about 48 miles from Key West. They're actually a few miles away from each other on opposite sides of the road—the Overseas Highway, or U.S. Highway 1.

The relatively short distances between anchorages and marinas in the Keys make it a popular cruising destination. About thirty miles south of Miami you'll find popular anchorages at Elliott Key and Angelfish Creek. Anglers will find paradise at both Tavernier and Islamorada, whether it's for tuna and dolphin on the Atlantic side or bonefish and tarpon in the backcountry waters of Florida Bay. Key Largo is home to the 21-mile long John Pennecamp State Park, the only living coral reef off the continental United States, and several marinas for visiting boaters.

Further south, on Duck Key, is one of the area's most luxurious marinas. Hawk's Cay Resort is an island paradise, with every imaginable service and luxury. At Marathon, on Vaca Key, you'll find a popular anchorage at Boot Key Harbor, and all the marinas and marine services you might need. You can buy fresh seafood from a local fish house or try one of the many fine restaurants along the shore.

Beyond Marathon you won't be able to miss the Seven Mile Bridge. It leads to Bahia Honda State Park, where there's a nice sandy beach for swimming. You can anchor or tie up to the marina in this well-protected man-made basin frequented by playful manatees.

Throughout the Keys you'll probably notice Conch Republic flags that celebrate the Keys' temporary secession from the Union in 1982. The mantra, "We seceded where others failed," is proclaimed by Conchs, or natives of the Keys. These are characters who enjoy the Keys' unique and quirky style of life.

And then there's Key West, one of our favorite destinations. It's expensive, it's hectic, it can be downright gaudy, but we go back for more whenever we can. The surrounding waters and harbor are always busy with traffic—gargantuan cruise ships jockeying for their moorings, tour boats bustling to and fro, sailboats slicing through the water, parasailors overhead, and of course, jet skis buzzing about looking for waves to jump. But most of the harbor activity slows at sundown when the main event is watching the sunset at Mallory Square. The time of sunset is clearly posted in town so you don't have any excuse not to be there.

The diversity of eateries, entertainment, and attractions appeals to any type of cruiser whether they're looking for a low-key, laid-back time at anchor or an action-packed week of shopping and partying. You won't find a better selection of restaurants, whether it's for a cheeseburger (in paradise à la Jimmy Buffett) or a gourmet Chilean coq au vin. Nightlife can be racy and raucous or quiet and subdued, with a good mix of everything in between.

Take a conch train tour to see the lush, tree-lined streets with beautifully restored homes and colorful cottages. Visit Harry Truman's Winter White House in Truman Annex and get a feel for quieter times. Take a side trip to Dry Tortugas National Park (on your own boat, ferry, or seaplane) to visit Fort Jefferson, a remote island steeped in history and surrounded by tropical waters just waiting to be explored. Fishermen and snorkelers find these waters filled with treasure.

Bring a good pair of binoculars so you don't miss the lush tropical foliage and wildlife. Swaying palms and rustling pines stand in contrast to the blue-green waters. You'll see a host of herons, spoonbills, and gulls at the water's edge. And the warm, shallow waters support a delicate ecosystem of plants and animals, making it a favorite spot for nature lovers.

Don't go to the Keys without good, up-to-date charts and software for your GPS. A recent edition of a cruising guide for the Florida Keys will give you the ins and outs of anchorages and out-of-the-way places. Appendix 3 lists websites where you'll find current information for planning your visit.

And to get a feel for the physical setting of the Keys and its many characters, pick up a novel by James W. Hall, Laurence Shames, or Carl Hiaasen. We always bring these authors along on a cruise to the Keys.

CHAPTER 37
Southwest Florida

The southwest coast of Florida is as close to island cruising as you can get. If you're looking for protected, pristine waters with good fishing, snug anchorages, and upscale marinas, you'll find them here.

Our favorite area on this coast is Pine Island Sound, a 25-mile stretch where the distances between stops are short and the choices are many. The waters are shallow, so be mindful of the markers that run north, beginning the Gulf Intracoastal Waterway in San Carlos Bay. This sound is one of the most accessible and delightful cruising destinations we know.

Pine Island Sound is bordered by Charlotte Harbor to the north, and the barrier islands of Sanibel and Captiva to the south and west. Pine Island makes up its eastern shoreline. Tour boats loaded with passengers cross the channel to the barrier islands, and a multitude of boaters passes to and fro.

Fishing boats of all sizes sit at anchor or make for their favored spots. The shallow waters support lush sea grass meadows called *flats*, providing breeding grounds for a host of marine life including sea trout, redfish, and snook. The sound is also known as one of the foremost areas for tarpon fishing. In fact, in the early nineteenth century, these islands were Cuban fishing *ranchos*, where fish were caught, dried, and transported back to Cuban markets.

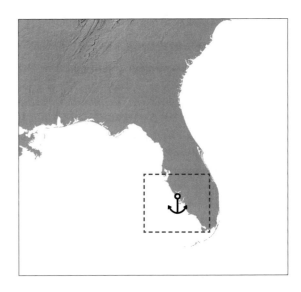

Cruisers love the area because they can make a lunch run to a marina, drop the hook for a swim, or find a quiet hidey-hole to anchor. Paddlers in canoes and colorful kayaks love it for the shallow, protected waters along the shore.

The landscape is lush and tropical, with vibrant foliage and colorful flowers. Charming fish shacks balance precariously on stilts on sandy keys. Lining the shoreline you'll see modest Old Florida shotgun cottages, contemporary new homes, and traditional white frame bungalows with wide porches, overhanging roofs, and widow's walks.

Nature lovers flock to the area to visit two popular destinations in particular. The Ding Darling National Wildlife Refuge on Sanibel Island covers 7,000 acres of forest and estuary, ideal habitat for water birds and other wildlife. You'll see spoonbills, herons, ibis, and white pelicans, as well as alligators, otters, and raccoons in this mangrove habitat. You can anchor along the shore of Tarpon Bay and explore by dinghy, or go ashore and walk the trails or rent a bicycle. Bring your camera.

While we're cruising this area we like to read Randy White's Doc Ford mysteries, which are set in Sanibel and the Southwest seacoast. They're always a good read.

Cayo Costa, a Florida state park at the northern end of the sound and just south of Boca Grand Pass, is another popular nature center. You can anchor at Pelican Bay. You'll find bird sanctuaries for frigate birds, ospreys, and bald eagles and lush vegetation along the entire 7-mile length of Cayo Costa. Take a short walk across the island to the Gulf side and you'll find beautiful white sandy beaches. Visitors and campers reach the island by ferry from Pine Island. Some stay for the day; overnighters use tent sites or rent rustic cabins.

A few miles south of Cayo Costa, the marked channel of the waterway passes by Cabbage Key, an island inn and restaurant, known for its funky atmosphere and lush forest of cabbage palms. Rumor says the place inspired Jimmy Buffett's song "Cheeseburger in Paradise." The dining room is wallpapered in dollar bills signed by famous, and not so famous, patrons. The unusual decoration gives this charming spot a unique personality, and makes it a popular destination for laid-back cruisers.

Just north of Cabbage Key is Useppa Island, an upscale private island for members only. In fair weather, many cruisers anchor off the island and cross the channel to Cabbage Key by dinghy.

On Captiva Island, connected to Sanibel at its northern end, we like Tween Waters Inn and Marina just off the waterway at the Roosevelt Channel. The resort has several restaurants, a tennis court, and pool, and across the road you're looking at the Gulf of Mexico, with white sandy beaches that stretch as far north and south as you can see.

It's no surprise that Pine Island Sound is often compared with the Abacos in the Bahamas. They both offer cruising in protected waters in a lush, natural setting.

CHAPTER 38
Northern California Delta

The Delta region of Northern California, located roughly between Sacramento in the north and Stockton in the South, offers some of the finest laid-back cruising grounds. The Sacramento River feeds in from the north, and the San Joaquin River from the south. More than 1,000 miles of waterways twist and turn through farm fields and friendly rural towns, whose residents are bent on keeping it as charming and peaceful as it is.

This vast area was once flood-prone swampland, but today it is fertile ground for corn, wine grapes, pears, and sod farms. The farms and orchards dotting the landscape are actually below sea level, protected by levees.

Fishing is a major pastime for residents and visitors alike, whether it's for the bounty of bass and sturgeon or their local crawdad, which are like crayfish. For many, fishing is a passion.

The miles of waterways and sloughs around the farmlands provide enough boating opportunities to fill a few days or a few weeks. One popular route that cruisers use is the Historic Delta Loop, a waterway that runs through a series of small rural towns, passing under bridges and crossing cable ferries. Cruisers can spend the night at anchor in a shady slough or a quiet cove, or tie up at a small town dock or full-service marina.

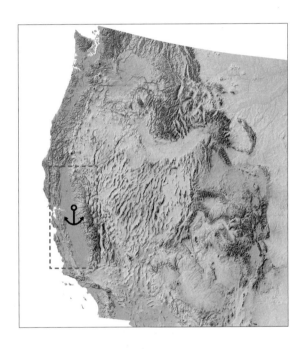

There's a relaxed attitude throughout the region: think Key West mixed with Country/Western. In Rio Vista, the walls of Foster's Bighorn Saloon, a bar and café, are decorated with 250 animal heads. They were taken by the original owner of the saloon while hunting on the plains of Africa or the Alaskan tundra. This is no ordinary local bar.

At Courtland, a charming little riverbank town, you can tie up at the town dock and walk to all the restaurants and shops. Or enjoy a quiet afternoon walking through neighborhoods with tree-lined streets and white picket fences.

At Walnut Grove you'll find farmhouses spread across acres of a family farm that have been there for generations of families. In the idyllic river town there are stately old homes and a general store.

From there it's a mile-long walk north to Locke, a small town that started out as a Chinese settlement. Locke was first built in the early 1900s when Chinese workers helped build the levees. A tragic fire burned most of the buildings. But some were salvaged and rebuilt, and are now on the National Register of Historic Places.

Ryde is another pleasant stop, with a riverfront hotel, restaurant, marina, and golf course.

In the town of Isleton many of the old store buildings remain intact and are home to antique and specialty shops and restaurants. The town celebrates the history and spirit of the California Delta with a rodeo and it also plays host to annual events celebrating crawdads.

This cruising loop is an inviting destination, whether on your own boat or on one you've chartered for the occasion. Don't be surprised if you feel a bit like Huck Finn on a backwater adventure where time seems to stand still.

CHAPTER 39
Puget Sound

Whenever we get the chance to explore unknown cruising grounds we jump at the chance, so brief though it was, we enjoyed a weekend on Puget Sound while visiting friends in the area. The busy harbor in Seattle was alive with ferries, freighters, cruise ships, and tugboats with their tows when we got aboard a small cruiser and joined the traffic plowing through the strong tidal waters of this central section of the Sound.

Our destination was Poulsbo, on the north side of Liberty Bay on the Kitsap Peninsula. Just a few blocks from the marina we found Poulsbo Village; its rosemaling-covered storefronts bespoke the town's Norwegian heritage. In the late 1880s, Scandinavians settled the area because it reminded them of the fjords of Norway. Today the town has more of an international flavor, with art galleries, specialty shops, and waterfront restaurants.

You'll also see signs of Poulsbo's Native American heritage at the Squamish Museum where carvings and clam baskets are beautifully exhibited. These open baskets for gathering clams, small fish, and oysters were intricately woven and made of cedar roots, split limbs, and bark.

You can take a walk on a nature trail or on the boardwalk along Liberty Bay or stop and rest awhile in one of the lovely parks in town.

The Marine Service Center is another popular destination. Its touch trays allow visitors to interact with all the plants and creatures of the chilly waters of Puget Sound.

Port Orange is located on the south shore of Sinclair Inlet across from the Bremerton Naval Base. The waterfront town offers a nice marina with plenty of docking space for visitors. Restaurants and interesting shops are all within an easy walk. There's also a farmers' market and a log cabin museum.

Blake Island State Park is one of the 43 state parks in Washington with moorings or floats for boaters. Some seven miles southwest of Seattle the island is one of the most popular for local boaters. Take the well-worn clamshell path to Tillicum Village and you'll see huge totem poles and a Native American longhouse. You'll also see carving demonstrations and native dances that illustrate the myths and legends of some of the Northwest Coast Indian tribes. And the intoxicating aroma of cedar-staked smoked salmon and warm grain breads can easily tempt you to enjoy an Indian-style meal.

You can simply enjoy the natural beauty of the place and walk along the beach with its view of the Olympic Mountains and Seattle's skyline. Or go inland and follow a forest walking trail.

We only scratched the surface of this expansive cruising area. We left with a resolve to return someday for an extended cruise to experience more of its captivating allure. A boater could spend a lifetime cruising Puget Sound and never tire of its breathtaking beauty, natural harbors, and pristine waters. You'll find more sources of cruising information listed in Appendix 3.

CHAPTER 40
Door County, Wisconsin

On the western shore of Lake Michigan, a narrow peninsula called Door County juts into the northern reaches of the lake and separates it from Green Bay. The high cliffs and quaint harbor villages of this peninsula offer boaters some of the best cruising grounds we know.

The area's limestone bluffs and rocky shoreline are dotted with towering lighthouses. With its close-together waterside towns, marinas, and anchorages, Door County is often compared to New England. The resort towns are busy all summer, welcoming visitors to a full schedule of art shows and music festivals. Fishermen will tell you the waters are renowned for walleye, rainbow trout, salmon, and some of the best smallmouth bass in the Midwest.

Large boats can choose from a nice selection of marinas and you can launch a trailered boat at several locations. Many marinas have motels and inns nearby, so it's an ideal destination for a "boat and bed ashore" cruise. This is a very popular destination, so if you like to anchor out, you'll find plenty of places to drop the hook, but plan to arrive early to claim a spot. Or, if you're headed to the marina, be sure to make a reservation.

Ashore you'll find public beaches, parks, and walking and biking trails. For maritime

history buffs the Door County Maritime Museum in Sturgeon Bay is a must-see. It features a chronological shipbuilding exhibit from the mid-1800s, with Native American dugouts and bark canoes, to today's navy vessels, ore carriers, and world-famous yachts. The collection includes impressive scale models of boats and ships built in the area.

If eating and shopping are your favorite diversions ashore, you won't be disappointed. Enjoy a Door County fish boil, an outdoor event centered on a steaming cauldron of whitefish steaks, potatoes, and onions that gives new meaning to the term "one-pot meal." There's also a variety of casual and elegant eateries throughout the area. The county is a haven for artists so you'll find homes and old buildings converted into specialty shops with one-of-a-kind gift items, and art galleries featuring traditional Norwegian arts, enamel jewelry, and scrimshaw.

Many cruisers enter Green Bay through the Sturgeon Bay Canal that connects Lake Michigan with Door County. The city of Sturgeon Bay is home to talented shipwrights who made the Door known for its shipbuilding. As you leave the canal and go north on the eastern shore of Green Bay you'll find a chain of towns and harbors.

Egg Harbor, with a resort and marina, is the first of several charming harbor villages. Just five miles north, Fish Creek offers restaurants, marinas, a summer playhouse, and a welcoming waterfront park.

Ephraim, just a few miles north of Fish Creek, is considered the center of the upper Door County peninsula. There you'll see neatly painted white houses and an eye-catching weather-beaten boathouse on the shore. First built for passengers waiting to board ships, the building now houses the work of some of the area's prominent artists. The names of hundreds of boats are painted on its siding.

Sister Bay, a few miles north, is another charming postcard-perfect harbor town reminiscent of its early Norwegian settlers, with specialty shops, inns, and restaurants. Nearby there are nice anchorages at Little Sister Bay and, our favorite, Horseshoe Island.

The harbor towns of Ellison Bay and Gills Rock lie further north and at the top of the peninsula there is Washington Island. The 6-mile strait, known as Death's Door, between the mainland and Washington Island is infamous—its unfriendly cross currents can make the passage perilous. Entering Detroit Harbor, on the south side of the island where the ferry boat from the mainland docks, you'll feel a strong sense of place among the island's rolling farmlands and orchards. Time seems to stand still here. In years past the island was the potato-growing center of Door County, but now it attracts visitors who like to fish and relax in a quiet atmosphere.

About 30 miles northeast of Detroit Harbor, across the entrance to Green Bay, is one of the most picturesque anchorages in the Upper Peninsula of Michigan. It's not in Door County, but we'd never go to Door without a return trip to Fayette—the historic town on the Garden Peninsula at Snail Shell Harbor. Nineteen public and commercial buildings and houses, and the stabilized ruins of the furnace complex, still stand here as a legacy to a mid-1800s iron-smelting operation. It's now a state park with a visitors' center, walking tour, and scale model of the original town.

You'll find information about the area and its marinas on the Door County's Visitor website listed in Appendix 3. For detailed cruising information look in either the Great Lakes Port O'Call or the Great Lakes Waterway Guide. The most comprehensive authority on cruising in Door County (and all the Great Lakes and their surrounding waterways) is The Great Lakes Cruising Club, also listed in the Appendix.

Appendix 1
Boating Resources and Information

BOAT CLUBS/ FRACTIONAL OWNERSHIP

Adair Yachts, 16832 Pacific Coast Highway,
Sunset Beach, CA 90742.
562/592-6220.
www.adairyachts.com.

American Yacht Share Management, Inc.,
One East Broward Blvd., Suite 700 Fort
Lauderdale, FL 33301. 954/745-5877.
www.americanyachtshare.com.

Bradford Yachts, 1800 SE 10th Avenue,
Suite 200, Ft. Lauderdale, FL 33316.
800/327-9719.
www.bradfordyachts.com/fractional.

Fractional Yacht Management, Inc.,
P.O. Box 410438, Melbourne, FL
32941-0438. 321/637-0312.
www.sharedyachts.com.

Freedom Boat Club,
1538 Stickney Point Rd.,
Sarasota, FL 34231. 888/781-7363.
www.freedomboatclub.com.

J/Port Annapolis, 213 Eastern Ave.,
Annapolis, MD 21403. 410/280-2083.
www.jportannapolis.com.

Sailtime Licensing Group, Suite 160-C-11,
10900 Research Blvd., Austin, TX 78759.
512/314-5600. Fax: 866/847-1386.
www.sailtime.com.

VIP Boat Club,
605 Orange Street South, Homeport Marina,
Palm Harbor, FL 34683.
727/789-2688. Fax: 727/789-0652.
www.floridaboat.com/membership.shtml.

BOATING ORGANIZATIONS

American Boat and Yacht Council,
3069 Solomons Island Road,
Edgewater, MD 21037.
410/956-1050. Fax: 410/956-2737.
www.abycinc.org.
The American Boat & Yacht Council (ABYC) is a not-for-profit membership organization that has been developing and updating the safety standards for boatbuilding and repair for 50 years. ABYC's membership includes boatowners, boatbuilders, surveyors, boatyards, insurance companies, law firms, trade associations, marinas, dealerships, government agencies, and equipment and accessory manufacturers.

BoatU.S.,
880 South Pickett Street,
Alexandria, VA 22304.
Member services: 800/395-2628.
www.boatus.com.

BoatU.S.—the Boatowners Association of the United States—has been providing savings, service, and representation to millions of boatowners nationwide since 1966. According to Richard Schwartz, Chairman & Founder, today BoatU.S. is the nation's most powerful advocate for advancing the interests of boaters and the single source to meet all boaters' needs.

Marine Trader Owners Association,
411 Walnut St., Green Cove Springs, FL 32043. www.MTOA.net.
The goals of the MTOA and its members include:
   Maintenance and repair problem solving.
   Training and education for captains and first mates.
   Ownership and resale of members' vessels.
   Activities and social events for members and guests.
   Information exchange and dialogue amongst the membership.

National Boatowners Association.
941/360-6777, 800/248-3512.
Fax: 941/360-6888.
Membership includes $1000 nationwide on-water emergency towing insurance and $150 on-road towing insurance, plus guaranteed low insurance premiums, marine financing, and an online ship store with great prices.

United States Power Squadrons.
888/FOR-USPS (888/367-8777).
www.usps.org.
Organized in 1914, USPS is a private, nonprofit, educational organization dedicated to making boating safer and more enjoyable by teaching classes in seamanship, navigation, and related subjects. USPS is America's largest nonprofit boating organization and has been honored by three U.S. presidents for its civic contributions.

United States Coast Guard Auxiliary.
Coast Guard Customer Infoline: 877/875-6296.
www.cgaux.org.
The United States Coast Guard Auxiliary was established by Congress in 1939 to assist the Coast Guard in promoting boating safety. Auxiliary members volunteer more than 2 million hours annually to benefit other boaters and their families. Membership is open to all citizens of the United States and its territories who are at least 17 years old.

Women Aboard,
816 Executive Dr., Oviedo, FL 32765.
407/328-1744, 877-WMN-ABRD.
Fax: 407/323-8051.
www.womenaboard.com. *Women Aboard's Mission Statement is this: to enhance the boating experience for ALL women aboard through information, education, camaraderie, and support.*

BOATING SCHOOLS

Chapman School of Seamanship, Stuart, Florida.
www.chapman.org.

Club Nautique, San Francisco Bay.
http://www.clubnautique.net/.

Florida Sailing & Cruising School.
www.flsailandcruiseschool.com.

Power Cruise School,
Southwest Florida. 888/851-0381.
www.powercruiseschool.com.

Sailing and Cruising School
at Southwest Florida Yachts.
www.swfyachts.com.

San Juan Yachting,
Bellingham, Washington.
www.sanjuanyachting.com/instruction.htm.

DISCOUNT MARINE SUPPLIES AND EQUIPMENT

Boatowners Warehouse.
www.boatownerswarehouse.com.

Defender Industries, Inc.,
42 Great Neck Road, Waterford, CT 06385.
800/628-8225. Fax: 800/654-1616.
www.defender.com.
This high-volume source has been satisfying mail-order customers for almost 70 years.

Hamilton Marine.
www.hamiltonmarine.com.

iboats.com.
The iboats mall stocks more than 100,000 marine products. If you can't find what you are looking for or have problems, questions, or comments, call Customer service at 800/914-1123.

Landfall Navigation.
www.landfallnav.com.
Nautical charts, cruising guides, marine electronics, plotting and weather software, and boating safety gear.

Mike's Marine Supply On-Line Store.
www.mikesmarine.com.
A discount marine store serving southeastern Michigan for more than 30 years.

Online Marine. www.onlinemarine.com.
888/933-BOAT.
Discount marine electronics, equipment, and supplies.

The Shad Connection, 111 Russell Drive,
Highland Village, TX 75077.
www.theshadconnection.com.

West Marine. www.westmarine.com.
This major marine retailer now has hundreds of stores nationwide. It has been in the mail-order business for years and still does a healthy remote business online. If you can't get to a store, or there isn't one near you, try the website.

DOCKOMINIUM INFORMATION

Dock Search. www.docksearch.com.
Docksearch is a place to locate boat dockage, and rent or sell your boat dock space or boat slip.

Frenchman's Bay Marina,
591 Liverpool Road, Pickering, Ontario,
L1W 1R1. 888/839-5036. Fax: 905/839-4380.
www.frenchmansbaymarina.com.
This marina is one of the few locations in Ontario where you can own your own dock in a condominium format.

Half Moon Bay Marina.
www.halfmoonbaymarina.com.
Located on the eastern shore of the Hudson River, 25 miles north of New York City and about 12 miles south of Bear Mountain and West Point, Half Moon Bay Marina is converting to a dockominium.

Kingman Yacht Center, 1 Shipyard Lane,
P.O. Box 408, Cataumet, MA 02534.
508/563-7136.
www.kingmanyachtcenter.com.
Many boat slips at Kingman Yacht Center are available for dockominium ownership through a 99-year leasing program. For details, call the Harbormaster.

Marinetrim.
www.marinetrim.com.
A service intended to provide early notification of pre-development opportunities to boatowners and investors who are interested in ownership of dockominium properties.

Portofino Harbour.
www.portofinoharbour.com.
Portofino Harbour is a marina on Clear Lake/Galveston Bay near Houston, Texas. At the time of this writing, it is selling dockominium slips.

The Dockominium Group.
www.thedockominiumgroup.com.
A licensed real estate broker whose slogan is "We sell homes for boats."

The Harborage at Ashley Marina,
P.O. Box 21408, Charleston, SC 29413.
866/WET.SLIP. Fax: 843/853-8857.
www.theharborageatashleymarina.com.

FINANCING

The National Marine Bankers Association,
200 East Randolph, Suite 5100, Chicago, IL
60601. 312/946-6260.
NMBA is a trade association of financial institutions that provide loans to consumers. Most financial services are members of NMBA, and the NMBA website should always be more up to date than any printed information we can provide. You'll find listings of lenders at www.Marinebankers.org.

GOVERNMENT RESOURCES

Coast Pilots are available for download at
www.nauticalcharts.noaa.gov/nsd/
cpdownload.htm.

FCC, the Federal Communications Commission, is found at www.wireless.fcc.gov/uls/.

Light Lists, the publications that identify and number all aids to navigation, are available at www.navcen.uscg.gov/pubs/LightLists/LightLists.htm.

National Ocean Service (NOS), a division of the National Ocean and Atmospheric Administration (NOAA), is at www.nos.noaa.gov.

National Vessel Documentation Center,
792 T J Jackson Drive,
Falling Waters, WV
25419-4527. 800/799-8362.
http://www.uscg.mil/hq/g-m/vdoc/nvdc.htm.

Rules of the Road,
U.S. Government Printing Office,
P.O. Box 371954, Pittsburgh, PA
15205-7954. 202/783-3238.
Tide and current tables can be downloaded at www.co-ops.nos.noss.gov.

Vector-based charts and free software can be downloaded at www.nauticalcharts.noaa.gov/mcd/enc/index.htm.

HEADS

Boatersland Marine.
www.boatersland.com/itt37045.html.

Groco.
www.groco.net.

ITT Jabsco.
www.jabsco.com.
(This site is also useful for other pump information, too.)

Lavac.
www.blakes-lavac-taylors.co.uk.

Microphor.
www.microphor.com.

Raritan.
www.raritaneng.com.

VacuFlush.
www.sealandtechnology.com.

Wilcox-Crittenden.
www.wilcoxcrittenden.com.

INSURANCE (GENERAL)

BoatLinks.
www.Boatlinks.com.
This is a resource listing of more than 50 marine

insurance companies, with links to company websites.

BoatU.S., 880 South Pickett Street,
Alexandria, VA 22304.
Member services: 800/395-2628
www.boatus.com/insurance.
BoatU.S. offers boat insurance with low rates, broad coverage, and fast claims service for recreational boaters nationwide.

GEICO.
www.geico.com/boat/.
This well-known auto insurer also offers insurance for boats.

National Boatowners Association.
800/248-3512. 941/360-6777.
Fax: 941/360-6888.
www.nboat.com/insurance/.
Since 1984, the NBOA Marine Insurance Agency has insured thousands of your fellow boaters with the finest possible boat insurance coverage at the most competitive premiums available. This continues to be the single most important function of our company.

Progressive.
http://watercraft.progressive.com/.
The Progressive Group of Insurance Companies ranks third in the nation for auto insurance, with more than 12 million customers. The group offers specialized boat insurance coverage.

INSURANCE (TOWING)

BoatU.S. www.boatus.com. See entry in "Boating Organizations" section above for more information.

National Boatowners Association. www.nboat.com. See entries in Boating Organizations and Insurance (General) sections above for more information.

Sea Tow Services International, Inc. www.seatow.com.
"Your Road .Service at Sea," is the international leader in the marine assistance industry, with franchise locations throughout the United States, Canada, Australia, Europe, Bahamas, Puerto Rico, and Jamaica. Sea Tow's members are backed by 24-hour service, regardless of where they travel.

Vessel Assist.
www.vesselassist.com.
Vessel Assist was recently acquired by Boat America Corporation (the provider of goods and services to members of BoatU.S.). This change in ownership will not affect service to Vessel Assist members.

LIGHTING

Boatowners Warehouse.
www.boatownerswarehouse.com.

Four Winds Enterprises, Inc.
www.fourwinds-ii.com.

Imtra Corporation.
www.imtra.com.

Marine Warehouse.
www.marinewarehouse.net/elec-lighting.html.

Yacht Lights.
www.yachtlights.com.

ONLINE BOAT LISTING SERVICES

Boats.com.
www.boats.com.

Boat Trader Online.
www.boattraderonline.com.

Boat Xchange.
www.boatxchange.com.

Iboats.
www.iboats.com.

Marine Source.
www.marinesource.com.

Marine Web.
www.marineweb.com.

Soundings Online.
www.soundingsonline.com.

Yachtworld.
www.yachtworld.com.

REFERENCE BOOKS

Armstrong, Bob. *Getting Started in Powerboating*. 3rd ed. Camden ME: International Marine/McGraw-Hill, 2005.

Brogdon, Bill. *Boat Navigation for the Rest of Us: Finding Your Way by Eye and Electronics*. 2nd ed. Camden ME: International Marine/McGraw-Hill, 2001.

Calder, Nigel. *Boatowner's Mechanical and Electrical Manual: How to Maintain, Repair, and Improve Your Boat's Essential Systems*. 3rd ed. Camden ME: International Marine/McGraw-Hill, 2005.

How to Read a Nautical Chart: A Complete Guide to the Symbols, Abbreviations, and Data Displayed on Nautical Charts. Camden ME: International Marine/McGraw-Hill, 2003.

Cutler, Thomas J. *Dutton's Nautical Navigation*. 15th ed. Annapolis: Naval Institute Press, 2004.

Eastman, Peter F. *Advanced First Aid Afloat*. 5th ed. Centreville MD: Cornell Maritime Press, 2000.

Chapman, Charles F. *Piloting, Seamanship, and Small Boat Handling*. Revisions by Elbert S. Maloney. 64th ed. New York: Motor Boating and Sailing, 2003.

Waters, John M., Jr. *A Guide to Small Boat Emergencies*. Annapolis: Naval Institute Press, 1993.

Wooldridge, John. *Chapman Boater's Log*. New York: Hearst Books, 2003.

SEMINARS AND EVENTS

www.boatshows.com

www.passagemaker.com (Trawler Port)

www.showmanagement.com

www.TrawlerFest.com

SURVEYORS

For listings of qualified surveyors, check out these organizations:

National Association of Marine Surveyors (NAMS). www.nams-cms.org.

Society of Accredited Marine Surveyors (SAMS). www.marinesurvey.org.

WATER FILTRATION SYSTEMS

Campbell Manufacturing.
www.campbellmfg.com.

Eden Engineering.
www.edenengineering.com.

Multi-Pure Water Filter System.
www.multipure.com.

PUR Filtration Systems.
www.purwater.com.

Pure Water Products, LLC.
www.pwgazette.com.

Sun Water Systems, Inc.
www.aquasana.com.

Whirlpool Corp.
www.whirlpool.com

Appendix 2

Cruising Boat Manufacturers and Websites

Acadia	www.acadia25.com
Afri-Cat	www.africatmarine.com
Aicon Yachts	www.aiconyachts.com
Albin	www.albinmarine.com
Altima Yacht	www.altimayacht.com
Altus	www.oceanalexander.com
American Tug	www.americantug.com
Antares	www.beneteaupower.com
Azimuth Yachts	www.azimutopen.com
Back Cove Yachts	www.backcoveyachts.com
Beneteau	www.beneteaupower.com
Bertram	www.bertram.com
Bluewater	www.bluewateryacht.com
Brenton Reef Yachts	www.aldenyachts.com
Buzzard Bay	www.mdcats.com
Cabo	www.caboyachts.com
Cabo Rico	www.caborico.com
Camano	www.camanomarine.com
Carver	www.carveryachts.com
C-Dory	www.c-dory.com
Chris Craft	www.chriscraft.com
Coastal Craft	www.coastalcraft.com
Cranchi	www.cranchiflorida.com
Crosswater	www.crosswatercats.com
Cruisers Yachts	www.cruisersyachts.com
Defever	www.acys.com

Donzi	www.donzimarine.com
DownEast Yachts	www.vicemusa.com
Doral	www.doralboat.com
Eagle	www.transpacificmarine.com
Egg Harbor	www.eggharboryachts.com
Endeavour Cats	www.endeavourcats.com
Fairline	www.fairline.com
Formula	www.formulaboats.com
Four Winns	www.fourwinns.com
Fountain	www.fountainpowerboats.com
Glacier Bay	www.glacierbaycats.com
Grand Banks	www.grandbanks.com
Grady-White	www.gradywhite.com
Great Harbour	www.mirage-mfg.com
Hampton Yachts	www.anchoryt.com
Hatteras	www.hatterasyachts.com
Hinckley	www.hinckleyyachts.com
Hunt Yachts	www.crhunt.com
Island Pilot	www.islandpilot.com
Jefferson	www.jeffersonyachts.com
Kadey-Krogen	www.kadeykrogen.com
Kanter	www.kanteryachts.com
Kelsall Catamarans	www.kelsall.com
Legacy	www.legacyyachts.com
Lagoon	www.lagoonpower.com
Luhrs	www.luhrs.com
Mainship	www.mainship.com
Manta Catamarans	www.mantacatamarans.com
Monk	www.monktrawler.com
MarineMax	www.marinemaxyachts.com
Maxum	www.maxumboats.com
Menorquin	www.gratitudeyachting.com
Meridian	www.meridian-yachts.com
Mickelson Yachts	www.mickelsonyachts.com
Navigator Yachts	www.navyachts.com
Nordhavn	www.nordhavn.com
Nordic Tugs	www.nordictugs.com

North Pacific	www.northpacificyachts.com
Novatec	www.novatec-yachts.com
Ocean Alexander	www.oceanalexander.com
Ocean Yachts	www.oceanyachtsinc.com
Pearson	www.pearsonyachts.com
Pershing	www.pershing-yacht.com
PDQ Power Cats	www.pdqyachts.com
Post Yachts	www.postyachts.com
Power Cat	www.portsmouthmarine.com
Prowler Yachts	www.prowleryachts.com
Regal	www.regalboats.com
Riva	www.marinemaxyachts.com
Rinker	www.rinkerboats.com
Rosborough	www.rosboroughboats.com
Sabreline	www.sabreyachts.com
Santa Cruz Yachts	www.santacruzyachts.com
Seaforth	www.seaforthmarine.com
Seawolf	www.seawolfmarine.com
Selene	www.portsmouthmarine.com
Sea Ray	www.searay.com
Sea Sport	www.seasportboats.com
Shamrock	www.compositeyacht.biz
Shannon	www.shannonyachts.com
Silverton	www.silverton.com
Sophie Yachts	www.sophieyachts.com
Stamas	www.stamas.com
Sterling Atlantic	www.sterlingatlantic.com
Symbol	www.heartmarine.com
Tiara	www.tiarayachts.com
Viking	www.vikingyachts.com
Wellcraft	www.wellcraft.com
Windy	www.worldwideyachtco.com
Zimmerman	www.zimmermanmarine.com

Appendix 3
Cruising Destination Information

ABACOS, BAHAMAS

Information on boating in the Bahamas: www.boating.bahamas.com.

Cruising and Fishing Guide for the Bahamas. Bahamas Tourism Office. 800/327-7678.

Cruising Guide to Abaco, Bahamas. New Smyrna Beach, FL: White Sound Press. www.wspress.com.

Explorer Chartbook Near Bahamas. Lewis Offshore Ltd., 12636 Selsey Rd., Ocean City, MD 21842. www.explorercharts.com.

U.S. Customs and Border Patrol's Pleasure Boat Reporting line: 800/432-1216.

CALIFORNIA DELTA

California Delta Chambers & Visitors Bureau. www.californiadelta.org.

Delta Boating. www.deltaboating.com.

The Cruising Guide to Central and Southern California. Brian M. Fagan. Camden, ME: International Marine. www.internationalmarine.com.

CHESAPEAKE BAY

Annapolis Visitors Bureau. 410/280-0445. www.visit-annapolis.org.

Baltimore Visitor Information Center. 888/BALTIMORE. www.baltimore.org.

Calvert County Tourism (Solomons, Calvert Maritime Museum, Calvert Cliffs). www.ecalvert.com.

Cambridge Lady. www.cambridgelady.com.

Chesapeake Bay Maritime Museum. www.cbmm.org.

Dorchester County Tourism Dept. (Cambridge and Richardson Maritime Museum). www.tourdorchester.org.

Guide to Cruising Chesapeake Bay. Chesapeake Bay Communications, Inc., 1819 Bay Ridge Ave., Annapolis, MD 21403. 410/263-2662. www.cruiseguides.com.

Kent County Visitors Guide (Chestertown and Rock Hall). www.kentcounty.com.

Talbot County Office of Tourism (St. Michaels and Oxford). www.tourtalbot.org.

Virtually Everything Annapolis. www.annapolis.com.

DOOR COUNTY, WISCONSIN

Door County Chamber of Commerce and Visitor Bureau. www.doorcountyvacations.com.

Door County Maritime Museum & Lighthouse Preservation Society, Inc., 120 N. Madison Ave., Sturgeon Bay, WI 54235. 920/743-5958. www.dcmm.org.

Fayette Historic Townsite. 906/644-2603. www.exploringthenorth.com.

Great Lakes Cruising Club, Suite 1300, 28 E. Jackson Blvd., Chicago, IL 60604-2284. 312/431-0904. www.glcclub.com.

Great Lakes Waterway Guide, 326 First St., Annapolis, MD 21403. 800/233-3359. www.waterwayguide.com.

Lake Michigan Port O'Call, 727 So. Dearborn St., Suite 812, Chicago, IL 60605. 312/276-0610. www.lakelandboating.com.

ERIE CANAL, NEW YORK

Cruising the New York Canal System. Skipper Bob, P.O. Box 391, Windsor, PA 17366-0391. 717/244-0081.

New York State Canal System Cruising Guide and Information. New York State Canal System. 800/4CANAL4. www.canals.state.ny.us.

FLORIDA KEYS

Cruising Guide to the Florida Keys. Capt. Frank Pappy, 108 Fox Island Rd., Bluffton, SC 29910. 803/521-9150.

Cruising the Florida Keys. Claibourne Young and Morgan Stinemetz. Elon College, NC: Watermark Publishing. www.cruisingguide.com.

Dry Tortugas National Park. www.dry.tortugas.national-park.com.

John Pennekamp Coral Reef State Park. www.pennekamppark.com.

Florida Cruising Directory. Waterways Etc., P.O. Box 21586, Fort Lauderdale, FL 33335. 800/749-8151. www.floridacruising.com.

The Official Tourism Council of the Florida Keys and Key West. www.fla-keys.com.

Southern Waterway Guide. 326 First St., Annapolis, MD 21403. 800/233-3359. www.waterwayguide.com.

INTRACOASTAL WATERWAY

Anchorages along the Intracoastal Waterway and *Marinas along the Intracoastal Waterway.* Skipper Bob, P.O. Box 391, Windsor, PA 17366-0391. 717/244-0081.

Managing the Waterway. Mark and Diana Doyle. Minneapolis, MN: Semi-Local Publications. www.semi-local.com.

The Atlantic Intracoastal Waterway Association. www.atlintracoastal.org.

The Intracoastal Waterway: A Cockpit Cruising Handbook. Jan and Bill Moeller. Camden, ME: International Marine. www.internationalmarine.com.

The Intracoastal Waterway Chartbook. John Kettlewell and Leslie Kettlewell. Camden, ME: International Marine. www.internationalmarine.com.

NORTH CAROLINA

Belhaven Chamber of Commerce. www.belhavenchamber.com.

Dowry Creek Marina, Bellhaven. www.dowrycreekmarina.com.

City of Elizabeth City, NC. www.cityofec.com.

Dismal Swamp Canal Visitors Center. www.dismalswamp.com.

New Bern Visitors Center. www.visitnewbern.com.

North Carolina Dept. of Transportation, Customer Service Office, 1503 Mail Service Center, Raleigh, NC 27699. 877/368-4968.

North Carolina's Coastal Boating Guide. www.ncwaterways.com.

Oriental Harbor Village Center and Marina. www.orientalharbor.com.

Oriental Tourism Board. www.visitoriental.com.

Pelican Marina, Elizabeth City. www.pelicanmarina.com.

Town of Edenton. www.visitedenton.com.

PUGET SOUND

A Cruising Guide to Puget Sound and the San Juan Islands. Migael Scherer. Camden, ME: International Marine, 2005. www.internationalmarine.com.

Northwest Boating Destination Guide. www.nwboating.com.

Waggoner Cruising Guide. 1803 132nd Avenue NE, Suite 4, Bellevue, WA 98005-2261. 800/733-5330. www.waggonerguide.com.

Washington State Parks. www.parks.wa.gov.

SOUTHWEST FLORIDA

A Guide to Anchorages in Southwest Florida. BAIL, Inc. (Boaters Action and Information League), P.O. Box 15014, Sarasota, FL 34277-1014. 941/922-5835. bailinc@home.com.

A Gunkholer's Cruising Guide to Florida's West Coast. Tom Lenfestey. St. Petersburg, FL: Great Outdoors Publishing Co.

Boater's Guide to Charlotte Harbor. Florida Sea Grant College Program, P.O. Box 110409, University of Florida, Gainesville, FL 32611.

Charlotte Harbor and the Gulf Islands Tourism Bureau. www.PureFlorida.com

Cruising Guide to Western Florida. Claiborne S. Young. Gretna, LA: Pelican Publishing Co.

Florida Boaters Guide. www.Floridaboatersguide.com.

Florida Cruising Directory. Waterways Etc., P.O. Box 21586, Fort Lauderdale, FL 33335. 800/749-8151. www.floridacruising.com.

Florida State Parks. www.FloridaStateParks.org.

Sanibel and Captiva Islands Chamber of Commerce. www.Sanibel-captiva.org.

Index

Numbers in **bold** refer to pages with photos or illustrations.